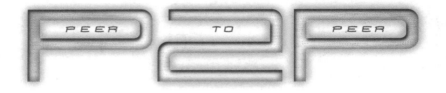

To order additional copies of *P2P,* call **1-800-765-6955.**

Visit us at **www.reviewandherald.com** for information on other
Review and Herald® products.

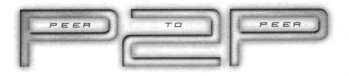

PEER TO PEER

LIVE LOVE JESUS

Stella Duncan Bradley, Editor

REVIEW AND HERALD® PUBLISHING ASSOCIATION

Since 1861 | www.reviewandherald.com

Review and Herald® titles may be purchased in bulk for educational, business, fund-raising, or sales promotional use. For information, e-mail SpecialMarkets@reviewandherald.com.

The Review and Herald® Publishing Association publishes biblically based materials for spiritual, physical, and mental growth and Christian discipleship.

The author assumes full responsibility for the accuracy of all facts and quotations as cited in this book.

Unless otherwise noted, all Scripture references are from the *Holy Bible, New International Version*. Copyright © 1973, 1978, 1984, International Bible Society. Used by permission of Zondervan Bible Publishers.

Texts credited to BBE from *The Bible in Basic English*. Published in the United States by E. P. Dutton & Co., New York. First published in 1949.

Texts credited to Clear Word are from *The Clear Word*, copyright © 1994, 2000, 2003, 2004, 2006 by Review and Herald Publishing Association. All rights reserved.

Texts credited to Message are from *The Message*. Copyright © 1993, 1994, 1995, 1996, 2000, 2001, 2002. Used by permission of NavPress Publishing Group.

Scripture quotations marked NASB are from the *New American Standard Bible*, copyright © 1960, 1962, 1963, 1968, 1971, 1972, 1973, 1975, 1977, 1995 by The Lockman Foundation. Used by permission.

Scriptures credited to NCV are quoted from *The Holy Bible, New Century Version*, copyright © 2005 by Thomas Nelson Inc. Used by permission.

Bible texts credited to NIrV are from the *Holy Bible, New International Reader's Version*. Copyright © 1985, 1996, 1998 by International Bible Society. Used by permission of Zondervan. All rights reserved.

Texts credited to NKJV are from the New King James Version. Copyright © 1979, 1980, 1982 by Thomas Nelson, Inc. Used by permission. All rights reserved.

Scripture quotations marked NLT are taken from the *Holy Bible*, New Living Translation, copyright © 1996, 2004, 2007 by Tyndale House Foundation. Used by permission of Tyndale House Publishers, Inc., Carol Stream, Illinois 60186. All rights reserved.

This book was
Edited by Kalie Kelch
Copyedited by Judy Blodgett
Cover designed by Trent Truman
Interior designed by Tina M. Ivany
Cover phots by Thinkstock
Typeset: Bembo 11/14

PRINTED IN U.S.A.

15 14 13 12 11   5 4 3 2 1

Library of Congress Cataloging-in-Publication Data

P2P : live, love, Jesus / written by students and staff of Mount Pisgah Academy ; Stella Duncan Bradley, editor.
    p. cm.
1. Christian children—Prayers and devotions. 2. Devotional calendars—Seventh-Day Adventists—Juvenile literature.
I. Bradley, Stella Duncan, 1968- II. Mount Pisgah Academy.
  BV4870.P88 2011
  242'.62—dc22
                      2011001935
ISBN 978-0-8280-2518-8

[Dedication]

In memory of my sister, Karen Leigh Duncan,
who had a poster on her bedroom wall that said,
Pass It On . . . Jesus Loves You,
and who shared this message every day.
(story on March 8)

Also
In memory of my dad, Garwood Duncan, an inspiration to all he met.

[Introduction]

Dear Reader,

Life has a way of exciting you and messing with you all in the same breath. We live in a sinful world filled with temptations, trials, sadness, and sufferings. But there is good news! Jesus has gone before us, giving us the example of how to live a godly life. And not only do we have His example of how to live, but we have the assurance of a Comforter, a Best Friend, a Savior who has promised to never leave us or forsake us! Jesus assures us that He will hold our hand and walk beside us through life on this earth.

But God doesn't stop there. He has also given us a community of believers to lean on and learn from. That's one of the greatest things about being a part of a church family—knowing that you always have someone you can talk to and get help from.

This devotional book is made up of hundreds of stories and thoughts from your "brothers and sisters" in academy. They are your family, and they want to help you grow in your relationship with God. They've experienced trials and joys. They've endured the death of family and friends and witnessed miracles. But above all, they've experienced God in their lives, and they want to share their thoughts with you so that you can learn from their mistakes and be strengthened by their victories.

You're embarking on a new year that will be filled with new challenges. Make sure you include God in your life every day. Read His Word, think about His commands, follow His advice, and surround yourself with people who will lift you up and point you toward heaven.

It is our prayer, the students and staff at Mount Pisgah Academy (MPA), that you will deepen your relationship with God this year. Time is short. Jesus will soon return to take us to heaven, and we want you to be there too!

What's New?

By Gary Bradley

What has been will be again, what has been done will be done again; there is nothing new under the sun. Is there anything of which one can say, "Look! This is something new"? It was here already, long ago; it was here before our time. Ecclesiastes 1:9, 10.

Many years ago a friend asked me, "So what's new with you?"
I thought for a moment and told him, "Well, I got a new car . . . and a new girlfriend!"
"Great," he said. "You're doing really well for yourself."

After he left, I thought to myself, *Yeah, I am pretty awesome.* But as the Lord often does to the proud, He quickly humbled me with the thought *Who told you that you are so awesome just because you have some new things?*

I thought about this for a while, and I realized that Solomon was right when he said in Ecclesiastes 1:9 that "what has been will be again, what has been done will be done again; there is nothing new under the sun." In my life there was nothing that I had that was really new, nor could I even do anything that was really new. Everything "new" that human beings have ever done or made has been derived from something else.

As we begin a new year, there is one thing that is certain—we will still have problems in this world. Famines will devastate countries; wars will continue; financial problems will shatter lives; families will break apart; disease will be rampant. These things are part of the continued decline of humanity, which is foretold in prophecy. But keep reading. There is good news!

Ecclesiastes 1:9 and 10 is not the only place that the Bible speaks about new things. It speaks of a new person (2 Corinthians 5:17), a new song (Psalm 40:3), a new heaven and earth (Revelation 21:1), and many other new things. When I look at these things, I realize that these "new" things are not created by humans. And when I look to God, the Creator of all things, I find something truly new—I find myself re"new"ed.

This is the best news in the Bible! Through Christ we have a new life to look forward to.

The Flower

By Brooke Wade

"For my thoughts are not your thoughts, neither are your ways my ways,"
declares the Lord.
"As the heavens are higher than the earth, so are my ways higher than
your ways and my thoughts than your thoughts." Isaiah 55:8, 9.

Once upon a time there was a beautiful little flower that lived in a red flowerpot in the window of the house of an elderly man. The man faithfully watered his precious flower every day. He did everything he could for her, because he loved her very much.

Every year he would replant her in a slightly larger pot, where she could stretch her roots and grow. The flower looked forward to the yearly replanting—her favorite part was being set right back on the windowsill. The window shone brightly, warming her through and through. She loved to look out and see the beautiful moving picture. And she loved the man for giving her such a wonderful home.

One day she awoke excitedly—it was Replanting Day! A new pot would be hers, and in ultimate comfort she could watch out her window. But something was wrong. The man did not have another pot with him. Did he not plan to replant her? She was quite alarmed when he picked her up and began to walk away from the windowsill—beyond the walls and windows.

Then he put her down and began to dig. She was so afraid! Was he going to leave her here? He took her out of her red flowerpot and put her in the hole he had dug. The flower's heart broke. She began to cry. How could he leave her here? Did he not love her anymore? Gently he packed the dirt around her and smiled. "My child," he said, "look up."

Amazingly, she was in the moving picture! It was incredible! The man stayed with her all night. He told her everything about the new place: about the sun, the breeze, and that her roots could grow deep beyond boundaries. He assured her that he would always watch over her.

"I love you so much," he said. "I want the best for you. I want you to be free."

Can you identify with the flower? I know I can. Sometimes we get so comfortable on our little windowsills that we fail to realize that our Master has bigger plans for us. When God moves us, He moves us to bigger, better, and more beautiful places. Trust Him with your life and see where He places you.

Is God Always With Us?

By Nicholas Ewing

And surely I am with you always, to the very end of the age.
Matthew 28:20.

Everyone knows that when students get sick they have a lot of homework to make up. During my junior year I got sick for a whole week. So when I left the dorm and headed home to recuperate, I took my books and homework assignments with me so that I could work on them if I felt up to it.

During my time at home I did get a lot of it done, but I still had so much to do. During that difficult time I felt so overwhelmed. I felt as if no one cared about me—and I even felt deserted by God.

One night I couldn't sleep, so I got up and started to read from my devotional book. I knew that by doing my part to get on track with God I would have a better chance at seeing my troubles through. After that the week just got better and better. I still had a lot of homework, but for some reason I didn't feel so swamped or overwhelmed. Of course, the homework got done and everything worked out well, but that experience reminded me of a story my dad had once told me.

The story went like this: A man and God were walking on a beach, and everything was going well. They were enjoying talking and spending time in each other's company. Suddenly they reached a section of the beach that was littered with stones and shells that hurt their feet. They moved in silence through the rough spots. When they got to the other side of these obstacles, the man looked back and saw only one set of footprints. He turned to God and said, "Why did You leave me when it got rough?"

Then God replied, "Those aren't your footprints; those are Mine. I was carrying you."

That little story helps to remind me that when times get rough, God is still with me.

He is with us through every experience we encounter. Continue to reach out to Him as He is reaching out to you.

Possessive

By Anders Markoff

Do not store up for yourselves treasures on earth, where moth and rust destroy, and where thieves break in and steal. But store up for yourselves treasures in heaven, where moth and rust do not destroy, and where thieves do not break in and steal. For where your treasure is, there your heart will be also. Matthew 6:19-21.

Possessions rule almost every aspect of our lives. We are constantly bombarded with advertisements telling us that we are not complete without a certain product. We are told that if we would just buy their unique product our lives would somehow be better. In reality, possessions are one of the primary problems we have in today's society. Things can slowly become our gods, taking our attention away from what is really important.

In the Garden of Eden Adam and Eve essentially owned nothing. The only thing that they had to "worry" about was taking care of the animals, but even then they were caretakers, not owners. This is very different from what life is like now. Today most people define others by their possessions; what you own represents you.

Someone once told me about an experience they had in Africa while witnessing the baptism of several dozen people. One woman, although wanting to be baptized, was demon-possessed, and even though she wanted to get into the baptismal pool, her body was trying to drag her in the other direction. It took several strong men to finally get her into the pool, where she was baptized, thus calming her down.

After watching the baptism, someone asked, "Why is it that nothing like this happens in more developed countries?"

Someone replied, "Satan already has those countries hooked. He doesn't need any of this to turn them away from God."

When I heard this story, I realized how true it is. With all of the tasks we must do, all of the things we need or want to buy, we are ultimately distracted from what is most important. Our possessions drastically pull us away from spending time with God. We need to make sure we are in control of our possessions, rather than the other way around. Take time each day to remember that serving God is the only reason we are here.

God's Joyful Heart

By Jessica Valenzuela

Light is shed upon the righteous and joy on the upright in heart.
Psalm 97:11.

Have you ever watched small kittens play or children running in a park? Have you noticed how carefree they are? Their attitude is one of happiness and contentment.

Have you ever had one of those mornings when you woke up and right away you knew that for some reason or another you woke up on the wrong side of the bed? Do you then spend your whole day focusing on all the mistakes you keep making? Those kinds of days are what we call "bad" days.

In the Bible God gives us the amazing promise that if we focus our attention on good things He will fill our heart with an overwhelming joy. I've witnessed the fulfillment of this promise in the life of my grandma, who, to me, is a saint.

My grandma wakes up every morning and starts her day with God. Her days seem to go smoothly, and when something does not always go her way, she stops and prays about it, asking God to fill her heart with peace and joy so that she does not have an angry heart. She is the person that I look up to the most. No, I don't always have the time to pray every time something goes wrong, but that is why I am so glad that our amazing Father in heaven can see everything we do. And although we may not always ask for joy or peace, God knows just the right thing to do without us even having to tell Him.

God tells us to fill our heart with good things, with laughter and joy, and not to focus on what is bad, or what may upset us. Don't think of God as someone who is always serious and never laughs. I mean, God did create the animals, and He had to have laughed some when He made monkeys. God is love, yes, but even more so, God is joy. He's the joy in your heart—He's that feeling you get when you get excited about something.

Focus today on finding joy through Jesus.

God and Butterflies

By Lorelle Evans

I revealed myself to those who did not ask for me; I was found by those who did not seek me. To a nation that did not call on my name, I said, "Here am I, here am I." Isaiah 65:1.

Life is full of trials and hardships. Often we stumble and fall along life's way. We may feel as if God is distant and impersonal. Other times we push God away and won't let Him be a part of our lives because of guilt, anger, or shame. No matter what we do, God wants to show us that He loves us, forgives us, and will never leave us.

The Southern Union Prayer Conference is an annual event in which schools in the union gather together at Camp Kulaqua, in Florida, for a weekend of prayer, sharing, and learning more about God. During my sophomore year a friend persuaded me to go, telling me it would be the best experience of my life. I honestly didn't have any desire to go. I was unhappy at home and unhappy at school—my life felt empty. The last thing I wanted was to go to a retreat and experience a God whom I felt had deserted me. Fortunately, I went.

I enjoyed the activities at the prayer conference, but I was battling against an internal struggle within myself. I felt unforgivable and unworthy of God's love. I couldn't grasp the fact that He cared about me. I needed proof, so I tested God, asking Him to show me a butterfly if He truly loved and forgave me. That evening I made my way to the prayer room, a quiet room with a cross, candles, and Bible verses on the wall. I reluctantly walked in, not sure what to expect. As I reverently took off my shoes and walked around the corner, the first thing I saw was a bulletin board covered with butterflies and Bible verses about forgiveness and love. I completely broke down in tears. God was there. He had shown me that He loved and forgave me even though I had so little faith. Many don't ask God to reveal Himself to us, and many others don't even seek Him. Think of how much more God might reveal Himself to us if we just asked Him. Don't wait another day. Wholeheartedly seek God, and He will answer!

Treadmills, Obedience, and Water Parks

By Colton Stollenmaier

The fear of the Lord is the beginning of knowledge, but fools despise wisdom and discipline. Proverbs 1:7.

It was going to be a great week. It was Saturday night, and I had a friend sleeping over. Even better than that, though, was the fact that in a couple days I would be going to the water park with my homeschooling association. We were sleeping in our family room where the TV and toys were. However, we soon got bored with all the usual stuff and found ourselves playing with the treadmill, jumping onto it and running at high speeds.

Unfortunately, a boy's hunger for adventure is not easily subdued, and we wanted more. Being the creative genius that I am, I was, of course, the one to come up with the idea to stack pillows at the end of the treadmill and not run when we jumped onto the treadmill. It was great fun being thrown off the treadmill again and again into the stack of pillows, until my mom stopped us. She appeared out of nowhere—as mothers do—told us it wasn't safe, and sent us to bed, or to at least lie down.

But my thirst had not yet been quenched. I convinced my friend—quite easily—that we should do it one more time. He did it and sailed into the pillows perfectly. I turned it up as high as it would go. As soon as I jumped onto the treadmill, my feet shot out from under me, and I landed with my lower back and right arm on the moving belt. Fortunately, I had the safety strap on, which turned the "human sander" off, but it took a long enough time to slow down from its top speed to take my skin right off my body. My back and arm were severely burned and cut—in some places muscle was showing through. Needless to say, I could not fall asleep, and the water park wasn't so much fun that week because of the holes in my body.

There are countless verses in the Bible, especially in Proverbs, that remind us that the wise accept instruction and reproof, but the foolish despise it and have a bitter end. There are also numerous verses that tell children to obey their parents. Having been a fool, I can assure you that the wisest man on earth and God Himself knew what they were talking about.

God Always Has a Plan
By Kris Kimbley

Be strong and take heart, all you who hope in the Lord. Psalm 31:24.

When I was 9 years old, I wanted to be the best baseball player ever. It was my dream to one day play for the New York Yankees, like all the rest of the great players before. So I joined a Little League team and was assigned the position of shortstop. I loved being part of the team, and I practiced hard, always doing my best.

One day we found out that our team would be playing games on Sabbath. As Adventists, this was obviously a problem for my parents and me. I quit the team. Although I understood why it wasn't right to play on the Sabbath, I was still upset that I was missing out on the fun of the game with my friends.

Baseball was not the only sport I loved. I was always playing basketball or football with my friends. I never really lost the desire to play on a team, but I was torn between my desire to be a part of something great and my beliefs. Every organized team for my age group played or practiced on the Sabbath. There was no way around it. I felt like I was being ripped off.

The years went by, and once I reached high school I started attending Mount Pisgah Academy. During my first year at school, I discovered that Mount Pisgah had a gymnastics team. At first I just thought of them as a bunch of cheerleaders. But as the year went by and I made friends with some of the team members, I began to realize that it was actually really cool. The next year my friends convinced me to try out. Even though the tryouts were difficult, I stuck with it and made the team. That year was so much fun. I learned a lot of things that I probably would have never known, and I made a lot more friends. We toured together and practiced together. I finally felt as though I belonged somewhere. I was finally part of a team.

Throughout academy I stayed on the team and loved it! And I never had a Sabbath conflict. God was looking out for me. Even though I didn't get to play baseball, I was able to be involved in a team sport, as I had always dreamed of. I think I am better off now than I would be if I was on my way to a professional career in baseball. God had a bigger plan for me. I stuck to my beliefs, and God blessed me with the opportunity to fulfill my dreams—maybe not exactly the way I had imagined, but He made it even better. God is good!

Witness for God
By Dustin Evans

We are witnesses of these things, and so is the Holy Spirit, whom God has given to those who obey him. Acts 5:32.

We can all be witnesses for Jesus through action and word. At different times in our lives we may be a passive witness or an intentional and active one. I believe that God loves us just for trying. Winning souls for Christ is not based on a total number count; our job is simply to live and to do our best for His service, letting Him do all the rest.

One summer I sold Adventist books, from cookbooks to Bible stories, door to door through the Magabook program. Many times I wondered why I had chosen this summer job—it was a little out of my comfort zone. The purpose wasn't to just sell books. The purpose was to share Christ with others. And I certainly needed courage from Christ Himself to do that.

At one house I visited, a woman invited me in. I could tell from her kindness that she knew God and was a Christian. After my initial pitch, we had a very interesting conversation about the Bible. When we were done, she bought all of the message books I had—*The Great Controversy*, *Steps to Christ*, etc. My heart was filled with joy. And I prayed that the Holy Spirit would convict her of the truths she held in her hands.

In addition to canvassing in residential areas, I tried visiting businesses. It was not my favorite venue. I had to work up a lot of courage to introduce my purpose to professionals. I wasn't always welcomed, and I think that was the most challenging part of my summer. But I did it anyway. By facing my fears and stepping out in faith, I was blessed. Despite the challenges, I did not, and I will not, stop witnessing for God.

You don't have to sell books to be a witness; you just need to be willing to step out in faith and live for Him in all you do. You may be met with opposition, or you may be welcomed with open arms. Either way, God knows your heart, and He will know that you didn't pass up an opportunity to share His love with those around you.

Edificación
By Hector González

Do not let any unwholesome talk come out of your mouths, but only what is helpful for building others up according to their needs, that it may benefit those who listen. Ephesians 4:29.

The Spanish word for "building," found in Ephesians 4:29, is *edificación*. I love this word and its connotation. In Spanish the same word is used for an actual building structure, such as an office building, a school building, etc. So when I read that our words should be for building others up, I picture my words being bricks and concrete that are to make the people that hear them be firm and strong. Wow! This is powerful stuff and an incredible responsibility.

This imagery takes me back to when I was in the seventh grade. Every year there seemed to be at least one person that got teased more than others, and that year it was Joanne. She was a plain girl who never dressed in stylish clothes. To make matters worse, Joanne in our estimation was not overly clean or organized, and she often smelled bad.

Because of these things, we teased her every day—often calling her names, and even making up and singing rude songs about her. Our teacher tried to solve the problem by allowing Joanne to leave school at the end of the day 10 minutes before the rest of us. But that still did not stop the boys, who would race to catch up with her and continue to heckle her the remainder of her way home. I know that the teasing words affected her deeply. She was withdrawn and sad. She probably had a low self-esteem and felt all alone.

For two years I witnessed Joanne being teased ferociously by the kids in our class. Even though I was not a participant, I never stood up for her. I now wish that someone had shared this Bible text with me then. I wish I knew that maybe my words could have helped reaffirm her, and maybe if I had spoken kind words to her, others would have joined in to help her feel better.

The summer after my eighth-grade year I was reading our local newspaper when I came across the story of a house fire that had killed a young girl. It was Joanne. My heart felt heavy with guilt for allowing her to be hurt so often. I read on and learned that, tragically, this was the second house fire that had taken a life in her family. Years before, a fire had killed Joanne's mother. Joanne did not have someone at home to help her match clothes or teach her how to brush her hair and put on makeup. I wish I had used my words for the "*edificación*" of Joanne.

God Is Strong Enough
By Clint Martin

My God is my rock, in whom I take refuge, my shield and the horn of my salvation. He is my stronghold, my refuge and my savior—from violent men you save me. 2 Samuel 22:3.

"Help! Help!" I yelled as my head went back under the water. I had only enough time to come up and get a breath of air and yell for more help.

I was on a mission trip with my church in Nicaragua. When we had finished working one day, we went to the beach, which was only 10 minutes away from our worksite. We had a lot of fun until we got caught by the riptide and undertow. When I started to go back to shore, I found that I wasn't going anywhere. I started to panic, just screaming for help. While I was under the water, holding my breath and being tossed around like a weightless object, I offered up a simple prayer—*Lord, help*. There was also this one thought that kept coming to my mind: *At least if I die, I know I am doing the right thing, being here in Nicaragua doing His work.*

For five minutes, although it seemed much longer, I went up and down in the water, repeatedly praying and yelling for help. Then my pastor, Rick Greve, who was behind me, came up and told me that it was OK. When I heard that, I felt a sense of security. It was as though the Holy Spirit had sent an angel down and comforted me. We all eventually made it to safety. And on that beautiful sandy beach we greeted each other with many hugs and tears. Everybody then quickly gathered around and had a prayer of thanksgiving.

God was strong enough for everybody that was in the ocean that day. He brought us all in safely. I know that I will never forget His gift to me.

If you ever find yourself in distress, know that you can call on Him for comfort and help. Nothing is too big and overwhelming or too small and insignificant to God. Let Him be your lifeline and Savior in every situation.

In My Father's Will

By Erin Gosling

And to know this love that surpasses knowledge—that you may be filled to the measure of all the fullness of God. Ephesians 3:19.

When Missy was a little girl, she would often go to her grandmother's house and play her music box. Missy loved that music box, and she always asked her grandmother if she could have it when she grew up. Her grandmother would just smile and tell her that one day, perhaps, she would will it to her. Missy loved the idea of being "willed" something, and every time she saw her grandmother she would ask, "What do you will me today, Grandma?"

"Love" would invariably be her grandmother's reply.

A few years later Missy's grandmother passed away. And she had indeed willed the music box to her granddaughter. But upon opening the music box, Missy found a note tucked neatly inside. "My precious granddaughter, I have very few possessions to will you, but please know that all of your life I have prayed for you. I hope that you will always search for your Father's will and be blessed."

I think we forget how awesome the will of the Lord is. We get so wound up in earthly things—such as Missy's music box and cars and money—that we lose sight of our spiritual needs. God has a precious gift for us—eternal life. Our heavenly Father wills all of us eternal life in the most glorious of places. How amazing is it that He has a plan and a new home just for you and me?

Don't miss out on the adventures and treasures He has promised for all who believe in Him. We know that not even one sparrow falls without His noticing (Matt. 10:29). So how much more, then, does He care for us?

I am so glad that I am in my Father's will.

The Master Plan
By Evan Paradis

"For this son of mine was dead and is alive again; he was lost and is found."
So they began to celebrate. Luke 15:24.

When I was 10 years old, my parents split up. Unfortunately, out of my brother, sister, and I, I took it the hardest. It hurt so badly, waking up knowing Mom wasn't home to cook me breakfast or maybe Dad wasn't there to play catch with me. I hated it. In addition to adjusting to a new home situation, I was moved from private school to public, where I found and was introduced to many worldly things very quickly.

After the divorce I changed drastically. I had always made good grades and saw school as a priority. Soon I fell in with the wrong crowd, which quickly took me away from Christ. Saturdays were spent playing hockey, friends seemed more important than family, and peer pressure made me make some horrible choices. In the seventh grade I started experimenting with different drugs. This introduced me to a new life that seemed to give me comfort away from reality. Because of wrong decisions, disrespect, and a growing addiction on my shoulder, I was in and out of juvenile detention without a care in the world—it was just another weekend, right?

Pretty soon I hit what I saw as "rock bottom." During my sophomore year my mom wasn't there to support me the way she'd always been (I'm sure she was weary), and the judge told me I was done. Sitting in juvenile detention, knowing I was headed somewhere I never thought I would ever see in my life, I felt lost. During that moment I realized what had happened—I had pushed God out of my life. I sat back and remembered my favorite memory verse. I fell back on it with assurance, knowing God was there with me, even with all my faults.

With God's grace I received one more chance to redeem myself, and I landed at Mount Pisgah Academy. I knew that I couldn't waste this, so I did my best to turn my life around. Thanks to a loving and supportive family and the staff at MPA, I rebuilt my relationship with my eternal Father. It saved my life!

I believe that whatever happens in life, that no matter how bad things get, God will not leave you. He loves each of us and wants what is best for us. He gives us many opportunities to get on the right path. Hold on to Him, and He will not let you fall!

Be Inspired

By Brittani Coleman

We continually remember before our God and Father your work produced by faith, your labor prompted by love, and your endurance inspired by hope in our Lord Jesus Christ. 1 Thessalonians 1:3.

Today you may be in your bed or on a chair staring at the ceiling or wall. You may think about all the things you should be doing right now, such as homework, a project you've started, or phoning a friend you promised to call. You may even be opening your Bible and actually reading it. Fifteen minutes pass, then 30. Finally a whole hour has been wasted, yet you are still there, staring and thinking.

Have you ever felt this way? Have you ever felt uninspired—as though nothing this world has to offer could possibly motivate you enough to get up and do something? I know I would much rather be sleeping most of the time.

So how are these sentences supposed to help you in your daily walk with God? Isn't the point of life to find God? What if you already have? What if you already believe in Him, and you know He will forgive and love you no matter what? Does that just mean it's smooth sailing until His second coming? Nope!

When you are a Christian, there are going to be situations in your life in which you are going to have to do stuff you don't want to do. God is going to call you to do something that you may not understand. There are going to be times you feel completely uninspired, but you are going to have to just do it anyway, because God is calling you to do more than just sit there, and because you were the one that asked God to call you in the first place. As a Christian, you have given your life away. It's no longer yours. It's God's.

But don't think of that as a burden. It's actually a huge honor and privilege. God trusts us to carry out His work in the time we have left on earth. There is so much to do, and time is too short to just lounge around. So listen for God's call, and follow through with His prompting. He has big plans for you!

What He Was . . .
What He Would Be
By Kari Mann

But you know that he appeared so that he might take away our sins. And in him is no sin. I John 3:5.

We often view Jesus with a detached notion. Yes, He died for us in a very painful way, but we find it hard to identify with Him because the life He lived was years ago.

Imagine sitting in a restaurant watching a man at a table catty-corner to yours. He is confident but quiet; He is neat in appearance. He is wearing a pair of jeans and a simple polo shirt. His hair falls to His shoulders. He has a slight smile on His face. He doesn't get upset when His waitress spills His drink on Him or brings Him the wrong food. He helps her clean it up instead of yelling or threatening.

Imagine watching Him talk sweetly with a 7-year-old mentally challenged child as if she were just like anyone else. Imagine watching Him send the child home with a new chance in life, with a perfect brain.

I like to think about what Jesus would be like today. Although He would look like us, He would not succumb to road rage, He would not be impatient with time, and He would have manners. I like to think of Him walking the halls of the ICU or cancer wards in the hospitals, leaving happiness in His wake.

In today's society it wouldn't be the Pharisees who would criticize Him—it would be the tabloids, the news, and the blogosphere that would tear Him down. And just like the people in His time, it would be our inability to have faith that would lead to His end. New medical advances or special effects would be to blame for His miraculous resurrection.

We claim Him, but I wonder if I would be able to accept Him if He were here now. If He were here, would I treat Him with suspicion? Would I be one to favor a court battle and the death penalty? Would I have faith? Would you?

Will There Be Attics in Heaven?
By Jonathan P. Michael

In my Father's house are many rooms; if it were not so, I would have told you. I am going there to prepare a place for you. John 14:2.

What's heaven going to be like? Well, for me, it's most likely going to be all about longed-for introductions and reunions initially. I'll meet the Trinity for the first time face to face, and They'll give me a chance to sit with Them on the throne (Revelation 3:21; 22:4). I'll have the opportunity to sit at a feast and chat with people I've always admired from the Bible, such as Abraham, Isaac, and Jacob (Matthew 8:11). I'll also be reunited with my loved ones and friends who died in Christ, and I will never ever be separated from them again (1 Thessalonians 4:13-18)—I especially hope to see my grandparents. However, one of the most anticipated reunions I look forward to is with Mrs. Johnson, mostly because of a special prayer we shared together.

Mrs. Johnson was an 83-year-old woman I met in 1993 when she opened her home in Ohio to me. I remember her age because we threw her a birthday party that summer, which included a cake with 83 candles! I spent less than three months at her house while serving as a student literature evangelist, but she made a lasting impression on me. I also have many special memories of the house itself, from having to take showers in the basement to eating granola in the kitchen with berries picked from bushes just off the back porch. There was one part of her house that I especially treasured—the attic. She had converted the upper floor of her home into a guest bedroom, which is where I and other students stayed temporarily. I will never forget this dear woman and her attic.

After that summer, I was given one last opportunity to stay in Mrs. Johnson's attic before she died. I had learned from a friend in school that she was fighting cancer, and so over Christmas vacation I traveled to see her. When it came time for me to leave, I opened my Bible and read John 14:1-6. From this wonderful passage I shared the promise that Jesus was building a special place in His Father's house just for her and that He was coming soon to take her there. I then asked Mrs. Johnson if she thought it would be OK if I prayed and requested that Jesus be sure to include an attic in her mansion. She thought that was a wonderful idea, so I did. Will there be attics in heaven? I'm pretty sure there'll be at least one. Just go to Mrs. Johnson's place!

Faith Like a Child

By Allissa Wright

And He said: "I tell you the truth, unless you change and become like little children, you will never enter the kingdom of heaven." Matthew 18:3.

I feel very privileged that I was able to go on my academy's mission trip to Kenya, Africa. When people say that mission trips are a life-changing experience, they are telling the truth.

I had never done anything like it before, and as I prepared for the trip, I was extremely excited about making a difference in the lives of those who lived there.

Upon arriving at the elementary school we were going to be working with, I was amazed by how many kids were crammed into one little classroom. The kindergarten room alone held at least 40 kids with their one teacher. The room did not have nice decorations or bins of school supplies. It was the most humble classroom I had ever seen.

But my attention did not remain on the bare walls or the lack of elbow room. My focus was on the kids. They were so cute and so full of happiness.

Every time my friend Addie and I would walk into that room, the children would start singing their welcome song to us. Most of them couldn't speak English, but their message was clear. They were glad we were there! These kids were the most trusting kids I have ever met. They all wanted to be near Addie and me—we were like instant big sisters to them all. They wanted to hold our hands, play a game, and simply share time together. Going to that classroom was the highlight of my day. Those small kids, most of whom lived in unimaginable poverty in dung homes surrounded by flies, were some of the happiest kids I have ever met.

If only everyone could be as trusting and kind as those little African kids, how different the world would be. If we let God come into our lives, we can have that awesome attitude, too! When I signed up for the African mission trip, I was expecting to make a difference in other people's lives, but a classroom full of 5-year-olds actually changed me. They made me want to be a better person.

Just Trust

By Ericka Wright

Trust in the Lord with all your heart and lean not on your own understanding. Proverbs 3:5.

The summer before my senior year of academy I had the opportunity to go skydiving. I had no second thoughts, because I had wanted to do this all my life. I arrived at Skydive Vermont bright and early, completed the 30-minute class, and got suited up. Since it was my first time jumping, I was required to jump tandem. I met my instructor, the man who would hold my life in his hands, and we boarded the plane.

As the tiny plane rose higher and higher, my heart began to race. I was psyched, but I was becoming a bit nervous as jump time drew closer. I began thinking, *Oh, no, what if my parachute doesn't open, or what if this guy doesn't know what he's doing?* I began praying like crazy.

Suddenly the doors of the plane flew open, and my instructor told me to place my feet on the step. The wind was blowing hard, and my heart was racing. Then we were given clearance, and I took a step into the nothingness. Within seconds I was falling faster than I have ever fallen in my life. I was flying face-first toward the ground thousands of feet below me. The sensation was terrifying and exhilarating all at once. It was almost surreal knowing that although humans don't have wings, here I was "flying" through the sky.

The presence of my instructor assured me that I would be OK, that I was in capable and experienced hands, and that we would have a safe landing. Without him I would have been in a lot of trouble! I just had to let go of my fears, enjoy the ride, and totally trust this man. That is exactly what we must do with God.

I think each one of us has had a time in our lives in which we're all wrapped up in doing something good for God, and then Satan throws that little bit of doubt our way, making us think we aren't doing the right thing or that we're not qualified to be doing what we thought would be a good idea. This may cause us to hesitate and even fall awkwardly away. But remember, stand fast for Christ—take that step out in faith. Grasp His hand and hold on tight, because He is all you'll ever need. We are tandem jumping with Him, and He will take care of us!

The Power of Music

By Rosa Chavez

I was young and now I am old, yet I have never seen the righteous forsaken or their children begging bread. Psalm 37:25.

Have you ever felt like something you longed for was just taken away from you in an instant? Have you ever imagined something to be a certain way, and when it happens differently from your dream it leaves you feeling disappointed? I know I have. Some of my senior year in academy was like this. The first reason was that my expectations for the year were very high.

Ever since my freshman year I had had idealistic dreams about how my senior year would be completely amazing. Each year my expectations became higher and higher. I was so looking forward to the blissfulness of being a senior.

But at the beginning of my senior year I realized that my dreams would not be fulfilled—so many things were different. Things that I thought were going to happen did not happen. At first I was very depressed. I did not know what to do. I actually got to the point that I wanted to go home and go to public school. One Friday was especially upsetting. I was about to call my parents before vespers and tell them that I wanted to come home. Thankfully, instead, my friends rushed me to vespers.

At vespers that night we had a song service, my favorite part of every program, which was longer than usual. We sang a lot of songs that I loved, and some of them really got me thinking. *Do I really want to leave this amazing place I call home? Do I really want to leave my friends that I have come to see as a part of my family?* I prayed to God and told Him everything I felt. I decided not to give up.

As the year continued, I gradually became more and more open-minded about the new changes. I accepted them and appreciated them. I finally realized that God has a plan for us no matter what it is. I also realized that nothing is impossible if you pray. God will hear our every prayer.

So when you are feeling down or feeling like things are not going the way you think they should, just go to God. He will always be there for you, and He may even send friends or a song your way to cheer you up and give you guidance.

A Glimpse of God's Delight

By Cheryl Grant

And hope does not disappoint us, because God has poured out his love into our hearts by the Holy Spirit, whom he has given us. Romans 5:5.

Anyone who loves dogs will agree that it is amazing how a dog brightens a home. Why is that? I know that with our family dog it's the whole package. We named him "Bo Gary," which fits his hound dog charm. He excitedly greets us before we can open the front door (even when we've stepped out for only a few minutes). Bo Gary never judges us, nor does he talk back when he is scolded for tearing apart a new bag of toilet paper. We are entertained each time we attempt to catch Bo as he darts in figure eight patterns across the yard. The real challenge is catching him when he bounces around the neighborhood chasing birds. I love that our dog's carefree nature does not hinder his willingness to learn new tricks. So far he's accomplished the basics—"sit," "shake," and "lie down."

I suppose our dog could fend for himself if needed, but Bo has learned we are his family and his master. He depends on us to supply his food and water and let him out to go to the bathroom. In return, we expect him to obey our commands, yet we appreciate his own personality. He is not some cold, unloving, robotic toy dog.

Thankfully, dependence on God doesn't mean we have to become a robot either. Our heavenly Father wants us to maintain our own individual personality. After all, that's what makes us such an awesome part of His creation. God desires us to be dependant on Him for our daily food, whether it's physical, a bowl of spaghetti, or spiritually, His Word. Choosing God as our Master supplies security in knowing we will always be cared for. As a result, we will find daily joy and energy that delights and entertains our God. How awesome it is that God enjoys me even more than I enjoy Bo Gary. I guess we brighten God's home, too. What a wonderful heavenly Father we have!

Don't Run Away

By Alexandra Roeder

In all your ways acknowledge him, and he will make your paths straight.
Proverbs 3:6.

We all feel like running away from our problems sometimes. During my freshman year I felt that way. I had lost a lot of friends and made a great amount of mistakes at school and in my own home. I had given up on things I should have stuck with, and I had given up on friendships I should have worked out. Honestly, by Christmas break I had a strong hate for my school, so I thought instead of trying to fix things I would just run away and leave my life there. I wound up going to another Seventh-day-Adventist boarding school in another state. Throughout the transition, I thought nothing of talking to God about my stresses.

When I got to my new school, it was great being with my brothers, but to tell you the truth, there was nothing that different or better about my new school, and I felt just as alone.

The next months were quite difficult. I was living in the dorm with no way to get home. My mother was very ill and in the hospital; my cousin had cancer; and an extremely close friend died all in a matter of months. My life seemed even worse than it had been when all I cared about was stupid drama. I finally realized the only way to get through this life is with God—I could not do it by myself. You can never put your happiness in the world's hands; it will only let you down. God has always been there for me, and I am just realizing it.

Things got a lot better in the following months. After school ended, I came back to Pisgah, my original school, and reconnected with great friends. I worked things out with the people I needed to, and I love my family so much. I still have stresses, as everyone does, but I know now that I need to pray and let God lead me through rough times. Running away doesn't help.

Snow

By Sarah Grissom

For the Lord will not reject his people; he will never forsake his inheritance.
Psalm 94:14.

Every year I look forward to the day when the first snowflake hits the ground. I've lived in Charlotte, North Carolina, for as long as I can remember. We don't get snow every year, as most of us hope we will. Some years we get lots of snow, some years it just flurries, and then other years we don't get anything at all.

While in boarding school at Mount Pisgah Academy, which is located in the mountains of North Carolina, a place more prone to snow than Charlotte, I was trying to get my homework done in the library one day. But I couldn't seem to stop looking out the window at the snow-frosted ground. I started thinking that the snow and Charlotte are a lot like us and God.

We hope and pray He'll come and be near us. We sit around waiting for Him to come. Sometimes we feel Him all around us, other times we see only a little bit of Him, and then there are the days we feel that He's left us. But then the thought came to me: snow (or at least water in some form) never really goes away. I'm sure you think I'm crazy, but it's true. It might not look the same, but it's always around. It's in the sky we live under, it's in the rivers we play in, and it's in the air we breathe.

Just so, God has promised never to leave us. He's all around us every day. In fact, He *is* the Water of Life. He wants to be the air that you breathe. He wants you to be dependent on Him. He wants you to look forward to spending time with Him. So instead of sitting by your window waiting for the snow to fall, go outside and take a deep breath. Let the fresh air fill your lungs. Then let God fill your heart. Breathe Him in.

Stop!
By Jamey Holder

I will instruct you and teach you in the way you should go; I will counsel you and watch over you. Psalm 32:8.

Many years ago my friend Steve had just turned 6 years old and was feeling quite grown and independent so he asked his parents if he could go for a walk in the woods by himself. Taking a cue from his confidence, and knowing that he knew the woods pretty well, they allowed him to go alone.

While he was out walking, he came to a hill. Since he was pretending to be Daniel Boone, he decided to jump off the ledge of the hill. As he jumped, he heard a voice say, "Stop."

He grabbed a nearby branch and swung back to the ledge. He then looked around but didn't see anyone. So he jumped again, and the voice said, "Stop." He grabbed the same branch and swung back to the ledge again. By this time he was getting angry, because he thought his dad had broken his word and followed him out into the woods. He walked around the area, but he didn't see anyone. In an effort to locate the voice, he decided to pretend to jump, but this time he'd listen for the voice so he could tell from which direction it was coming.

As he did so, he heard the voice say, "Stop."

He quickly got on more solid ground and proceeded to try to find the source of the voice. He searched over rocks and behind trees. He called out to try to get a response from whoever had said "Stop." When he didn't find anyone in the woods, he looked over the ledge. And there, just where he would have landed, was a six-foot rattlesnake.

He knew then that the voice he had heard was definitely a messenger from heaven. Whether it comes as a startling command from above, or a still small voice, we should listen to God. He always has our best interest at heart.

Do I Have Something in My Eye?

By Michelle Dannenberger

You hypocrite, first take the plank out of your own eye, and then you will see clearly to remove the speck from your brother's eye. Matthew 7:5.

Have you ever sat in a room filled with people and overheard some of their conversations? Have you ever realized how often you hear "You will never guess what he did!" or "Did you see what she was wearing?" We, as humans, are so quick to judge and criticize people, but how often do we look at ourselves with the same eyes we use to look at others?

I remember one day in class there was a discussion going on about people and their gifts from God. I specifically remember someone saying how their gift was to notice details. They continued on, saying how they loved to pick out details in people—especially their flaws and how they loved talking about it. Then they said, "Yes! I am a gossip, and I'm not afraid to admit it!" This is something that stopped me in my tracks. How could someone who loves to pick out the flaws of others and talk about them behind their back say that it's a gift from God? Yes, I do believe that God has given this person a gift, but I'm not so sure that's it.

As Christians we sometimes are so busy trying to do the work of God that we forget what that really means. Instead of blathering on about "a certain someone who hasn't shown up at church for the second week in a row" or getting our feathers in a ruffle because "they're playing the wrong instrument for praise time again," I think we need to focus more on our own relationship with God and not everyone else's. We need to be good Christian examples for others. If we let small matters like these distract us and cloud our minds, we will soon lose perspective of what the real meaning of being a Christian is about. So instead of pointing out the specks in our neighbors' eyes, let's try checking out the log in our own.

God's Plans

By Jonathan Harris, Jr.

May he give you the desire of your heart and make all your plans succeed.
Psalm 20:4.

I had just returned from an amazing mission trip to Peru. It was a gift from the organization called Pathways to Success, and it was definitely the trip of a lifetime. I had never traveled much at all, and never out of the country before. So this foreign trip, with an incredible group of cool Adventists, really opened my eyes to the world and God's work. It was a remarkable experience I will never forget.

After that trip I thought my summer was complete, but then I got a big surprise. I was checking my e-mail for the first time after my trip and saw a message from a guy offering me a job. The e-mail said that this guy wanted me to help out on his race team. Now, you've got to understand that racing is my passion—anything even remotely having to do with NASCAR would be my dream job! I read the e-mail through thoroughly (three times in a row) just to make sure it was true.

I then quickly e-mailed him back and told him that I would most definitely work for him. He wrote me back and told me when and where to meet him at the track. My summer could not have been more fulfilling.

I think it is really awesome that God has plans to keep blessing me and keep helping me grow closer to Him. He gave me two wonderful gifts that summer—gifts that I didn't even ask for or wouldn't even have considered asking for. That is why I chose this verse: it helps me know that God has plans for me and that He wants me to be successful in my life.

Just remember that if you are having a bad day, or even a great day, God has unexpected blessings just waiting for you. Enjoy the surprise!

Attitude Is Everything
By Briana Richards

All the days of the oppressed are wretched, but the cheerful heart has a continual feast. Proverbs 15:15.

Have you noticed that if someone is in a bad mood everything appears to go wrong, and if they are in a good mood life is great? Their situations haven't changed, only their perspective on the situations.

Attitude is everything. I see this best illustrated in my life. If I'm studying in my dorm room and hear my friends talking and laughing outside, I can think, *They're having fun without me and are excluding me on purpose.* If I let myself dwell on those feelings, I'll end up moping around while doing homework, and my friends won't have any idea how I'm feeling. My negative attitude will affect the rest of my day and could even cause damage to my friendships. These thoughts are a result of me just feeling sorry for myself.

Or I could think, *Hey! It sounds like they're having so much fun; I'll go join them*! This option—going outside to spend time with my friends—allows me to take a break from my homework, hang out with my friends, and have a good time! Now I have a positive attitude, so I am able to look at the situation in a different way.

It is the same situation, but a bad outlook creates problems, while a good mind-set builds healthy feelings.

Just as attitude determines what we are going to think and do, our outlook decides if our lives will seem as if they're going wrong or right. Life is full of problems, so you might as well meet them with a happy attitude instead of having a bad attitude that makes going through a crisis more difficult.

This is my challenge to you: for the rest of the day, consciously choose to have a good attitude. Yes, there will be challenges. But when you face them with cheerfulness, the difficulties won't seem as hard. And remember, when you accept the love Jesus gives, happiness is guaranteed!

Preaching Love

By Melissa Couser

Accept one another, then, just as Christ accepted you, in order to bring praise to God. Romans 15:7.

For many of us just the thought of witnessing is pretty scary! It brings up images of knocking on doors or attending your church's evangelistic meetings every night. Don't get me wrong—those things are great. But there are other ways.

I recently went on a mission trip to Panama, and before we left, I had grand images of witnessing to the people there. Boy, was I wrong! While we were in Panama, we worked during the day constructing a local church, and at night we held evangelistic meetings in town. All the students on the mission trip, including me, worked every night at the VBS. We met so many cute kids. One girl in particular, Chanelle, and I got really close.

After working all day, most of us were really tired, and the kids sometimes got annoying. One night I was in a particularly bad mood. I had worked really hard that day and was tired. To make matters worse, one of the other girls from our group and I weren't getting along. I just wanted to sit down and sulk—certainly not my best moment! But I still prayed that God would use me.

At the meeting that night, Chanelle came up to me and tried to pull me outside. I brushed her off and went to sit down. Then I heard, "Go outside." It wasn't an audible voice—it was just an idea that popped into my head that I know hadn't come from me. So I went out back, and Chanelle came running up to me in tears. She was really upset and just bawling. I didn't know what to do, so I just hugged her and tried to comfort her. She cried for more than an hour, but eventually she calmed down. She just needed, literally, a shoulder to cry on, and I was able to be there for her.

I didn't share scholarly doctrine with her or preach at her. I just let God use me to witness to her in the way that she needed. Sometimes that's all we need to do—just be available for people. Preaching and stuff isn't bad, and if that's what God calls you to do that's great, but sometimes all God requires is a willing heart to share His love.

Encircled With Fear

By Danielle Grandy

For you have been my refuge, a strong tower against the foe. Psalm 61:3.

Excitement overwhelmed me as my family and I trekked deeper into the African grass-lands. We saw elephants, giraffes, and zebras; however, a crucial piece was missing from our daily game drives. We had not yet encountered the "king of the jungle." We were on a quest—one that we didn't realize would lead us straight to a den of lions.

We were visiting my uncle and his family, who were missionaries there. This was quite the adventure for my family, and we tried to soak up every detail. As we continued on our safari, I kept a hopeful spirit and a watchful eye. Despite every bump, jolt, and crash along the rough roads, we kept our eyes peeled, not wanting to miss anything, especially the illusive lions. The sun had almost set and rain began to fall, but we pressed onward. The mud road was extremely slick and dangerous. We ran into a large pothole, causing us to lose all control of the vehicle, which sputtered to a stop. When the car would not start back up, I realized that this was only a small part of the problem. As I looked out the window, all I could see surrounding me were big, scary lions and their cubs.

I felt as if my life might possibly end in a few short minutes. A sense of fear came over me. My family all came together and said a prayer. We asked God for wisdom and courage to face our dilemma. While my mother served as watch guard, my uncle got out of the vehicle to check under the hood. My heart was racing, and I sat there for what seemed like hours. In no time at all, the car started, and we quickly drove to safety. The lions never moved closer to our car, and I managed to take fabulous photographs that I cherish. But the situation could have been much different. God protected my family and me that day, and I am extremely thankful.

Fear is something no human lives without. Nobody likes to be afraid or unsure of what the future may hold for their lives. Whether it's a great or small fear, remember God knows and cares about each one of us. He will always be with us. He can bring us comfort and peace to overcome anything, and He promises to give us blessings along the way. Isn't God good?

What's Your Story?

By Brandy Johnson

But he said to me, "My grace is sufficient for you, for my power is made perfect in weakness." Therefore I will boast all the more gladly about my weaknesses, so that Christ's power may rest on me. 2 Corinthians 12:9.

Have you ever heard those people who come to speak for a chapel or vespers service and tell powerful stories about how God saved them from the depths of despair? That seemed to be all I heard growing up—stories about people following Satan and the world when wham! God rescued them and immediately turned them into perfect Christians.

How was I ever going to witness to someone? I hadn't killed anyone or had premarital sex or taken drugs or drunk alcohol. Sure, I'd sinned, but just little things like yelling at my brother and refusing to clean my room. Likewise, I certainly hadn't survived a near-death experience where I met the hand of God or an angel. I'd just been living my life, going to school, attending church services. Nothing exciting or "witness worthy." I mean, who would want to listen to such a boring testimony?

That used to really frustrate me. It was as if everyone was telling me that I had to have this horrendous sin that I finally relinquished to God in order to share the good news effectively. So what if you're like me, and you don't have a spectacular story to tell?

It took me awhile, but I finally realized that I was missing the whole point. I had to look deeper to understand that it wasn't what the person did or even who they had become since then. The point was that God cared enough to love them, and He was using them to fulfill His plans. Regardless of what "little" or "big" sins I have committed—because in God's eyes, any sin is SIN—God can and will use me as a witness for Him.

When I am nervous, His knowledge will put words in my mouth. When I am angry and lash out, His wisdom can focus me back on Him. When I am weak, His power is strong. As long as I allow Him to change my heart and live through me, His amazing glory will prevail in everything. And just think what a powerful testimony that will be!

Let Your Love Define You
By McKennan Cook

By this all men will know that you are my disciples, if you love one another.
John 13:35.

Most people would say that my defining feature is my height. I'm six foot four, so I tower over most. Often the first thing someone says when they meet me is "Wow, you're tall." And they know me thereafter as "the tall guy." It doesn't bother me that people initially identify me this way, but what does bother me is what people seem to initially notice about Christians. A couple of people I used to work with turned down my invitation to come to church, because they said that the people there were too stuck-up and that they would feel judged. As you can imagine, this disappointed me greatly. I became even more disappointed after watching a couple of videos in which random people from off the streets of major cities were asked about Christians and gave similar responses.

It's not that I think all or even most Christians are overly judgmental. Actually, I feel that Christians are, in general, more accepting than most, but somehow society has still gotten the wrong impression. So maybe we do already love each other, but we obviously need to do a better job of showing that love to the world. People should see a Christian and think, *Wow, they are really loving.*

Often we let our beliefs define us. We say, "We're the people who go to church on Saturday," or other things that set us apart from other churches. Some people come to know us as just another religion or denomination, no different than any other. If we could do a better job of loving each other, I think people would notice that love very quickly and would recognize that they want to be a part of something like that. That's how Jesus did it. He made people realize that He loved them, and that simple act of loving them made them want to be one of His followers.

So if you are a Christian, help me show the world how loving we are by being more loving toward fellow Christians and toward all others. If you aren't a Christian, know that Jesus loves you, and I love you, and the rest of God's followers love you, too.

Life's Little Delays

By Joy K. Pelto

Do not withhold your mercy from me, O Lord; may your love and your truth always protect me. Psalm 40:11.

A few years ago my husband, Ed, and I were making a trip from Andrews University in Berrien Springs, Michigan, to Lincoln, Nebraska. It was raining heavily, and we had just entered rush-hour traffic on Interstate 80/90 near South Bend, Indiana. The windshield wipers were working as hard as they could, but the wipers on our little Dodge Omni were having a difficult time keeping up with the heavy rain.

Suddenly the driver's-side windshield wiper flew off the car and onto the side of the road. Ed momentarily panicked as he realized he was driving blindly at 65 miles an hour in heavy traffic. He quickly leaned to the right to see out the passenger side of the front window as he worked to maneuver the car to the side of the road and out of traffic. Ed got out in the heavy rain, removed the wiper from the passenger side, and put it on the driver's side so he could see well enough to get us to the next exit. When he got back in the car, he was soaked, and we were both somewhat annoyed by the inconvenience of having to stop somewhere. At the next exit we purchased new wipers from a large truck stop and were able to continue our journey. The whole incident took approximately 25 minutes.

We had been driving almost 20 minutes again when traffic came to a stop. Not too far ahead there had been an accident. We don't know what had caused the accident, but we know multiple cars were involved. After we passed the accident scene, we realized that if we had not had to stop to replace the windshield wipers, we would have been at, or near, the spot where the accident occurred, and we could have been involved. What we had thought was one of life's little annoyances now seemed like divine intervention.

I often wonder what the conversation was between God and our guardian angels in the moments before that windshield wiper flew off. Did God tell an angel to yank it off, or did He just say "Delay them," leaving it up to the angel to figure out the best way? Did the angel have fun watching us see that wiper fly off? These questions will have to wait until I meet my guardian angel face to face, but I do plan to ask.

My Story
By Kyle Dennis

I will be glad and rejoice in your love, for you saw my affliction and knew the anguish of my soul. Psalm 31:7.

As far back as I can remember, God has been with my family and me. Through every hard time He has always showed that He is in control. One occasion that sticks out in my mind is when I was about 6 years old. My mother and I had just moved to Charlotte, North Carolina. We lived in a small townhome in south Charlotte, and we didn't have a lot of money.

I remember my mother being offered a job with the company her sister worked at. When my mom had first taken the job, things seemed to be heading up for us. But as usual, something had to break up our newfound happiness. My mom kept the job for about three years and then quit. We then found ourselves on food stamps and living off my aunt and child-support checks. My mother floated around from job to job for about three more years until she landed a job as an interior decorator for a local homebuilding company.

Up until this time we had stopped going to church and had really lost touch with the Adventist community. But we did have God in our lives and prayed daily for financial help. During my eighth- and ninth-grade years we started going to church a little more. And the job situation began looking up. My mom, who had never been to college, got a good job over a person with a degree, we were feeling pretty good. Life went on as normal until the summer of 2004, when we met Ken Hodges and his son, Brett. This was an answer to our prayers.

Ken and my mother dated for eight months and were married September 5, 2004. We then moved from Charlotte to Hendersonville, North Carolina. And this is the happiest we have ever been. We have security, a complete family, and the Lord in our lives. God is good!

Please, dear friends, remember the Lord, for He will deliver you from all hardships. "These things I have spoken unto you, that in me ye might have peace. In the world ye shall have tribulation: but be of good cheer; I have overcome the world" (John 16:33, KJV).

I So Hate Consequences

By Eileen Rojas

My son is here—given up for dead and now alive! Given up for lost and now found! And they began to have a wonderful time. Luke 15:22, Message.

We've often heard stories of children running away from home. I never actually ran away, but recently the thought didn't seem like such a bad idea. I wasn't actually planning on running away physically, but I did decide to run away from everyone around me. I didn't want to face the consequences of some of my recent actions. I had messed up in a few areas of my life, and I didn't want anyone to know—I felt so ashamed. I didn't even want to talk to God about it. I thought that if I ignored everything long enough, it would just go away. Or maybe if I fought hard enough on my own, I could overcome it. We humans usually make that mistake. We always want to fix everything ourselves. But I couldn't run away from my sins no matter how hard I tried.

Then one day I listened to a song by Relient K called "I So Hate Consequences," and it really hit home. It's sort of the story of the prodigal son, who realizes that he can't escape the mistakes he's made and that he can never run away from God. My favorite part of the song is the very end:

> "I said the words I knew you knew
>
> Oh God, Oh God, I needed you
>
> God all this time I needed you, I needed you."

I stopped running. Will you?

He Promises to Love You Freely
By Lorelle Evans

I will heal their waywardness and love them freely, for my anger has turned away from them. Hosea 14:4.

When I was 13, my family moved to the next town, which was closer to an Adventist elementary school and academy. I had been taking voice lessons from a woman for a couple of years, but it hadn't been going well lately, and with our recent move my parents and I decided it would be better to quit and maybe find a new teacher closer by. When my mother told my teacher I would no longer be taking lessons from her, she got angry and told my mother that I acted as if I were a prima donna but that I really wasn't any good and would never be able to go professional.

Have you ever had someone tell you that you're not good enough? Have you ever had someone give up on you? Maybe a parent has told you, "I've done my best, but this is it. You've gone too far this time. I want you out of my house." Or maybe your coach has told you, "You'd better pull yourself together. If we don't win tonight, I don't ever want to see your face again!"

Limits. Limits. Limits. Humans have a hard time loving without limits, so it can be hard to imagine a God who does. But that's exactly what He promises—to freely love you beyond anything you have ever experienced. He sees your scars, hurts, and tears. He's even been hurt by your sin and by the times you've rejected Him. Yet He still loves you. He will never kick you out, never love you and leave you, never throw you off the team, never tell you that you're not good enough. He has sacrificed everything for you, and He will do all that He can to spend eternity with you. We humans just can't grasp a limitless love like that. But if you trust Him, He will prove it. Imagine the possibilities.

Prayer

By Olivia Williams

Our Father in heaven, reveal who you are. Set the world right; do what's best—as above, so below. Keep us alive with three square meals. Keep us forgiven with you and forgiving others. Keep us safe from ourselves and the Devil. You're in charge! You can do anything you want! You're ablaze in beauty! Yes. Yes. Yes. Matthew 6:9-13, Message.

During my senior year of academy I got the chance to go to the Southern Union Prayer Conference at Camp Kulaqua in Florida. I was so excited. There were going to be lots of kids from other academies, and the activities were going to be super fun! I was also looking forward to it because it would be a chance to grow in my relationship with God.

We were at the conference for three days. With a total of 11 academies represented, we had about 300 kids there. Each day we had worship in the morning before breaking into our prayer groups, where we would talk and get to know each other. We also discussed subjects that academy and high school students face on a day-to-day basis. We prayed, but I kept thinking the whole time I was there that we weren't praying as much as I thought we were going to. Sure, we prayed a fair amount, but it was a "prayer" conference.

On the way back home I was sitting, thinking about the week, and I realized something: it's not how much you pray, even though we should pray often. It's how you pray to God.

When you're praying, do you find yourself distracted? I often do. So I thought, *If I pray to God the way I talk to my best friend, maybe I won't get distracted as much*. Talking to Him about anything and everything, in the way I talk to my friends, also helps me pray more often, and more comfortably, to Him.

So go and pray to God the way you would talk to a friend and see how much more you tell Him about your day, your friends, and your life.

Never Leave You

By Rebecca Anderson

"For I know the plans I have for you," declares the Lord, "plans to prosper you and not to harm you, plans to give you hope and a future."
Jeremiah 29:11.

It was Tuesday, February 5, and I was on a choir trip to Greenville, South Carolina, when I succumbed to a bad stomachache. But I felt uneasy. Something just wasn't right. My pain became so great that I had to be excused from my classes the next morning. I was sick on the couch when I heard my mom come through the door with a tone of voice that sounded down. She informed me of the death of a good friend from my freshman year. I then knew why I had felt so uneasy the night before.

Tears flooded my eyes, and Mom stroked my cheek while she told me about his untimely death. Will Eglinger was 17 years old and had a full life ahead of him. I started questioning God, and I was angry about the tragedy that had taken place.

I didn't sleep much that night, but I looked over at my nightstand and saw my Bible. I opened it, searching for some type of comfort. I settled on the verses in Matthew 18 about the lost sheep. The Shepherd never leaves His sheep and will go in search of the lost one. I was astonished how much of an impact this parable had on me. I then realized that God never left Will and only He knows the big picture.

The memories of Will and his love for others made people want to reach out to others who were hurting. I believe now that even in tragedy God works to impress our hearts. Will's short life reminded people that we need to live every day for God.

When something unexpected happens in your life, and especially when something sad or traumatic happens, remember that God did not cause it, but that He does have a plan to help you get through it. Even if you don't realize what His plan is right away, know that God can provide emotional healing and help you work through any situation. Let Him help you turn tragedy into triumph as you do all you can to live for Him and share His message with others so that you can enjoy the reunions that He has planned for us when He comes again.

The Courage to Be Gentle

By Amanda Skilton

Let your gentleness be evident to all. The Lord is near. Philippians 4:5.

The word "gentle" may not be something you like to hear in accordance with a description of your character. I never understood how being called a "gentle spirit" could be a compliment. I always wanted to be someone who wasn't afraid to step up to the plate and say what was on my mind. Aren't Americans taught to be assertive, and sometimes even aggressive, to establish ourselves as independent? Well, I was never that way. I always thought of myself as a coward since I could never really work up the courage to actually say anything.

As I was reading a daily devotional I had received as a gift, I started to believe differently. I came to the realization that maybe I didn't have to be forward with my thoughts to affect others. Maybe all it takes is a simple act of gentleness: a smile, a hug, or a sincere "How are you doing?" We don't have to get up in front of the entire school and give a sermon to have an impact on someone, but rather we can simply be a gentle spirit and be willing to be available for others when they need a friend.

Often we have no idea what those around us are struggling with. Rather than getting defensive or angry when someone says or does something offensive, show them gentleness and be a friend. Henry Wadsworth Longfellow put it this way: "Every man has his secret sorrows which the world knows not; and often times we call a man cold when he is only sad."

Remember that what may be considered a virtue in our society can differ greatly from that of God's ideals. So swallow the words that may first come to mind in the heat of a debate and show someone some gentleness.

Destruction of the End
Chris Janetzko

Blessed are you when people insult you, persecute you and falsely say all kinds of evil against you because of me. Rejoice and be glad, because great is your reward in heaven, for in the same way they persecuted the prophets who were before you. Matthew 5:11, 12.

I used to be afraid of the end of time. When I was younger, I had bad dreams about the end of time. In one of these horrific dreams I saw my family get murdered—that was not cool. The thought of this time period would bother me, especially since everyone would say it would likely happen during my lifetime. I wanted to grow up and have a normal life. I didn't want to live in the worst time period of all history. Recently, though, I found comfort about the end of time, and I'm not so afraid of it now.

I'm not saying that the end of time will not be a scary time, but I have found comfort in the Bible. The Bible says not to be afraid, for when we are put on trial, it's for the glory of God, and He will speak through us. Mark 13:11 says, "When ever you are arrested and brought to trial, do not worry beforehand about what to say. Just say whatever is given you at the time, for it is not you speaking, but the Holy Spirit." Even though we may be placed in scary situations, we are not alone and never will be. God will always be there, helping us through tough times.

If you watch any news, you can't help seeing terrible crimes, disasters, immoral behavior, and misplaced values. All of the signs that were predicted to happen before Jesus comes have been fulfilled. But think of those as the thorns on the rose. We know the Second Coming is soon—do not be afraid of the days ahead. Jesus will watch over you through everything. Something better is coming. We will soon be with Jesus, and that is what counts!

God Answers Prayers

By Leydy Reyes

Be joyful in hope, patient in affliction, faithful in prayer. Romans 12:12.

When I was in grade school, I really looked forward to going away to the adventure of a boarding academy. The first time I ever heard of Mount Pisgah Academy was about fifth grade, because the big kids at our school were planning to attend. Years passed and Mount Pisgah Academy Creative Ministries came to my school. They did puppet numbers and what I thought was the coolest thing, Mr. Parra doing Christian illusions. I remember talking to them and saying that I was going to attend Pisgah.

Later that day I went home and told my mom that I wanted to go to Pisgah. I was so sad because she told me I couldn't go because there was no way we could afford it. Sadly, I had to give up my dream, and I tried not to think about life after eighth grade.

Later, the Mount Pisgah Academy Acrosport team came to Raleigh SDA Elementary, and after watching their program and meeting the students, I again got excited about the possibility of attending. I went home and told my mom that Pisgah had came to the Raleigh SDA school, and she told me that it could have been a sign from God that He wanted me to attend Mount Pisgah Academy. We prayed that night and asked God for a sign during the summer that one person from Mount Pisgah Academy would come to the Raleigh area and talk to my mom and me.

During summer vacation after seventh grade, Mr. Hindman and Coach Lighthall, teachers from Mount Pisgah Academy, came to my house and invited us to go out to eat with them. Wow! It was an answer to our prayer. They talked to my mom about my brother, Oscar, and me attending Mount Pisgah Academy. My mom finally said yes, and we put our financial faith in God that He would provide the way.

I am happy to say that God did provide a way. Oscar and I worked hard to earn money. And with the help of financial aid, we both attended academy. We had a wonderful experience—it was more than I had hoped for.

I know that God listened to the prayers of a little grade school girl, and I know that He cares about my future. Trust Him to provide for you, too.

Life Everlasting

By Eli Rojas

For He chose us in him before the creation of the world to be holy and blameless in his sight. In love he predestined us to be adopted as his sons through Jesus Christ, in accordance with his pleasure and will—to the praise of his glorious grace, which he has freely given us in the One he loves. Ephesians 1:4-6.

Life is such a fragile thing. Every day thousands of babies are born, and every day thousands of people pass away. It's the cycle of life. Whether it's the death of a beloved pet or one of your closest relatives, everyone at one point in life has to cross this bridge. I've had many friends and close family members pass away, and the consolation is always, "As long as they had Jesus, we don't have to worry." But it wasn't till I almost died that I realized what that meant. I've had my share of close calls, and the scar on my hand is one of the biggest proofs. (But that's another story!)

In March of 2007 I had been visiting my family (several hours from school) during spring break. On Sunday we were to meet the school transportation bus and other students at the mall to head back to campus. But I was running a little late that day. The Pisgah bus will wait a total of about 10 minutes beyond leaving time, and if you're not at the bus, you're left behind. (They have scheduled stops at other places, so timing is an issue.)

As I said, I was late. When we got to the mall, I jumped out of the car and ran across the parking lot. Suddenly, out of the corner of my eye I saw a speeding van. I knew it would be a close call—it would either hit me or barely miss me. But in that second of wondering what would happen, I heard a voice say, "Don't worry; you'll be just fine." I relaxed, and at that moment I felt the mirror slide across my back.

I know that as long as I'm following God, even though I make a lot of mistakes and am very much human, I never have to worry about what's going to happen in this life. God will either protect me or I'll rest in Him. Either way, I know that we'll see Him very soon. Nothing beats the peace and assurance of knowing everything will work out in the end.

Freshmen Victorious

By Hector Gonzalez

But God chose the foolish things of the world to shame the wise; God chose the weak things of the world to shame the strong. 1 Corinthians 1:27.

It is almost impossible for the undersized, underexperienced freshmen to beat the seniors in any campus class event, but this one time made up for all the times that the freshmen were seen as unable to tackle the mighty seniors—an experience that should make all freshmen proud.

Scene 1: David, a freshman, and Neely, a senior, come to my office. Neely is upset and almost at the point of needing to be restrained, not at all violent, just attempting to be intimidating. His claim is that David owes him money because he lent him a fan that was later broken while in David's possession. David argues that he does not owe Neely any money. At some point in the argument, Neely says that he should take David to "The People's Court." I agree and ask them if we hold our own court if they will agree to the outcome. They do.

Scene 2: Each of them is to select a lawyer. David selects his buddy Angelo, a freshman, and Neely selects his buddy Greg, a senior. They're each sent to their rooms for one hour to prepare their cases. Neely and Greg leave with a confidence and assurance that they are going to win this case. In this hour a jury is selected as well as a judge. The jury is made up of selected students of each grade, but the people's choice for judge is Alain, a senior. Neely feels even more confident as he hears the choice of judge—his friend and classmate.

Scene 3: All sides are ready. The lobby is converted into a courtroom. Greg opens up the trial with his client's clear and to-the-point demand for payment of a broken fan. Angelo follows with an acknowledgment of his client's responsibility for the broken fan but astonishes the jury with his introduction of depreciation. He calls in witnesses who testify of the condition of the fan at the time of its being loaned to David, and they testify of how it had been damaged on other occasions while in Neely's possession. He enters into evidence a receipt of a similar fan purchased by another student and calculates with depreciation a fair settlement of what the fan is believed to be worth at the time of its damage.

Scene 4: After deliberation, the jury and judge side with David. Neely and Greg sit in surprise and disappointment. David and Angelo sit as victorious freshmen.

You might feel like an underdog in society, but in God's kingdom you are victorious.

God's Comfort Zone
By Ross Knight

I can do everything through him who gives me strength. Philippians 4:13.

My freshman year of high school I went to a junior academy in Charlotte, North Carolina. My class was very small. There were only about 12 kids combined in the ninth and tenth grades. Sometime during the year we were told that we were going on a mission trip to New York City. That got everyone excited, thinking about all the fun we'd have in the city. I was pretty scared, however, because I had never been on a mission trip before.

It was an experience I'll never forget. When we first got to the dormitories where we would be staying, we were immediately thrown into action. We found out that we would be engaged in a new urban ministry, and we were encouraged to try and go outside of our comfort zone and be the Lord's hands as we participated in the daily activities.

Yeah, that sounded great and all, but what they had us doing first threw me outside my comfort zone for the rest of the trip. The woman in charge took us to a costume room where we were to dress up like clowns. We had the funky hair, face paint, and huge colorful pants and shirts. Then I found out that we were heading to Wall Street, in the middle of the city, to pass out tracts about our faith in our clown suits. It was definitely an interesting day.

This first test to my comfort zone really prepared me for the rest of the trip. During our stay in New York City we visited kids' shelters, mental health homes, and even drug rehab centers. At the drug rehab center, I even got to preach a sermon (through an interpreter because the men all spoke Spanish). That trip was such an eye-opening experience, and no other event, thus far, has made me grow closer to God than that trip.

Remember, even when things are outside of your comfort zone, God promises in Philippians 4:13 that "I can do all things through Christ who strengthens me" (NKJV). Don't be bashful or afraid; instead, let Him use you to fulfill His work. I'm sure an adventure awaits you.

Just Let Go

By Anna Grissom

There remains, then, a Sabbath-rest for the people of God; for anyone who enters God's rest also rests from his own work, just as God did from his.
Hebrews 4:9, 10.

For as long as I can remember, Sabbath has always been a very special time in my family. I can remember as a little kid always looking forward to Friday nights. At the time, my dad was working at the conference office as the assistant treasurer. He would work late all the time, and I didn't get to see him very much. But Fridays were different. He would come home about the same time that I would come home from school. This became the most relaxing time of the week. We would always do something fun on Friday nights. I can remember singing and dancing around our living room to the King's Heralds, going over to a friend's house for supper, or just having fun with my family. I looked forward to going to church the next day and seeing all my friends. I always considered Sabbath as a time for relaxation and fun.

It wasn't until I got much older that I realized the real importance of the Sabbath. The Sabbath is a day for us to relax from our normal everyday life and just spend time with our loving Creator.

It wasn't until I got older that I also noticed the people in my extended family who are not Adventists anymore doing whatever they want on the Sabbath. The Sabbath to them is just another day of the week—Saturday, not Sabbath. They didn't have a day to just relax, and I could tell that they really needed that time to just let go and not worry about where the next paycheck was coming from or whether or not the grass had been mowed.

God has a reason for everything. He knew that we needed one day a week to just let go. He also knew that in our busy lives it would be very easy to forget to stop and spend time with Him. So today, on this Sabbath, just let it all go. Let God worry about what is going to happen. Let Him show you what the Sabbath truly is all about.

My Not-So-Happy Valentine's Day

By Stephanie Thomas

Your love, O Lord, reaches to the heavens, your faithfulness to the skies.
Psalm 36:5.

Excitement filled my day as I started pondering what special thing I could do for my boyfriend. Valentine's Day, one of my favorite holidays, was coming up, and I wanted it to be special. Some things in my life were not going very smoothly, but I still held my head high. I could not wait for all the flowers, chocolates, and love that would be spread. Plus, it was going to be the first year I had a "real valentine." But a few days before February 14, out of nowhere, BOOM, my boyfriend, whom at the time I thought I was madly in love with, dumped me. I was crushed—I couldn't believe my ears. He didn't love me anymore, and he just wanted to be friends. How could this happen?

When Valentine's Day arrived, I didn't think I could get through it. No valentine, roses, chocolates, or anything. Why did I have to be heartbroken on a day that's supposed to be about love? Our breakup had happened at the worse possible time, and I didn't understand—I thought everything had been going fine. Some stuff at my church and with my friends wasn't going well at all, and now this. I was miserable. But that night one of my best friends called. She told me that I didn't need a valentine or a boy in my life. Weeping, I explained how I felt. The lingering feeling deep inside me was like I did not matter and no one cared or loved me. This is when she told me that I should remember that God will *always* love me and be there when things get rough. Even though it was difficult to see, this was just a part of God's plan for me. And maybe, my now ex-boyfriend and I were better off just being friends. Perhaps if we had kept on dating, we might not have been able to keep our friendship as strong.

I am so glad that she called me—I had totally forgotten to trust God! I prayed to God to help things work out and help me get through the difficult time. No, things did not all get resolved that second, but I felt a lot better. God helped me get through that hard time, and as time passed, my heart healed, and I am happy to say that I am now great friends with my former boyfriend.

We all need to remember that although humans may fail us, and we may not understand the timing of events in our lives, God will *always* love us! We need no other valentine.

Spreading the Love

By Lorelle Evans

The King will reply, "I tell you the truth, whatever you did for one of the least of these brothers of mine, you did for me." Matthew 25:40.

During my junior year of academy, our entire class went on a mission trip to Tennessee to help people whose homes had been destroyed by a tornado.

It all happened one Monday morning in the middle of math class. Our principal and class sponsors waltzed in and announced that we would be leaving the very next morning for Tennessee and wouldn't be back until that Friday. I was a little upset. I was going to miss Valentine's Day, which meant that I would miss spending time with my amazing boyfriend whom I rarely got to see. I had plans, and this trip was ruining them. All day I complained and dreaded the next day's journey.

But as we drove through the neighborhoods of western Tennessee and I saw the destruction and loss of many homes, I changed my attitude. I met people who were left with nothing but crushed up pieces of what was once their home. All of a sudden I felt guilty. I had been so mad because I had to miss a day of chocolate, kisses, and hearts, but these people were missing their belongings, their treasures, and their warm, comfortable homes. My Valentine's Day was spent picking up trash and pieces of what used to be a family's home, and I have to say it was the best Valentine's Day I have ever had. I felt so much happiness knowing I was doing something for someone else.

I think God knew that this experience would open my eyes to reality and help me realize that life is not about me. I think that life might just be about what I do for others instead of what I do for myself. God knew that Valentine's Day wasn't about the love I could receive but the love I could give to someone else by helping and showing the hand of God.

A Box Bite and Seven Hours
By Alyssa Pelto

We know that anyone born of God does not continue to sin; the one who was born of God keeps him safe, and the evil one cannot harm him.
1 John 5:18.

It was February 15. My whole family was in a cleaning frenzy at our house the whole day. About 6:00 p.m. we finally decided that we really needed to eat. As my mom was cooking supper, she saw a box on top of the refrigerator that looked like it had a rag draped over the side, so she reached up to see what was in the box.

As she grabbed the box, she squished the "rag," which turned out to be a bat. It hissed at her, and she yelped. There had been a bat living on top of our fridge! We threw the bat outside. What a mistake!

After a little research, we realized that we should have taken the bat to get tested for rabies. We piled into the car to find out if we needed to get rabies shots. When we arrived at the ER, they said that only my mom needed one. Unfortunately they didn't have the proper vaccine available, and they told us that we would have to go to another hospital.

The following day my mom called the Department for Disease Control and they said that we *all* needed to get the shots, since bats have very small mouths and razor-sharp teeth that can bite a victim without their ever knowing it. Plus, bats can secrete rabies through their skin and in their droppings. That day we spent seven hours just waiting to get our shots, but it was all worth it.

I look back at that experience and realize that if my mom had not grabbed the box we could all be dead now. Why? We would have never seen it coming! We do not know how long the bat had been in the house or how long we may have been exposed to rabies.

Just so, we don't always see Satan sneaking into our lives. It sometimes takes something bad to happen to us for us to actually realize that we need spiritual saving. God works in mysterious ways, but He always has a plan for us!

For Richer or Poorer
By Luke Hudgins

Better to be poor and honest than to be dishonest and a fool.
Proverbs 19:1, NLT.

Throughout my life my parents taught me that there were more important things in life than money. When I was young, though, I wanted everything technology and money could offer. I longed for the day when I would have a high-paying job and could buy the kind of life I wanted. As I've grown older, I've learned that handling large sums of money requires determination and talent—and that getting money requires a lot of hard work.

With assurance, God says that He will never give us tasks we cannot handle. From a financial standpoint, God's words mean to me that if we truly need money, He will supply it. For example, when I was deciding to go to Mount Pisgah Academy, my parents did not have enough money to pay for my tuition. But they knew that sending me to a Seventh-day Adventist school was what God wanted, so they stepped out in faith. As crazy as it may seem, every year we had just enough money for me to stay. It is my belief that God will also help me when I go to Southern Adventist University.

When Jesus was here on earth, He made sure people understood the true power of money. The widow who gave two mites was considered richly generous. Her treasure will be in heaven! The story of the rich young ruler reminds us that earthly wealth cannot fill an empty heart. And Jesus called folks from all walks of life—from simple fishermen to a doctor—to be His followers. They all gave up their jobs to live selflessly and completely follow Christ. And they didn't go hungry—they always had just what they needed because God provided for their needs.

Jesus teaches us not to store up treasures (cars, money, electronics, clothes, etc.) here on earth, but to live our lives for Him. What He has for us in heaven makes everything we can imagine in this world inconsequential.

As you go about your day, remember to thank God for the money you have—and if it doesn't seem like enough, don't worry. Live for Him, and He will provide just what you need.

Never Fear, God Is Here!

By Emily Milliner

I call to the Lord, who is worthy of praise, and I am saved from my ene-mies. 2 Samuel 22:4.

I love all water sports! I love to swim, sail, ski, snorkel, and pretty much all other water sports. But there is one problem—I'm deathly afraid of sharks! I hate anything that swims and has sharp teeth. This is a problem, since I like to spend time in the ocean where there are sharks.

When I was about 11 years old, I took sailing lessons with my older sister in St. Petersburg, Florida. We would often take our little sailboat out into the bay. I was never scared of being out there until one day!

It was really windy outside, and usually that means it is perfect sailing weather, but the waves were high and the water was really choppy. After being out in the bay for a while, I started to head back to the dock, but that's when I saw it! It was a shark circling my boat! I was so scared! I was the only one still out in my boat—everyone else had already started to head back to the dock. I was alone in a boat with a shark circling around me, and no fast escape. I began to pray that God would keep me safe and help the shark to go away. I tried to ignore my fears and keep going, and the next thing I knew, the shark was gone.

Even though the shark probably had no intention of hurting me, I was still afraid of it. I was by myself in the wild ocean, and I had to rely on God alone. And as soon as I had asked for help, the shark left. How amazing is that?

God doesn't just protect us from danger; He even cares about our feelings and can calm us and reassure us with a peace that passes all understanding. I am so thankful that He is only a prayer away and that He promises to protect and save me from my enemies, even if it is a shark.

Why?

By Rosella Age

Cast your cares on the Lord and he will sustain you; he will never let the righteous fall. Psalm 55:22.

Our family suffered a tragic loss when my siblings, Sara and Nathaniel, were victims of a freeway accident. (They were staff at Nosoca Pines Ranch for many years. You might remember Nature Nate or Sara at the ski beach.)

I found out about the accident when my mom woke me up early on a Monday morning with a grave look on her face. She told me to follow her. Some very close family friends were sitting in the living room, but I didn't catch the hint that something was wrong until I saw my dad sitting with his elbows on his legs and his hands clasped together. When Daddy explained what had happened, my first reaction was "No!" Like everyone else, I was in shock. Then I began to ask the tough questions: "Why, God, why?"

Being so vulnerable at this time, I realize now that Satan was trying to turn me against God and blame Him. I can't count the number of times I cried out in anger at God for taking my brother and sister away, for not preventing the accident. Of course, what I, and my family, *really* needed was help to get through this—help from God. It seemed like the right thing to do, so I prayed for my family, for His presence, and for Him to take away all my grief. I didn't feel as though I should have had to experience something like this at 10 years old. What a horrible thing. That event shaped my childhood and changed my life. The way I think is different. The way I act is different. Even the way I dress has leaned toward my sister Sara's style. It's as though God was working on my faith when I really could have used it. Casting my burdens on Jesus relieved me, so I depended on Him a lot more.

Now I feel pretty confident and consistent in my bond with God. The accident was something I ended up accepting and maturing from. I think I have a better understanding of death, after thinking it through over the past years. It's definitely not something I could handle on my own, and I am grateful that God stood by me through all of my emotional ups and downs.

In times of trouble, we must turn to God for support. I think about my siblings a lot, and occasionally I still cry, but I find comfort in knowing we'll all be going home soon.

The Whole World Is in His Hands

By Cheryl Grant

Be at rest once more, O my soul, for the Lord has been good to you.
Psalm 116:7.

"Mommy, does He really got the whole world in His hands?" Kaitlyn, age 4, had sat quietly as we drove around town completing our ordinary weekday errands. We were at our last stop, pulling into the grocery store parking lot, when Kaitlyn spontaneously inquired about the lyrics of this song. She had apparently been singing it to herself for quite some time. A smile came to my lips as I thought of how simple and wonderful her question was.

Before I could answer, Jakob, her big brother, replied very candidly and with reassuring confidence, "Yeah. I can feel His palms." I couldn't have given Kaitlyn a better answer.

Life stays so busy, and stress hits us over and over like waves in an ocean. Weekly tasks are never ending—laundry stays piled high, there are expenses to pay, deadlines to finish, and school projects to start. Most of us are constantly juggling all the time. A friend said to me that she was juggling so much that she was afraid to stop, in fear of everything falling apart. Sound familiar? This is a familiar feeling to most people. When I start getting overwhelmed with life's chores, I remember Kaitlyn and Jakob's conversation. God has the whole world in His hands. He is in control. Everything runs smoother and falls into place better when I take a breath, put God first in my mind, and ask for Him to lead.

Talk to God and keep Him first. Have a daily relationship with Him. If you seek to have a relationship with our heavenly Father, not only will you feel an ever-growing love for Him but you, too, will be able to feel His palms.

So Help Me God

By Brian Hindman

*You gave me life and showed me kindness, and in your providence
watched over my spirit. Job 10:12.*

When I was in elementary school, George Washington was my hero. After I learned to read, my grandma gave me a series of books full of interesting stories about the American presidents. George Washington captivated me the most. He was brave in some of the most frightful situations. Once while fighting as a young soldier, Washington had two horses shot out from beneath him and four bullet holes in his coat, yet he survived unhurt. He wrote a letter to his brother giving credit to God for his protection. Washington believed that God was all-powerful and cared about his safety.

Later in life Washington was a general in the Revolutionary War and found his army almost completely surrounded and heavily outnumbered at the Battle of Long Island. In a daring attempt to survive, he ordered his entire army to be rowed across a river during the night. When daylight came and the army still hadn't been fully evacuated, an unusually thick fog allowed the remaining soldiers to cross to safety. Washington had managed to remove his army of 9,000 men without the loss of any soldiers. One account of the story says that Washington and his men knelt and thanked God for miraculously rescuing them.

There are other events in Washington's life that show he trusted in God's care. After many years of military service, he was elected the first president of the United States. At the ceremony when he was sworn in, he is said to have added the phrase "so help me God" at the end of the oath to become president. Since then, many U.S. presidents have repeated the same words when they take the solemn oath.

God is just as interested in your life as He was in George Washington's. Are you facing difficult battles? God promises to watch over you and give you strength. Are you uncertain about what the future may hold? God promises guidance for every situation. We can have the same bravery President Washington had. In every situation you face today, pray, like Washington, "so help me God."

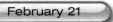

Watch Over

By Junho (Daven) Kim

I love you, O Lord, my strength. Psalm 18:1.

When I was 5 years old and living in Korea, my family and a couple of other families went to East Beach. All of our families were really close to each other because we were all members of the same church. It was a windy day and quite dangerous to swim because the wind made the waves very high. But we went into the water anyway. I had to come out earlier than the others because my mom was worried about me since the waves were so much bigger than me. So I lay on the beach just watching everyone else play. After a while everyone came out of the water and sat on the beach with me.

We were all hungry, so our moms began getting everything ready for lunch. About 30 minutes later my mom called me and told me that the meal was ready. I ran toward my mom and the delicious food she had prepared. All of us enjoyed a great meal, finishing it off with watermelon for dessert, and then all the parents started talking about adult stuff.

Quickly getting bored of this, I quietly went into the water and started playing. I was having a lot of fun, but after a while a wave forced me down. When I came up, I realized that I was getting pulled farther and farther from the beach. I tried to stand up, but the water was too strong. I started feeling afraid and began to cry. Suddenly my back hit something hard. I turned around and saw that it was a huge rock. Climbing up on the rock, I called to my parents for help. My father ran to me as fast as he could. He hugged me and carried me out of the water.

I still remember that moment clearly. If there hadn't been a huge rock at that place, I would have been drawn into the water with the riptide current. But God was with me and He saved me. I am so grateful to Him!

Cost of Salvation

By Michael Huskins

It is for freedom that Christ has set us free. Galatians 5:1.

What if, after Abraham Lincoln had proclaimed the Emancipation Proclamation, a former slave had come to him and wanted to pay for his freedom because he didn't think it should be a gift? The conversation might have gone something like this:

Lincoln: "Well, how much do you want to pay for your freedom?"

Former slave: "I reckon about $30."

Lincoln (after pointing out to the former slave some of the people who had sacrificed so much for him, including a woman who had lost her husband and all of her sons, and a man who had lost both of his legs): "These people fought to give you this gift. Now how much are you willing to pay?"

Former slave (with tears in his eyes): "I can't pay that price."

Lincoln (giving the former slave a heartwarming smile): "That's right; no one could pay that price."

We can't even begin to understand the price that Jesus paid for us on the cross. If the price He paid was enough to bear all the sins we have committed, how can we expect that earthly things will even come close to matching Jesus' gift?

Galatians 5:1 says, "It is for freedom that Christ has set you free." When Jesus died on the cross, He gave us an amazing gift, because He loves us. He sacrificed everything to give us what we needed most. He gave us freedom from a world of hatred and sin.

Let us not discard the most precious gift, thinking that we don't deserve it. Instead, accept it freely and live as if you own it. Be thankful, and be proud of your place in God's kingdom.

God Provides

By Nicole Dannenberger

If anyone speaks, he should do it as one speaking the very words of God. If anyone serves, he should do it with the strength God provides, so that in all things God may be praised through Jesus Christ. To Him be the glory and the power for ever and ever. Amen. 1 Peter 4:11.

All my life I have been asked the same question: "What do you want to be when you grow up?" For most of my life I never had a good answer. Even after starting my senior year of academy, I felt lost and didn't know what direction to take the following year. I asked God for His help and guidance.

At the beginning of the year, the seniors took a Friday off to go to a college fair at one of our neighboring schools. Many colleges were there with so much to offer. I approached one of the representatives from Kettering College of Nursing who told me that nursing was a very competitive career to get into. He also told me that I should look into getting my CNA (certified nursing assistant) license, because that would help me get into nursing school. Of course, up to that time I had never considered becoming a CNA. However, I prayed about it that night and asked God to show me what He wanted me to do.

By that Sabbath afternoon I had decided to look into becoming a CNA. That Sunday I called a little nursing home that was 15 minutes from my house. I asked them if they could give me any information on CNA classes. They said that a class was starting the next day and all I needed to do was bring a pen. I was so excited! But that's when the decisions got hard. Taking this opportunity would mean missing out on several days of school, and I would have to work a 12-hour shift on the weekends. I prayed that night for God's help in showing me what I should do. It didn't take long for me to receive an overwhelming feeling that God wanted me to pursue this path.

God helped me through the few months it took to complete the course. And although I was extremely busy taking the CNA course, working weekend shifts, as well as keeping up with my homework for all of my senior classes, I always seemed to have just enough strength to make it through the week. Now I am certified, and love it!

If you are having a hard time deciding what to do with your life, ask God to help. He will provide you with the answer. Just be patient and open-minded—and be ready to act.

Again

By Teddi McAllen

And I—in righteousness I will see your face; when I awake, I will be satisfied with seeing your likeness. Psalm 17:15.

Loving and kind mothers are wonderful people to have in life. Mothers are usually the ones who sing us to sleep when we're little. They also often cry at various important occasions: baby's first steps and words, birthdays, graduations, weddings, and the birth of their first grandchild. When you think of home, while you are on a school trip, living in a dorm, or moving away for the first time, usually you imagine her face, her voice, the things she said, and things she always does for you.

Today is my own mother's birthday. What you do not realize is that 10 years ago she passed away of ovarian cancer. It did not take me that long to understand what was going on. What did take time for me was being able to think about her and not be sad every time I did. February 14, 2007, marked the tenth year without her in my life. Ten years without her lovely face, beautiful voice, and loving heart. In those 10 years I have gone through life wondering why it had to be my mother, why it had to be my life that was turned completely around.

It took someone saying what day it was in the middle of my senior Bible class, while talking about marriages and why they have problems, to remind me that my life without her had reached a decade. Standing out in the hallway between classes, crying on one of my closest friend's shoulder, I let out things I had not said before. It hit me that I was not going to have my mother at my graduation, and I would probably not even have my father there. It hit me how much I was really going to go through without her. I had already missed having her around at those big birthdays, and there were many more to come. And she wasn't going to be there to celebrate my graduation from Mount Pisgah Academy, finding the man of my dreams, and my wedding day. With those events running through my mind, all it took was one calming set of words to warm my heart. "You'll see her again," my friend reminded me. I thank God for that promise.

Stay Awake!

By Ryan Johnson

The bridegroom was a long time in coming, and they all became drowsy and fell asleep. At midnight the cry rang out: "Here's the bridegroom! Come out to meet him!" Then all the virgins woke up and trimmed their lamps. The foolish ones said to the wise, "Give us some of your oil; our lamps are going out." "No," they replied, "there may not be enough for both us and you. Instead, go to those who sell oil and buy some for yourselves." Matthew 25:5-9.

Early one morning my brother, Eric, my father, and I were courageously braving the highway. To survive the horrors of modern-day traffic, one must stay alert and be ready to react to any danger. My father and I were vigilant. Eric, however, was falling fast asleep in the front seat.

In front of us was a semitrailer towing two other trucks. The two others were being pulled backwards, so their fronts were facing us. My brother, unaware of this, was enjoying his nap. Struck by a moment of mischievous inspiration, my dad came up with the idea to give him a little scare. He drove up real close behind the truck, and when we were about 10 feet away, he started screaming for us to hang on. My brother woke up from all the noise and saw the truck facing us and panicked. Thinking we were about to be splattered by the 18-wheeler, he almost started to cry.

My brother got a good scare because he wasn't paying attention. He wasn't aware of what was happening, just as the 10 virgins who waited for the bridegroom. The foolish virgins were unaware and lost their guard, unprepared for what might happen. The bridegroom came and went, and they were left out because of their lack of attention.

We have to remember to be alert at all times, because we don't know when the end will come. Whether it is the end of our lives on this planet or Jesus' second coming, we must always be ready. Instead of sleeping your life away, start preparing for what your future may hold.

Laughing at the Cross?

By Kathy Brannan

So, as the Holy Spirit says: "Today, if you hear his voice, do not harden your hearts." Hebrews 3:7, 8.

They were standing by the cross. The thud of the hammers swung by the Roman soldiers resounded sickeningly. The wails of the women who had followed and the mocking, jeering cries of the crowd echoed across the hill. Jesus was being crucified. But many people were laughing! These same people were talking loudly about who knows what and turning their backs from the scene. I stood there, momentarily stunned. How could this be? True, this was just a reenactment—it was not really Jesus, and the soldiers were not really hammering nails into his hands—but this was a very vivid, action-filled portrayal of the most serious, decisive moment in all history!

Why are we sometimes so casual and even calloused to the Crucifixion events? One reason is expressed well in the old spiritual "We Didn't Know Who You Was." We forget that He is the answer—sometimes the only answer—to our needs and to our optimum well-being. We forget that He is the ruler of the universe, yet He cares about each of us as though we are His only creation. We cannot grasp how deep and wide and everlasting is the love of the One who hung on that cross. We forget that Jesus was willing to give up heaven and being with His Father forever if that was what it took for us to have eternal life.

A lot of us know who He is, but we do not want to accept His answers or guidance. His ways are not our ways and His will is not our will, so we resist that still small voice. And each time we resist, it becomes easier to do so. Gradually, almost imperceptibly, we could end up in the same sad condition as the Pharisees who crucified Him. But if we let Him mold us, God promises, "I will give you a new heart and put a new spirit in you; I will remove from you your heart of stone and give you a heart of flesh" (Ezekiel 36:26).

Someday God will have everyone's attention riveted on His Son! He will not be on a cross in humiliation and pain. And it will not be simply a pageant. The real Jesus will be riding on the clouds, surrounded by billions of angels! At that event "every knee should bow, in heaven and on earth" (Philippians 2:10). I want to bow because I love Him, know Him, and adore Him.

Love From the Hated One
By Brooke Wade

Praise be to the God and Father of our Lord Jesus Christ! In his great mercy he has given us new birth into a living hope through the resurrection of Jesus Christ from the dead. 1 Peter 1:3.

Once upon a time there was a little boy. This boy was poor—he was born in one of the most humble places imaginable. No one really liked him, except his parents, and some even tried to kill him. When he grew up, most people rejected him, and his friends never really understood him. He told them about his life, but they were too caught up in their own lives to worry about what they were missing. When he died, most never even saw it coming. Shocked, they watched him die a criminal's death—the worst there was.

I'm sure by now you've figured out that this boy was Jesus. And to the joy of the universe, He rose three days later to give hope and peace and salvation to us all.

Through Jesus' great mercy we have the awesome ability to live new every day. He came down to this sick earth just so we could be born again. He chose to love us more than anything, risking His life—life that we can't even begin to understand—so that He could save us. He came and was born in a stable—filled with the stink and contamination of dirty animals—to be a helpless baby. He encountered life as we do. He got sick, was hurt, and experienced hatred—just so He could save the world.

Throughout the ages humanity continues to discard Him, but He loves us so much. Praise God for His mercy and grace! He sent His Son to do this for us because He loves us. God's heart broke the day His Son died, but three days later Jesus rose to life. Now we have the awesome hope that we can have new life in our God. So, in praise to my Lord and my Savior, I choose today—and forever—to celebrate that day that He was born to die, so I could one day pray for Him to save my life.

Jesus Is Our Love Story

By Lauren Lowe

Surely goodness and love will follow me all the days of my life, and I will dwell in the house of the Lord forever. Psalm 23:6.

Teens often dream about finding someone who will love them completely—a boyfriend or girlfriend who will complete them; a person who will love them forever; someone they can always count on. However, this usually causes disappointment when the person they think is their charming prince or the girl of their dreams turns out to be exactly the opposite. Usually it's better to stay out of these unrealistic relationships and just wait for the right person to come later. Easier said than done, I know.

What really matters is that God has a plan for each one of our lives. He knows even when we don't understand. I know how frustrating this can be as a young person. We all have lots of decisions to make: what college to attend, what major to choose, what the rest of our lives will hold. That's a lot to take on when we're teenagers. But God knows whom you'll be with, where you will go, and what you'll do.

Jesus is the true lover of our souls. He is the one who will never stop caring or listening to us. He promises to help us through whatever our future holds. We may look to a significant other for love, but Jesus is really the lover we need to look to. He'll never break up with us, never leave us alone, and never forsake us as long as we live.

And the best news is that He has given us an invitation to spend eternity with Him, the ultimate lover of our souls.

Leap Year

By Stella Bradley

He has made everything beautiful in its time. He has also set eternity in the hearts of men; yet they cannot fathom what God has done from beginning to end. Ecclesiastes 3:11.

Do you know anyone who has a birthday today? People born on February 29 technically have a birthday only every four years. Yet they continue to get older. When a leap year baby celebrates for the fourth time on February 29, we don't say that they are only 4 years old. No, that person is already a teenager, ready to get a driver's license.

Time and age are funny partners. My cat is now more than 21 years old. In cat years that makes him equivalent to a 100-year-old man. We have a fish that's about 1 year old. So in "people years" that makes him 30 years old. And did you know that a 200-year-old Galapagos tortoise is equivalent to a 25-year-old person?

It takes awhile to wrap my mind around the concept of age on this earth. The antediluvians (people who lived before the Flood) thought nothing about blowing out 400 candles on their birthday cake. And they weren't arthritic and bent with age. They had newborn children and could run and jump and look forward to several hundred more years of vibrant life.

But what is even more mind-boggling is the concept of eternity. I once heard someone describe eternity this way. Imagine a planet as big as the sun and made out of solid steel. Now imagine a little gnat flying around in space near this steel planet. (Obviously this is impossible, but just go with it.) The gnat gets just close enough to the planet to lightly touch the surface with its wing. Then it flies away to wander in space. After flying around for 100 years, it makes its way back to this steel planet and lightly touches the surface with the delicate tip of its wing. Then it flies off again for another 100 years. By the time that steel planet is worn away by the touch of a gnat's wing, we have just passed the first second of eternity.

I certainly can't comprehend it. But we know that it is possible to live forever! Eternal life with Jesus will be exciting and adventurous. We will never be bored. I don't know how time will be measured in heaven or the new earth, but in my limited concept of time, I don't want you to miss out on your 400th, 1,000th, or 1,000,000th birthday. Get to know Jesus as your personal friend; He's looking forward to spending time with you!

Trust in God
By Sarah Milliner

Those who know your name will trust in you, for you, Lord, have never for-saken those who seek you. Psalm 9:10.

Have you ever had to make a hard decision and it seemed as if both of your options were terrible? During my sophomore year I was faced with a dreadful choice. I had to choose where I wanted to go to school for the next two years. You see, my little school went only to tenth grade. I had two choices.

The first choice included going to a local public school where I could stay at home with my family. I was terrified, because I had always attended a Christian school; in fact, the same school since kindergarten. I also didn't want to leave all of my friends.

The second choice was to go to a boarding academy. I wouldn't be able to be with my family, but I would be in a Christian, Seventh-day Adventist, environment. I was scared because I wouldn't know anyone, and I would have to make all new friends.

If you are a worrywart like me, you'll understand why I began to freak out. I felt as if I were trapped in a cave, and the way out was blocked by deadly lions. One day I was talking to one of my teachers at school, and they mentioned to just keep praying about it. How could I be so dumb? How could I make such a big decision and not ask God to help me? I began to pray.

My answer didn't come immediately, but eventually I began to believe that a boarding academy was the best place for me. And after experiencing it, I am sure I made the right decision. I made amazing friends, and I grew in Christ. I am so thankful that I handed my decision over to God.

God cares about you and every dilemma you face. He already has the best plan chosen for you; just ask Him to help you realize His will for your life.

Unchanging Truth

By Kaylee Couser

I will give you a new heart and put a new spirit in you; I will remove from you your heart of stone and give you a heart of flesh. Ezekiel 36:26.

For me, going to camp was a life-changing experience. God showed me that I needed to be cleansed and commit myself to Him. At camp the staff did a play on Jesus' resurrection—it was so overwhelming that I cried. I knew then that He was the only one who could make me happy. Instead of having a heart of stone, He gave me a heart of flesh.

For girls, getting clean is more than just scrubbing with soap and water. We don't just shower or bathe; we indulge. Indeed, we have made "getting clean" an art form. No matter how much we scrub, however, our cleansing goes only skin-deep (literally). When we need cleansing from sin, we need far more than a scented bubble bath.

The Israelites needed to get clean also. They had dirtied themselves with sin and idolatry; many of them had been taken into captivity in faraway Babylon. At the same time Jeremiah was telling the people in Jerusalem about the coming destruction of their beloved city, Ezekiel was giving the same message to those already in captivity. You see, the people were certain that because God loved Jerusalem, the city would never fall to a foreign nation.

What they didn't understand was that God was willing to let the nation fall in order to teach His people an important lesson about their sin and His holiness. God also gave Ezekiel a message of hope. One day God would gather His people back and cleanse their hearts. He would give them a new spirit and a new heart to love and serve Him.

After you shower once, are you clean forever? Nope. In the same way, you need to keep coming to God, asking Him to cleanse you from sin. Even though I have committed myself to God, I still need to ask Him for help and to cleanse me from sin—every day.

Making a Difference

By Lorelle Evans

You are the salt of the earth. But if the salt loses its saltiness, how can it be made salty again? It is no longer good for anything, except to be thrown out and trampled by men. You are the light of the world. A city on a hill cannot be hidden. Matthew 5:13, 14.

In the sixth grade, after being homeschooled for a while, I enrolled second semester at the private school I had attended in the past. But I didn't know many kids very well, and being shy, I had some trouble making friends. But a few weeks later another new girl came—her name was Krystal. She had some major problems. She smelled awful; her hair looked greasy; her words were slurred; and her clothes looked like they had once belonged to her grandma.

Everyone was so cruel to her, often treating her as if she weren't even human. Sometimes when I had no one to hang out with, I would play with her. But I would feel so embarrassed, and in an effort to fit in, I would talk bad about her behind her back. I would say terrible things about the way she dressed and the weird things she would do that totally grossed me out.

Soon I stopped hanging out with her because of peer pressure. Other kids told me that she was too weird. After I ditched or ran away from her several times, she stopped trying to hang out with me. I felt terrible and so ashamed of myself. She was a person just like me, yet I was treating her unkindly just to hang out with people who were mean and never stayed true friends. I know I didn't make a positive difference in Krystal's life. I made life seem cruel and unwelcoming for her—and I regret it.

As Christians we need to be a light to the world to point people down the right path leading to Jesus. I have learned from this experience that God wants me to make a difference in the lives of *all* the people I meet. He wants me to go boldly into the world and let others see Jesus in me.

How to Get Rich Quick

By Katie Oates

If you remain in me and my words remain in you, ask whatever you wish, and it will be given you. This is to my Father's glory, that you bear much fruit, showing yourselves to be my disciples. John 15:7, 8.

Now that I have graduated from academy I have to decide what I want to do with my life. However, I have to make the decision whether or not I am going to let God take control of it. Everyone has their own idea of what they want their life to be like. Some people want to become doctors; others may want to be animators or singers—the list could go on forever. Yet we have to remember that God has a plan for our lives, and through this plan He wants to bless us and give us everything we need. He not only wants to bless us, but wants our lives to be a blessing to others.

And though I wish that God would write it on a piece of paper, or give me an audible message of direction, things just don't work that way. Instead, I have to earnestly pray for guidance and that God will impress me with the direction He wants me to go. We all have to make this choice and be willing to pray this prayer. Sometimes He will open clear doors; sometimes He will "speak" through the advice of trustworthy people; sometimes He will perform a miracle on our behalf to provide opportunities or finances. Whatever He has in store, we can be sure it will be an adventure suited just for us.

In order to let God lead, we need to actually ask for help, daily humbling ourselves to His will and being ready to follow His lead. John 15:7, 8 says, "If you remain in me and my words remain in you, ask whatever you wish, and it will be given you. This is to my Father's glory, that you bear much fruit, showing yourselves to be my disciples." In this verse I learned that God wants to give us all the things our hearts desire, but we have to daily commit ourselves to Him in everything we do. Doing this will bless not only us but others as well.

This isn't a simple task, and God knows that in this world it is really easy to get sidetracked. We just have to remember that as long as we stay focused on Him, He will give us the directions we need to follow the plans He has for us.

Faith Game

By Brittany Foster

But when he asks, he must believe and not doubt, because he who doubts is like a wave of the sea, blown and tossed by the wind. James 1:6.

Every Wednesday my grade school had joint worship with all the classes together. I must have sat through hundreds of them, but only one lesson still remains with me now. It was my seventh-grade year, and the speaker was Pastor Zane. He told the coolest story of a man who prayed for a country in Africa for a whole year. At the end of the year he received the chance to visit that nation. He met many important officials and toured everywhere, including the jails. One particular jail held American hostages. He told the native officials that they should let the hostages go, and amazingly, they listened and freed the men. Upon his return to the United States he received a letter from the government thanking him for helping release the prisoners. You see, the United States had been trying to negotiate the prisoners' freedom for some time. As the story concluded, he challenged us to strengthen our faith.

So I did just that. I chose the country I thought would be the most fun to visit: Australia. About six months later I stopped praying, thinking that it was a ridiculous notion. A couple of years went by and then, during my freshman year in academy, my parents announced that we were going to Australia the coming summer. I was so excited—it worked! How awesome is that! I could use half the prayer and half the faith and God would still answer. I wish I could end with a cool story from "down under"; however, the plans fell through, and I spent my summer in Tennessee. That summer I learned something I will never forget: half the faith will get you half way, and God doesn't go halfway. From that moment on I promised to always give 100 percent.

Now four years later I play the faith game daily. Sometimes I'm not sure about things and doubts cross my mind, but then I think of how much fun Australia would have been, and I step forward in faith.

Where are you going for God?

Right Beside You

By Makoto Mori

Evening, morning and noon I cry out in distress, and he hears my voice.
Psalm 55:17.

Stanford, Duke, UCLA . . . My goal was set, and I was very excited about this new challenge. During the summer after my junior year in high school, I decided to aim for these prestigious colleges. I knew it was a long shot, and I would have to sacrifice a lot to achieve this goal; however, nothing held me back. That was all I wanted: to get accepted by the most competitive colleges. That summer I spent most of my days studying in the library. School started, and I kept studying. I forced myself to sleep no longer than four hours each night for one month because I had to deal with schoolwork on top of my own studying regiment. During that time my SAT score improved almost 500 points. I gradually started to feel confident and started to look forward to receiving the decision letters from colleges.

I applied to five colleges, and all the decision letters started with the same sentence, "We regrettably notify you that we are not able to offer you admission to . . ." Every time I opened the envelopes, I had to bite my lips to hold back the tears. All the work was in vane.

Furthermore, I had compromised friendships and lost the most precious relationship I'd ever had by immersing myself too deeply in pursuing my goal. Earlier I hoped that getting accepted to some of the colleges would justify what I had done and compensate for the loss. But the realization that I had spent so much time for nothing, and lost such an important relationship, tore me apart. Why? Didn't I deserve something better than this? I could not get up for a long time—until I read Psalm 55. The passage reminded me that God was standing right next to me, and He heard my cries. That was a relief. The Creator of the universe actually cares about me and feels my sorrow.

God is always right next to us no matter what we are going through. Isn't that good to know? So I will continue to make plans and pray that God will open the doors that He wants me to walk through.

The Road

By Anna Grissom

I run in the path of your commands, for you have set my heart free.
Psalm 119:32.

I was walking down a beautiful country road that was flanked by trees all decked out in their spring dresses. They all seemed to be thanking their loving Creator for releasing them from their winter prisons. The flowers joined them in their celebration and were swaying in the cool breeze.

In some places the road was smooth, as if no one ever traveled there. It was in these places that the trees seemed to glow and the flowers sparkle. Then there were the places where the road was scarred with deep ruts. Some of these ruts weren't very deep, and if I hadn't been paying attention, I could have missed them. In these places the trees and the flowers were still very vibrant, but they didn't shine quite like the others. As I walked I noticed that the ruts were getting deeper and there were more and more places I could see that someone had gotten stuck. I saw old shoes that looked as if they would never come loose. I wondered who owned this land, because it seemed to me that if so many people were getting stuck, something should be done to the road.

It was at that time that I saw a man sitting by the road. He was watching me, and when I got close enough to see his face, he stood and faced me. It was then that I realized who it was. He was the Creator, the one who had made all of the trees and flowers that I had marveled at earlier. I asked Jesus, "Why doesn't someone fix the ruts in the road? Why has something not been done to keep people from getting stuck?"

He turned and said, "Anna, I have not fixed the ruts because they are there to remind people that they will not make it though this road without My help."

Are you walking by yourself, or will you walk with Him?

Everything Matters

By Linda Duncan

For the Lord himself will come down from heaven, with a loud command, with the voice of the archangel and with the trumpet call of God, and the dead in Christ will rise first. After that, we who are still alive and are left will be caught up together with them in the clouds to meet the Lord in the air. And so we will be with the Lord forever. Therefore encourage each other with these words. 1 Thessalonians 4:16-18.

It was a sunny Sabbath afternoon in March. Karen, a ninth grader, had enjoyed a walk in the woods with two of her friends, taking pictures, climbing trees, and just talking. As evening approached, they changed clothes and headed to a King's Heralds concert at church. Her friend's mom was driving and had just pulled out of the neighborhood and onto the main road. A man who had been drinking was also driving on that same road. His truck hit them head-on, crushing their car against an embankment, resulting in the deaths of Karen, her friend, and her friend's mom. This happened just one month before Karen's fifteenth birthday.

I don't know why God allowed this to happen. (We can ask Him someday.) But I do know that there are sin and evil in this world, and bad things do happen to good people. So I choose to trust our heavenly Father and find joy and comfort in His love and promises.

Because of this tragedy, I learned the following lessons. Live each day with a purpose for good and with joy in your heart. Let your family and friends know you care. Enjoy life. Talk to Jesus throughout each day, and take time to listen to Him. Find ways to share kindnesses. Pass on Jesus' love to others. And live a clean, healthy life.

Karen had shared with her parents and big sister just weeks before that if anything ever happened to her, she wanted to be an organ donor. Because of her healthy lifestyle and choices, she qualified as a donor and helped many people.

We know Jesus is coming again soon. We don't know when. We don't know if we will be translated or resurrected when He comes. But by staying close to Jesus and knowing He is always our very best friend, we will be ready. I believe the next thing my daughter Karen will hear will be the real King's herald of trumpets on resurrection morning!

Satan: The Biggest Con Artist
By Emily Abernathy

Be that as it may, I have not been a burden to you. Yet, crafty fellow that I am, I caught you by trickery! 2 Corinthians 12:16.

I recently saw an episode on Oprah Winfrey's show about con artists. Oprah was talking to normal people like you and me who had been tricked into sending money to fake organizations. One woman had received an e-mail from someone who had supposedly gotten in a logging accident and needed $10,000 to go to a special hospital for surgery. The woman felt sorry for the man, so she sent the money. Unfortunately, he kept asking for more and more until the woman had emptied out her entire savings account. When she realized she had been scammed, she was in total shock.

Some people make a living by tricking people out of their money. They are so careful in their wording, and convincing in their tone, that their e-mails and letters sometimes deceive even professionals who can't detect the trickery.

In some ways I think Satan is like those con artists. He is always lurking around, trying to trick someone into sinning or straying from God. Satan, like these criminals, has only one purpose: to trick people. You need to realize that Satan studies us. He knows our weaknesses and can make a scheme just for us—one so convincing that we cannot detect the forgery. Although con artists try to trick us out of earthly money, Satan tries to trick us out of the luxuries of heaven and eternal life. He knows he will never enjoy it again, and he doesn't want us to either.

Even though we all have sinned, fallen short of the glory of God, and listened to Satan's temptations, the love Jesus has for us is everlasting and will never end. And if we ask Him, God will give us wisdom and strength to identify and resist Satan's tricks.

When Satan tries to *scam* you, pray to God and ask Him to make Satan *scram*!

Glow

By Brittany Foster

Neither do people light a lamp and put it under a bowl. Instead they put it on its stand, and it gives light to everyone in the house. Matthew 5:15.

You're a Christian," he stated.

I looked up from washing tables to see a middle-aged man eating a few tables away. That summer I had the opportunity of a lifetime, one that takes talent, smarts, good people skills, and basic math. I, Brittany Foster, worked at Wendy's. OK, so anyone can work there, but I chose Wendy's because they were hiring smiling faces. My smile quickly landed me the position of supervisor of taking orders on the right side of the front counter (in layperson's terms—a cashier). I was also known as the good girl. I was different, and the big managers knew it—I wasn't like them. Whatever it was about me, it carried over into my work and showed through to the people around me.

Staring at the man who spoke to me, I said nothing—my mind was racing. How did he know? What did I say? Did I know him? "Yes," I said.

He simply replied, "I could tell."

I never said any more to him. I was thinking, not about how joyous a Christian I was or how I could share God, but what was it? In my uniform I seemed like the others.

Then Matthew 5:14 came to mind—"A city on a hill cannot be hidden"—and I knew then what I hadn't realized before. I couldn't be like them; I had Jesus. You can't be normal with Jesus. How cool is that! How awesome is it that He really does change us. I studied my coworkers—every day was the same for them whether it was Monday, Thursday, Saturday, etc. The days made no difference. Their purpose in life was dim. Trust me, none of their goals sound as good as heaven. I see people with crosses around their necks and cars with fish bumper stickers, but take these away and can they glow? When everyone's wearing the same uniform, will you glow?

A Little Boy's Prayer

By Aaron Haah

Call to Me, and I will answer you, and show you great and mighty things, which you do not know. Jeremiah 33:3, NKJV.

It was winter, and I was hoping for something special. It was almost Christmas—the trees were decorated, and the streets shone beneath their beautiful bright lights. I was living in a small apartment with my family in Suwon, South Korea. I'd been praying for a very long time that we could have a Christmas tree. We had never had any Christmas decorations before, and I really wanted them.

One evening I asked my parents if we could buy a small, fake Christmas tree that we could use every year—there are no real Christmas trees in Korea. They agreed to think it over, but they warned me that it wasn't a definite yes. I told myself, *It's not a big deal. I know when Dad becomes a doctor one day we will be able to afford a Christmas tree.* I decided to forget about it after that.

A couple weeks later I woke up in the middle of the night from a noise. I had to listen very carefully because it was so soft I could barely hear it. I heard someone say, "Aaron's going to be so happy when he wakes up. I'm so glad we've decided to do this for him!" I was eager to know what was going on, but at the same time, I didn't want to spoil the surprise, so I closed my eyes and went back to sleep.

When I woke up the next morning, I was really amazed! I didn't see a tree, but what I saw was even better. I saw beautiful multicolored lights all over the ceiling. They surrounded me. I couldn't stop smiling, and I thanked my parents over and over. But mostly I thanked God because He had listened to my prayer.

At all times God is listening to us. He may not answer just the way we think He should, but He always wants what is best for us. And sometimes He just gives us wonderful little surprises and blessings simply to make us happy.

Why Someone or Something?

By Cindy Flores

The light shines in the darkness, but the darkness has not understood it.
John 1:5.

During the time Jesus was with us, He felt many things. Sometimes I wonder how discouraged He got when He saw all the sins we had in our lives. How did He feel when He saw ungrateful people who ignored His pleas and purpose? We know that Jesus loved them anyway, but it must have made Him sad.

Do you think it still makes Him sad to see us behave in ways that are unkind today? Have you ever noticed that there is always someone or something that tends to put us down? Sometimes we are having a good day and suddenly we come in contact with that person or that thing that puts us down and causes us to want revenge or to give up. We react so quickly that our true sinful nature comes out before we have time to make a conscious decision.

But we must remember that our actions have consequences. The words from our mouth and the gestures with our hands should always be a reflection of Jesus' character. I know that acting appropriately isn't always what first comes to mind, but we need to do all we can to try. We also need to spend time thinking about the mercy that God shows us every day. And perhaps if we would think about that more often, we could more easily take on the character of God. If we didn't seek revenge or do things our own selfish way when someone upsets us, things would be so much better.

So next time someone puts you down or upsets you, give your burden to God and pray that you will react as God would have you. To help you have a successful day, ask yourself these questions:

What am I thankful for today?

What can I do to help someone today?

How can I thank Jesus for His promise of salvation?

How will I react when things don't go my way today?

Will I behave like a child of the King today?

Don't Hate . . . Appreciate

By Richard Lawrence

I have told you these things, so that in me you may have peace. In this world you will have trouble. But take heart! I have overcome the world. John 16:33.

Quite often I find myself frustrated about many things, and seemingly everything. But as a Christian who tries to follow God's will, shouldn't I be immune to troubles?

The realization is this: being a Christian doesn't necessarily mean that we will not experience trials and tribulations. God makes it crystal clear in His Word that at times life will be frustrating and difficult. But as a God of love, He has so graciously provided us a way to overcome these tough times. That way is found in following Christ's teachings and totally surrendering our lives to Him.

His love is amazing, and the peace you will find in Him is unmatched. You can rest and trust that He is working all things for the best. As the apostle Paul wrote: "And we know that all things work together for good to them that love God, to them who are the called according to his purpose" (Romans 8:28, KJV).

Victory through tough times comes by staying connected to other believers, reading God's Word, trusting Him, worshipping, and communicating with Him through prayer. Striving to model your life after that of Christ's life is also a positive step.

If you're feeling troubled today, lift your head up and stand strong on the Rock, solely depending on the love your Savior has for you. The next time you get stressed out, don't hate your life or the people around you; appreciate what you are going through, because it is an opportunity for you to learn and grow. No matter what you're going through, just remember that Christ has promised never to leave you.

Don't Give Up

By Moses Haah

If you need wisdom ask our generous God, and he will give it to you. He will not rebuke you for asking. James 1:5, NLT.

Do you believe in miracles? If not, read this and believe! This is a true story about a boy I'm calling Ji. One day while in the sixth grade he had a math test, and guess what score he got? He earned a 34 percent. Does that look similar to your test scores? I hope not. Ji didn't like studying, but he loved playing football.

Ji kept sliding by in school until he was old enough to move on to high school. About that time rumors began circulating about the high school kids and how they were all gathering at a place called Fire Fly (named for how the cigarettes looked at night) to smoke and hang out. In Korea high school students start classes at 8:00 a.m. and do not leave school until 10:00 p.m. Worrying that Ji might get influenced by the kids who were smoking, his father decided not to send him to high school.

So Ji was forced to study at home. As homework his dad made Ji read the encyclopedia, but as an incentive his father offered to pay Ji one dollar for every three pages he read. Ji studied as slowly as a moving slug, but his father had great patience with him.

Finally, a year passed and Ji was sent to a high school. In spite of having to save every penny for Ji's tuition, his family still decided to send him because of their beliefs in education. Before Ji left he promised he would study hard to become a medical doctor and to devote his life to being God's healing hands.

Ji has now been accepted at the University of Texas at Austin. God has taken care of his grades and other things. Ji, who at one point and time didn't care that he scored a 34 percent on a math test, now would get upset if he didn't get an A.

Grades aren't everything, of course, but through hard work, prayer, and God's help, the impossible can be achieved. With God, impossible means *nothing*! If you want to know what God has planned for you, ask Him, and He will prepare you in various ways. Let this be your prayer today.

Movement

By Brooke Wade

"For in him we live and move and have our being." As some of your own
poets have said, "We are his offspring." Acts 17:28.

Proudly, Paul proclaims this message to the people of Athens. As he declares the wonders of the Lord to them—in hopes they will finally know Him—Paul taps into this wonderful truth: in God "we live and move and exist." What an amazing thought! We all know God guides us and has a plan for us, but this goes one step further.

Paul tells us that we exist in God. Not a bad thing—life wouldn't be too great if we didn't exist through it! But even better than existing, we live in God. He loves us so much that He wants us to think and experience and return His love. He has allowed us to live in Him so we can move in Him. We move forward. Yes, there are a few side trips we sometimes choose to take, but there is always forward motion. As God's children, we have the spectacular privilege of holding His hand all the way.

Today we continue moving forward. Another school year will come to a close in a few months. With it comes a million new possibilities—God is in all of them. Some may lead us to disregard God's presence and try to move within ourselves. We may travel somewhere and forget who God really is—even though He's constantly whispering it in our ears. But let us not forget the paths that are straightforward. They are the ones in which we move in God completely.

I want more than anything to let God move me. In Him, I know He will lead me where life can be fully lived—not just an existence. I, His child, choose now to move in Christ—from now until forever. I pray you will do the same.

Read Your Devotionals!

By Joy Shin

For God is not a God of disorder but of peace. 1 Corinthians 14:33.

This experience happened one summer when I was in Korea visiting relatives with my parents. It was fun to travel, but I was ready to get back to my country, my state, and more important, my home. But there was a problem. I didn't have a plane ticket. My parents and I called many airlines, but no one had a ticket for me. Luckily, one of the workers at the airline suggested that I should go to the airport first thing in the morning and get the plane ticket that they save up for emergencies. So my mom and I left around 5:00 the next morning. I said goodbye to my father, who had swollen eyes from crying. He told me that he was going to miss me so much, and I was going to miss him, too, but I just couldn't wait to go back to Georgia.

When I got to the airport, I ran to get in line for the plane ticket. The airline steward checked my passport and told me to have a seat and wait. I never prayed so hard in my life. I became exhausted and couldn't stop crying. Every second felt like hours to me. A couple of hours later, while sitting in the busy airport, I began to get very angry with God. I questioned Him. Why was this happening to me? I was just so furious! Then something told me that I hadn't read the Mount Pisgah Academy summer devotional that day. I had gotten in the habit of reading it daily during the summer. So I took out my devotional book and started to read the one for that day.

My friend Emily Abernathy had written it. It was about how Satan likes to trick us so that we can turn away from God. After I read this wonderful story, I felt very guilty and asked God to forgive me and to get Satan off me. Then I told God again and again that I loved Him. Right afterward I felt much better.

A little while later a steward called out my name—she had a ticket for me! If I hadn't read Emily's devotional, I would have stayed mad at God and maybe not have gotten the plane ticket! Maybe God was testing me, or Satan was trying to trick me. Anyway, I was extremely glad that I had read that devotional. The Mount Pisgah Academy summer devotional book, written by my peers, helped me every day that summer. Since my parents are not Christians, I never attended a single church service the whole summer, so I learned to depend on this book for spiritual food. Thank You, God, for knowing just what I need, even before I realize it.

New Memories

By Stella Bradley

Behold, I will create new heavens and a new earth. The former things will not be remembered, nor will they come to mind. Isaiah 65:17.

Some day soon God will make a new earth just for us. And all of this world's sadness, crime, and grime will not be remembered or even tickle the corners of our mind. What a nice thought! Not only will we not have all of the sinful things of this earth to plague us, but we won't even have to think about them. We won't be haunted by the sins of our past. We won't need to remember the pictures of the Holocaust, starving children in Africa, the homeless in our cities, the pain of disease, or fatal earthquakes and floods. God will erase all wrongs. In our new heavenly home, we will be happy, cared for, loved, and without guilt or sadness. What a merciful God to think of that promised gift.

What will our new earth be like? It is awesome to try to imagine the possibilities. Oh, the people we'll meet and the places we'll travel . . . the possibilities are far beyond our comprehension. James Weldon Johnson, an American poet, painted a vivid picture of a brand-new world in his poem "The Creation."

"Then the green grass sprouted,
And the little red flowers blossomed,
The pine tree pointed his finger to the sky,
And the oak spread out his arms,
The lakes cuddled down in the hollows of the ground,
And the rivers ran down to the sea;
And God smiled again,
And the rainbow appeared,
And curled itself around His shoulder."

God's rainbow of promise reminds us that His unconditional love for us is the most significant component of both the former and the future creations. What a kind God—He delivers us from any thought of corruption and lavishes us with gifts.

March 18

Giving Up

By Brittani Coleman

Distress that drives us to God does that. It turns us around. It gets us back in the way of salvation. We never regret that kind of pain. But those who let distress drive them away from God are full of regrets, end up on a deathbed of regrets. 2 Corinthians 7:11, Message.

I think you learn the most from times of struggle. I'm not saying that you can't learn from the good times, but at least for me I've learned the most from my moments of defeat, from the times when it seems nothing else could possibly get worse, from the times when loneliness seemed to be an everyday occurrence. These times, when we are at our lowest of lows, is when we should depend on God the most. I've learned that even when everyone seems disappointed in me because of my grades or messy room that God doesn't care about those things. Those earthly things are insignificant to Him. He cares only about the relationship that we share.

This does not give me permission to not do my homework. Nor does it allow me to slack off in keeping my room clean or on my other daily tasks. Those things, while not important to my salvation, show respect and responsibility. God blessed me with a brain and body able to help myself. But everyone gets overwhelmed sometimes. And when that happens, I need to remember to turn to God.

I used to beat myself up over everything—all the homework I need to do, a deadline at work, etc. Since everyone else made a big deal about it, I did too. I would cry in my room because I felt that I couldn't do anything right. Then I played the song "Praise You in the Storm," by Casting Crowns. I realized that even when I think nobody cares, God cares. Even when everything comes crashing down, there is one thing I can do right, and that is pray. God still loves me even when I mess things up. Even when I have given up on everything else, God still cares. Talk to Him about what's going on today. He's always listening.

Any Little Thing

By Haruka Mori

Be joyful always; pray continually. 1 Thessalonians 5:16, 17.

Knock-knock. "Good morning. May I clean your room?"

One summer, in my native Japan, I worked in a hospital, and my job was housekeeping. I would clean the lobby and then go to the fourth floor, which was the hospice ward, to complete my work for the day. I always paired up with one or two women who worked there. When we went to the hospice ward, sometimes a patient would be yelling, or families crying. I had never realized how many people suffer from cancer. During the months I worked there many patients who were in the hospice ward passed away. It was really hard to see the people that I had become close to become weak and sometimes die.

But many things kept me smiling. There was one elderly woman who didn't really talk much but always told me "Thank you" with all her might, a big smile on her face. I loved to go to her room. Another woman down the hall chattered the whole time I cleaned. She asked me about school. She wanted to know my career plans. She always told me to say thanks to my parents and listen to them and to be strong even if things were tough. Going to either of their rooms always cheered me up.

These dear women were dying of cancer, yet they looked happy. And although they were physically very weak, I thought of them as powerful. They were so influential in my life. Just like them, I want to be appreciative of everything and always thankful for the people around me.

In Shakespeare's *Hamlet*, Prince Hamlet says, "There is nothing either good or bad, but thinking makes it so." Please know that I'm not saying that cancer, or any ailment, is in any way good. But the way we approach life's challenges can be either inspirational or tragic. It's really all about attitude.

I have discovered that when we appreciate even a little blessing we can find happiness, even in the midst of troubles. And when you are thankful for little things, it can bring happiness to other people who are around you, just as those women did for me.

It's Our Job

By Carolina Diaz

In the same way, I tell you, there is rejoicing in the presence of the angels of God over one sinner who repents. Luke 15:10.

I often wonder about God coming back to earth and what He wants from me. Can I do anything to help people until He comes? Luke 15 features three parables that explain our most important jobs on earth.

The first is the parable of the lost sheep. A man searched for his sheep until he found it. He then rejoiced. The second parable is about the lost coin. A woman searched for it until she found it. She then rejoiced. The third parable is about the lost son. He left home and broke his father's heart. In the end he returned home, and his father rejoiced.

This made me think about how the church needs to go out and find the lost people, too, because there are people out there like the sheep. The sheep knows she is lost—probably crying, scared, hungry, cold, hurt—but she doesn't know how to get back home. That's why we need to go out and look for the lost people and help them get back home.

There are people like the coin. They are in the dark; completely lost, they don't know that they are missing. It is our job to go look for them and help them get back home.

There are people like the younger son—people who leave the church. They know they are lost, and they also know the way back. But they may be too ashamed or afraid to return. When they do make their way back home, the church needs to show them love and, like the father in the parable, be sincerely happy that they are back where they belong.

All three of these stories have happy endings. Let's do all we can to help others find their happy ending—which exists only through Christ Jesus.

The Blood That Was Shed

By Katelyn Gonzalez

They stripped him and put a scarlet robe on him, and then twisted together a crown of thorns and set it on his head. Matthew 27:28, 29.

Blood. Is it just a word to describe the bodily fluid that keeps us alive? To me, it is a powerful expression proclaiming to everyone that all we need is God.

The first time I saw the movie *The Passion of the Christ*, I cried. It wasn't just my eyes watering; my heart was in pain. The scene that got to me was when Mary, mother of Jesus, was reminiscing about Jesus as a child. She wanted to hold Him. She wanted to help Him as she did when He was a child. It hurt her to see Him beaten and covered in blood. Mary knew that she couldn't help Him. She knew that Jesus came to this earth for a purpose—to save her and all humanity—but she still anguished over His death. The blood He was covered in had to be shed in order to secure our salvation.

There is a song that talks about blood and how it was shed through pain. It provides strength and power that will never be lost. It soothes the soul, calming all fears. The song is called "The Blood." That's it, and that's enough. All we need is the blood that was shed for us, sinful humanity, on the cross.

I have sung this song since I was a small child. When I lived at Garden State Academy, the students would sing it for vespers. It is my favorite worship song because it is true, and it is my prayer. I want to get my strength from the blood that Jesus shed.

I pray that everyone who reads this is blessed today. May God give you strength to make it through your struggles. Look to the cross when you feel alone, in pain, or just want a place to belong.

Naked as a Jay Bird

By Jake Nielsen

*For I was hungry and you gave me something to eat, I was thirsty and you
gave me something to drink, I was a stranger and you invited me in, I
needed clothes and you clothed me, I was sick and you looked after me, I
was in prison and you came to visit me. Matthew 25:35, 36.*

It was a crisp and beautiful Sabbath morning in Kenya, Africa. My father was sitting on the back porch watching the birds around the feeder. He went into the house to get a hot drink and asked my mom if she wanted to join him. She declined, so he went back outside without her. After a while, out by the fence, he noticed a man who appeared to be naked. Dad went back into the house to ask mom if she would like to look at the birds. She again said no. Dad then proceeded to ask, "How 'bout a naked man?" She immediately changed her mind and ran outside to see what my dad had been talking about.

Using binoculars, she verified that the man was indeed naked. Dad headed toward the man to see what was going on, but he kept his distance because of the threat of an ambush. As he got closer, he could tell by the cuts, scrapes, and bruised and swollen face that the man had been beaten. Dad sent my mom back to the house to get the man some clothes. The man said he had been dumped behind our house and didn't know where he was. My dad gave him directions back to Nairobi. When my mom got back with the clothes, they tossed a little money to the man so he could catch a ride on his way home. The man thanked them and left.

My parents went about their daily business and soon forgot about the naked man. Later the same day a campus guard informed my dad that some people were looking for him. It was the naked man and one of his friends. He had returned to tell my dad his story.

Joseph was a newly converted Christian. His mosque had been very angry at his decision to leave the church, and they had shunned him. He was threatened, had all of his belongings stolen, and was finally beaten for his beliefs. That is how he had ended up in our backyard.

After hearing his story, we saved his life by relocating him to a safer part of Kenya. Joseph helped me and my family learn the importance of giving to needy people. We didn't know he was a Christian, and we certainly did not know what he had been going through, yet God used us to bless him. God doesn't miss anything.

Perseverance

By Brandon Peggau

That is why I am suffering as I am. Yet I am not ashamed, because I know whom I have believed, and am convinced that he is able to guard what I have entrusted to him for that day. 2 Timothy 1:12.

When I was a baby, I was just like every other average kid, happy and innocent. But one day when I was getting my picture taken, my mom noticed a lump on the side of my leg. This turned my life upside down.

There isn't a cure for cancer, and most victims die from it, but that's what I had. Soon afterward, when I was about 3 months old, I had to have surgery on my leg. The doctors felt that there was no way to save my life without amputation. The doctors advised my mother of their recommendation, but the decision was hers. After much prayer, she agreed with the doctors, and they proceeded with the surgery.

My leg was removed below the knee, and the cancer is gone. Now I live life like a normal person—I don't feel any different than other people. I do have a prosthetic that enables me to play sports, drive, and be a functioning normal person. I do not dwell on my "disability"—and I really only use it to get me and my friends in the fast line at amusement parks (it comes in handy then).

I'm sure all of us have challenges—some are just more obvious than others. But don't let any challenge get you down. Become the person God wants you to be. He can use you no matter your circumstances.

God has blessed me with life, and I don't regret a second of it. I body build, power lift, and live life like I want. And I thank God for giving it to me. I feel that if you put your faith in Christ He will help you overcome any obstacle that you encounter—I know He has for me.

A Big Turnaround

By Dustin Evans

Then he said to the man, "Stretch out your hand." So he stretched it out and it was completely restored, just as sound as the other. Matthew 12:13.

As a sophomore in academy, I severed a tendon in my pinky finger. I cut the tendon one day while I was cleaning a bus. I was asked to close all of the top hatches; however, I had no idea how to do that. When I tried to close one, the hatch came down and sliced my finger open. As a result of this injury, I had to get stitches. A week after I got the stitches taken out, I realized that I couldn't bend my pinky finger all of the way.

I went to a doctor and had X-rays done. He told me I had a severed tendon—something that would not heal on its own. But the doctor was confident that he could fix it surgically.

When surgery day came, I had a fever, so we had to reschedule. The second time I went in I still had a little fever, but they said that they could do the surgery anyway. The surgery, however, was not a success. The doctor told me that the tendon had disconnected from its proper place and had gone into my hand. He told me that there was nothing he could do about this. He did tell me that he was able to move a type of muscle from where it had originally been attached to a spot where it could make my finger have a slight bend. I was glad to hear this, even though I was told that I would never be able to have full function in that finger again.

Despite this injury, I can still play violin, and I look forward to majoring in music in college. I am thankful that God healed my wound—even though it was not in the way I first expected.

Sometimes God answers our prayers with a yes, sometimes with a no. And then other times He may answer with a not yet or in another unexpected way.

Even if He doesn't answer the way you think He should, trust in Him and know that He will do what is best for you. He may be trying to teach you a lesson (such as patience, faith, forgiveness) as you go through the process. And one day, in heaven, if not on this earth, you will understand why He made the decision He did or allowed a certain circumstance to happen to you. Hold fast, and keep trusting in the Great Physician.

Fear

By Anna Grissom

The steps of a good man are ordered by the Lord: and he delighteth in his way. Psalm 37:23, KJV.

Have you ever felt afraid to move forward? Have you been afraid to try something new? I feel like that all the time. I remember the summer before my freshman year. I was terrified to go away to academy. I remember asking myself an endless stream of questions. Am I going to make any friends? Am I going to have fun? Are the classes going to be hard?

As the year started and I got used to the life of an academy student, I realized that I was having fun and that I was making friends.

Now as I look back on those several months, I realize that there was really nothing to be afraid of. Even though I was afraid of what was to come, God knew exactly what was going to happen and what I was going to go through.

After academy every student faces the same thing over again. Going to college, starting a new job, maybe even moving to a new state . . . all of these new beginnings, while a little scary for us, are part of God's plan. Don't be afraid. Just pray that you will know His will for your life. And if you communicate with Him through prayer and Bible study, He will reveal Himself to you.

As you finish this school year and gear up for summer, remember that God has a plan and that nothing surprises Him. He knows where you are going to be next year, and no matter where you go, He has a plan and lots of blessings in store for you!

Stand Above the Crowd!

By Jessica Koobs

God is not unjust; he will not forget your work and the love you have shown him as you have helped his people and continue to help them.
Hebrews 6:10.

The lights were everywhere on this very dark night. The ambulance had just rushed someone I didn't know to the hospital. And the police were trying to get the crowd to go home, telling us that the victim was going to be OK, but I knew in my heart that it would not happen.

Moments before, I had witnessed a truck smash into a small sports car. When I saw the paramedics pull out the unfortunate victim, I wanted to gag and put my hand over the eyes of all the small kids who were watching. His face was covered in blood and glass. His body was mangled so much that I couldn't see how he could still be alive.

I often ask myself, Did he make it? If not, did he have a family he left behind? Why would God let something so bad, so cruel, happen? But then something tells me that it's not "God." Things happen because of sin, and there is someone—Satan—roaming this earth who wants us dead. Then it seems better. Our unfailing, loving Father God doesn't want this to happen, but He has to allow certain things to happen. Satan "owns" this world, and God wants us to know the cruelty that sin brings.

We need to live our lives as if this day is our last. We need to be heroes in this world. We need to stick up for others when they don't have the power. When you see someone struggling to survive, put yourself in their place. What would you want someone to do for you? Sometime in the future you will need someone to be a hero for you. You never know when it's going to be someone's last moment in this life. Stand above the crowd and be a hero.

Nathan

By Lauren Kenemore

The Lord is close to the brokenhearted and saves those who are crushed in spirit. Psalm 34:18.

My day started out like every other day. I woke up early, went to class at 7:00 in the morning, had lunch in the cafeteria, and then went to work. I got off work early that day because my grandparents were passing through on their way to Tennessee. They were in a hurry, so they stayed only long enough to say "I love you" and "Have a good day." As soon as they left, I went to supper with my friends and then back to the dorm. Later that evening we went to rec. As usual, it was fun being with friends and just hanging out. After rec, as I was walking back to the dorm, I got a phone call that changed my life.

Grandma was crying on the phone and talking very fast. I couldn't understand everything she said, but I could gather that something had happened to my brother. I had so many questions: Was he OK? Was he in the hospital? How serious was it? Was he going to live? And then she told me that they were on their way back to campus to pick me and my cousin Stephen up from school. That's when I knew things were serious.

As I was waiting to be picked up, my friends and some staff members hugged me, prayed with me, and helped me pack. It felt good to have the support of my school family. Shortly before my grandparents arrived, I got a phone call from my dad. I was glad that now I would be able to get more information. But when I asked questions about Nathan, Dad didn't answer me. After a long pause, he said the four words that I never wanted to hear—"He didn't make it."

March 27, 2008, was the day my brother died. He was only 6 years old. Nathan was doing what every little boy does at that age, something that is very harmless, or so it seemed. He was climbing a big tree with lots of branches. I guess he didn't see the power lines, or maybe he did and was trying to avoid them, but whatever the case may be, he didn't have the opportunity to climb down like other kids.

Some days it feels like it is just a bad dream and I will wake up from it and he will be back. But I know that Nathan is safe from this world. Now it is up to me to live my life like God would want me to so I can see my brother again. Thank You, God, for comforting me and giving me the blessed hope of Your soon coming and the resurrection.

God Always Cares for Us

By Carina Herrera

Here I am! I stand at the door and knock. If anyone hears my voice and opens the door, I will come in and eat with him, and he with me.
Revelation 3:20.

People tend to forget about God during the good times. And only when we have a problem do we remember that we have a God who is mighty and waiting for us to ask Him for help.

Several years ago my grandmother had open-heart surgery. Three of her heart arteries were 100 percent blocked, and only one was functioning correctly. We were told that she had a 10 percent chance of making it through the necessary operation because of the infection she had developed in her liver and stomach, and her diabetic issues. I really felt bad for her, but I felt that I could not do anything to help her because she always rejected God. The day came when she was supposed to have surgery, and as I visited with her, I was happy when she asked me to pray that God would help her through surgery. It really touched my heart, knowing that my grandmother seemed to be accepting God at last.

She survived the surgery, and we were all full of joy and happiness. And since we saw such a direct answer to prayer, my family expected that my grandmother would want to go to church with us and maybe even ask for Bible studies.

However, when we asked her to come to church with us, she said no. She made it clear that she didn't want to know anything about God. We were all astonished by what she had said, but she just kept telling us that it was not God who helped her in her surgery, but the doctors. We continue to pray that she will have a change of heart.

What I learned from this experience is that even if things don't turn out the way we planned, God is always there in every aspect of our life looking out for our well-being. Even when we reject Him, He is always waiting for us with open arms. He never gives up on us.

And He loves us no matter what!

Guitars and Chocolate

By Rosella Age

He will swallow up death forever. The Sovereign Lord will wipe away the tears from all faces; he will remove the disgrace of his people from all the earth. The Lord has spoken. Isaiah 25:8.

Once upon a night in a dorm far, far away, an overwhelmed, hormonal teenage girl sat on her bed and sobbed. And cried. And whined. She cried about school and peers, but most of all she mourned about the loss of her brother and sister in a tragic accident that had happened five years before.

Seeking relief, she went off in search of chocolate but found none, and thus she resorted to playing the guitar, which always put her in a peaceful mood. Strumming and singing, singing and strumming. After a while the young junior's fingertips were ailing and her voice pleaded for a rest. She resumed her miserable state. As was her custom, she kept to herself and rarely shared her sadness with the other girls around her—the act commonly known as "venting."

Desperate for some form of encouragement, she picked her Bible up off the floor and whispered a prayer: "Dear Jesus, I am struggling right now. Please show me something in the Bible that will give me comfort. Amen."

Following that prayer, she opened the Bible and flipped through it randomly until she happened upon a heading in Isaiah that read "Praise to the Lord." Scanning down a little, a verse appeared that concurred with what she was searching for: "He will swallow up death forever. The Sovereign Lord will wipe away the tears from all faces; he will remove the disgrace of his people from all the earth. The Lord has spoken."

The adolescent was very excited about the verse and how it applied to her. She became encouraged and made it a point not to rely on her guitar or chocolate, but to go to God first, because it was He who wiped away her tears.

And she lived happily ever after . . .

Jesus' Blood

By Chris Janetzko

This is how we know what love is: Jesus Christ laid down his life for us. And we ought to lay down our lives for our brothers. 1 John 3:16.

I do a lot of my thinking in bed before I fall asleep. One night I was thinking about something—I can't even remember what it was now—but I ended up telling God I was mad at Him and that I even hated Him.

Almost immediately afterward I thought about what I had said, and I realized that even though I had just told God I hated Him, He loved me just as much as He did before I said that. Once I thought of that, I couldn't be mad at Him anymore. How could I? He died so I could have eternal life. There is no greater love than that.

I also realized that because of His example of love, we should be nice to others even though they may be cruel to us. I understand that this is not an easy thing to do. Being nice to those who do us wrong is a hard thing, but Jesus did it when He was on earth, and He wants us to show kindness to all of His children.

This, of course, does not mean you have to tolerate an abusive relationship or hang around people who demean you or reject you. In some situations you may need to love people from afar. But that kind of love still takes a big measure of forgiveness and inner peace—as Jesus puts it, a peace that passes understanding. The world would have us stewing over personal injustices, concocting plans of subtle revenge, or blatantly "telling off" those who do us wrong. But don't fall for Satan's traps. Rise above by asking God for help in overcoming the situation and plan to trade in revenge for kindness. And then ask Him to help you love.

The next time someone makes you mad, just think of all that God has done for you and do your best to follow His example.

The Power of Prayer
By Ross Knight

If you believe, you will receive whatever you ask for in prayer.
Matthew 21:22.

I was really excited. I was in Florida at Camp Kulaqua with a group from Mount Pisgah Academy at the Southern Union's annual youth prayer conference. It was my first time going, and I had been looking forward to this week for a long time. So many of the kids who had gone before had told me about all the fun they had had in years past. Getting to be at a camp and being able to swim, drive go-carts, and play football with kids from all the other academies represented was half the fun. Also, I knew I would probably grow spiritually while on the trip, but that was not my main focus for heading down there.

As I was leaving the first night's meeting, my phone rang. It was my dad. He told me a little hesitantly that my mom had been to a doctor for a checkup, and the doctor diagnosed her with a form of breast cancer. He tried to play things down like it wasn't that serious, but all I really got from the conversation was that my mom had cancer. Almost instantly my excitement about being at the prayer conference was gone. I was scared and mad at God for letting it happen. However, I talked and prayed with my close friends, and I also prayed with our school chaplain, before deciding to put the issue aside and continue the week as if nothing was wrong. I forced what I had found out to the back of my mind and continued with my activities.

On Friday night we had a special service. Each of the prayer groups split off by themselves and began sharing testimonies and things they needed prayer for. I felt what I believed to be God tugging at my heart, and I decided to tell my group what was going on with my mom. When I finished telling them, each person laid a hand on my head and said a special prayer for my mom. I really appreciated the spiritual support that evening.

Not much more than a month later my mom was declared cancer-free after a successful surgery. The doctor who performed the surgery said it had been his best work as a surgeon. My mom didn't even have to receive radiation treatment. I knew things couldn't have gone so perfectly had it not been for the prayers of my group and the prayers of friends and family. (And I also realize that not every praying family has the same outcome.) God is so good to us. Always remember to give all your problems, big and small, to God.

Without Him We Have Nothing

By Leah Killian

I love those who love me, and those who seek me find me. With me are riches and honor, enduring wealth and prosperity. My fruit is better than fine gold; what I yield surpasses choice silver. Proverbs 8:17-19.

Have you ever looked into the eyes of someone who has nothing?

In 2006 I spent a week in the Dominican Republic with people who had absolutely nothing. Each day our group would go out into the towns and spend time with people who were more destitute than I ever imagined. As I photographed their beautiful faces, I noticed that there was something in their eyes that was so inspiring. I didn't understand it, but it captivated me. It wasn't until I visited a place called "The Dump" that I actually understood so clearly what I saw in their eyes.

The Dump is a place where many people spend their lives. It's literally a dump full of trash. As we entered, I didn't know what to expect. The smell was so horrendous. I felt as though I was going to vomit or pass out. All I wanted to do was get out of there. As we got off the truck and started walking around, visiting with the people, a man invited us into his home. His "home" was disgusting to me. Inside, the smell grew stronger. I couldn't even stand up straight. I didn't want to touch anything. *This isn't a home*, I thought to myself. At first I felt sorry for him. But this man was so proud of everything he had. He was so happy and full of joy. We began to sing songs about Jesus together. It was at that moment that I saw something I hadn't seen before. As I looked into his eyes, it was like looking into his soul. It was beautiful. There was such happiness and contentment in his eyes as we sang about Jesus together. I could see God in him. This man, whom I thought had nothing but a small collection of trash, had everything.

I feel that God sent me to this man to teach me something. Why can't we be more like him? Why do we always have to want bigger and better things? Things don't give us happiness. God does that. God is everything! Without Him we have nothing.

Day by Day
By Ethan Williams

In his great power God becomes like clothing to me; he binds me like the neck of my garment. Job 30:18.

Have you ever wondered whether there is actually a God? I have struggled with this issue through much of my life, and I've tried testing God to see if He would answer. (I believe I'm not the only one to go through this stage.)

It has taken me several years in high school to sort out my problems and give them to God. God, though, does not always answer in ways I expect or look for. I have learned that the only way to have a relationship with God is not to doubt and test but simply to trust in Him and give your life to Him. This does not mean I never struggle. There are times I don't want God's opinion or I just ignore Him. However, God puts someone in my path every day to remind me of Him and help me refocus my attention on Him.

Have you ever seen people without God in their lives? They don't have anything together. I see God as glue. When we break down or lose control, He is there to bind us to Him and heal our wounds. I now try every day to find something that God is in and put it close to my heart.

If you are having trouble finding or listening to God, look around—there are people who reflect Him. This helps me know that God is not just a Bible character from the past. He is here every day, and He is everywhere.

Parents Do Care

By Latavia Rose

Honor your father and your mother, so that you may live long in the land the Lord your God is giving you. Exodus 20:12.

I know that parents can often be a pain, and sometimes I think that they know nothing at all. But they do. Even though some of us can't seem to wait to move out of our parents' house, because we'll be on our own and won't have to listen to them, we are not seeing the whole picture.

Going out into the real world will not change the fact that we have to answer to somebody. And what we may not get out in the world is the unconditional love that our parents will always have for us.

No matter how old or young our parents are, they are always going to know more than we do. They have had a lot more experiences than we give them credit for.

Parents try their hardest to raise their kids in the best way possible, but a lot of us don't appreciate the love our parents give us. Our parents try their best to make us happy, but we disrespect them when all they are trying to do is help.

Romans 1:30 says to avoid being "backbiters, haters of God, despiteful, proud, boasters, inventors of evil things, disobedient to parents" (KJV). Yet that's how a lot of us treat our parents and God—with no respect.

One day when I was living in the dorm I walked by another girl's room and heard her yelling at her mom. That made me think twice about that person, and it also made me think twice about how I treat my mom.

No matter how upset our parents get with us or we get with them—no matter what—they are always a part of us. We young people need to realize that our parents are right about a lot of things, and we need to appreciate their wisdom and our connections to each other. Our parents really do care about us a lot more than we think.

Live Well
By Rachelle Shook

Then you will win favor and a good name in the sight of God and man.
Proverbs 3:4.

Bonnie was a dear friend of mine in the fifth grade. She was the class clown and had a real knack for making people laugh. Her grades were as perfect as her attendance. She hadn't missed a day of school in her life, and the teachers loved her dearly. Everyone thought well of Bonnie. Our elementary school even made an award in honor of her behavior: The Student of the Year Award. Yes, Bonnie was very good in the eyes of people.

I knew something shocking about Bonnie, though, something very unexpected from such a well-behaved young girl. She was a pill popper. No one could tell she had this problem, and I was totally amazed when she confided in me. She didn't take them regularly—only if she got stressed or worried. I soon started to notice that every time we had a test, Bonnie would be the most relaxed and calm person in the room. The teachers thought it was confidence. I knew better.

She and I had many talks about her problem. We were both Christians and believed that our bodies were a temple, not to be misused in any way. We both knew that this act of pill popping could become a habit for her and eventually become a serious addiction.

I'm not trying to say that prescribed medication, under a doctor's authority, is a bad thing. But pill popping as a general coping method is not a healthy way to live. It is OK to feel a gamut of emotions, but instead of relying on outward sources for security and happiness, we should turn to Jesus, who is the only true source of comfort and coping.

After many years of praying, learning about herself, and walking with Jesus, Bonnie finally stopped taking pills and earned a reputation for living well in God's eyes, as well as in the eyes of her peers.

The Power of Prayer
By Anthony Hunt

Therefore I tell you, whatever you ask for in prayer, believe that you have received it, and it will be yours. Mark 11:24.

When a lot of people pray, they just recite the same prayer again and again. In fact, in some religions it is the customary way to do things. But many of us just get in a habit of mumbling our same old food blessing or going through our ritualistic prayer of blessing so and so and "what's-her-name." Some people pray only when they need or want something. Have you ever noticed that our prayers usually consist of more requests than thank-yous? Why do you think that is?

I can remember when I was about 10 years old that I asked God to help my mom stop smoking. It never happened. Sometimes we don't get what we want when we want it, and sometimes we think God is not going to answer that prayer. But instead of pondering on the prayers He hasn't answered, we should take time to praise Him for the ones He has.

In the middle of my freshman year of high school, my mom had surgery to remove a blood clot. We thought everything had gone great, but then a week later she ended up in the hospital again. I didn't find out until after she had been readmitted, and I was so worried. A week after that, I went home for Christmas break. I found out that my mom was scheduled for another surgery, which would be the Monday after I left for campus, so I couldn't be there.

That Monday I prayed so hard because, as it usually is, the most risky surgery offers the most promise, and that was the option my mom chose. She was supposed to have a room by noon (and then I could talk with her), but they didn't have one for her until 9:27 that night. During those nine hours and 27 minutes I prayed more than I usually do in a month.

About a week later my mom was able to go to work again, and now she's perfectly healthy and working out again like she loves to do. And she has stopped smoking! It was around the time she started working out again that I realized God had answered my prayer from so many years ago.

The next time you think about the prayers He hasn't answered, try to praise Him for the ones He has, because you never know when He is going to answer your next prayer.

Guide Me Through Hard Times
By Abbie Carrillo

Let the morning bring me word of your unfailing love, for I have put my trust in you. Show me the way I should go, for to you I lift up my soul.
Psalm 143:8.

Life is not always easy. We will always face challenges in life that will hurt us at times. Before I moved to South Carolina, I lived in Virginia. I loved it there. I always thought I was never going to leave for anything in the world. But things changed so suddenly and painfully. My oldest sister, who had just turned 18, ran away from home with a guy. We begged her to come back, but she insisted that she wanted to live her own life. It hurt our family to see her leave like that. It hurt us so much that we moved.

We all packed and moved to South Carolina without my oldest sister. It wasn't easy for any of us, but we knew that God had a plan for us and that we were to put everything in His hands. We started to go to church again as we began our new life.

As time went by, many of the church members and kids knew "our family story." Many of the kids would come up to me and ask me about it. Then they started to tell me that I was going to be like my oldest sister—that I was just going to wait until I was 18 and then run off with some guy. At first the comment hurt, but I knew deep inside it shouldn't bother me, because God is the only one who can judge.

We are not bound to any pattern in life. While circumstances may dictate some situations, our reaction to those circumstances is our own choice to make. Someone who has a family trait of addiction, or who comes from an abusive background, does not have to repeat the problems of their family. No, with God's help they can overcome any circumstance and be their own person. We are made as independent thinkers, and through the grace we are shown, we can lead lives that will glorify Christ. Let's remember that we are His children—we can't ask for a better heritage.

I know that Jesus has a plan for me and for my oldest sister. I just have to pray for His guidance in all that I do and then put everything in His hands.

The Desires of Our Hearts
By Beth Anderson

Trust in the Lord and do good; dwell in the land and enjoy safe pasture. Delight yourself in the Lord and He will give you the desires of your heart.
Psalm 37:3, 4.

Faith and prayer are at the core of my belief in God. It is truly amazing how God looks after us and gives us the desires of our hearts, if it works into His plan. Again and again, from my childhood to now, I can see how God has led in my life.

I believe that God brought my family to Mount Pisgah Academy several years ago. We had been at another school, in another union, for two years. Although we loved our students and had good friends there, I felt ready to move on. We looked at a map, talked about what region of the country we would like to live in, prayed, and left it up to God.

It looked like an opening was coming up at a sister school in the Southern Union. My husband had an interview scheduled. Then a call came that there wasn't an opening after all. I had been so excited and now I cried as I planted flowers that spring, figuring that I would have to make the best of things. We prayed again, and I had renewed faith. God either wasn't finished with us there yet, or He had something even better planned for us.

A few weeks later my husband got calls for interviews at two schools. They were both really good jobs in good locations. Both jobs were in the Southern Union, where we really wanted to be. Although he got offers for both jobs, our family decided the beautiful mountains of western North Carolina were the best place for our family. God knew the desires of our hearts. He heard our prayers, and He answered in a bigger and better way than we could ever have anticipated. All three of our children completed all four years of academy at MPA. God had it planned all along. What a blessing!

Rejoice!
By Julian Foster

So the soldiers took charge of Jesus. Carrying his own cross, he went out to the place of the Skull. . . . Here they crucified him. John 19:17, 18.

Crack! Lena had heard the sound all morning. Now her curiosity was getting the best of her, as it usually did. "Khia, don't you hear that? We should go see what it is," Lena said.

"Father said to stay put in the house while he fetches water," replied Khia.

Lena knew that her father had her and her twin sister's best interest in mind, but something about the crackling seemed to draw her attention outside.

"I know what Father said, but aren't you the least bit curious?"

Khia put her hand to her head in thought. She had been put in this situation by Lena before, and Khia knew there was no way to change her sister's mind.

"We can go, but only for a little while. Father will be back anytime," Khia responded.

The two girls made their way out of the red clay house to the main road. They quickly saw the large crowd formed along the road. As they rushed to the front of the multitude to see what all the ruckus was about, they heard loud chatter and the shrieking cracking noise.

"Look, Khia, they are beating that man while He carries a piece of wood!" uttered Lena.

"I see," Khia whispered. "He is looking our way."

"His eyes look so kind and softhearted. What could He have done?" asked Lena.

"I don't know, but I sure feel sorry for Him," Khia ventured.

"Don't feel sorry for Him, young lady. If anything, be rejoicing to God in heaven for having mercy on us humans," said an older woman in the crowd. "He is the Son of God, sent to the earth to take the punishment of our sins. He wouldn't want you to be sad or enraged, but thankful and willing to spread His message throughout the world."

I often forget this story when I go throughout my day. I take for granted the sacrifice Christ made for me on Calvary that Friday. I go through my day not treating it as if it was special. But I have come to the conclusion that every day is special. Not just because it is another day to talk to that dream girl, excel at that new job, or watch that new movie, but another day to tell someone about the Man who gave me the gift of eternal life before I even lived.

Wrapped Up, Tied Up, Tangled Up

By Zachary Bradley

So if the Son sets you free, you will be free indeed. John 8:36.

One of my favorite songs in Sabbath school goes like this: "Well, I'm wrapped up, and I'm tied up, and I'm tangled up with Jesus . . ." As we sing the song, we do motions that illustrate being wrapped up, tied up, and tangled up. It is fun to try to keep up with the motions when the song speeds up. I also like the song because we often talk about getting tangled up in Satan's snares, but it is so much better to be tangled up with Jesus.

This song reminds me of a trip my family took to Charleston, South Carolina, one of our favorite beach destinations. We like to catch hermit crabs and have them race on the beach. We like to find starfish, anemones, and minnows in the tidal pools. We enjoy watching the sea creatures up close before releasing them back to their homes. One day at the beach we saw a lot of ghost crabs scurrying about. They are fun to watch because they are cute when they run sideways into their sand holes and then peek out at you.

My dad thought it would be cool to hold one so that we could see it up close. It was funny watching Daddy run around with a net trying to catch one. They seemed too fast for him. But one crab surprisingly ran right into his net. At first we were excited and were fascinated to see how its eyes worked and its pinchers snapped. It was very interesting. When it was time to set the little crab free, we realized that it was quite tangled in the net.

When my dad tried to untangle it, the crab sliced open my dad's finger with its sharp claw. The crab didn't know that Daddy was trying to help it. Finally we got it untangled (partly by cutting the net) and tried to release it, but the crab held on to the net with its pincher claw. It could have been free, but it didn't want to let go.

This story reminds me of a good lesson. Jesus tries to set us free from our tangled mess of sin. And even when we could be free, we sometimes hang on to the net. Instead, we should avoid Satan's net and accept Jesus' help. It's much better to be wrapped up, tied up, and tangled up with Jesus. Being tangled up with Christ means true freedom!

Thankfulness and Humility

By A. J. King

In his pride the wicked does not seek him; in all his thoughts there is no room for God. Psalm 10:4.

Pride, arrogance, greed, and selfishness can take over all Christians at one point. This world has trained all of us to look out for ourselves and fight for what belongs to us. But God tells us to be humble and thank Him for the blessings we have.

Humbling ourselves is as simple as making the decision to suppress our pride whenever it might get in the way of doing good. In Luke 18:9-14 Jesus tells a story of two men who went to the Temple to pray. One was a Pharisee, and the other was a despised tax collector. The Pharisee went far away from the tax collector and said this prayer: "I thank You, God, that I am not a sinner like everyone else. For I don't cheat; I don't sin; and I don't commit adultery. I'm certainly not like that tax collector! I fast twice a week, and I give You a tenth of my income."

At the same time the tax collector was in the corner repeating, "O God, be merciful to me, for I am a sinner!"

The Bible then says, "I tell you, this sinner, not the Pharisee, returned home justified before God. For those who exalt themselves will be humbled, and those who humble themselves will be exalted."

In order to be truly humble, we must resist our natural tendency to exaggerate what we deserve. Being humble is closely related to being thankful. Jesus died on the cross for our sins, making us all equal in His eyes. It is not our place to criticize any other person.

So step out of the world's comfort zone—the zone that teaches you to look out for and promote yourself. It won't be easy, but make an effort to practice a little humility today. You might actually be surprised by the blessings you will receive.

The Storm

By Stephanie Thomas

I sought the Lord, and he answered me; he delivered me from all my fears.
Psalm 34:4.

On the way to the lake with some friends, we noticed that the sky was turning gray. We hoped it was just a small rain cloud that would pass by. After we unloaded our equipment at the landing, we got everybody on the Sea-Doos and boat and headed off to go "beach hunting." While looking for a secluded beach, we saw a few boats rushing toward the landing and were curious about why they were in such a hurry. But we didn't pay attention to them and just kept looking for a beach.

By the time we had reached an island with a beautiful secluded beach, the rain had started. While the dads were tying up the boat and Sea-Doos, the wind became stronger and the trees started swaying back and forth. Suddenly we started feeling hard objects the size of marbles falling down on us. It was icy, cold hail—and we had no shelter other than the trees. That's when our pastor, who was with us, decided to pray. I had never felt so scared in my life. I really thought the storm would never end. In the middle of my worry, I decided to say a personal prayer. I prayed that God would keep us safe and that He would calm the storm. As soon as I finished praying, I got an amazing, peaceful feeling, like no matter how bad the storm was, or how scared I was, that it was going to be OK. The fear I had during the storm disappeared, and I felt safe. Suddenly the wind died down; there was no more lightning; the hail stopped; and the rain slowed to a drizzle. Then the clouds opened and the sun started shining.

Later we found out that we had been in the outskirts of a tornado, which had been less than a mile away from where we had been stranded on the little island. We were so grateful for God's loving protection of us that day!

I now look back and realize that God had been with us the whole time protecting us. He had to be—nothing else could have helped us get through safely. Now, when I get scared or feel alone, I always remember that I can talk to God, and He will never leave me. As a song says: "Sometimes He calms the storm, and othertimes He calms His child." I know that in God's hands I will be all right.

Faith and Patience

By Lillian Williams

So that your faith might not rest on men's wisdom, but on God's power.
1 Corinthians 2:5.

I have a big problem with patience and faith. For example, as a junior in academy, I had had my driver's permit for more than two years. I could have gotten my license only six months after my permit, but it didn't happen. I thought I was a pretty good driver. Also, I did well in school, and I had a good attitude, just as my parents asked of me. In spite of this, my parents chose not to let me get my license right away. Why? I'm not sure.

It was really frustrating for me to wait and be patient, because I wanted my license for so many reasons. The main attraction, of course, was the freedom that accompanies a license—the thought that I could go where I wanted to go when I wanted to go was very enticing. I'm sure my parents had good reasons for making me wait, but it was still difficult for me to realize that when all my friends had their licenses, I still had only my permit.

The Bible tells us we need to have faith and be patient with God. I know I am impatient waiting for God to come. I can't wait to see Him, but I know that He has a plan, and He will come when He is ready! It is hard to have faith sometimes, because we cannot see Him. And we don't always see the big picture as He does. Just as I had to have patience with my parents and faith that they would one day let me get my license, we need to learn to put our faith and trust in God! He is smarter than we are, and His timing is perfect.

By the way, I did get my license. And I know that God will fulfill His promises too. He is coming soon! And what freedom we will have after His return—we will be able to go anywhere in the universe, and time will not be a factor. Until then, have patience and be faithful!

Foolish Friday

By Michael Daily

There is a way that seems right to a man, but in the end it leads to death.
Proverbs 14:12.

Friday the 13th is sometimes viewed in secular society as a day of misfortune and bad luck. I believe that Friday the 13th is no more unlucky than any other day of the year. By thinking that it is and by looking for unfortunate circumstances, we allow Satan to have more control over the situation.

This is illustrated in the story of Saul when he visited the Witch of Endor. The story is found in 1 Samuel 28:7-25. As we see the story unfold, Saul begins to feel that the Lord is no longer with him in his battle against the Philistines. The reason he feels this way is that God is no longer answering him through dreams or prophets. In Saul's great distress he seeks the council of a witch who conjures up a demon who resembles the deceased prophet Samuel. The demon tells Saul of his upcoming death. By allowing this demon to deceive him into believing he would die in the battle, he denied God's power to intervene in his life. If he had only trusted in God and not betrayed him by turning to Satan, he may have won the battle. But by going to see the witch, he gave control to Satan, and ultimately ended his own life.

In the same way we allow Satan to have control over events when we minimize the occult influences found in popular television shows, movies, or books or when we buy into superstitions such as Friday the 13th. (In actuality, this day is no different than any other day. To me it is the best day, because I was born on Friday the 13th.)

We should always look at the positive side of life and all the good things that happen, not at all the misfortunes. We should allow God to lead in our lives and trust in Him to carry us through our problems. And like it says in 1 Corinthians 10:13, God will never allow us to face a problem that we cannot overcome, no matter how unlucky the situation seems. Every day, even Friday the 13th, remember, "Today is the day the Lord has given us." Celebrate every minute of your day as you live in Christ!

Where Is God?

By Anders Markoff

Have I not commanded you? Be strong and courageous. Do not be terri-fied; do not be discouraged, for the Lord your God will be with you wher-ever you go. Joshua 1:9.

People often wonder where God has gone. The events around us seem to continually spiral downward as time continues. Everyone has heard about God's huge displays in the Old Testament—flashing thunder and lightning bellowing profound words to His people. We wonder why we don't see anything like that today.

Hurricane Katrina is known as the most devastating storm in recent history. Shortly after the storm passed through, I had the opportunity to go with all of the Mount Pisgah Academy staff and students to Waveland, Mississippi, where the center of Katrina passed over. We went to a relief center each day and handed out food and water to everyone who came through. At night we stayed in the "open air" gym at Bass Memorial Academy. The BMA campus was torn up, but we were glad to have a safe place to stay in the midst of such dreadful conditions.

Toward the middle of our trip, our principal took us on a bus ride to see the destruction and the circumstances that the families we were helping were dealing with. Everything was gone. I don't remember seeing one house still standing when we got near the shore, and the houses that used to be directly on the beach were nothing more than a few cement blocks scattered about. I just remember thinking, *How could God let this happen to so many people?*

Many people wondered where God was after Katrina hit New Orleans and the rest of Louisiana. I wondered that until someone told me, "Just imagine how bad it would have been if God hadn't been there." We often ask ourselves why God couldn't have done more. But I think that He already does more than we could ever ask. In fact, He cries to see all the terrible devastation that the devil has unleashed here, and He promises to see us through the storms of life, if not physically, at least emotionally.

I am sure that God is even more eager than we are to restore this world to perfection and to give us eternal life, with no more suffering or pain. One day all will be made perfect.

God Is Our Guide

By Kris Kimbley

For this God is our God for ever and ever; he will be our guide even to the end. Psalm 48:14.

Through the years I have faced many trials and temptations. During high school I was suspended three times, I almost failed my junior year, and I have been written up (part of the discipline system at MPA) countless times. It's not that I am a troubled kid, but I have just been caught on the wrong side of the fence a few times. I attended Mount Pisgah Academy for four years, and I learned a lot through what I experienced. I have actually changed quite a bit since I first started high school. In the beginning I didn't have any ambitions or goals—I just wanted to hang out and float through the rest of my life. But as a senior, I started to formulate goals and dreams. I realized that I had a lot of opportunities I wanted to pursue. I also realized that I would never meet any of my goals if I continued to slack off and not start standing up and becoming a responsible citizen.

I am very thankful for all of the help I have had, for without good guidance and encouragement, I don't think I could have turned things around. Of course, God guided me through a lot of tough times. He would speak through a vespers program, a Sabbath school, a family member, or a friend. I am blessed with the best group of friends—they have always been by my side. And my grandparents have always helped me out when I have needed it and sometimes even when I didn't think I did. Because of all of these influences, I have realized how important life is.

Everyone goes through tough times in life. Remember that God, with quality friends and your family's help, will always guide you and help you face your problems. And if you make a few poor choices along the way, know that God's love for you will not fail. Just learn and move on to better things.

Stand Firm in Faith

By Megan Coffey

Be strong and courageous. Do not be afraid or terrified because of them, for the Lord your God goes with you; he will never leave you nor forsake you. Deuteronomy 31:6.

Throughout our lives we often run into situations in which our faith is tested. When that happens we have to make sure that others know we are a Christian and that we aren't afraid to stand up for what we believe. We have to be courageous and stay strong, knowing that God can help us through anything whenever we need Him.

My friends and I often talk about God. Somehow He usually comes up in our conversations. We talk about the circumstances when we pray to Him, even about the simplest things. He answers our prayers and is always willing to listen. Sometimes I sit down right before a test and ask God to help me remember everything. Sometimes I pray to Him to help my friends who are sick or struggling with certain things in their lives. I always know that He is willing to help me through anything if I just ask Him and have the courage to believe.

Sometimes it is difficult to talk about faith to people. It feels as if they're going to judge me and not care about what I have to say. It's probably one of the hardest topics to just bring up in a conversation because it doesn't seem important to most people. People often say that it is hard to understand and think about something they can't see. It's hard to explain what something looks like if they can't see it or touch it, and I think that this is the image that most people get in their heads when they think about God.

God gives us the Bible to let us know how He feels about us. He tells us that we must have faith and courage in Him so that we can be strong in our faith and stand up for what we believe in. As we go throughout the day, we just need to remember that God is always there for us and that we must believe that He will never leave. We have to be ready for anything that comes up and be ready to stand up for the Lord!

An Hour Spent With a Gift From God

By Rachel Sheridan

Every good and perfect gift is from above, coming down from the Father of the heavenly lights, who does not change like shifting shadows. James 1:17.

There I was in the hospital waiting room, everyone around me crying. Questions of confusion ran through my head. *What's going on?*

It was in November when we got the news that my mom was pregnant with a sweet baby boy. I was so excited! I was going to have a real baby to play with instead of a plastic doll. At 4 years old, I was going to be a big sister.

It was many months later that my mom visited the doctor, like she had many times before, but this time they noticed that my mom was bigger than normal. So they decided to do an ultrasound, because they thought there might be twins, which was even more exciting. Soon after they took a closer look at the pictures they found there was only one baby. They also found there was something wrong. My baby brother had Pallister-Killian Syndrome, which meant he had a chromosome problem. This caused a hole in the diaphragm. His colon was pushed up, and his heart was pushed over. Without a doubt this didn't allow room for lung development. So he couldn't breathe. Therefore, my baby brother wasn't going to survive.

Finally, the time had came for my mom to go into labor. When we arrived at the hospital, they took my mom in a room while we waited outside. After delivery we went in to see my mom and brother. When we entered the room, my mom was crying, and I just sat on the chair. I still didn't understand why everyone was crying. Then the nurse walked over and placed him in my arms. As he laid his little hands and fingers across my arm, a happy feeling ran over me. Those few minutes with my baby brother I'll cherish forever. Then the nurse took him out of the room, and he died within three minutes. His entire lifespan was only about an hour.

This experience changed my life forever. I've learned to cherish every moment I spend with friends and family because life is precious.

Great Is Your Faithfulness

By Brian Hindman

Great is your faithfulness. Lamentations 3:23.

The world we live in today is filled with uncertainties. At times friends and even family let us down. We can be overcome with sadness and disappointment. But this is not how God is. He has promised, "Never will I leave you; never will I forsake you" (Hebrews 13:5).

After my wife and I were married, we decided to get a dog. We purchased a furry tan mutt from a student of mine. The student had already named him "Peekin," so we kept the name. Peekin would follow me wherever I went, so much so that sometimes it was even annoying. One evening when Peekin was still only a puppy, about 3 months old, I walked across campus from my house to the boys' dorm. As usual, the dog faithfully followed me. After spending an hour or more visiting with some of the boys, I left and walked back home. It was late in the evening so I went to bed.

The next morning my wife, who was working the night shift at a hospital, called me and asked how our new puppy was doing. To my complete horror, I realized Peekin was gone. I had completely forgotten about the young puppy when I went into the dorm. Frantically I called and searched around the house and around campus. Nothing. As my mind raced, I decided to retrace my steps back to where I last saw him. And there was my dog—sleeping beside the back door of the boys' dorm where he had last seen me. I had forgotten about him and went out the front door when I left. He had spent the entire night in the cold waiting for me.

In a small way that puppy illustrates God's faithfulness. Wherever we go and whatever we do He is there, watching us and waiting for us to call upon His strength and mercy. May we never forget Him, for He has promised, "I will not forget you!" (Isaiah 49:15).

Obstacles, Choices, and Asking

By Michelle Dannenberger

Then Asa called to the Lord his God and said, "Lord, there is no one like you to help the powerless against the mighty. Help us, O Lord our God, for we rely on you, and in your name we have come against this vast army. O Lord, you are our God; do not let man prevail against you.
2 Chronicles 14:11.

Many people ask, "How could God let this happen?" I have also asked this question, and I was determined to find an answer. And this is what I found.

One time, long, long ago, life was without trouble, pain, and misery. This of course was in the Garden of Eden before Adam and Eve sinned. I'm sure you all have heard the story of how Eve chose to disobey God and eat the forbidden fruit.

Some people ask, "Why even make a tree? No tree, no temptation, no sin, right?" Yes, that is true, but if God didn't give us the choice to disobey, then we'd have no choice but to do His will. We can't truly love something we're forced to love.

God knows what's going to happen in the future. He knows everything. He knew that Adam and Eve would fall into sin and succumb to the temptations of Satan. Thousands of years later we face the same decisions that Adam and Eve had to make—sin and disobedience are still an option. Yes, this life we live as Christians and followers of Jesus isn't an easy one, but all we have to do as Christians is ask for God's help—ask Him to be with us every day and to give us strength to make it through the obstacles of life.

Sometimes we fall and don't always do what God tells us, but that doesn't change His mind. He never leaves us. As cliché as it may sound, He's only a prayer away. And that's the beauty of the whole thing—God loves us despite our failures. He has given us a choice—an amazing gift of freedom—and He loves us no matter what. Unfortunately, some people will choose to ignore Him and will perish, while others will choose to follow Jesus and will gain eternal life. But Jesus died for all so that we may have life if we want it. What a generous blessing—the opportunity to choose (no force involved) our own fate.

I pray that we will all make the wise choice and enjoy all of the blessings that God has prepared for us! Thank Him for your freedom of choice today.

What Is It
With These Hummingbirds?

By Linda Duncan

Look at the birds of the air; they do not sow or reap or store away in barns, and yet your heavenly Father feeds them. Are you not much more valuable than they? Matthew 6:26.

What is it with these hummingbirds? One feeder with fresh, rich sugar-water nectar hangs on our front porch, and another one hangs outside a huge window at the back of the house. Now, wouldn't you think that would be plenty for the two, sometimes three, hummingbirds that visit our yard? These tiny birds are so beautiful with shimmery feathers, green and ruby red. But in their case it seems beauty is only skin/feather deep. One will sit on a nearby limb, looking and waiting. When it sees another one approaching the feeder, he immediately goes into defense mode. He maneuvers his 0.124-ounce body (less than the weight of a nickel) better than a stealth helicopter, diving and chasing the guest from the food source. Often they are so preoccupied with keeping other hummingbirds from the feeder, either in the air or just sitting on the feeder constantly looking for an invader, that they don't even get a drink for themselves. And the sad part is there is plenty for all.

Wait . . . am I like that sometimes? So busy looking at others and preoccupied with a meaningless, selfish mission that I miss the blessing that God has waiting for me?

But there is another amazing event in the hummingbird's life that illustrates God's tender love and mercy and guidance. These tiny little birds migrate every year to Central America to stay warm in the winter. They can travel 1,500 miles, including more than 500 miles nonstop over the Gulf of Mexico, to reach their destination.

He cares for all His creatures, including me, even with our faults. WOW! What an awesome God!

Life Is Hard

By Brittany Trosino

Though he stumble, he will not fall, for the Lord upholds him with his hand.
Psalm 37:24.

Sometimes life challenges us far beyond what we think we can handle. Yet even though these challenges are hard, God has promised that He will not give us more than we can handle.

For some of us, life may be harder than what our peers can imagine. I've been through a lot. Despite all the bad things I've lived through, there are two events that stick out in my life.

First, being "raised" by a bipolar mother meant being abused physically, mentally, emotionally, and verbally. My mother had constant mood swings, so taking care of myself and my younger sister was left up to me. Life sort of seemed impossible. I never knew how my day was going to turn out.

The second event that shaped my life took place when I was 12 years old. The man who had been like a father to me raped me. This seemingly ended every possible hope and dream of my future.

Right after my life had changed forever, God opened up the doors for me to live with my grandmother. She showed me how much God loves me and reminded me every day how much she does, too. After living with her, I had the chance to go to an amazing school, Mount Pisgah Academy. What a journey I've been on. I am just glad that God saw fit to open the doors so that I could get a new start. I've had my ups and downs, but it's a blessing for me to be at academy, a safe place.

Still, during the middle of one school year, I got down. When I felt as if I had hit rock bottom, my dean got me in touch with author Cheri Peters. (If you haven't read her book yet, you should.) She has been through a lot of what I've been through, and even worse. She told me just a small bit of what she's lived through and how she's found God through all of it. This gave me so much hope. I really appreciated her taking the time to talk to me.

Every time I'm really down, God directs me to someone who can give me hope. So I know He cares for me. He loves us all so very much. The next time you feel like your life is not worth living, just remember, there is nothing you and God can't get through together. Life is hard, but you are not alone.

Your Best Friend
By Katie Thrash

A man of many companions may come to ruin, but there is a friend who sticks closer than a brother. Proverbs 18:24.

One thing I know for sure, I love my friends! I have so many I can't even count them. They are a huge part of my life.

I thank Jesus every day for my friends, and I know that He has given them to me because He loves me. He knows I couldn't survive without them.

Jesus gets to watch everyone have fun with their friends, but do you ever stop and have fun with your friend Jesus? He says He wants to be your friend, too. He is the kind of friend who will be there even if you go crazy. He will listen no matter what, and for me that is great. You will always be excited about seeing a friend, but how about getting extremely excited to talk to your friend Jesus?

Just because Jesus doesn't go shopping or skating with you in person doesn't mean He is not always there. Stopping and talking with Him throughout the day is a great way to get help, and no, you don't have to stop and get on your knees. Just talk to Him when you are walking the dog or cleaning the dishes. I know it isn't the same as having someone standing there giving you feedback, but Jesus can give you a lot more than feedback. He will never move away or get "better" friends. He will be there. He is waiting to become one of your very best friends forever.

Baggage
By Bonny Musgrave

For the wages of sin is death, but the gift of God is eternal life in Christ Jesus our Lord. Romans 6:23.

Countdowns have always engaged my imagination, whether they are for music, celebrities, or events. Perhaps it is the challenge of trying to predict who is going to be in first place that intrigues me so. Whatever the reason, recently I was watching the E! network's countdown to the top 101 most shocking moments in entertainment. The list included the deaths of celebrities such as J. F. Kennedy, Jr., Marilyn Monroe, and Anna Nicole, as well as other events, such as celebrity hookups and breakups. My personal guess for number one was the tragic death of Princess Diana, but she was edged out by the trial of O. J. Simpson for the top spot.

What really caught my attention, and had me thinking long after the show's conclusion, was an event that took place in August 2001. Aaliyah, the 22-year-old Grammy-winning R&B singer, who just happened to also be a dancer, model, and actress, was killed when her small plane took off from the Bahamas. The entertainment world was shocked. But it was the final two sentences in her story that caught my attention: "It was later determined that the cause of the crash was the excess baggage brought on board by the passengers, causing the small plane to crash upon takeoff. The passengers had been asked to leave some of their belongings behind, but nobody was willing to do so."

What fools! I thought to myself. *Who would be so stupid as to put their own life in danger with a few personal belongings?* But of course, they didn't know they would lose their lives over this decision. When the airline officials said they needed to lighten the load, they didn't take them seriously. But wait, don't I make the same mistake in my own life? What "baggage" do I cling to that may cost me eternal life? Which grudges do I refuse to let go of? What material things is God trying to pry from my clenched fingers?

For each of us, the answer to these questions will be different, but all of us need to ask God to show us what "baggage" we need to let go of so that our lives don't come crashing down around us. Let's let Jesus take our "baggage" and lighten our load so that we can make that final flight to heaven with Him!

God Is There for You!

By Tiffany Weber

In the same way, the Spirit helps us in our weakness. We do not know what we ought to pray for, but the Spirit himself intercedes for us with groans that words cannot express. Romans 8:26.

Do you ever have a hard time trusting or even believing in God? It's sometimes hard to believe in someone you can't see. We often hear about Him and the miracles He has performed. But is it personal to you? Sometimes it takes an extreme circumstance to help us realize how much He watches over us. I know that God is always right there when I need Him, even if I can't see Him.

When I was 7 years old, I was at school playing on the monkey bars. I decided to climb to the top. When I got up there, I decided to sit down and put my legs on the bar across from where I was sitting. When I did, I slipped and fell straight through to the bottom. As I went down, my head hit each bar and finally hit the rocky bottom. My teacher saw me fall and rushed over to see if I was OK. She took me inside and called my mom to tell her to come get me. Mom came to pick me up, and then she took me to the emergency room.

I remember lying down in the back seat on the way to the ER just wanting so badly to go to sleep, but my mom kept saying, "Don't go to sleep. Stay awake." We arrived at the hospital, and while in the waiting room, I slipped into unconsciousness. Then after a while, I woke up and they took X-rays to make sure nothing was terribly wrong. After a long day, I walked out of the emergency room with a golf ball-sized hematoma on my head.

I know I was young at the time of my accident, but every time I think about it, I am grateful for my health and safety. This story is a reminder of God's mercy that touches our lives all the time—even when we don't realize it. We often brush off a close call in the car or a small head injury we recover from quickly as a "lucky break." But we need to remember that God is in control of everything, and He should get the credit for every day that we live.

Where Was God?

By Shawntese Smith

Jesus said to her, "I am the resurrection and the life. He who believes in me will live, even though he dies; and whoever lives and believes in me will never die. Do you believe this?" John 11:25, 26.

Aric is dead." These were the most horrible words I had ever heard over the phone. A few summers ago my mother got a new boyfriend. And guess what? I hated him. I wanted my real parents to get back together again. This was my dream, and I was not willing to let it die, even though I knew Aric loved me and my sisters. He was so good to all of us, and most of all, he loved my mom.

Finally I let him into my heart. I realized what a great father he would be, and I began to truly love him. I began to look forward to our future as a family.

Sadly, on January 21, 2007, Aric died. He was driving home when he was shot at, causing him to accidentally drive into a street pole. He was pronounced dead there on the street.

After this horrible event I questioned God so many times. Aric was a righteous, innocent man. I didn't understand why he died, especially just as things were going so well. Why wasn't he spared?

However, God gave me a message on the day of Aric's funeral. I picked up my Bible that day and felt renewed after reading John 11:25. "He who believes in me will live, even though he dies." The Bible clearly promises that death for the righteous is not permanent. We know that my stepfather, who is dead, is only sleeping. We know that in the near future Christ will return to resurrect the faithful. I can hardly wait until that day.

The night of the funeral I slept peacefully, knowing that God has promised a happy ending to our story if we love Him. Won't you be His faithful follower now so that you will be ready to be reunited with your loved ones who went to sleep in Jesus, and together, spend eternity with God?

The Golden Dollar
By Ryan Gillen

Finally, all of you, live in harmony with one another; be sympathetic, love as brothers, be compassionate and humble. 1 Peter 3:8.

The summer after my sophomore year of high school I had the privilege of working in Valdez, Alaska. I know what you are thinking, "How did that Carolina guy get a job in Alaska?" Well, my great-uncle actually lives up there. He owns a quaint bed-and-breakfast and a construction company. Because summer is the peak of the Alaskan tourist season, he was in need of some extra help running the bed-and-breakfast. My dad and I answered his call for help.

Needless to say, my summer was extremely interesting and quite life-changing. This was not only because I was in Alaska, far away from my home and all the other comforts I know and love, but also because I was in a new town, which meant lots of new people to meet.

One day in the middle of the summer I was tired of work and slightly homesick. I had been there for a month, so I was accustomed to the work, but the job had not turned out the way I had envisioned. There were also some other unforeseen circumstances that caused things to be a little different than had been expected. I was especially frustrated this particular day, and I was regretting having decided to work there.

While I was watching the desk, a couple of women came in, and I proceeded to check them into the bed-and-breakfast. I conversed with them briefly and then handed them the key to their room. As they were leaving, one of the women asked me to put out my hand, so I did. In it she placed a brand-new golden dollar. Then she said, "God bless you," and walked out smiling.

This small action and token meant a lot to me because it showed me that even though I thought God wasn't listening or watching, He was. Sometimes He sends people just at the right moment to lift our spirits. It just may not always be in the way we expect Him to. Keep your eyes open for glimpses of God working in your life.

Patience, God Loves

By Jacob Ballew

Give thanks to the God of gods. His love endures forever. Psalm 136:2.

All people have some similar questions in the back of their mind. What is our purpose? Are we loved? Does God hear us? Sometimes I wonder these things.

In the Bible God says that He loves me, and in my heart I know it's true. But on a day-to-day basis, especially when things are going well, I sometimes forget that God has an active role in my life. I speak to Him every day in prayer. I pray for Him to bless and keep my family and friends safe and well. So far He's answered yes to that request. But perhaps all of my requests or wishes are too much to ask, or are just selfish. Does God want to be bothered with my prayers?

I know I should appreciate the things He's already given me, and I do, but I don't always make the connection between my blessings and God's part in giving them to me. Until one day . . .

My brother Kyle and I were working on his car. I was standing between my brother's car and my mom's car. It was late, and I was tired. While I stood there, Kyle told me we'd check the car while in neutral and then go on a test drive. I trust my brother's knowledge about cars and felt very safe in front of the started car. But while I stood there, knowing the car couldn't move in neutral, something told me to move out of the way, so I did. When Kyle put it in neutral, it somehow slipped into drive and rammed into the back of my mom's car. If I hadn't moved, I could have been hurt very badly.

After experiencing this, I felt stupid for doubting God and His presence in my life. I now know for certain that He loves me and takes care of me. So don't doubt God. Whether it's in a time of crisis or during your ordinary day, God loves you and will not leave you.

Embracing Love

By Tressa Perry

Come to me, all you who are weary and burdened, and I will give you rest. Take my yoke upon you and learn from me, for I am gentle and humble in heart, and you will find rest for your souls. For my yoke is easy and my burden is light. Matthew 11:28-30.

In April 2007 I hit one of my lowest times spiritually. I was tired of worship and almost anything to do with God. My grandma had sent me a devotional book, and I read it for a while before stopping. I knew Jesus loved me, but I couldn't feel His presence. I didn't truly believe that He could help me with all my problems, because I felt like I had messed up too much in my past. At summer camps and spiritual retreats, I would accept Him as my personal Savior. Yet a couple months later I would go downhill spiritually again.

April 3, 2007, my day started off very badly. I was late to work, and my "friends" weren't being friends to me at all. It was just a bad day. I was so fed up with everything by the end of the day that, after worship, I decided to call one of my best friends who loves God with all his heart. I told him how I was tired of guys looking at me in a dirty way and how I was tired of not being right with God.

While we read a few Bible texts together, I really felt like God was talking to me though my friend. Because of all the verses we read and the things he said, I realized that I shouldn't let guys get away with making me feel insecure about my body. My friend said that if I was ever depressed, I could read Matthew 11:28-30. And whenever I needed someone to talk to, Jesus would always be ready to listen to me. That was the night I accepted God back into my heart.

I know that everyone goes through ups and downs, but I thank God for friends who help me keep my priorities straight, my self-esteem in check, and my relationship with God unwavering. God understands me and wants to be a part of my life no matter what I go through.

A Niece Instead of a Brother

By Denis Kasap

Remember your word to your servant, for you have given me hope. My comfort in my suffering is this: Your promise preserves my life.
Psalm 119:49, 50.

You will have a little brother soon," my dad said to me one evening. I was 12 years old and living in Russia at the time. I was so excited! That was my dream—to have a little brother or sister. But something happened.

Two brothers from a small city near Moscow were living in our church. One Sabbath we had some visitors in the church, and they asked me to show them the nearest subway station. I couldn't do that for some reason, so I asked one of those brothers to help them. Auris, who was younger, was glad to help them. They left the church and went to the subway station. Later in the evening my dad got a call from the church. They said that on the way back Auris had been hit by a car and was in a coma in the ICU. All my family was shocked. We prayed every day for him, but five days after the accident, he died. As a young man who wanted to be a pastor, I kept asking God, "Why . . . why did You let this happen?"

My mother got really depressed. She knew that it was really bad for her unborn baby, but she couldn't do anything. She lost the baby. "Why?" I asked God again. I had lost a friend and now my unborn baby brother—I didn't even have a chance to see him, to hear him, to hold him.

That tragedy changed me. I was 12, but I didn't play with my friends outside anymore; I didn't cry; I didn't talk like a child. That tragedy made me grow up faster. I began to think differently. Auris' brother, Gedrius, was also really depressed. My oldest sister wanted to help him to get through this tragedy. She began to talk to him every day, and they began spending more and more time together. They married after three months. And a few years later they had a baby girl, so I now have a niece! God is good.

On this earth we will never understand why bad things happen. But we must trust in God to get us through the rough times. We should build our faith in Him so that we can be reunited with our loved ones in heaven someday soon.

The Day I Was Saved
By Blin Richards

You are my hiding place; you will protect me from trouble and surround me with songs of deliverance. Psalm 32:7.

When I was in second grade and living in California, my family and a few friends decided to go to the beach for an afternoon of fun.

We were enjoying the beautiful surf and sand at the beach when some of us kids decided to go climb on a rocky cliff right by the edge of the water. The tide was coming in, and the only way we could see to get on the rocks was to go right down where the waves were crashing and, in between waves, run right along the rocks for about 10 feet and then climb up onto a small rock that allowed us to get up onto the larger boulders. So one by one we waited for our turn. The wave would crash against the rocks, and then someone would run and climb up it as fast as possible—no one wanted to be smashed onto the rocks and washed away.

Finally, it was my turn. As I waited for the wave to break on the rocks, I felt a little uneasy, but I wiped that thought out of my mind and started running. I reached the rock and started climbing, but I slipped and landed back on the ground. I looked out at the wave racing toward me, but there was nothing I could do to get out of the way. So I just braced for impact and hoped for a soft collision with the rocks.

Just then I was jerked into the air. The wave crashed into the rocks below, and the overflow washed around my feet. I looked around, and standing right beside me was my dad. He had been watching me. And when I needed help, he came to save me.

God is exactly the same way. He is always watching us, and He saves us when we are in messes that we cannot get out of on our own. The Bible says He will never leave us nor forsake us. So when you are in trouble, know that God is there with you, holding out His hand, just waiting for you to grab on and be saved.

The Game of Life

By Derek Youn

Similarly, if anyone competes as an athlete, he does not receive the victor's crown unless he competes according to the rules. 2 Timothy 2:5.

Everyone close to me knows that I love sports. I often put sports in front of things that I shouldn't. Athletes, including myself, try to find that edge on our opponent, something that makes us a better athlete than we had been before. Many athletes will try to do it by pure effort—working out and training harder than anyone else. This would be the honest way to gain that edge, but unfortunately, it's not always the path taken.

In today's age of modern medicine, athletes have access to many performance-enhancing drugs that alter their bodies, and sometimes mental abilities. It seems as though every time I turn on SportsCenter, one of the main headlines for the day is that another star athlete is accused of taking steroids or growth hormones. These athletes apparently do not think things through. Those who take steroids not only endanger their health; their career could be thrown away in one instant.

In 2 Timothy 2:5 we learn that we will not receive the victor's crown unless we compete according to the rules. How will we ever be able to make it to heaven unless we abide by God's rules? He gave us 10 commandments as guidelines for our lives. We may disregard a few of these commandments to get ahead in this life, but I think we sometimes forget how short a time we have here on earth.

So don't try to take shortcuts that could be detrimental to your immediate well-being or to your long-term reward. Next time you face a decision in life, remember that God has offered you the victor's crown, and He wants you to join Him soon in heaven.

Desperate Decisions and Answered Prayers

By Jonathan P. Michael

Your ears shall hear a word behind you, saying, "This is the way, walk in it,"
whenever you turn to the right hand or whenever you turn to the left.
Isaiah 30:21, NKJV.

Decisions, decisions, decisions. Life is definitely full of them. It's a never-ending array of choices. What will I wear today? What will I eat? Should I say this or do that? And what's behind door number 3, anyway? One of the biggest dilemmas I wrestled with after graduating from high school was what college I should attend. By the end of the summer I had narrowed it down to two schools, but I felt that these two options would lead me down two very different paths. This left me feeling like my whole life was hanging in the balance. I even had a nagging fear that this decision might actually have some impact on my eternity. That's strange to think now, but that's the way I felt at the time. Needless to say, I really wanted to make the right choice.

School A was well respected and spoken of highly by the majority of people I talked with, including my parents. But over the summer I had made some new friends who were strongly pulling me to go to School B. My parents were deeply concerned; they too saw that this decision would impact my future, but they were respectfully leaving the choice to me. What should I do? I had prayed and prayed and prayed and prayed, but I still did not feel as though God had shown me a clear direction. "Lord, which school should I choose? This decision is entirely my call to make!"

I had delayed the decision long enough. It was now the end of the summer, which meant it was choosing time. With two days left to spare, something clicked in my mind. I finally realized I really did *not* want to make the choice myself. I honestly and wholeheartedly wanted to know God's preference. I then sent up a new desperate prayer: "Father God, I believe Your will is best. Please have the school of Your choice call me tomorrow. I will joyfully go there."

The next morning the phone rang. It was the school of God's choice.

I learned that this is the confidence we have in approaching God: that if we ask anything according to His will, He hears us. And if we know that He hears us—whatever we ask—we know that we have what we ask of Him (1 John 5:14). There seems to be a definite connection here between God's will and answered prayer. Do I really want God to direct my life? If so, then I must be willing to know and do God's will! After all, answered prayers are His call to make.

The Sneaky Creature

By Jacquelyn Plested

No temptation has seized you except what is common to man. And God is faithful; he will not let you be tempted beyond what you can bear. But when you are tempted, he will also provide a way out so that you can stand up under it. 1 Corinthians 10:13.

It was a beautiful, sunny spring day, so my sister and I decided to play outside in the yard. We had just moved from town out into the country, and our house was across the road from a field that was full of daffodils. I was 7 years old at the time, and my sister was 3.

On this particular day we heard that it was supposed to freeze that night, which would kill all of the beautiful flowers. So my sister and I set out to pick a bunch of the flowers before the frost came.

I was walking along, picking flower after flower, when all of a sudden the grass moved right beside my foot. I stopped and peered down to see what creature was in the grass—it was a snake! I was so scared. I went running and screaming back toward the house, leaving my sister standing in the field curiously looking at the snake.

This experience reminds me of Satan. We go about our day so innocently. Then the devil pops up with a temptation or a disaster. But we need to remember that God will help us through it. He promises to be with us at all times, and if we have a growing relationship with Him, He will help us do the right thing and make the right decisions.

Next time you run into one of Satan's temptations, be like me and run away. Don't be like my curious sister, who stuck around looking at the snake, because you could get hurt.

Who You Gonna Call?

Brittani Coleman

No one will be able to stand up against you all the days of your life. As I was with Moses, so I will be with you; I will never leave you nor forsake you.
Joshua 1:5.

No one here on this earth can promise that they will be with you 24/7. I, however, will be with you always. I know sometimes, or maybe all the time, you feel as though you can't talk to Me the same way you do to your other friends. But that's just it! It's not the same—it's better. You never have to think twice about whether or not I'm going to spill the beans; you never have to worry about someone listening in on our conversation. I understand any problem because My Son has been through it all and more—and I never left Him either!

I know that things can weigh heavily on you, that life in the twenty-first century is difficult. You are actually living in some of the most corrupt times earth has ever seen. And although you are bombarded with troubles and temptations, don't think that I've left you. Talk to Me about your stresses and your trials. I want to comfort you and give you hope. Soon we will be face-to-face friends—and oh, the surprises I have waiting for you! I am so excited about you joining Me in My house. The universe is My backyard—we'll explore it all!

I am always available to talk to you. You will never get a busy signal; you will never be put on hold. You don't have to deal with sarcastic remarks, odd looks, or being laughed at. The greatest thing of all, though, is that I want to talk to you! I can't wait to hear you say, "OK, God, today was the absolute worst/most fantastic day of my life . . . " Even though I already know what happened, I just want to spend time with you! Consider Me like the frantic friend who leaves a thousand messages on your phone begging you to call Me back. I have so much I want to share with you, and I am eager to be closer friends with you.

So when the time is convenient for you, please return My call. I'm always available.

—God

The Fawn
By Sheldon Safrit

The wolf will live with the lamb, the leopard will lie down with the goat, the calf and the lion and the yearling together; and a little child will lead them.
Isaiah 11:6.

One day my brother and I decided we would take a walk in the woods. We got dressed and headed out. After walking awhile we came upon some brush, but we saw something moving in it. We sneaked to get a closer view and found two tiny fawns. We didn't want to spook or endanger them, so we backed away slowly, hoping the mother wouldn't detect our smell.

We were excited about our find, and as we headed toward home, we talked about the unique encounter. As we walked toward the road to go back to the house, I heard something behind me. I turned around to see what it was, and there was one of the fawns following us. I tried to make it go back, but it didn't; it just kept following us to the house. I told my brother to go inside and get Mom.

Mom, apparently just hearing that a deer had followed us home, quickly ran out of the house, afraid that a big deer could hurt us. But as soon as she saw the fawn, she went inside and got a towel to pick it up. We carefully retraced our steps and put the fawn back where we had originally found it.

To be that close to God's creation was an amazing experience—I will never forget it.

God is good to give us such variety and beauty in nature. What a gift when we can witness the wild animal kingdom in person, because it is a rare thing to have such encounters. On this earth wild animals fear people (and for good reason), and people (also for good reason) often fear wild animals. But I look forward to the day little children will lead lions and deer side by side, and we will never have to be afraid.

God's Little Wierdo

Leena Zepeda

And so we know and rely on the love God has for us. God is love. Whoever lives in love lives in God, and God in him. 1 John 4:16.

God loves you and cares about you regardless of what you look like or what people think about you. When I was about 7 years old, I attended a private Catholic school. I was the type of person who would sit by myself and not make much effort to get to know others. I was very quiet. Consequently, I did not have many friends. But loneliness wasn't my only problem. Because I was so painfully shy, other kids made fun of me. I felt like a complete loser because every day in class my classmates would talk badly about me, and it made me feel worthless.

Then my life took a different turn. My mom and I moved from Spain to America, which didn't help matters for me. In fact, I felt even worse because not only was I the shy weirdo, now I was the shy weirdo foreign girl who didn't understand or say a word in English.

I have been in America now for a few years. My English is still a work in progress, although I do all right. I have made some good friends here, and I continue to try to break out and be more assertive, although it does not come easy for me.

But over the past few years I have gotten to know God. I have realized that God loves me no matter what, and He thinks I am special in my own way. He can give me internal confidence, and I don't need the approval of others. Maybe you know someone whose life is similar to my story, or maybe that person is you. You know how hurtful words can be from people who think you are not special, that you're not attractive enough, that you act strangely, or that you are worthless. Know that God loves you and sees the true person you are. God loves you no matter what, and you don't need anyone else's approval.

Our Talents

By Kaylee Couser

We have different gifts, according to the grace given us. If a man's gift is prophesying, let him use it in proportion to his faith. Romans 12:6.

I was homeschooled from first through eighth grade. For the first couple of years, I didn't mind it, but once I was in seventh grade, I wanted out. I really wanted to go to school and meet some friends. For my ninth-grade year, I was allowed to attend our local academy. I was so nervous. I remember asking myself, "Should I really go through with this? Will I make any friends?" Even now I am still shy, and I get really nervous around people I don't know.

Since I have a really hard time going up to people and saying hi, I wondered if being shy meant that God couldn't use me. Luckily, though, I realized that God can use anybody. Surprisingly, He has used me.

During a retreat with Kenneth Cox, an evangelist, a few friends and I were asked to sing for the meeting. I was so nervous, but I got over my nerves and finally agreed to sing with them. After we finished our song, everyone said amen, and I felt very happy that I had stepped out in faith.

Even though we may not be sure what God has in store for us, we have to use the talents He gave us. Just because I am shy doesn't mean I can't do something for God. I have to use my talents and step out in faith to help others find Jesus.

According to Wayne Rice in *Hot Illustrations for Youth Talks*, "we have all experienced rejection and failure in life, but God has gifted each one of us with unique talents and abilities that enable us to make a significant contribution to the world. What are your gifts? Unless you attempt to use them, you will never discover how God prepared you to contribute. We need to be like the little boy in Scripture who offered Jesus his lunch. Jesus in turn used it to feed a multitude."

Read Romans 12 again, and be assured that God has chosen a special gift just for you. And if you will let Him work through you as you use your talents, you won't regret it.

Protector

By Megan Couser

For he will command his angels concerning you to guard you in all your ways. Psalm 91:11.

Occasionally, when I was a child, my siblings and I would put on shows for our parents. A day I remember well was the day my sisters, Melissa and Kaylee, my brother, Drew, and I were practicing a circus skit down in our basement. We decided to put two chairs, center stage, in front of the fireplace. Kaylee sat on one chair and Melissa on the other. Since I was the smallest, I stood on both of the armrests. While practicing our skit, I lost my balance, fell back, and hit my head on the fireplace. For a second I lay there, wondering what had just happened. As I got up, I felt the back of my head and then looked at my hand—I saw blood! Scared, I lay on the couch, and my sister Melissa ran upstairs to get our parents. My mom went to the refrigerator to get an ice pack for my head. We then headed to the hospital.

In the hospital waiting room, my mom told a nurse what happened. Shortly afterward, we were ushered into a room. The doctor stitched my cut and said that everything would be fine. On our way out, the nurse gave me a little pack of M&Ms. I fully recovered, but I know that my injury could have been far worse. My angels kept me from serious harm, and I thank God for that gift.

How many times are we spared serious injury and go on about our day, munching our M&Ms, not thinking about the reason we are all right? How many accidents do we not have, thanks to a miraculous occurrence of which we are not even aware? Do we thank God when things go well? Or do we just turn to God in times of trouble?

Take some time today to thank God for sending a personal guardian angel to get you through each day.

A Clear Blue Sky

By Kyle Hano

The heavens declare the glory of God; the skies proclaim the work of his hands. Psalm 19:1.

When I walk outside, I have the tendency to look up at the sky. However, to me it is more than just the sky; it is a constantly changing portrait from God that is always new and surprising. Some days the sky is clear and blue as far as the eye can see. On other days the sky is filled with billowy cotton candy clouds. Still other days, clouds are heavy with rain. The sky makes me think of God. He's always going to be a constant in my life. And just like the sky, God also surprises me almost every day.

Sometimes my relationship with God can seem like it's not going so well—like a cloudy or rainy day. Other times my relationship with Him seems as though I am on cloud nine, and my day just couldn't be any better. The prophet Paul says in Romans 11:33, "Oh, the depth of the riches both of the wisdom and knowledge of God! How unsearchable his judgments, and his paths beyond tracing out!"

I know that sometimes people think they have God all figured out. I sometimes think that I am having a clear blue sky day, but in reality that is just how I feel. The next day I feel different, like a cloudy day. My weather changes from sunny to cloudy, and my relationship with God will have its ups and downs. But the important thing to realize is that He doesn't change. It's just our perceptions and mood that change—and we shouldn't let that affect our relationship with God. He is not just a fair-weather or even a foul-weather friend. He is with us always!

The Bible says, "Drop down, ye heavens, from above, and let the skies pour down righteousness: let the earth open up, and let them bring forth salvation, and let righteousness spring up together; I the Lord have created it" (Isaiah 45:8).

I know that my spiritual life may seem to change as often as the sky patterns. I also know that when my spiritual life may seem cloudy, Jesus will be with me and the clouds will soon part and reveal a clear and sunny blue sky.

It Wasn't Worth It

By Hector Gonzalez

What good is it for a man to gain the whole world, yet forfeit his soul?
Mark 8:36.

I was playing in an intramural flag football game one night when I experienced a spiritual lesson. I was playing on the opposite team of one of my friends. Our two teams were evenly matched, and on this day it was a very close game. We were running out of time before the end of recreation and the beginning of worship.

There appeared to be a bias by the referee this day toward my friend's team. On two consecutive plays the referee called the exact same penalty on his team. The referee threw the yellow flag and blew his whistle. Each time, the referee called my friend's name, announced his offense, and advanced the ball in favor of our team. Each penalty brought our team closer to our end zone. I watched him as he grew increasingly agitated. He questioned the penalty, always careful not to display disrespect to the referee's authority but attempting to plead his innocence.

I placed myself closer to him and watched the following play more intently. I saw him stand his position. I heard our quarterback yell for the hike of the ball, and then I saw him cross the line as he was required to do. But for the third consecutive time the referee threw the flag, blew the whistle, and called out his name. Again my team was the beneficiary of the infraction, but I saw none. I looked toward him and saw him taking off his flag belt and begin to leave the field. I rushed over to him at the sideline and pleaded with him not to leave like this. And he said to me, "Dean, I have to leave now." The words that followed impress me as much today as they did when they were first spoken. "This game is not worth me losing my salvation." Wow!

He was right. What shall it profit a man to gain the whole world but lose his own soul? (Mark 8:36). Nothing. At no time. In no way.

You may meet Moses Eli if you enter my office. There is a picture of him on my door. If you are ever in New Jersey, you may visit the church he now pastors in Newark. If not here, please look up this incredible Christian in heaven.

Judged

By McKennan Cook

Do not judge, or you too will be judged. Matthew 7:1.

I have a tendency to judge people before I really know them. I can meet a person and then instantly form an opinion of them.

I remember going to a Bible conference once where we were separated into groups. The groups were designed to mix together students from other schools so that we could share with new people. There was a girl in my group whom I had met but never really talked to. Based on the short time I was with her each day, I judged her to be shallow, not really a deep thinker. I went through the week thinking that she really didn't have much to add to anything, and I continued to judge her.

At the end of the week, we were in our groups and were assigned to make little pledges of what we would continue in our lives that we had practiced at the conference. As we went around the circle stating our pledge goals, I said that I wanted to try to stop judging people, not even remembering that I was judging her.

This girl was the last person to speak up and I thought, *That figures. She couldn't think of anything good to say.* But when she finally started to talk, she said, "I don't know how to let people know who I really am."

I felt like a jerk.

I guess what I'm trying to say is that judging people is wrong, and we usually come to the wrong conclusions. We could actually miss out on some good friendships by not really trying to get to know new people.

When Jesus walked on this earth, He did not judge others. He was friends with the rich and the poor. Just look at the original occupations of His disciples. Jesus set the example that we should follow. So let's not miss out on an opportunity to get to know someone new, and let's spend our time doing something other than being judgmental.

Remember Me

By Julian Foster

Jesus answered him, "I tell you the truth, today you will be with me in paradise." Luke 23:43.

The sun hid itself behind the clouds as if it were mourning. The stars hung low in the dreary sky as if they were tears falling. "If you are the Christ, save yourself and us," yelled one of the criminals. The three of them had been hanging there for many hours, and the two criminals saw something different in the third man among them.

"Do you not even fear God, seeing you are under the same condemnation?" pleaded the other criminal. "And we indeed justly, for we receive the due reward of our deeds: but this man has done nothing wrong." The foolish criminal listened but didn't quite understand like the other criminal. "Lord, remember me when you come into your kingdom" (see Luke 23:39-43), the criminal said.

Jesus had been listening all along to the sneers, the jokes, and even to His fellow brothers on the cross. With the pain, the anguish, and the weight of our sins, He replied, "Assuredly, I say to you today, you will be with Me in Paradise."

We live in a society of selfishness and greed. The world tells us that we always need more—that nothing is ever enough. We can never work hard enough, look good enough, or have enough. This way of life has warped our view of the grace of our heavenly Father. We feel we can't come to Him unless we have everything right in our life. But we could never be more wrong. God urges us to come to Him as rough and torn as we are. He wants all of our junk. He asks that all the problems in our life be put into His hands.

He is waiting for us with His arms open wide to receive us into our true place of dwelling, our true way of life. All we have to do is ask. Just like the criminal told Jesus to remember him, we, too, need only to ask God for the free gift of eternal life. Why wait? Take time right now and ask God to remember you.

A Mother's Love

By Beth Anderson

As a mother comforts her child, so will I comfort you;
and you will be comforted over Jerusalem. Isaiah 66:13.

I know from experience that teenagers do not always think it's "cool" to admit that they really like their parents and that they actually listen to their advice, but that is the kind of relationship I had with my parents, especially with my mom. My friends always liked her. She was fun to talk to, and she actually listened to me. I knew she cared deeply even when she got angry with me for something I did. Even though my mother and father had different parenting styles, they always presented a united front and expected me to be respectful.

Some say that parents cannot and should not be friends to their kids. I disagree wholeheartedly! I knew my parents were in charge and had authority over me, but they didn't misuse that power; they didn't lay down rules arbitrarily. They made sure I understood why things were done within the big picture. They gave me room to think and make decisions as I grew older and took on more responsibility.

Honestly, I didn't always take my parents' advice, but many times I did. My mother always empowered me to seek answers and prayerfully make good decisions. She encouraged me to talk to other adults and get spiritual advice. I saw my mother living a life of faith. She could be nosy and pushy, too, but what an amazing role model she has been in my life!

When I was a sophomore, I attended the local public high school. My mother was concerned about some of my decisions. She started coming into my bedroom every morning before 5:30 to read to me from *Messages to Young People*, by Ellen White. Most mornings I pretended to be asleep and not listen. But I really was listening. Although I was obstinate, she kept coming back. She didn't give up on me. Her care and attention during those cold, winter Maine mornings was life changing for me. She showed me the unconditional love and desire that Jesus has for me and for each one of us. She didn't give up on me, a rebellious teenager, and that made me realize that God doesn't give up on me either! He is always there—caring, loving, and wanting a relationship with me. I thank God for a mother who taught me that lesson in a very practical way.

Hope and Healing

By Anna Romanov

And we know that in all things God works for the good of those who love him, who have been called according to his purpose. Romans 8:28.

When I was little, I loved to crawl into my grandfather's lap and listen to him tell me the story of his life. I loved watching his expressions when he spoke. I could see every emotion as he would tell me about his experiences. His eyes would lighten with joy when he spoke of God's gift of hope and joy. His voice would rise and he would almost shout to me how God was able to deliver him in his despair.

He was just 20 years old when the KGB forcefully took him to a labor camp in a desolate place. You see, he was a Christian, a young pastor in the church, and this was unacceptable to the Communist government of the former Soviet Union. The conditions were harsh, emotionally and physically pressing. The officers would insult, humiliate, beat, and ridicule him and his faith in God. He was treated as the worst criminal and betrayer of the government. As he would share this with me, I would become filled with anger at the officers. I would start imagining myself in his place and how I would react. It would seem right to blame the KGB, to become depressed and hopeless. But my grandfather chose a different response. He decided to put his trust in God. While he was in prison, he learned the original Hebrew from the Jewish rabbis that were there. They too were persecuted. While he was in prison, he shared God and His hope and His joy with the discouraged people.

Now he is working on translating the Bible into modern Russian. There is only one version of the Russian Bible, and it is very old. Publishing a new translation would allow the people to read and understand the Bible. God has worked out even the most horrible situations and used them for the good of His people. If we humbly allow God to lead and direct us in all situations, we can be used by God in the most amazing ways. If we let God humble us, He will mold us for His kingdom in heaven.

Is there a situation in your life that is testing your faith? Do you feel like you are trapped in the prison of a difficult situation? Trust God to lead you and show you that everything works out for the good of those who love Him.

Diving In
By Devin Suarez

Stop judging by mere appearances, and make a right judgment. John 7:24.

Everyone has played the game of tag. There are many versions of it: freeze tag, flashlight tag, off-ground tag, water tag, and others. As a kid I played tag a lot. I also seemed to get hurt a lot. I guess most active guys have a few scars from playing.

Once, at a Christmas party, while all of the adults were inside talking, all of the kids decided to go outside and play tag. It seemed like a great idea at the time.

We'd been playing for some time when I finally got tagged. I was "it," but I was determined not to be "it" for long. As I was running, trying my best to catch someone, one of my friends darted right in front of me. As I dove for him, I quickly realized that not only would I miss him (he darted to the left just as I was about to tag him), but I would land right in a big bush. No worries. The bush looked soft—I expected that it would cushion my fall and provide a nice landing. I was wrong. My face smacked into the bush, and I fell hard to the ground.

I must have been quite the show to the other tag players. Blood dripped down my face as I struggled to stand. Inside the house I was examined by a couple of people who worked in the medical field and easily determined that I would live to play tag another day. But I did have to get three stitches in my eyebrow.

The point is that things aren't always as they seem. Even though something (like what I thought would be a soft landing spot) may seem soft and innocent, it could be harmful.

Satan likes us to believe that sin is harmless. Cheating on schoolwork; not respecting our parents; trying drugs, alcohol, or tobacco; living a promiscuous lifestyle—all of these things are made to seem harmless and even acceptable in the world's view. But they will hurt us, sometimes with immediate consequences, sometimes in the long run.

It is not fun to get hurt, but we can heal and do better. So if you've run headlong into problems, perhaps under the guise that it was all in innocent fun, learn from your mistakes and have God "stitch" you up and apply His healing touch. He is the Great Physician who is always available.

To Swim or Not to Swim

By Jennifer Beckham

Remember the Sabbath day by keeping it holy. Six days you shall labor and do all your work, but the seventh day is a Sabbath to the Lord your God. On it you shall not do any work, neither you, nor your son or daughter, nor your manservant or maidservant, nor your animals, nor the alien within your gates. For in six days the Lord made the heavens and the earth, the sea, and all that is in them, but he rested on the seventh day. Therefore the Lord blessed the Sabbath day and made it holy. Exodus 20:8-11.

When I landed a lifeguarding job at Carowinds Theme Park near Charlotte, North Carolina, for the summer, I was completely excited. I couldn't wait to work out in the sun and in the water with all those people. My excitement was bubbling at the thought of saving someone from drowning. I was even more excited to wear the hot lifeguard uniform and stare at my guy coworkers.

But I was a little apprehensive after I got called into operations, which is where all of the park's staff converse and plan everything. Most of the people in my training group had already been called into Chris's (my boss) office to go over scheduling. Everyone was talking about how Chris wasn't giving certain days off because those were the days most people wanted off. This got me really worried, because I needed Saturdays off. As a Seventh-day Adventist, I believe that the seventh day is God's holy day, and that is when I go to church.

When I finally got into Chris's office and told him that I needed Saturdays off, he asked me why. I didn't hesitate in saying that Saturday was my day of worship. Even as I said it, I knew that if they required me to work on that day I would have to decline and possibly lose my dream job for it.

But God blessed. Chris gave me Saturdays off, and I never had to worry about working on the Sabbath, because I remembered God's commandment and stayed strong for Him.

When faced with a "Sabbath dilemma," have faith that God will take care of you no matter what the immediate outcome is. He will use the experience to strengthen your faith and to witness to others.

Judge Not

By Allison Bradley

Judge me, O Lord my God, according to Your righteousness, and do not let them rejoice over me. Psalm 35:24, NASB.

Every year I enter items to be judged at our local fair. I have entered flower arrangements, baked goods, pottery, handcrafts, photography, drawings, and other things. Every year I anxiously await the judges' decisions to see how many ribbons I won. Every year I have entered I have come home with many ribbons of every color (blue, red, and white). Ribbons mean both the prestige of being chosen as well as cash prizes.

It is very exciting to receive ribbons that announce "Best in Show" and "Judges' Choice." While these don't carry any extra monetary value, receiving one of these coveted ribbons shows that the judges thought my entry was extra special. One year I was even featured with my winning cattail arrangement on our local television news broadcast. It's pretty easy to get a big head with a lot of positive attention.

When I was 9 years old, I worked very hard on a charcoal drawing for the fair. I spent hours on the shading and details of the piece. I just knew that it would win a blue ribbon. But when I got to the fair to count my winnings, I was disappointed to see that another entry won first prize in the charcoal category and that I had gotten only a participant ribbon (which means "thanks for trying"). The winner's piece, in my opinion, was far inferior to my art. I couldn't understand why the judges didn't pick mine. Even though I collected blue ribbons for some of my other entries, this loss really bothered me.

It took some time before I could realize the lesson from this experience. But here is what I learned. I need to be unselfish and supportive of everyone's efforts. I also learned that I shouldn't weigh my value by other people's opinions. I need to learn to get my value and self-worth from doing my very best for Jesus.

When Jesus comes to take us home to heaven, He will not count the number of blue ribbons I have won at the fair. What will matter is my attitude, my relationship with Jesus, and how I have shared Him with others. The ultimate prize—an eternity with Jesus in heaven—is waiting for each of us. Let us do our best work now to make Him proud!

God Says, "Tell!"
By Stella Bradley

And this gospel of the kingdom will be preached in the whole world as a testimony to all nations, and then the end will come. Matthew 24:14.

The story of Jonah is very intriguing. In the beginning Jonah clearly received a directive from God to go to Nineveh and preach God's message. And then Jonah, deliberately disobeying, tried to hide from God by getting on a ship headed to another city. Jonah went through a lot of effort to avoid God's command.

Next comes every child's favorite part—the big storm came and Jonah was thrown overboard in an attempt to appease God and calm the storm. And of course the Bible tells us that a big fish came and swallowed Jonah, and he lived in the fish's belly for three days and three nights. Imagine what that would have been like: terrifying, gross, and definitely unforgettable. God got his attention.

Then after those three days—which Jonah spent in prayer—the fish temporarily beached itself and spit Jonah out on dry land near the town of Nineveh. God didn't even make Jonah swim to shore—how convenient. (That's just the first half of the story; go to the book of Jonah and read it in its entirety.)

We know that God could have placed Jonah near Nineveh in many ways. But He chose a very creative and memorable method. God was not kidding when He told Jonah to share God's message with others.

Today we have the same commission. We are to share God's messages in the Bible with the world. Do not be bashful, afraid, or ashamed to proclaim the good news that Jesus loves us and that we need to live according to His Word.

Soon Christ will return and take us, His family, to a wonderful new home in heaven. Let's share that good news boldly so that no one can say, "Why didn't you tell me?"

God can (and does) use extreme methods of getting His Word out (as in Jonah's case). But the simplest way is for us to share it and live it. We are privileged to be a part of that process— what an honor we have to be His messengers.

I challenge you to share your story, and His story, with others.

God's Helping Hand
By Nicholas Ewing

The Lord will protect him and preserve his life; he will bless him in the land and not surrender him to the desire of his foes. Psalm 41:2.

Many people often wonder if God ever reaches down His mighty hand to save or heal someone. I know He does—a few summers ago it happened to me.

I was helping my dad with the cows one Monday morning, and he told me that a bull was angry. He told me that the day before he had tried to push the bull into another pasture, but the bull had chased him and his horse whenever my dad got close to him.

My dad pointed the bull out to me, and we proceeded to move the cows into the cow pens. As we got close to the pens, the bull seemed extremely happy and was not causing any problems. As we pushed the herd into the pens, my dad rode his horse into the pens with the herd, and I got off my horse to close the gate. As he pushed the herd farther into the pens, the bull turned and charged at my dad and his horse. My dad immediately turned his horse and galloped toward the gate. I was holding my horse's reins in one hand, so I opened the gate with the other. After he flew by me on his horse, I did my best to get the gate locked, but the bull hit the gate and slung it open. At this point the bull was about five yards away from me. I was lying on the ground still holding my horse's reins. I could tell that the bull was ready to charge anything that moved. I did my best to be completely still, and I hoped that my horse would do the same. Eventually the bull moved on out to the bigger pasture. My dad said that when he came up to me, my face was as white as paper.

God watches over us in all sorts of ways, whether it's protecting us from bulls or protecting us as we drive in the car.

Let us never forget to give credit where credit is due—thank God for always having our best interest at heart.

When and How It's Needed Most

By Timothy Iuliano

Blessed are those who hunger and thirst for righteousness,
for they will be filled. Matthew 5:6.

Many people talk to God only when they need something—lost keys, a friendship restored, good health, etc. People ask for what they want, and they expect God to give it to them exactly how and when they think He should. But God, in His wisdom, answers things according to His will.

At the beginning of my junior year, Ricky Schwartz led a Week of Prayer at our school. Just like any other overexhausted, sleep-deprived high school student, I just sat in the middle of the pew, in a semiconscious state, waiting for the speech to end. I did want to get a spiritual experience out of his stories—I even prayed for one. But I expected God to do all the work. Even after the second day of meetings, I still hadn't experienced anything like I had hoped.

At the end of Tuesday's evening meeting, I sang the closing song, bowed my head very respectfully for the prayer, hugged all my friends, left the church, and went back to my room. However, when I got there I found my roommate with an unusual expression on his face. When I asked him what was wrong, he told me that the meeting had really moved him and that he wanted to be closer to God. All the speeches, all the songs, and the pretending to be paying attention gave me nothing, but at that moment, with my roommate's revelation, I felt the Holy Spirit move, and I felt the closest to God I had felt in a long time.

That very night my roommate and I started reading a devotional book his father had sent him. The title of that day's devotional reading was "Finding God Where You Least Expect Him."

We can pray all we want, but if we don't try and let God answer it His way, we might not ever notice that He answered it. Ask God to give you a willing heart, and then act on it.

Seek the Lord

By John Ratzlaff

This is what the Lord says to the house of Israel: "Seek me and live."
Amos 5:4.

My wife and I are big fans of geocaching. For those who are not familiar with this, I will explain. Geocaching is a game in which somebody hides an item, called a "geocache," and then they publish the GPS coordinates for the cache on a Web site (www. geocaching.com). Then anyone else can get those coordinates and use a GPS receiver to go and find the cache. This game has been called "high-tech treasure hunting," but generally the contents of the cache do not deserve to be called "treasure." If there are any desirable items found, the finder can take something, provided they leave something else of equal or greater value. Many times, however, the only item to be found is a paper on which the finder signs their name, giving proof to the find.

One of the things that continues to impress me about geocaching is the wide variety of caches to be found. Ranging from urban micros (tiny caches hidden in, say, a film canister in a shopping mall parking lot) to ammo boxes in the woods, from "park 'n' grabs" to scenic hikes or puzzles or multistage adventures, caches are as varied as the people who enjoy the sport.

I've learned that the act of finding something hidden is the part that appeals to me. I'm rarely interested in whatever trinket might be there for me to trade, but I am compelled to find more and more caches just because finding them is fun. (As of this writing, I have found 3,600 caches!) And just like anything in life, this doesn't seem to appeal to everyone equally—some people find it a pointless waste of time. But that doesn't keep me from being a "caching evangelist," and I count a number of people as my "converts" to geocaching! For some people, caching approaches a religion. We do it as much as we can, invite others to join us, get together in meetings to talk about it, and even devote a significant amount of money to its pursuit.

All of which has made me wonder: Am I as devoted to Christ as I am to geocaching? Well, yes, certainly—much more so! But am I as willing to teach people about Jesus as I am to teach them about geocaching? That's a little harder to answer. Knowing about geocaching might bring some enjoyment to some people, but knowing Christ can bring eternal life to anyone. Despite the fact that not everyone will respond positively, we all need to share our love for Christ and help others find life by seeking Him, as He invites us to do in today's text.

Shark!

By Michael Brackett

Therefore he is able to save completely those who come to God through him, because he always lives to intercede for them. Hebrews 7:25.

On Friday, July 6, 2001, at 8:30 p.m., a young boy, Jessie, was playing in shallow water off the coast of the Florida panhandle. All was going well. The water was warm, the air was nice, and he was on vacation, enjoying life. Just when things couldn't get better, a seven-foot bull shark suddenly attacked him! The shark ripped into Jessie's leg, causing a deep gash. Worst of all, the shark bit his right arm completely off between his shoulder and elbow! Jessie was in serious trouble!

But praise God that Jessie was not there alone. His aunt and uncle were with him. His uncle (who must have been a big, bad dude) ran into the water to save Jessie from being killed by the shark. In an effort to free Jessie, his uncle grabbed that huge and muscular animal by the tail with both arms and dragged him to shore! Can you believe that?

A medic helicopter flew Jessie to a nearby hospital, and after a National Park Service ranger who arrived on the scene shot the shark, they pried the shark's mouth open and rescued Jessie's arm and rushed it to the hospital. There at the hospital, the doctor successfully reattached Jessie's arm!

Now, let me ask you: If Jessie's uncle wanted to save his nephew that desperately, how much more does God want to save us? We are God's children! With the tenderest love He has watched us grow from the womb to where we are now. The Bible says that God will save to the uttermost (Hebrews 7:25), and He would have none to perish (2 Peter 3:9)! Praise God we are not alone in these shark-infested waters of Planet Earth! We have a God who loves us and who has gone to extreme measures to give us eternal life through His Son, our Savior, Jesus Christ! The only question is Will you let Him go the extra mile for you?

Thank God for Angels

Josh Wright

Guard my life and rescue me; let me not be put to shame, for I take refuge in you. May integrity and uprightness protect me, because my hope is in you. Psalm 25:20, 21.

About 7:00 Friday night, January 2, 2009, my sister Ericka and I started driving back to our school in North Carolina from our home in Vermont. We knew we had a long drive ahead of us, and we planned to take turns behind the wheel. I drove from Vermont to the Pennsylvania line, but I was too tired to drive any farther without sleep.

So at 12:30 in the morning I pulled into the parking lot of the Pennsylvania Welcome Center and woke my sister up to let her know that she needed to drive.

It was cold, but the roads were clear. Ericka started driving while I fell asleep in the passenger seat. About an hour later I awoke to our truck swerving on a snowy road. Our truck slid into another truck, causing that vehicle to go off the road. We spun around, hit the guardrail at 70 miles per hour, and then came to a stop in the middle of the road.

Ericka panicked, so I climbed into the driver's seat and drove us to the shoulder of the road, where we made sure we were all right, checked on the man in the other truck, and inspected the damage to the vehicles. Miraculously, everyone involved was safe. We breathed a prayer of relief.

We know that our angels were watching over us. After the accident we saw that just 20 feet from where we landed there was a 30-foot drop-off and no guardrail. Had we been just a few feet farther down the road, our truck would surely have rolled down that embankment, causing us to be seriously injured or killed.

God protects us more than we know. His angels are constantly at work keeping us safe on this earth. Praise Him!

My First Prayer

By Teddy Lin

If your brother sins, rebuke him, and if he repents, forgive him. If he sins against you seven times in a day, and seven times comes back to you and says, "I repent," forgive him. Luke 17:3, 4.

Everybody makes mistakes. I made a pretty bad one that almost cost me my future. But my story has a happy ending.

During my sophomore year of high school, I attended an Adventist school in Palau, a small American-owned island in the Pacific Ocean. While in school, I met a lovely girl named Jane. She became very special to me, but the school did not allow high school students to date. But we "secretly" dated anyway. The principal found out and talked with me more than 10 times, telling me to break up with Jane. But we didn't listen.

One day the principal caught us kissing. We were in a lot of trouble! According to the rules, we deserved to be kicked out of school. I was afraid that if I got kicked out of school I would have to go back to China, and I would never be able to study in America. Studying in America had been a dream of mine since childhood. At that time I was feeling lonely and scared. I thought I had no one on my side. I was getting desperate.

But then the school pastor came and talked with me. He told me to pray and to trust in God to do what's best for my future. He said that God answers prayer. I didn't know whether he was right or not, but I thought I would try—it was the only thing I could do to help Jane and me.

I prayed. Approximately 30 times a day I said: "God, please help us. We are in terrible trouble. Please forgive us. We will never do that anymore. Please give us a chance to stay; this opportunity is really important for us. I beg You for help. Amen." I said that many times a day for many days. And a miracle happened. The principal allowed us to finish the year. At the end of that school year, God led me to Mount Pisgah Academy in North Carolina.

If we trust God, worship God, and love God, He will answer our prayers. That is why I am a Christian. Thank You, God, for giving me such a good opportunity to attend school in America.

An Unexpected Blessing

By Anna Wurster

And the peace of God, which transcends all understanding, will guard your hearts and your minds in Christ Jesus. Philippians 4:7.

Right before my freshman year of academy started, I was trying to decide what campus job to take. I had never had a "real" job before, besides babysitting. I looked at the list of jobs, and one stood out to me—a job at Pisgah Manor, the nursing home on campus.

I wasn't supposed to work at the Manor because I wasn't on a scholarship. And I didn't know a thing about working there; all I knew was that's where I wanted to be. I fought for that job, and I got it. I didn't have a clue what I was getting myself into.

It is a great facility with a great staff, but after two weeks of working as a nursing student there, my feelings changed, and I desperately wanted to quit. I'm not exaggerating when I say that working as a nursing student is one of the hardest jobs on campus. Nursing students work an hour longer than most other students who work in the cafeteria or the dorm. I had to work many weekends and vacation leaves. When I tried to help some patients, they sometimes yelled at me. I always tried to treat them with kindness and respect, because I knew that if I were in their situation I might be upset too. Most of the residents were not able to walk and had to stay in bed all the time. And then when a beloved patient died, it was so sad. The emotions I felt working there were sometimes overwhelming. I tried to quit many times—but there wasn't another job available. It wasn't fair. Why did I want to work there in the first place?

Even now, I can't explain my original desire to work at the Manor, but I do have a theory. I think God planned for me to work there. Even though I was completely miserable at times, God still blessed me. During my time there I had some incredible experiences, and I met some amazing people. There was one woman I took care of to whom I grew very attached. When she died, I took it pretty hard. I remember her always saying, "Enjoy life while you're young; no one wants you when you're old." In a way, she was right. After we die, people may eventually forget us. But God will never forget us. And one day He'll restore His faithful and there will be no more nursing homes. But until then, I will heed her advice—live a good life and do my job well.

We Are All the Same

By Stephanie Leena Zepeda

There is neither Jew nor Greek, slave nor free, male nor female, for you are all one in Christ Jesus. Galatians 3:28.

Throughout the years I have noticed how people tend to treat each other differently depending on social status, race, and religion. When I was younger and attended a Catholic church with my family, I remember seeing a homeless beggar outside my church after the service every weekend. I saw how people would look at him in disgust and would stop, stare, and then keep walking—going on with their lives. I thought people, especially churchgoers, were supposed to feed the poor, give them a place to live, give them comfort, and above all, give them love. I was confused by the mixed messages I received.

Growing up in Spain, I remember my dad talking about a new guy in the neighborhood, an African immigrant, whom my dad did not like at all. Just because the new neighbor was a different ethnicity, my dad would talk about him in a very rude and hurtful way. Over time I started feeling the same way as my dad did. Years later when I came to America, I accepted Christ as my Savior. It was then that I realized I had been hurting people and was treating others very unfairly.

Depending on your background and friends, ridiculing certain people or groups of people may be an acceptable practice. It is all too easy to get pulled in to the crowd mentality of putting others down. But pray for strength and courage to stand up for what is right. The Holy Spirit will help you.

What does God want us to do? It doesn't matter if we are rich or poor, young or old, Black or White, Jew or Gentile. We are all the same to God; we are all created equally in the holy image of God. We need to start thinking about others and stop treating them differently just because they are not like us. Each of us is unique, special, and loved by our amazing Creator. Simply love one another!

Roommate

By Shavana Lloyd

If one falls down, his friend can help him up. But pity the man who falls and has no one to help him up! Ecclesiastes 4:10.

When I first arrived at Mount Pisgah Academy, I didn't know anyone. The students were friendly enough, but I found it hard to make close friends. The culture of North Carolina is very different than that of Hawaii, my home state, and I felt like I didn't fit in. I had my own room in the dorm, so unlike most of the other girls I did not have a roommate to talk to and become good friends with. Pretty soon I was feeling very homesick.

Then, three weeks after school started, some new girls came to the dorm. Most of the rooms were already full, so the dean said that since I wasn't paying to room by myself, I would be getting a roommate. At first I was rather resentful. I enjoyed having my own room and didn't want to share it. However, Reyna, my new roommate, turned out to be really awesome. We had the same interests, likes, and dislikes. We began hanging out all the time. She quickly became my closest friend at the academy—I could trust her with anything.

Having made friends with Reyna, I guess it boosted my confidence. I stopped being shy and began making more friends and talking to more people. With my newfound attitude, I made many friends. And as my circle of friends grew, I found that getting through the days and weeks and months were much smoother.

When we're down in a pit of despair, good friends don't just throw a rope down to help us, they crawl down in beside us and then boost us up to higher ground. That is what my friends did for me.

Sometimes in life we may feel alone or discouraged. We may feel that we have no friends and that no one cares. But even if our earthly friends are not to be found, there is one Friend who is and will always be there. Jesus is constantly searching for a relationship with us—all we have to do is accept Him. He loves us so much. He gave up His own life so that we could live. Now, that's a true friend.

Are You Ready for Battle?

By Stella Bradley

Endure hardship with us like a good soldier of Christ Jesus. 2 Timothy 2:3.

My grandfather, George Smith, from Salem, South Carolina, was a true hero. He served his country in World War II by leading reconnaissance missions on the European front. He was on the beaches of Normandy; he was wounded in battle and consequently lost sight in one eye; and he was taken as a prisoner of war. He survived many attempts on his life and lost many good friends to the effects of war.

Once, while patrolling on an abandoned street in Germany, Sergeant Smith was faced with a P-47 bomber flying straight toward him. It carried a bomb bay, of course, and eight .50-caliber machine guns. The plane was so low that he could see the pilot's eyes. Bullets from the gun turrets ripped through the road on a trail leading straight to him. Unbeknown to the American pilot, this was his comrade. As Smith yelled to his troops to take cover, the plane rained artillery right over him, miraculously missing him, but blasting a hole in the street large enough to bury a car, which covered him in dirt. On the second pass through the town, the pilot of the plane finally realized that he was firing on Americans. He tipped his wings in apology.

For all of the amazing war stories I have heard from my grandfather, I am more impressed by what he did in his daily life after the war. He, along with my grandmother, lived a life of Christian service and thoughtfulness, a witness for Jesus to the community. My grandfather was a brave soldier on the military and spiritual battlefields. Just as the scars and shrapnel he carried throughout his life were a constant reminder of the physical hardships he endured, he, as we all do, had the scars of hurt and rejection from standing for God and truth against all else. But draw courage from our Leader. The war is almost over!

On this Memorial Day we sincerely thank our soldiers and veterans. We appreciate their sacrifice. But more important than being a soldier of an earthly war is to be a soldier for Christ Jesus. We must all boldly march onto the battlefield each day—clear in our purpose, never shying away, properly armed with the Word of God. Of course we may endure hardships, some from the enemy, and perhaps even some from "friendly fire," but let's not be distracted in our purpose. We know that soon Christ will conquer the enemy once and for all.

The Joy of the Lord
By Ryan Gillen

Do not grieve, for the joy of the Lord is your strength. Nehemiah 8:10.

The summer between my junior and senior year I had the privilege of working with the Mount Pisgah Academy recruiting team. We traveled all over the Carolina Conference visiting churches and their members and helping them take care of various needs such as yard work, Vacation Bible School, maintenance projects, etc. Along the way we met many wonderful people who opened up their homes to us and made our trip interesting and enjoyable. One little girl, in particular, sticks out in my mind.

We were in New Bern, North Carolina, at the time, helping with a VBS program, being crew leaders and teaching the Bible story. One little girl took a special liking to Andrew Grissom and me. She would follow us around and ask to be picked up and spun around all the time. Every time we would accommodate her request she would just laugh and ask us to do it again.

We eventually found out that her dad was actually serving a second term over in Iraq and that she had not seen him for 18 months. Her mom told Andrew and me that her dad was the one who usually spun her around and that she missed that time with him. Once we found that out, we were even more willing to spin her around and make her laugh, no matter how many times she wanted.

In Psalm 68:5 it says, "A father to the fatherless, a defender of widows, is God in his holy dwelling." When I read this, I thought of that little girl. Even though her dad was gone she could still be happy, because she has a Father in heaven who will always be there for her. I know she was too young to realize this, but it just showed me that even in tough situations God will be there to return the joy and happiness to our lives.

Pray today that you can be an ambassador for God and help Him fulfill this promise.

Getting Through It All

By Chloe Howard

The Lord himself goes before you and will be with you; He will never leave you nor forsake you. Do not be afraid; do not be discouraged.
Deuteronomy 31:8.

Over the past few years events have happened that have changed my life forever. I believed my little world was perfect—my family, friends, everything. But within a flash it all turned upside down.

Issues arose between my parents, and before long they were no longer considered a couple. My life came crashing down and shattered into a million pieces. Everything had changed. Everything was different. I woke up every day wishing and hoping I was younger, back in the happy days, but it was all still the same. I hated my life.

The time passed by, slow as molasses. I needed something to happen. I needed a serious change. I couldn't keep living like that, and I began to pray daily, asking God to comfort me and help me get through all the sadness. Eventually things began to clear, like the clouds after a thunderstorm. My parents lived separately, but the fighting was less. The stress had decreased, and I was not nearly as sad.

My life is completely different now, and it will never be the same. Before my parents separated I was living in a fog, believing my life and family were literally perfect. In the long run I truly am grateful this has happened because it has woken me up. There is no way I could have survived without my Leader, Jesus Christ. He led me though it all, and He can get us through anything. Trust me.

We cannot always stop bad things from happening to us, but He has promised to carry our burdens for us—we just need to be willing to hand them over. And that is sometimes the hardest part. So often we clutch tight to our stresses and can't see Christ through our tear-filled eyes. But He is there, ready with strong arms to pick us up, hug us tight, and lighten our load. Won't you let Him do that for you today?

Temptation

By Dustin Evans

Then Jesus was led by the Spirit into the desert to be tempted by the devil.
Matthew 4:1.

The devil has many ways of tempting us. He can tempt us in ways that we could never imagine. We can avoid these temptations by holding on to God and His teachings. He is the way, the truth, and the light. Jesus was even tempted, but He never gave in to it.

In the story of Jesus being tempted by the devil in the desert, we find out that Jesus knew what was right and what was evil and wrong. The devil thought he could get Jesus to do something against God's Word. He knew that he wouldn't be able to defeat Him, but he thought he would try anyway. Jesus listened to God and didn't give in to the false statements of Satan.

I have been tempted in my life many times. I have had to decide whether to follow God or Satan. There were many times that I didn't listen to God. I haven't always been the brightest person, but God loves me anyway. I have had to make a lot of tough decisions many times. It isn't easy making tough decisions, but when I pray about it, God helps me get through it.

Jesus came to this earth to die for us all. He came to die for our sins. If He hadn't died for us, we wouldn't be able to go to heaven. He could have said no and not died, but He wanted each of us to be with Him in heaven. What love!

The devil knows that he doesn't have much time before the end. That is why he is trying to drag all of us away from God. We need to hold on to God and stay away from the devil.

Jesus calls every one of us to be His followers. What a joy it will be when we all get to heaven.

A Plan for Everyone

By Cassi Sommerville

Blessed are those who wash their robes, that they may have the right to the tree of life and may go through the gates into the city. Revelation 22:14.

Jenna was so excited! She was going to the park with her friends. It was three weeks before school was out, and she was ready to get outside and be free. Everyone was going to meet for a picnic and then just hang out at the park. Jenna's dad was going with her to supervise the outing, and she couldn't wait to get going.

At the park Jenna and her friends had lunch and then ran around playing on the playground. Jenna loved the swings and asked her dad to push her so she could go high and touch the tree limb that was hanging over the swings. She had done it before and loved it. He agreed, and she started going really high. All of a sudden Jenna felt really dizzy! "Stop the swing!" she shouted, and her dad quickly stopped her. "I'm really dizzy; I thought I was going to fall," Jenna said. They began to walk away so Jenna could sit down and rest. They hadn't gone far when they heard a loud CRACK! The tree that Jenna had been trying to reach had just fallen right where she and her dad had been.

"Jenna," her dad cried, "do you realize that Jesus sent an angel to make you feel dizzy so you wouldn't be hit by that tree?" Jenna nodded slowly and then really did need to sit down. All of Jenna's friends were very glad that she hadn't been crushed; Jenna was amazed that Jesus had saved her life.

Lots of times we don't feel like God truly has a plan for us, but He does. I believe that we have all been saved more times than we can count, even if it doesn't really feel like it. When we get to heaven, we should definitely ask our angels how many times they saved us from getting hurt, or even dying. I think it will be many more times than we would ever have imagined.

Undeniable Presence

By Candis Watterson

A thousand may fall at your side, ten thousand at your right hand, but it will not come near you. Psalm 91:7.

Imagine a normal Monday at work. What awaits you? Is your boss handing out excessive paperwork or calling a surprise meeting? As a marine deployed to Iraq, my brother could only wish for so simple a workday.

Moses joined the Marine Corps in the summer of 2003, and he finished boot camp as an honor graduate. We were hoping they would send him somewhere safe like Hawaii or culturally fascinating like Japan. However, with September 11 still hovering in the background, his first deployment was to Iraq. When he was sent back a second time, we stopped watching the news so we wouldn't worry every time they announced more casualties.

An amazing thing happened during that time, though. Late one night my mother awoke with an urging to pray for Moses, and so she did, including his friends in her prayer. She spoke with him later and nonchalantly mentioned the incident. He was shocked, because that exact same day his squadron had been patrolling the streets where they were located and were ambushed. The fight lasted more than two hours, but not one of the marines were killed or wounded. Moses said that during the skirmish, he felt a powerful presence around them and what felt like angel's wings against his face.

While Moses has completed his third tour in Iraq, there are many others who are just getting started serving their country, and still others who have fallen and are sorely missed and fondly remembered by their families. I pray for the day when God will appear in the sky and there will be no war, no death, no regrets, and no worries. What a day it will be when all is at peace!

Until then, for those who have served, or are currently serving, in our armed forces, we appreciate your work and we honor you for your service. May God bless you all.

Power of Thoughts
By Anna Romanov

Finally, brothers, whatever is true, whatever is noble, whatever is right, whatever is pure, whatever is lovely, whatever is admirable—if anything is excellent or praiseworthy—think about such things. Philippians 4:8.

Last night I could not fall asleep. Many different thoughts filled my mind. These were not pleasant positive thoughts, but thoughts of despair. I began to worry about what the future may hold. My sense of direction was not clear at all. What if this bad thing happened or what if that bad thing happened. I became restless. It was late in the night, and I still couldn't fall asleep. I decided to read a verse from the Bible. I was hoping that I could obtain some strength from it. I opened to Philippians 4:8: "Whatever is true. . ." Whatever is true? All the nightmares I was stressing about were not true. They were just things that *may* happen. They were the thoughts of a person who didn't trust in God. I realized then that my focus should be on true things. And these are the things of God, which stand firm forever. I realized that I should turn my eyes to the things that are true, noble, right, pure, lovely, admirable, and praiseworthy.

God knew that we would be battling with our thoughts and feelings. He knew that we would become discouraged easily by dwelling on thoughts of despair. Jesus Himself was tempted to think that His Father had left Him in Gethsemane. Jesus knew that we would face these temptations. And that is why we are told to think about the true things and pure things so that we can take our thoughts off ourselves and our troubles and focus on the glory of God. Focus on the blessings He bestows on us. Focus on the constant presence of His Holy Spirit. When I start thinking about the goodness and love of God, I can start praising God. I start seeing how my God is at work to show me how much He loves me. When I start seeing God, I lose sight of my trials.

Do you have times your worries cloud the greatness of God? Are there times you become discouraged and dwell on your trials? Remember to start praising God when you are overwhelmed, and He will make His presence known to you.

Me, Lord?

By Ross Knight

[Make] the most of every opportunity, because the days are evil.
Ephesians 5:16.

I woke up that Sabbath morning wishing I was sick. I really did feel sick, but I think that was only because I was so nervous. I didn't want to do this; I couldn't believe my teacher had volunteered me to do such a thing. I, this very day, had to go up front and not just lead the singing or read a Bible verse, not even just take up the offering or play a special music. No, this was far worse. I had to preach the sermon!

My church is not a small one—it has about 800 members. And I was supposed to give every one of them God's message that they had waited all week to hear, which was usually from a professional such as our PASTOR! *I'm not a pastor*, I thought. *I'm only a freshman in high school.* To me this could not be done. I knew I had prepared well and even thought my sermon was pretty good, but maybe someone else could read it or better yet, just leave it to the pastor.

I was so scared because I know I have a stuttering problem when under pressure. I also have a tendency of having my mind go blank right as I'm about to say something. In addition to those worries, I had the added stress of friends driving from other parts of the state just so they could hear me. I was afraid to let all these people down.

When I actually started thinking straight, though, I realized I wasn't doing this to impress anyone. I was doing it to honor God, and He really had given me this opportunity to work for Him. It's kind of funny, and ironic, because my sermon was actually about how God calls at unexpected times in our lives and how He can use us at any point in our lives. I began to get excited, and I ended up doing pretty well, aside from stuttering just a couple times.

When you're given an opportunity to work for God, remember to let Him lead. Just be His vessel. Keep this verse in mind: " 'For I know the plans I have for you,' says the Lord. 'They are plans for good and not for disaster, to give you a future and a hope.' " Trust in Him to work through you.

The Glass Is Half Full

By Beth Anderson

Whatever you have learned or received or heard from me, or seen in me—
put it into practice. And the God of peace will be with you. Philippians 4:9.

Each school year brings its own rewards and challenges. One recent school year started out a bit stressful with some transitions in our community. Then a large percentage of our student body became sick with strep throat. We as a staff had to be flexible and creative.

As a counselor (or any other staff member for that matter) on a boarding school campus, the workload, discipline issues, and long hours can get discouraging. It is difficult, if not impossible, to leave work at the office. Many hours at school and at home are spent in thought and prayer for students, the school, staff, and church.

That particular year I was really letting things get me down. But I prayed to God about my stress and discouragement, and then I felt so much better as I handed my burdens over to Jesus. He helped me through it. I felt blessed the rest of the school year.

I have made the Bible verses Philippians 4:8, 9 my aim and motto. Each day I strive to fill my mind with truth, joy, beauty, and praise for my Lord. I take time to cultivate friendships on and off campus, read, exercise, and connect with God.

It is easy for us as humans to see the glass as "half empty," but God has given us the ability to choose to live positively. Choose to see the glass as "half full," and fill your minds with what is "true, noble, reputable, authentic, compelling, and gracious."

Coincidence? I Think Not!

By Rosella Age

Then Jesus answered, "Woman, you have great faith! Your request is granted." And her daughter was healed from that very hour. Matthew 15:28.

"Have faith in God," Jesus answered. "I tell you the truth, if anyone says to this mountain, 'Go, throw yourself into the sea,' and does not doubt in his heart but believes that what he says will happen, it will be done for him." Mark 11:22, 23.

I find God's answers to my insignificant prayers amusing and encouraging. I have had several experiences in which God has responded immediately to my quick, three-second prayers, one of which was fairly recently. My aunt Pat, my friend Ryan, and I ventured over to Cold Stone Creamery for some soothing ice cream in preparation for the ACT test the next day. I ordered mint chocolate chip, and my companions both got "Coffee Lovers Only," decaf of course. I wanted this afternoon delight to be my special treat, but only because I had a $10 gift certificate given to me by my generous faculty family. So I proudly handed my certificate to the cashier, who swiped it, but it wasn't accepted. So she swiped it again. And again. And again. She tried punching in the number multiple times. Finally the cashier summoned the shift manager for some assistance. That's when I did what anyone automatically does in that kind of situation: make excuses. "This woman must be new; it's probably her first day . . . I know I haven't used that card yet . . ."

We had already begun eating our frozen treats, and I didn't want Pat to have to pay, so I said a prayer out loud: "Dear Jesus, please help the card to work so we can carry on. Amen." Ryan was staring at me, so I told him confidently, "Now it will work." And I kid you not, the very next attempt made with my gift certificate was successful. Not five seconds after breathing amen God answered my prayer. I know it wasn't just a coincidence.

You can't go wrong when you put your faith and trust in God. Prayer is not a trivial thing. Anytime we talk with God, chatting as a friend, in sincere petition, or in a quick request or thanks, He hears us. In fact, He wants to be a part of our life in big and small things. Won't you let Him?

Faithfulness

By Melanie Bethancourt

May he be enthroned in God's presence forever; appoint your love and faithfulness to protect him. Psalm 61:7.

What is faithfulness? The dictionary defines it as being trusted, worthy, and reliable. I love my parents. And to me they are the perfect example of faithfulness. They may have had their ups and downs, but they have made it through them all. They have always been true to each other. They want only what is best for each other. They care for each other, and that to me is true faithfulness.

God is the same way. He is always faithful to us. He always lends that helping hand, that shoulder to cry on, or that listening ear. God is so in love with us that He will go to any extreme to make sure our needs are met. As a matter of fact, He went to the extreme to save us and give us everlasting happiness. He sent His only Son to die on the cross for us! How many parents would willingly give up their precious child?

Faithfulness is powerful, and it can be really hard, too. It can be tough to stay committed to something, but with God's help we can do anything. Philippians says, "We can do all things through Christ Jesus who strengthens us." Isn't that amazing? Jesus stretched out His arms on Calvary and took all of our sins, debts, hatred, and unfaithfulness—everything we struggle with. He took it upon Himself so we could get beyond this sin-filled world. Jesus took the weight of the world on His shoulders so we wouldn't have to pay the price for our own sins. Jesus gave His life for us.

What more can we ask of the God of this universe? He gave it all willingly. God is forever faithful concerning our needs. Why can't we be faithful to His?

Topsy-turvy at Tumbling Rocks

By Jonathan P. Michael

Then they were eager to let him in the boat, and immediately they arrived at their destination! John 6:21, NLT.

Life is like a river. And we each have a boat.

One of my favorite memories as a Boy Scout was our annual weekend-long canoe trip down the Greenbrier River in West Virginia. We would pair up in canoes and then paddle all day long down the river until we reached our camping spot for the night. After some sleep we would wake up the next day and do it again. Whenever there was any calm spot in the river, we would engage in all-out water wars between canoes, which was always fun. But what we really lived for was the rapids. The most anticipated spot was a place in the river called Tumbling Rocks. Two large rocks caused the entire river to forcefully squeeze between them. This meant speed. This meant rapids. This meant . . . trouble. One particular year there had been a lot of rain. The river was high. The rapids were fast. And Tumbling Rocks was intimidating, to say the least. If the canoe didn't hit the exact middle, the river would throw the canoe up against one of the rocks, turn it over, toss everyone out, and then swallow them whole.

Our leader was pretty skilled with a paddle, so he offered to jump aboard anyone's canoe who wanted help to ensure they successfully hit the sweet spot between Tumbling Rocks without capsizing. My partner and I decided against this; we thought we could handle it on our own. Needless to say, we had a close encounter with the rock on the right. Tumbling Rocks turned us over, tossed us out, and swallowed us up—we went under and were down for the count. I noticed something very interesting that day: the canoes with the leader on board made it through Tumbling Rocks right-side up, and the canoes without the leader on board went topsy-turvy. Things definitely went a lot smoother if the leader was in the boat.

There are some stories recorded in the Gospels that give us the same insight. Waters threatened to turn over, toss out, and swallow the disciples, too. Having Jesus in their boat made all the difference in the world. The winds died down, and they reached their destination.

Life is like a river. And we each have a boat. Jesus is offering to climb aboard. Saying yes to Him is the only real way I've found to stay right-side up and reach our eternal destination!

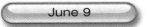

Thank You

By Michelle Stollenmaier

*For God so loved the world that he gave his one and only Son, that who-
ever believes in him shall not perish but have eternal life. John 3:16.*

Recently my brother, much to my family's surprise, joined the Army. He had always talked of joining the Army, but we never thought he actually would. When he started filling out all the paperwork, I was a little shocked.

It took a few months before he left for basic training. During the months before, it didn't really hit me that he was leaving and would be serving our country. When the day finally came, all the things I hadn't thought of hit me: my big brother was leaving—not just to go to college, but to train and serve people who sometimes aren't even grateful.

That day I hugged my brother tight and cried on his shoulder. He was in basic training for 10 weeks. He called every few weeks, letting us know he was doing great and passing with flying colors. Ten weeks later he graduated. I was so proud at his graduation. My brother looked so sharp in his uniform, ready to serve his country. There were so many men and woman graduating with him; some were as young as 17 and a few as old as 42. I was a little sad, yet at the same time happy, that so many people would give up an easier life to do a thankless job like serving people they didn't know. We don't know how much they sacrifice just so we can have a safer country.

The saddest thing of all is that every time one of them messes up, people blame the soldiers who try to protect them. It reminds me of how Jesus gave up His life for us, but when things start to go badly, we blame Him. I understand we are all selfish humans, but sometimes we need to stop and realize how much other people are suffering and sacrificing for us. I would like to thank every man and woman who has given up their time, and some even their lives, for me and my country. That's the least I can do. The greatest thing we can do is pray. Pray for all the men and women serving our country. Pray that Jesus will come soon so that they can stop sacrificing so much.

A Bad Way to Waste Time

By Cassandra Dannenberger

A new command I give you: Love one another. As I have loved you, so you must love one another. John 13:34.

There are some people I just love to be mad at. I used to think it was OK, because it let me settle my anger without a total loss of self-control. As long as they didn't know, I thought, *No harm done, right?*

Later I found out the person I was mad at didn't like me so much either. But instead of acknowledging the anger, I just held a grudge, which is what most people do.

The rest of the year I was mentally mad at the person while they were verbally and physically mad at me in their own way. What I realized a little too late was that instead of confronting the person and making peace with them, I wasted a lot of time trying to get them back for all the pain they had caused me. And I tried to make their life miserable instead of trying to enjoy mine.

It took us a while, but we eventually both came to our senses and worked things out. I am friends with this person now, but every time I look back on our relationship, I don't have many pleasant memories as a foundation. But we are building that good foundation now, and I am so glad.

I learned the hard way. But save yourself some trouble and take a minute to stop and think every once in a while to remind yourself of how much time you're wasting just being needlessly mad at someone. Then think of how much time people waste when they hate the world—yeah, it's a lot.

Don't waste any more time being mad or worrying about making your enemies' lives miserable, because in the end your life is the only one that will end up miserable.

Jesus Is Coming Soon!
By Stella Bradley

Behold, I am coming soon! Blessed is he who keeps the words of the prophecy in this book. Revelation 22:7.

I really believe that we are nearing the final days of earth's history. This is a comforting thought to me. I want to spend time with Jesus. I can hardly wait to be reunited with loved ones (especially my sister, dad, and grandparents) who are sleeping in Christ. I want to meet my guardian angel. I want to eat the tasty fruit from the tree of life. I want to talk to my Bible heroes. I want to travel the galaxies with God and finally understand all of the things my mind can't comprehend here on earth. I want to feel what it's like not to have a schedule or deadlines. I want to play with lions and bears. I want to see my kids grow up in a place that is free of pain and suffering.

Until that glorious day when we are rescued from this weary world, the Lord says to be faithful. In 1 Thessalonians 5:12-24 we find some final instructions: "Now we ask you, brothers, to respect those who work hard among you, who are over you in the Lord and who admonish you. Hold them in the highest regard in love because of their work. Live in peace with each other. And we urge you, brothers, warn those who are idle, encourage the timid, help the weak, be patient with everyone. Make sure that nobody pays back wrong for wrong, but always try to be kind to each other and to everyone else.

"Be joyful always; pray continually; give thanks in all circumstances, for this is God's will for you in Christ Jesus.

"Do not put out the Spirit's fire; do not treat prophecies with contempt. Test everything. Hold on to the good. Avoid every kind of evil.

"May God himself, the God of peace, sanctify you through and through. May your whole spirit, soul and body be kept blameless at the coming of our Lord Jesus Christ. The one who calls you is faithful and he will do it."

As we look forward to Christ's return, let's endeavor to follow these instructions. We can do it with God's help.

He Gave Me Peace

By Shawntez Smith

Turn from evil and do good; seek peace and pursue it. Psalm 34:14.

I cannot find the words to tell you all the things that God has done for me. I can only tell you that I've been touched, transformed, and have become stronger. In elementary school I did not feel the peace that I have now. I attended public school. While there, I was not the best student. I did not listen to the teacher, and my grades were unexplainable. It probably didn't help that my friends were more like family to me. I got along with my grandparents, whom I lived with, but not as I wished to. To me, life was just daily life. I really did not have a goal. My only plan was to plod through high school and join the Army, but all of that changed the summer I went to Nosoca Pines Ranch, one of our Adventist summer camps.

I attended camp for a week, and I became curious about what God wanted for my life. I had been raised in a Christian home, and I believed that the seventh day is the Sabbath. I went to church, and I knew the difference between right and wrong, but I didn't always have God in my heart! The last night at camp our counselor told us, "God has a plan for each of you; He has a reason you are here. You were put on this earth to serve Him."

I kept asking myself what God wanted from me. Then something told me to stop asking myself and ask God. For the first time in my life I prayed and really meant it. I told God that if He had a reason or a plan for me, then please show me. I told Him that I would back off and let Him lead the way. Believe it or not, I did let go. I wanted to change my old ways. I was tired of living my life the way I wanted to. It was time for a change.

That's when I was given a chance to attend academy—an opportunity I had never even considered before. Several years have passed since then, and I have to say I am not the person I was back then.

While attending Mount Pisgah Academy, I decided I wanted to be a pediatrician. But more important, I strengthened my faith in God. First, I gave God my attention and He gave me hope. I was nothing in the beginning. I had no life. Now that I have given God complete control over my life, I not only have a future—I have peace.

Attitude Change

By Daniel Lee

For the Son of Man came to seek and to save what was lost. Luke 19:10.

In the spring of my junior year in academy, I went on a mission trip to a Navajo Indian reservation in Arizona. About 20 of us from Mount Pisgah Academy went to work in a youth center there. About 250,000 people live on the reservation we visited, but very few are Christians.

The youth center had been vandalized, and it was really a mess. We spent a lot of time clearing out the trash and cleaning up. We also poured a new cement floor, painted the walls, and shoveled the snow that had piled up around the center. In the afternoons we worked with children from the reservation. Most of the little kids did not know anything about God. So we told them Bible stories and taught them songs about Jesus. Everyone enjoyed our time together.

The area that the center was in was very poor. And it was obvious that many of the people did not take pride in their neighborhood. I saw many empty bottles of liquor lying around. I also saw many kids and adults drinking alcohol and doing other bad things. It was sad to see their poor choices.

However, I was impressed by the difference in attitude between the people who did not know Jesus and those who did. The Christians were happy and had a good attitude. Those who got drunk seemed so sad and hopeless. The difference was obvious.

This reminded me of the verse that says if we are in Christ we are a new creation (2 Corinthians 5:17). This passage goes on to say that God gave us the work of bringing everyone into peace with Him. When I saw the change in attitude and lifestyle of the people who had a relationship with Jesus, I could understand how important it is for us to tell everyone the good news about Jesus. I am really thankful that I had the chance to go and help on the reservation. It made me want to continue to help other people. I am very grateful for the difference Jesus makes in people's lives.

I'm Alive and Well!
By Shawntese Smith

But all of you who held fast to the Lord your God are still alive today.
Deuteronomy 4:4.

As I look back over my life, I can see all the blessings that God has provided for me. Remembering the lies and self-pride I took upon myself, there have been times when I felt useless, and all I depended on was my friends. Sometimes I've let my friends run my life. In fact, at times I felt that my friends were even more important to me than God. If something bad happened to me, I thought God was punishing me and I, in turn, would punish myself.

In hindsight I know that sounds ridiculous. A relationship is a partnership between two friends. And I realize now that I was not holding up my end of the friendship. God never left me; I just backed away from Him.

From my very beginning God has not given up on me—He has a plan for my life. To begin with, He put my life in the hands of my great-grandparents. He gave them the wisdom and knowledge to control me, a bit of a rambunctious kid. He gave them the strength to lead me in the right direction, socially and spiritually. I thank them so much. They raised me to be all I can be, and I have never been able to thank them enough for it. They are my biggest blessings.

I am also blessed to have brothers and sisters, because I cannot picture my life without them. My family is my most valuable treasure. My identical twin sister is so wonderful and kind. My life is forever shaped around her, for she is my other half, and I love her with all my heart. I have so many blessings that I cannot count them.

I cannot wait to see what God has in store for me in the future. I'm a living testimony for Him, and I am proud to say it. God is the light that shines in me, and there is nothing in this world that can top that!

Prayer Changes

By Cheryl Grant

Answer me when I call to you, O my righteous God. Give me relief from my distress; be merciful to me and hear my prayer. Psalm 4:1.

As a young girl growing up with my mom and my brother, I was very shielded and protected. But at the age of 11 I was almost molested by my mom's best friend's son. After that incident I began having trust issues with a lot of men. At the age of 13 I met my father, and seeing him for the first time in my life brought me so much joy. Developing that relationship helped me forget about my previous issue.

However, things took a turn for the worse. When I was 16, my dad got drunk one night and also tried to molest me. I was devastated, so my mom moved us to a different state. She got married, and life seemed like it should be normal, but it was very difficult for me accept another man in our lives. When I finally did, he also tried to take advantage of me. When I tried to tell someone, no one would believe me.

No one was there to have my back, so I decided to turn to God to give me the strength I needed to make it through. It did not seem to work, and I started wondering if my prayers were being heard. After a while I stopped talking to God and tried to do things on my own.

A couple of months later my mom and I finally decided that I would be attending Mount Pisgah Academy. My first couple of months here were very challenging, and I was ready to leave. I had constant nightmares about what had happened to me; it was a very miserable experience. What I did not know was that God had a way out for me. At Mount Pisgah Academy I could really feel the spiritual atmosphere, and as it began taking hold of me, I began talking to God more and giving my problems to Him. As I began to talk to Him, I felt this calmness and assurance come over me.

Now as I look back on what happened earlier in my life, I think about how far I have come, and I thank God for giving me a safe and spiritual haven. Praise Him!

Student Life

By A. J. King

In your unfailing love you will lead the people you have redeemed. In your strength you will guide them to your holy dwelling. Exodus 15:13.

My days are filled with happiness and fun with friends, but I still feel empty. Do you ever feel like something is missing? I started going to a Seventh-day Adventist boarding school when I was 16 years old. Not long after arriving, I started to get in trouble for small things—things such as skipping class and not doing homework. These tiny problems started getting bigger and bigger, and soon I did not even think about school. *It didn't promise me anything!* I thought.

Later I was expelled for multiple reasons and started to attend a public school. Public school did not interest me, either, and again I was caught up in the wrong crowd.

After a year at my local public high school, I felt compelled to reapply to Mount Pisgah Academy. After all the trouble I had been in, I did not expect to be accepted. However, the Lord always has a plan—and I was accepted. I recognized this second chance for what it is worth, and I did all I could to prove to the staff that they had made the right decision by allowing me to come back. I thank the Lord for leading me through my troubles and for the opportunity I was given.

God always has a better plan than you think. I thought that I would not graduate from an Adventist high school, but with God's help I did it! And let me tell you, where there is a will, there is a way. An Adventist education is a wonderful chance to change your life.

Always remember that Jesus Christ will lead you down the right path if you let Him. We may not always follow the best path He had in mind for us, but God is a master at offering us a Plan B, Plan C, Plan D, etc. He never gives up on us. And it is never too late to turn to Him. He also promised that we would not be given trials that, with His help, would be too much to handle. And part of preparing for those inevitable trials is through good training from family, school, and church.

Appreciate the God-sent opportunities you have, and remember to thank Him for all of the blessings in your life today.

No Matter What

By Callie Adams

But while he was still a long way off, his father saw him and was filled with compassion for him; he ran to his son, threw his arms around him and kissed him. Luke 15:20.

There is something about this world, something about being young and inexperienced, that makes humans want to go out and make their own way. When I was 21, I went overseas to a school to learn Spanish. I didn't go with the intention of getting into trouble, but once I was on that campus, I knew that I could do whatever I wanted and no one would ever know. With this mind-set, I tried drinking for the first time. I dated the wrong kind of guy and eventually put myself in a very compromising situation. That night I finally realized that this wasn't how I wanted to live my life. A sinking feeling came over my heart. I called my parents, and my mother bought me a ticket to come home. I had to wait three days before I could make the trip—those were the hardest three days I have ever had.

During that time I listened to Christian music and cried over all the mistakes I had made. Until that time, I had, in my own mind, a perfect record. I was pure and clean. How could I have tainted myself this way? Would I ever be clean again? I showered again and again, trying to wash the "dirt" off my soul.

My biggest worry was that my father would not see me the same ever again. The flight was longer than I remembered, and I thought of how I could possibly make up for the choices I had made. I had wasted Dad's money. I had wasted valuable time. But most of all, after all the "good raising" he had done, I had wasted myself.

When I got off that airplane, there was my father, waiting for me with his arms open wide. He hugged me, and I knew that everything was going to be all right. He whispered in my ear, "You can always come home."

My First Date

By Mandi Skilton

Come near to God and he will come near to you. James 4:8.

The weather was brisk, and the sky was smooth with not a cloud in sight. As I drove my car around the switchback roads leading to an open field on top of a mountain, I could not figure out what had led me to this idea. One minute I was trying to take a nap on a Sabbath afternoon, and the next I was speeding away. I knew God must have a reason for impressing me to do such a spontaneous thing.

At the time my relationship with God was good, but I felt there was something missing. After driving for a while, I arrived at my destination. I then settled down on the grass with my Bible and began to read, but something told me that was not why I was there. For a while I sat in silence, and then I was overwhelmed with the desire to pray and listen. For hours I talked with God about my friends, my plans for the future, and the ordinary details of my life. On that mountainside I had my first date with God, as I like to refer to it. Being up there with no distractions and opening myself up to His presence was an incredible experience. I realized that what had been missing from my relationship with God was true intimacy.

Love is not something that occurs in one day; it requires time to grow. Beginning a new relationship requires attention and nurturing. The same is true for a relationship with God. Getting to know God is not just about going to church and reading the Bible, but is also about building a lifelong relationship. Creating time to be intimate with God gives us the chance to really focus on who He truly is. We sometimes spend so much time and energy devoting ourselves to our human relationships that we have little time for God. The opportunity to build a friendship and an intimate relationship with God starts by first spending one-on-one time with Him. Now I love and appreciate every moment I get to spend with God.

Forgive and Forget

By Josias Flores

Be kind and compassionate to one another, forgiving each other, just as in Christ God forgave you. Ephesians 4:32.

Sometimes people get so caught up with their own problems that they forget to look at situations from different points of view. We say that we forgive and forget, but when it comes down to it, do we really?

At the beginning of the school year I unfortunately went through an annoying and time-wasting experience. I had a serious ear infection that started rather simply. We were cleaning the boys' dorm thoroughly one night, so they gave us all cleaning sprays. Like the teenagers we are, we started spraying them at each other. Suddenly my friend came from behind and sprayed me in the ear. I thought nothing of it, but the next day my ear was clogged up. I decided to go to the nurse, and she gave me pills to unclog it.

The pills worked wonderfully, and within the hour my ear was draining the liquid. It was Sabbath, and I was kind of embarrassed that my ear was draining, so I wiped off the liquid with my finger every five seconds or so. In the afternoon my ear started draining a yellowish liquid, and the next morning it was still draining the liquid along with blood. After four or five doctor's appointments and a week at home, my ear finally healed. But I still had to deal with a ruptured eardrum and a little bit of hearing loss.

You may think that I was really mad at the person who did this to me, but early on I decided to look at it from his point of view, accept my responsibility, and forgive him.

Still, my forgiveness is nothing compared to the love Jesus has for us. He, being perfect and sinless, had to go through the worst possible death and ridicule. He died in the ultimate sacrifice to forgive us of all the sins we have committed. We have all hurt many people and even God—sometimes intentionally and sometimes carelessly. But all because of His amazing love and forgiveness, He came down to give us the chance to have eternal life. He did more than we could ever imagine.

Perfect Companion
By Megan Coffey

If I rise on the wings of the dawn, if I settle on the far side of the sea, even there your hand will guide me, your right hand will hold me fast.
Psalm 139:9, 10.

I recently got a new puppy, and much like bringing a new baby home, my puppy captured my heart. Many people say a dog is the best companion, and I was definitely smitten.

For weeks all my attention and free time was spent with the puppy. He was so special. It took my family almost a week to name him because his name had to be perfect. Our decision was finally complete when we named him Max.

Max was the newest addition to our family, and definitely the cutest! However, after the first month of cleaning up his messes, feeding him, walking him, and taking him to go to the bathroom every few hours, I was getting quite annoyed, especially after an exasperating day full of school, work, gymnastics, friends, and family.

Nevertheless, when I came home with a bad attitude, my puppy was always happy to see me. Even if I yelled at him or punished him, he never stopped trying to get my attention. All he wants is love.

It is the same way with God—all He wants is to know more about you. He cares! He wants you to seek Him, love Him, and, most of all, need Him. Although we all have our "bad days" and sometimes ignore Him, He waits patiently for us. He never stops trying to get our attention; He wants a deeper relationship!

No matter where you are in life, ups or downs, God will stay with you. He will continue to try to capture your heart.

Widow in Need

By Michael Brackett

To those who by persistence in doing good seek glory, honor and immortality, he will give eternal life. Romans 2:7.

A widow named Juliet once lived in Wandsworth, England, a small town southwest of London. She cried herself to sleep for almost three years after her beloved husband died of cancer and left her alone with her two young children. To make matters worse, one of the largest financial institutions in England refused to pay her husband's life insurance policy, which was worth hundreds of thousands of dollars.

The insurance company claimed that Juliet's husband had not disclaimed that he had knowledge of the possibility that he had lymphoma. The couple, however, had indeed disclaimed that possibility when they first signed the paperwork for the insurance. What happened? Well, it turned out that the agent who sold them the policy conveniently didn't report that fact to the insurance company, so that the policy would go through.

After Juliet's husband died, the insurance company didn't pay. But Juliet didn't get down, and she didn't give up. She got persistent. Juliet appealed the insurance company's decision, but they turned her down again after their review. She then took the matter to a financial judge, who initially shot down her claim against the insurance giant. She continued to go before the judge, taking more and more evidence. She went so far as to dress in a black widow's dress and visit the financial institution's annual general meeting in Glasgow. She was escorted off the premises by security guards.

Finally, after three years, the judge conceded and recommended that Juliet receive the full amount of the policy's death benefit, and the financial institution agreed to pay in full!

Jesus is well aware of the battles we go through in this life. And He is concerned about our battles. Sometime today read the parable found in Luke 18:1-8. In this passage Jesus tells an almost identical story about a widow not being treated fairly.

Be persistent with Jesus in prayer and don't lose heart! He asked us to do it! If you're not being treated fairly on this earth, there is a righteous Judge who says that in the end the judgment will be overwhelmingly in our favor!

Many Missionaries

By George and Linda Grow

It was he who gave some to be apostles, some to be prophets, some to be evangelists, and some to be pastors and teachers. Ephesians 4:11.

During a school vacation I drove a busload of students and sponsors to the Atlanta airport so that they could catch a plane to Kenya for a mission trip. I pulled the Mount Pisgah Academy bus up to the mostly deserted terminal at 4:30 a.m. After all the missionaries and equipment were unloaded, Chaplain Witas gave me $100 as a gift for driving. Just before I left the terminal, Jesus impressed me to give the $100 to a trip sponsor, Ken Cook, to use as needed. My wallet was empty again, but I was happy. I later learned that one of the students hadn't brought enough money, so Ken gave her the $100 saying, "An angel gave it to me!"

Back outside at the bus, airport security was getting agitated: "The bus is not allowed to park that close to the terminal. You have to move it NOW." But then I discovered the batteries were dead and would need a jump start. You can imagine how I felt telling security. They called for a huge tow truck, the proper size for buses. When he arrived, the driver needed $100 just to hook up, plus hundreds more to tow. I explained that I didn't have any cash, just a credit card, and that all I needed was a jump start.

He said, "You don't need me, so I'll call someone who can help." The driver assured the increasingly anxious police officer that we should wait for a jump start. Generously, he waived any of his usual fees and kept security off my back until the battery truck arrived.

I explained my no-cash situation to the second driver. He started the bus and told me to follow him to the company office to use my charge card. Because of rush hour traffic, I lost him. When I returned to campus, I found the company on the Internet and called them. The company said they would fax an invoice, but to this day we haven't seen one.

I've come to the conclusion that drivers of huge tow trucks and battery-charging trucks must have fun being missionaries too.

Responding to Symptoms or Curing the Illness

By Rick Anderson

Nevertheless, I will bring health and healing to it; I will heal my people and will let them enjoy abundant peace and security. Jeremiah 33:6.

Ricky was 10 years old when simple cold symptoms caused little concern for his mother, Beth, me, and his babysitter, JoAnn. But stomach pains grew into fever and nausea, as well as fatigue. After a visit to the doctor and a thorough exam, we were given prescription medications to relieve his symptoms and were told that Ricky could return to his daily routine at the sitter's and play with his friends. Days passed, and the symptoms not only continued but increased with a vengeance (especially the stomach pains). As parents we became increasingly concerned, as did JoAnn who suggested that we take him back to the doctor for reevaluation. This time the doctor sent him to the hospital's emergency room. Within what seemed a few minutes of a typical checkup, things turned into a state of grave concern as the doctor told us Ricky would need immediate surgery for an appendectomy. When I called Beth, who was at home with our other children, she could hardly believe the news and was in the car on her way before I could hang up! The doctors told us it was routine surgery and would take only about 20 minutes.

An hour and a half into surgery a nurse came to the waiting room to inform us that the surgeons had run into some complications. There is nothing more disconcerting to parents than to hear this type of news. In addition to removing his appendix, six inches of Ricky's intestines needed to be removed. After much prayer and mutual comforting, we were relieved when the surgery was finally complete. It took weeks of recovery time, but things ended positively.

What began as common cold symptoms ended up being a much more complex issue. Isn't that the way with life at times? We treat the symptoms of our pain and misery without really dealing with the root of our illness. God alone can bring healing to our innermost ailments and pain. We can relieve the symptoms of hurt by leaning on friends, or coming up with our own solutions, but final resolution can come only through Jesus—trust only in Him!

Darcy

By Victoria Crawford

I praise you because I am fearfully and wonderfully made; your works are wonderful, I know that full well. Psalm 139:14.

One time a group of my closest friends and I all read the same book. A character in the book named Darcy always got what she wanted. She was the most popular girl in school. She could date any guy she wanted, and she had money. Every time I picked up the book, I found myself extremely jealous of her.

Do you ever feel like absolutely nothing can or will go your way? I feel like that at least once or twice a week. I find myself screaming into my pillow at God, asking Him why He let something happen to me, why I can't be as pretty as someone else, or why I have to study for what seems like forever just to make a C. It's hard, but usually after I'm finished being angry with Him, I try to remember that God has a purpose for my life.

Maybe I'm not supposed to be the prettiest girl in school because my future husband will think I'm perfect just the way I am. Maybe I'm supposed to learn something from the experiences God puts me through to make me wise enough to handle tough decisions I will have to face later on in life. Things happen for a reason.

I also have to remember that in a fictional book the characters may have a charmed life, but reality is never like that. Everyone, with no exceptions, faces many trials. Some people may hide their challenges better than others, but book characters do not portray real life.

The next time you're faced with a "Darcy" in your life, remember that you are just as good as the prettiest, richest, funniest person in the world to God. In fact, to God no one is more important or special than you. So be happy with who you are. Count your blessings and know that God has given each person their own gifts and talents. Who cares if no one else likes it? God loves you just the way you are—and that's what counts!

The Missing Retainer

By Joy Shin

And call upon me in the day of trouble; I will deliver you, and you will honor me. Psalm 50:15.

On a cold Sabbath during Christmas break, my friends Kelsi, Grace, and I were having a very good day. We all sat together at Sabbath school and during worship service. Then we went to Kelsi's house. That afternoon we went to the park and took a lot of pictures. It was just a perfect day!

And it got better. That night we were planning to go ice skating with all the youth from our church. We were so excited! We had planned for this night for days! When all of us were ready to leave the house, Kelsi stopped us and said, "Guys, I can't find my retainer!" Grace and I looked at each other and thought it wasn't a big deal. Losing retainers was one of Kelsi's many talents. But when she told her mother that her retainer was missing, her mom was very upset. She told Kelsi that this was unacceptable and that she couldn't go ice skating with Grace and me! We immediately started to search the whole house.

We checked Kelsi's room, the living room, and every other room in the house! But we had no luck. Kelsi ran into her room and started to cry. We thought her mom was being so unfair! The whole day we had talked about how much fun we were going to have that night—all three of us together! Grace and I went inside and tried to comfort Kelsi, and Kelsi said, "It's just a stupid retainer! I don't get how it could just ruin my whole evening!" Grace and I gave Kelsi a big hug, and we started to pray. We asked God for help, and we also told Him that we loved Him and thanked Him for our friendship.

After we had finished, we all walked downstairs. Then Kelsi went into the dining room and did a quick search. I had already checked every inch of that room, so I thought it was just hopeless. The retainer couldn't be there! Then I heard a gasp—and there it was. The tiny clear retainer we had been looking for was sitting on Kelsi's hand.

Grace, Kelsi, and I learned a very good lesson that night. God cares about every single thing, and He's always willing to help us out if we ask Him—even if we lose our retainer.

Angels With Machine Guns
By Paul Musgrave

God is our refuge and strength, an ever-present help in trouble. Psalm 46:1.

In March of 1977 a group of students from Fletcher Academy raised the funds and provided the labor to help finish a construction project at a mission academy in Honduras. We left on a Sunday morning in a bus loaded to the gills with 24 students, six staff, a 55-gallon drum of drinking water, and enough food to feed us for the round-trip of 9,500 miles.

The plan was to drive straight through and arrive at our destination on Friday, but some mechanical problems along the way slowed us down, and we spent Sabbath in Guatemala with some missionaries at the union headquarters. Saturday night we continued on our way. The roads in Honduras were not in great shape, and it did not take us long to figure out that after coming upon three consecutive piles of brush on the road we had better keep our eyes open for danger. I was driving in the wee hours of that Sunday morning when we came to yet another three piles of brush. I slowed the bus to a crawl, watching for any signs of danger, but after creeping along for a while, I decided that whatever the problem was it must have been cleared. I cautiously proceeded down the road.

Suddenly three men armed with machine guns jumped out of the bushes beside the road and started yelling and waving their guns at us. I didn't know what they were saying, but the message was clear: I was to stop! After we waited anxiously for half hour, an army jeep appeared, leading a caravan of several cars. The driver turned, motioned for me to follow, and then led us down a very steep, winding trail. After a mile or so, he turned, waved us on, and disappeared.

It wasn't until our return trip, which was in daylight, that we saw the reason for the "detour." The mountainous section of that area had been left devastated by the earthquake of 1975. The road we had been traveling on that night crossed a valley on a very high bridge, a bridge that had the center section completely knocked out by the earthquake. There were no barricades, no signs. The road just abruptly ended in midair not too far from where we had been stopped.

I will always be thankful for what I call my three "angels with machine guns" and the protection that God provided for us that night.

Mickey, Meet Tony

By Michael Brackett

He performs wonders that cannot be fathomed,
miracles that cannot be counted. Job 9:10.

On a beautiful Sunday, November 12, 2000, cameraman Mickey Pfleger was going about his awesome job of taking pictures of the 49ers/Chiefs game. By halftime it seemed to be just another day on the job that he had been accustomed to doing for 25 years. However, one minute and 50 seconds into the third quarter tight end Tony Gonzalez for the Kansas City Chiefs came barreling toward the sidelines right at Mickey! The 249-pound player hit Mickey at full steam, knocking him flat on his back and sending his cameras flying like missiles in every direction.

Mickey was hit so hard that he was unconscious for two minutes. During that span of unconsciousness, Mickey had a seizure. He was taken off the field by stretcher and rushed to the emergency room. Because of his condition, he underwent a CT scan. The scan didn't show anything abnormal from the impact on the football field, but it did show something the doctors were concerned about. A follow-up MRI helped diagnose Mickey with a large brain tumor. He was faced with the decision of whether or not to have surgery to remove the tumor. Mickey said that the decision was easy. He said, "I really believe that things happen for a reason.... I was never supposed to get hurt from the 'hit' by Tony Gonzalez. I couldn't find any bruises on my body the day after being hit full force by Tony, a 249-pound tight end in full football pads. I didn't even have a headache the next day, even though I suffered a concussion and seizure and was unconscious for two minutes. And none of my camera equipment was damaged in any way, even though my cameras went flying in three different directions." "I was supposed to be knocked out by Tony Gonzalez at the football game. I was supposed to go into a seizure so that...the emergency room doctors [would] do a CT brain scan on me. . . . I thank God that I am alive, and I am looking forward to the future. I feel great!"

Are you facing a bad situation? Always remember Romans 8:28. The Bible says, "And we know that all things work together for good to them that love God, to them who are the called according to his purpose" (KJV). Sometimes it takes longer to see what God intended, but the Bible promises that it is for our good.

God's Mushroom Patch
By Bonny Musgrave

For he satisfies the thirsty and fills the hungry with good things.
Psalm 107:9.

Recently I listened to a speaker on the radio discuss the question of whether or not God is a personal God who wants to be bothered with the insignificant details of our lives. A few days later I had an experience that affirmed for me once again how much God really does care for us.

We were spending the weekend at our place in Virginia. Sabbath afternoon my husband and I went for a walk in the woods below our house. At one point I looked down to see where I was stepping and was surprised to see a single morel mushroom on my path. You have to understand that we both dearly love morel mushrooms. For those of you who have never had the privilege of discovering the morel, there is nothing quite as good, or as hard, to find. The season for morels in Virginia lasts about two weeks, and if you are lucky enough to find some, the location is a very heavily guarded secret.

On this particular day we searched and searched for more, but there was only the one lonely mushroom to be found. We decided to take a drive up on the Blue Ridge Parkway to a location that we knew sometimes had morels growing in a ditch beside the road to see if we could find enough for supper.

Since the area where the morels grew was only a stretch of 500 feet or so, Paul let me out at the beginning and drove to a wide grassy shoulder past the other end to wait. Dusk was fast approaching, which made it hard to see, and try as hard as I could, I didn't find a single mushroom. Filled with disappointment, I trudged back to the car. As I was getting in, I glanced down at my feet and couldn't believe my eyes! Paul had pulled the car over in the middle of the biggest patch of morels I had ever seen! And it was an area where we had never found mushrooms before. We both got out and picked every mushroom we could find. Strangely, there were no mushrooms before or after where the car was parked, only those right at my door.

As we feasted on sautéed mushrooms that evening, we couldn't help feeling that God had grown that patch just for us and then led Paul to park right in the middle of it so I couldn't miss them! Does God care about the little details in our life? You bet!

Heaven on Earth

By Leah Killian

But in keeping with his promise we are looking forward to a new heaven and a new earth, the home of righteousness. 2 Peter 3:13.

Many people imagine what heaven is going to be like. They envision flying over the ocean or sleeping with a tiger. Heaven seems to be the place where the impossible becomes possible and dreams become realities.

Mount Pisgah Academy (MPA) had the privilege of hosting the Great Lakes Adventist Academy (GLAA) acrobatics team for a week of prayer during the school year. The meetings were wonderful and many students were touched, but Thursday night was a night to remember on the MPA campus. The GLAA team performed a Passion play, the story of Jesus' crucifixion. After the play many students came to the front, giving their hearts to the Lord or simply recommitting their lives to Jesus. But this night did not end like any other night. As the whole school gathered in the front of the sanctuary, something incredible happened—the Holy Spirit worked in and spoke to each individual. Many were crying and many were comforting, but we were all there, praying and praising the Lord. The room was alive with the love of God.

As I took a minute and stepped back to observe what was going on, I saw heaven. I looked around and saw people who had never spoken to each other hugging and loving each other. I saw broken friendships being repaired. And I saw the love of Jesus in each person. That night it didn't matter what grade somebody was in, what school they were from, or what social status they might have. All that mattered was that they needed to be loved, and each person was willing to love them.

The rest of the night we all sat together in the front of the sanctuary praying, singing, and embracing each other. I couldn't help thinking that this was what heaven is going to be like—full of love. I started thinking how, as Christians, we could bring a piece of heaven to this sinful earth by simply loving and accepting each other a little more.

Next time you walk by someone, smile at them, hug them, or say a prayer for them, but above all, do something to show them the love of Jesus and bring them a little heaven on earth.

The Vase
By Devin Suarez

Weeping may remain for a night, but rejoicing comes in the morning.
Psalm 30:5.

The accident had mangled his arm to an unrecognizable mess; it would never work the same again. He had just reached the peak of his painting career, and after the wreck his career came to an abrupt stop. Feeling like there was no point in living anymore, he attempted suicide, only to fail. The hospital sent him to a therapist to help with his depression. The therapist told him to paint a self-portrait with his other hand. She watched as he painted a beautiful vase with a crack in the side of it.

Time passed and he found himself falling in love with his therapist. He explained to her that before the accident, he had been so consumed with his work that he had never had time for love. After he was injured and broken, he had time to see what he had been missing. They eventually got married and had a good life together.

While suffering from depression, he had been missing a light in his life. It was only through the crack in the vase that he could see a glimmer of light. Just so, it's only when we are broken that we realize what is really important in life.

Most of us are pretty spoiled and have very few actual needs. Do you think that is why we sometimes don't lean on God? Then in more dire times we realize we really are missing a very important element in our lives. And that realization leads us to depend on God. But then, when things are going well again, do we forget about Him?

Even a physical therapist will tell you that the more you move, the stronger you will be, and the stronger you are, the easier it will be to get up. Strength training, spiritual strength training, is very important for everyone. In other words, even in our strongest times we should continue to build up our spiritual muscles—we should "exercise" regularly by studying our Bible and talking with God in prayer.

Then we can have a more constant, and a more meaningful, relationship with Christ. If you are broken, or if you are not, make God your first priority.

Leave Me Alone!

By Kristina Forrest

Then you will understand what is right and just and fair—every good path. For wisdom will enter your heart, and knowledge will be pleasant to your soul.
Proverbs 2:9, 10.

After my sophomore year of high school, I thought I had it made. First off, I was going to be a starter on my school's varsity basketball team. Next, I was happier than ever because things were going good with the guy I liked at the time. Then there was the fact that it was summer break! My sophomore year at school had been one of the toughest so far, and I made it out alive! So as you can see, I was living large. However, my joy was short-lived. With summer plans formulating in my head, my mom picked me up from school and announced that I was leaving the next day for Lake Junaluska and the Carolina Conference's camp meeting. I was not excited!

Instead of going to the beach for a week, I had to go to camp meeting. Let's just say I wasn't the most chipper girl to be around. I didn't like the idea of going to an unfamiliar place where I knew no one. Overall, I knew I would feel extremely uncomfortable. Being stubborn, I did everything to make my parents' time there as completely miserable as mine. However, something very strange happened the first afternoon we were there.

While I was wallowing in my self-pity, three kids my age walked over and started talking to me. Their names were Andrew, Shana, and Lucas. They told me they were students from Mount Pisgah Academy. The whole time they were talking I was thinking, *Just get away from me, because I don't want to talk to you. I don't even want to be here!* Well, God obviously had other plans for me that day, because something ignited a little interest for MPA. These students were genuinely interested in me, and they had a very spiritual spark to them. They got my attention. Shana told me to text her if I had any questions. Well, as it turned out, I had quite a few questions. But she was reassuring and told me how the academy had changed her life.

Now I am a graduate of MPA, and I am so glad I gave the academy a chance. I made so many great friends there, and I know that I grew spiritually. Those three people who introduced themselves to me became amazing friends. I know I made the right choice!

If you are in a dilemma about your high school future, contact your local academy. Give them a chance. It just might change your life for the better!

Giving In to That Godly Impulse
By Ian Brewer

Whoever acknowledges me before men, I will also acknowledge him before my Father in heaven. Matthew 10:32.

How many times have you seen someone with a certain look in their eyes, one of quiet desperation in a world that doesn't care? Something in you causes you to connect with that person on a level you don't entirely understand. Thoughts such as *What can I do to help?* and *Does this person know my Jesus?* enter your mind.

Suddenly, without realizing it, you feel an impulse deep in your heart—a godly impulse. In your heart you know you should walk up to them without hesitation and share the love of God as we are commanded to do. The thought is so perfect—it seems nothing could be better. This is the way sharing Jesus with the world feels.

Then a new feeling creeps in. That feeling is nervousness, doubt. You begin to shy away from the idea of sharing the priceless gift you've been given simply because you can't overcome something as silly as a little stage fright. There's nothing standing in your way but yourself.

At this point in the story, which you've doubtless experienced firsthand, a juncture of sorts has been reached. There are two choices to make. There is no option C. Either you will give in to the human impulse to ignore conscience or you will give in to the divine impulse to do what is right. This "fork in the road" is where you should reinforce your resolve with scripture. Matthew 10:32 turns things around on us. We are the defendant in heaven, and Jesus is confessing before His Father. What do we want Jesus to say about us? Will it be "I never knew you," or will He tell His Father that you are just like Him?

Let's show God to everyone we meet. Let's give up that human feeling of doubt and trade it for God's divine feeling as He enters our hearts. Pray for the opportunity first, and then pray for the strength to tell everyone about the great God of love we serve.

Missing Photos
By Elizabeth Wilson

Cast all your anxiety on him because he cares for you. 1 Peter 5:7.

The summer before I entered third grade my family and I went to Disney World with some of our friends. Disney is a very fun place, and to capture all of the memories, my dad, as usual, was ready at every corner to snap our pictures. At that time we did not have a digital camera, so Dad carried around an ample supply of undeveloped film in the camera bag.

Our friends had a 4-year-old daughter, so they had a stroller with them. We were getting ready to go on a ride, and we put the camera bag in the stroller, hidden with some other stuff, thinking that things were safe enough. After all, it was a family-friendly park. Who would steal a stroller?

When the ride was over, we went to get the stroller, but it wasn't there! We looked everywhere and asked people if they had seen it, but we couldn't find it. So our little group huddled together and prayed that we would find it.

We continued to enjoy the park, but with a constant prayer sent up for our lost things. As we strolled into the entrance of the Pirates of the Caribbean ride, my dad spotted our camera bag on top of a trash can. We could hardly believe our eyes. And amazingly, it still had everything in it. What a miracle! It was a reminder that God cares even about the smallest things, such as family vacation photos.

A few weeks later our friends got a phone call from the people at Disney. Some employees had found the thief going through the stroller in the back of a restaurant. They caught the thief and confiscated the stroller. Everything was still there.

We certainly sent up many prayers of thanks to God for returning our belongings.

In all things, ask God for help. Nothing is too big or small to take to Him in prayer.

The Big Bang
By Alyssa Pelto

We wait in hope for the Lord; he is our help and our shield. Psalm 33:20.

On a recent Independence Day my family and I went to a Fourth of July party that some of our friends were having. It was fantastic, with all sorts of good food and yummy desserts. As the sun was setting, we brought out some sparklers and fountain-type fireworks. After a little while an elderly woman who was with us decided that it was time to go home, so we said good night and sent her on her way.

After she left, a few of our friends decided to "enhance" the party with a little more bang. They pulled out a different type of firework—the launching type. At first it started out wonderfully. Then . . . *boom!*

I watched as the firework exploded, and instead of going up, it shot toward the side, hitting our friends' house. I began screaming. Then another firework shot out, hitting a light post. The force of its fire made the container fall over, pointing the rest of the artillery straight at the rest of our friends who were watching. Fireworks shot out right at them! I screamed again, telling everyone to look out. The fireworks exploded all around us. I watched as everyone dove, rolled, and ran out of the way.

Miraculously, no one was hurt except for a few small burn marks on pants. We found out later that one of the missiles had launched right at the chair where the little elderly woman had sat just minutes before the accident. We were so thankful that God had protected us.

Our guardian angels were watching out for us that evening. I look back and realize that if it hadn't been for them a lot of us would have been seriously wounded or worse. This story reminds me not to be afraid. I know that God will always protect me and will always love me. All we have to do is trust Him. I thank God every day for His loving protection. (And we've learned our lesson about fireworks safety!)

Celebration

By Ben Steinkraus

From the beginning, the Word of God was there. The Word stood by the side of God, and the Word was fully God. John 1:1, Clear Word.

Our family has had a tradition for as long as I can remember. Every year on July 3 and 4 we hunt down all the local fireworks displays within 25 miles. We carefully schedule our time so we can see as many as possible. (Sometimes the ride there is more exciting than the fireworks show—I guess it's just good family time.) On our way home we all share our opinions as to which one we liked the best and why.

On July 5, the day after all the fun and celebration, the day after we, as a country, celebrate our independence and freedom to be one under God, we have a celebration of our own. We invite family and friends over, enjoy good food, and have a great time continuing the holiday. My dad and I arrange and set off our own fireworks display, and we compare it to the professional shows. We always save the sparklers and snaps for last so that everyone can participate in the grand finale.

I can only imagine the fun Jesus had when He and God the Father created this world. What a light show of creativity that must have been! Blasts of color and textures suddenly filling a void—and all of it intended to be the perfect location for God's created people to enjoy a life of peace and enjoyment.

And can you even comprehend how fantastic it will be to be in heaven as we celebrate our independence from sin? I am sure it will be a spectacular festival, like nothing we've ever seen—better than any fireworks and sparkler show down here. I can hardly wait.

Won't you accept the freedom God is offering you so that you can be a part of the greatest Independence Day ever?

Power of Prayer

By Denis Kasap

This is the confidence we have in approaching God: that if we ask anything according to his will, he hears us. And if we know that he hears us—whatever we ask—we know that we have what we asked of him. 1 John 5:14, 15.

Prayer is one of the most amazing gifts from God. You can't find a better way to talk to Him. As our chaplain once said: "Prayer gives more opportunities to God to help you in your life. He can't just always help us, because Satan will blame God for doing something people don't ask Him for. Satan tries to keep God's help away from people. But when people pray, it gives God many more opportunities to help people. Then Satan can't do anything about it."

This idea of prayer reminds me of a story. The summer after my junior year of academy I traveled to Russia, my home country. My grandparents live in Moldova, a small country between the Ukraine and Romania. It is a 35-hour drive from our home to my grandparents' home.

On this particular trip my dad and sister were taking turns driving. We were only three hours away from our destination when my sister, who was driving at the time, briefly lost focus, and our car veered off the road. Thankfully our car wasn't damaged badly, but the front wheel was shifted back from where it was supposed to be. We were stuck. It seemed as if there were no life around us. That highway was really old, and nobody used it much. We got really scared, because there was nothing we could do. We were in the Ukraine. We didn't have insurance in that country. The only thing we could do was pray. So we did—and in five minutes we saw an old car coming. The driver told us that there was a small village five minutes away. They had a mechanic there. The driver promised to bring back help with him. After 20 minutes he came back with a truck and took our car to their small shop. The driver was really kind and invited us to stay at his house while our car got fixed. We spent two days in that small village. When we finally left and got back onto the highway, nobody was disappointed about the expenses we spent on the car. Everybody was thankful to God for His help.

It's so amazing that we can just pray and get what we ask for free! God doesn't charge us. His Son paid for everything.

Words of Love

By Jacob Ballew

This is how we know that we love the children of God: by loving God and carrying out his commands. 1 John 5:2.

A lot of people mistake infatuation for love, but those are two very different things. Infatuation is seeing the other person as perfect. When you are infatuated, you want your needs met, you spend all your time with the other person, and you quickly "fall" for the other person. You then let other relationships and friendships deteriorate. It includes feelings of jealousy and often short-term emotions. Infatuation is often based on a physical relationship, and distance will put a strain on, and often an end to, the relationship.

Love is different. This may sound like a cliché, but love is not a feeling—it's a choice. Although real love is often accompanied by strong feelings, love does not equate with the sense of floating on clouds. Unlike the type of love that television and songs portray, people in love don't always feel "ooey gooey" around each other. In fact, a relationship does not last long on emotions alone. Love takes effort. Sometimes distance can even strengthen the relationship. Love is trust. Love is patient, kind, does not envy, boast, and is not proud. It is not rude, not self-seeking, not easily angered, doesn't keep record of wrongs. It doesn't delight in evil. It always protects, trusts, hopes, and perseveres (1 Corinthians 13).

Recently I've wondered what love is and if I truly love my girlfriend. I've found all the things above to be true for me, but I left out one thing: God. The Bible says that we cannot love unless we love God. So I spent some time studying the Bible and trying to build a better relationship with God. As I did this I noticed that my feelings toward my girlfriend grew stronger. I believe that if you love God and try to know Him, He will give you love, real love.

Apparent Christian

By Haruka Mori

I know your deeds, that you are neither cold nor hot. I wish you were either one or the other! So, because you are lukewarm—neither hot nor cold—I am about to spit you out of my mouth. Revelation 3:15, 16.

What is the definition of a good Christian? Someone who prays a long time? Someone who pays a faithful tithe? Someone who goes to church every Sabbath? Probably everyone has their own opinion in the matter, but I believe we need to connect to Jesus personally first, then our actions follow naturally.

One summer my friends and I were planning to sing a song for special music. The song had eight parts and was a cappella. It was a challenging song, but we were excited. However, there was a problem that we did not realize then. Because of too much excitement, the most important part, giving our hearts and our song to God, slipped from our mind. All we cared about was how well we sang, and we concentrated on our techniques and harmony. One day our choir teacher came to talk to us. He said that we were singing a praise song without praising God. I was shocked. I was ashamed of how little importance I had attached to God.

It is easy to act like a good Christian on the outside, and since no one knows what is actually happening in our minds, nobody would judge us for wrong motives.

But God wants us to act the way we really are. He wants to have a real relationship with us—not just a surface relationship. We need to go to church because we want to, play special music to praise God, pray to God to talk to Him—not because everybody else is doing it or expects it of us.

Do you have a good relationship with God, or are you pretending that you have one?

Serving God Everywhere
By Kris Kimbley

Serve wholeheartedly, as if you were serving the Lord, not men.
Ephesians 6:7.

During my freshman year in academy I was blessed with the opportunity to serve God on a mission trip. Our chaplain planned a trip to Bequia, an island off the coast of Saint Vincent and the Grenadines in the Caribbean. It is a very small island. We stayed for a week and built a roof on an Adventist grade school. The people were extremely hospitable and kind to us. I was young, and it impressed me a lot. After that I decided I wanted to serve as a missionary sometime later in my life.

During my junior year I had another opportunity to serve God on a mission trip. This time we went to Panama. I was a lot older, and I wanted to help as much as I could. We stayed and worked in David, Panama, for a week. We began to build a church. We worked all day, returned to where we were staying to clean up, and then went to a different church to help with an evangelistic series. I decided to help out with the children's meetings. I loved every minute I spent with those kids. Even though they spoke Spanish and I didn't understand anything they said, I had so much fun! I grew closer to the friends who went with me, to the sponsors, and most important, to God. Everyone there was so open, humble, nice, and genuine. I met a lot of cool people on that trip. It was an experience I will remember forever.

I have been on only these two mission trips so far, but I plan on going on many more. Those experiences helped me grow in God and learn more about myself. How is it that I signed up to help bless someone in a foreign country yet I ended up receiving so many blessings? My life has been changed! I want to be a missionary in college, after college, or whenever I get the opportunity. I love working for God and learning about other cultures.

If you ever get a chance, I encourage you to go on a mission trip! You will never be the same again.

By Your Side

By Madeline Wade

But God demonstrates his own love for us in this: While we were still sinners, Christ died for us. Romans 5:8.

Everyone feels deserted some time in his or her life. There isn't any one person who goes through life without a day when something goes completely wrong. It seems as though the times we are most in need of love, no one's there. This is how I felt one January morning.

Nothing was working out the way I wanted. I felt alone. Later that day while I was listening to the radio, I heard the song "By Your Side," by Tenth Avenue North. I listened to the lyrics, and it hit me—I had been trying to obtain the ability and grace to take away the bad days in my life on my own. This song showed me that God is the only one who has the grace to help me. He had been trying to give me His love and grace, but I just wouldn't take it. I kept turning away from Him and looking for something else, as if God weren't enough. God was right in front of me, wanting to give me everything.

There was one part in the song that especially stuck in my head. It said, "I drank the world's sin so I could carry you in and give you life." The more I thought about this song, the more I felt the presence of God in my life. I had never really understood the meaning of what Jesus did for me until I heard those lyrics. He didn't give up His life because I had to be saved or because it was His duty. He allowed Himself to be hung on the cross because He wanted to. I realized that God loves me. I had no reason to feel lonely and deserted. He was there during my bad days, and He will always be there.

Now, whenever I have a bad day or start feeling lonely, I remember this song. I know that God is there for me, and He knows what I'm going through.

God cares. He wants to be with you. He loves you. Don't turn away from Him. God wants to give you so much. He's just waiting for you to accept it and give your life to Him. He will always be by your side.

M&Ms Are Awesome!

By Reyna Torrez

You judge by human standards; I pass judgment on no one. John 8:15.

M&Ms are awesome! They're so chocolaty, crunchy, and amazingly satisfying. They all have an "m" on them and come in different colors! Isn't that just awesome? Another reason I like M&Ms is that they once taught me a valuable lesson.

One Sabbath morning my Sabbath school teacher, Mrs. Ancheta, called a girl up to the front of the room. Mrs. Ancheta said, "Close your eyes, eat this M&M, and tell me what color it is."

So the girl closed her eyes, ate the M&M, and guessed. "Is it red?" asked the little girl. The class yelled, "No!" We all got so excited. We wanted her to get one right.

She tried it again. "Blue? Orange? Brown?" None of those answers were correct.

As the girl sat down in disappointment, I began to think. *What does this have to do with Jesus? What was the point of all that?* But after the teacher explained it, I completely understood.

I have never liked how people judge each other. I have never liked how people put others down because of their race, background, or religion. Or maybe they criticize people for the way they dress, talk, and walk. How can people do that? How can they push others aside just because they seem different?

M&Ms remind me of people—we are all like M&Ms. It's true. We are all different colors—we even come in different shapes and sizes. But on the inside we are all valued the same. God made us all equal. We all have chocolate inside of us. I find it hilarious when I find a big, chunky, deformed M&M in the bag. It's like a bonus—something extra unique. M&Ms are amazing no matter the size or shape or color. And people are too!

God created us all, and God has purpose for each one of us. It shouldn't matter what color or ethnicity we are. We shouldn't judge one another. God sees us all the same. I thank Him for that.

Dreams

By Anna Grissom

But I trust in you, O Lord; I say, "You are my God." Psalm 31:14.

Dreams are something everyone has from a young age. I am no exception. I have hopes and dreams for my future, just as everybody else does. What if all the things you had ever hoped for suddenly became impossible? That is exactly what happened to me.

Toward the end of my junior year I started to make plans for the summer. I applied for jobs at two summer camps, and I applied to be part of the MPA recruiting team. I had already gotten a job offer from one of the summer camps, and I had planned to take it. I was going to be working with one of my classmates, and I was looking forward to it. Then it all came apart. Everything changed in one instant. My dream of working at summer camp was shattered, and even my plans for the future were crushed.

I had been told by a doctor that something was wrong, and then he gave me a list of things to do to get better. None could easily be done at a summer camp. I had to call the director of the summer camp and tell him that I was not going to be able to work for him. It was the hardest thing I had to do, because I had really wanted to work there.

After that phone call, I was mad—mad at God for letting this happen and taking away my dream job. At one point I remember sitting on the swings outside the girls' dorm yelling at God. I was crying as I yelled, saying, "What about my dreams! What about working at summer camp! Why did You take away my dreams?"

Suddenly I heard something clear as day: "Those are your dreams; what about My dreams for you?" In that moment I learned what the promise in Jeremiah 29:11 is really about—even if your dreams fall apart, He has other plans designed for you. I can promise you that whatever His dream is for you it is far bigger and better than anything you could ever imagine.

Are You Crafty?

By Stella Bradley

This is what God the Lord says—he who created the heavens and stretched them out, who spread out the earth and all that comes out of it, who gives breath to its people, and life to those who walk on it . . . [has] called you in righteousness. Isaiah 42:5, 6.

I have always admired crafty people. I love their creativity, their daring out-of-the-box thinking, and their skilled and practiced handiwork. My grandmother could whip out any sewing project with seemingly endless patience and energy. I liked looking at patterns and choosing fabrics—I didn't even mind cutting out around the onion-skinned paper—but my mind just couldn't wrap itself around how to put all of the pieces together. My grandmother was also good at woodworking, and after cutting out a design, she would bring it to life with paint. With a swoosh of her brush, she would say, "Just do it like this; it's not hard, see?" I would swoosh, trying to mimic her, but it would look nothing like hers.

I have taken two woodworking classes. I really enjoyed them both. But I can honestly say that I didn't complete any project (paper towel holder, bookends, step stool, or end table) on my own without the teacher's capable help. My specialty turned out to be cutting cedar hearts and smoothing the edges with a sander. I'm not so sure that qualifies as a woodworking project.

(And let's not discuss my pottery wheel escapades—so much fun, but such a warped bowl.)

Through all of this, I've come to three conclusions. People are meant to create. Even if my end result is not the vision I had originally hoped for, if I enjoy the process, it's worth it. Even better, crafting is just another reason I'm looking forward to heaven, where I will be able to sculpt, paint, arrange, and build with more patience and skill than I have now. But most important, I am in awe at the skilled craftsman God is. He works with more stubborn materials than clay, wood, rope, or grass. Yet everything in His hands turns out beautifully. I am so thankful for the amazing artistry of our Savior and the work He has done in me and you.

Meet Thomas—Part 1

By Hector Gonzalez

For there is nothing hidden that will not be disclosed, and nothing concealed that will not be known or brought out into the open. Luke 8:17.

I met Thomas during the summer at camp meeting. He was quiet and reserved; however, he made an immediate impression. He walked funny. He had a limp, yet he walked very fast. Every time I saw him he looked to be in a hurry, yet I later realized that this was his everyday walking style.

I met Thomas again at the start of school as he enrolled and entered the dormitory for a room assignment. I recognized soon enough that Thomas was most comfortable left alone. It took considerable effort to engage him. I entered his room one day and found him painting. I talked to him for a while and informed him that I could use some artwork to decorate my office. He later gave me the painting he was working on and said it was Moby Dick. The colors were very dark, and they ran together. I asked him about his use of dark colors, remembering what I had learned from an art therapist I had worked with. Then I hesitantly told him how I would interpret his painting if I were an art therapist. I was worried what his reaction would be, but he put his head down and went on to talk to me about his experience.

He related to me how, when he was young, he was on a motorcycle ride with his father when a car pulled out in front of them. His father held him as they were thrown off the motorcycle, twisting his body to receive the force of the impact as they hit the ground. His father was killed, and Thomas received major injuries. He was in and out of the hospital over the next few years, and he spent a lot of time alone. His injuries caused one arm and one leg to be shorter than the other. This caused his limp as he walked. His desire not to be seen caused him to hurry to get to his destinations.

Thomas shared with me his feelings of anger with God after his tragedy. I listened and learned, grateful that I had taken the time to talk about his painting.

Meet Thomas—Part 2

By Hector Gonzalez

Again, I tell you that if two of you on earth agree about anything you ask for, it will be done for you by my Father in heaven. Matthew 18:19.

Every student I have ever supervised as a dean has a special place in my memory; however, now and then a student leaves his or her mark a little more indelibly so that he or she is even more unforgettable. Thomas was one of those.

Another experience we shared occurred when I learned that Thomas had been teaching himself to play the guitar. I asked Thomas if he would be interested in playing a special music for a dorm worship. I was shocked and impressed when he said yes. I did not think to ask Thomas if he knew how to play anything spiritual. I assumed that he did. However, when he played for our dorm worship, I could tell from the chuckle of the guys that it was not. I was later told that it was a song by a secular rock group. I thanked Thomas for his musical contribution to our worship.

Another day while I was talking to Thomas, he shared with me how he would sometimes see our chaplain walking on campus with his son on his shoulders and how this made him think about how his dad used to carry him that way. I shared this with our chaplain, Pastor Ed Keyes. I remembered that Pastor Keyes also was a guitar player, and I asked him if he would be willing to give Thomas lessons. He agreed to do so. Over the remainder of the school year, Pastor Keyes gave Thomas guitar lessons mixed with Bible lessons and encouragement.

I was not too sure one day when Thomas asked me if he could play another special music for a dorm worship. I did not want to hurt his feelings, so I told him that would be fine. Thomas went on to play for us a song that he had arranged with Pastor Keyes' assistance, a beautiful rendition of "Amazing Grace." God's grace is sweet, and it heals all wounds if we let it.

Meet Thomas—Part 3

By Hector Gonzalez

But now you must rid yourselves of all such things as these: anger, rage, malice, slander, and filthy language from your lips. Colossians 3:8.

It was a cold, snow-covered winter night. During study hall time all of the gentlemen were in their rooms. The RAs were patrolling their halls when Juan, the RA of Thomas's hall, ran to my office and asked me to follow him. There was something I needed to see. When I got to his hall, I noticed that all of the boys who roomed on the left side of the hall were in the rooms of the boys who roomed on the right. I entered a room and looked with them out the window. Running around in the snow was a screaming, and naked, Thomas. The boys were already a little intimidated by Thomas. He walked funny. He hardly ever spoke to anyone, including his roommate, and now this.

I attempted to direct everyone back to their own rooms and away from the windows. Juan and I stood by the door until Thomas noticed our presence. I held the door open for him, and Juan handed him a blanket. Not knowing what to say to him then, I asked him if we could talk in the morning, and I encouraged him to call it a night.

The following morning Thomas was already sitting in front of my office door before I opened it. I didn't invite him in; instead I sat down next to him, and we talked. He apologized for his display and told me it was what came to mind to prevent him from releasing his anger. He told me that he was angry with something that had been done to him. He went on to say that he was not a fighter, but he was a curser. He did not want to get into trouble and decided to release his anger by running around in the cold. I complimented Thomas for wanting not to curse and not to get into trouble. But I informed him that he worried us out in the cold with no clothes on, and I asked him if we could discuss other anger-management techniques, and he agreed. I also asked him if we could pray. Once again, he agreed, but after I finished praying, he prayed for the first time with me.

Meet Thomas—Part 4

By Hector Gonzalez

Make sure that nobody pays back wrong for wrong, but always try to be kind to each other and to everyone else. 1 Thessalonians 5:15.

Thomas's senior year was coming to an end when one day I questioned him about his plans after graduation. I was pleasantly surprised, and reminded of how far he had come, when he answered that he wanted to serve as a missionary in the Philippines for a year. He went on to tell me that he was going to be meeting a representative to be interviewed. I told Thomas that I was extremely proud of him. I went further and asked him if it was important enough for him that he would be willing to do whatever it would take to go. He answered that he would.

Thomas had long hair. Thomas loved his long hair, and when addressed about his hair length, he would proceed to cut it to meet the academy's absolute minimum expectation. I questioned Thomas, asking if cutting his hair was a barrier to his going to the Philippines. He immediately protested and said he would rather not go than cut his hair.

Thomas graduated from academy, checked out of the dormitory, and said his goodbyes to me and the rest of our staff.

Several years passed before Thomas returned to visit us. When I saw him, there were two things I noticed immediately. First, he smiled, and I realized I had never seen his smile before. He was truly at peace and full of happiness. Second, his hair was cut military short. I asked him if he had gone into the military, and he said no. He reported that he had gone to the Philippines and that it was important enough for him to do whatever it took, even cut his hair.

It has been a really long time since I have heard from Thomas, but I pray that he still loves the Lord with the fire that he loved God the last time we spoke.

Becoming Personal

By Stephen Herren

What do you think? If a man owns a hundred sheep, and one of them wanders away, will he not leave the ninety-nine on the hills and go to look for the one that wandered off? And if he finds it, I tell you the truth, he is happier about that one sheep than about the ninety-nine that did not wander off. In the same way your Father in heaven is not willing that any of these little ones should be lost. Matthew 18:12-14.

It was the summer of my eighth-grade year, and I had no idea where I was going to go to high school. To be honest, I had not really given it any thought; I had put it completely in my mom's hands.

About halfway through the summer my mom sat down with me and told me about Mount Pisgah Academy and how there was a good chance I might be able to attend if I really wanted to. But to be honest, I didn't really want to go to a boarding school—I wanted to stay with my family. So the summer went on, and about two days before Pisgah's registration we jumped in the car and went to Walmart. There we got everything I would need for my dorm room and classes. While shopping, I realized how much this was going to affect my life and how I might not be able to have the comfort of my parents with me on a daily basis. Life would change.

Registration day had come, and I was scared. I registered, was assigned a roommate, and settled into what was to be a new home for a while. Within the first week, the new experiences slowly started to change me. I became more outgoing and responsible. And I made some great friends.

Fast-forward the story. I attended academy for four years, and it was a great experience. But something specific has happened to me that is even more amazing. I have realized who God is and that He has been searching for me. Before I started academy I had worshipped God my whole life, but I didn't have a reason for doing so. Now things are different for me. I have learned the importance of a daily, personal walk with God. Maybe it's because I had to become more independent and make choices for myself. But I know that I will never be the same again. Jesus is my best friend, and I'm glad!

The Story of John

By Jesse Nielsen

Even though I walk through the valley of the shadow of death, I will fear no evil, for you are with me; your rod and your staff, they comfort me.
Psalm 23:4.

I was raised as a missionary kid in Kenya, East Africa. My childhood was definitely an interesting one, not at all boring. I have so many stories from my experience overseas, but here is one that sticks out in my mind. This is a story about a 15- or 16-year-old teenager named John whom I used to know from the Masai tribe.

One day John was herding his family's livestock (as all boys his age did) in the vast savannah of the Masai Mara. Out of the silence came the bleating of one of his goats. Immediately he turned around, and to his horror, he saw a full-grown leopard snatch the goat and start dragging it up a nearby tree. In a flash, and out of sheer courage, John grabbed his spear and let it fly! The spear made its mark on the leopard, entering one ear and exiting out the other, immediately killing it. The leopard fell to the ground, dropping the goat. Fortunately, the goat was unharmed and returned to its family.

This story, of course, reminds me of the parable in the Bible that talks about Jesus being our protective shepherd. As our shepherd He will protect us from all evil. And He has gone through so much to ensure that we can have eternal life. We are so vulnerable on this earth—leopards stalk us every day. But remember that all we have to do is cry out for help. Jesus will hear our cries and run to our rescue. Every individual is important to Him, and He would, and did, give up everything for every person in this world.

Even though you walk through the valley of the shadow of death, you don't need to fear. Jesus will never leave you nor forsake you.

Trust in God

By Fabiola Diaz

Some trust in chariots and some in horses, but we trust in the name of the Lord our God. Psalm 20:7.

It seems that problems never cease, and when one problem is over, something else comes along to cause even more trouble. When I was younger, I decided that I wanted to be more independent, not in the I'm-leaving-the-house-to-live-on-my-own way but in an I-don't-want-people-to-worry-about-me way. I wanted to become someone who mattered and was important based on my own abilities. So when I faced hardships, I would try to get through them by solving them the way I thought things should be solved and managed. But that actually caused many more problems—sometimes I didn't have good judgment, and my decisions only compounded my problems.

Once, as I read my favorite story in the Bible, the story of Joseph, I began to wonder what it would have been like to say to God, "Take my life and do with me what You know is best." Just by that little decision of giving himself to God, Joseph became great.

As I considered that story, I realized that all we need to do is simply follow the path Christ has set for us. All those times I had become frustrated looking for an answer, all I had to do was pray, "God, please help me with this and show me what I'm supposed to do so I can glorify Your name in everything I do." Of course, not all answers are as direct as we'd like them to be. We may have to be in some pretty low times in order for God to use us and teach us a lesson. Joseph was completely humbled as a slave and prisoner before he was called to be the second in command of all of Egypt. But through all times, good and bad, he followed God's leading and stayed faithful to Him.

Now that I've realized this, I feel more free and liberated from all those burdens that I have tried to carry on my own for so long. There are still many problems awaiting me in life, but now I know I can rely on Someone to help me through them. Maybe I'll have to spend some time in jail, as Joseph did (although I hope not), but I know that God has big plans for me and will use me no matter what.

Immanuel, God With Us!

By Lilly Mitchell

For the Lord your God is a merciful God; he will not abandon or destroy you or forget the covenant with your forefathers, which he confirmed to them by oath. Deuteronomy 4:31.

What else could go wrong? My grandma was really sick; my grades were not good; and my friends were pretty much ignoring me. I was discouraged and didn't know where to turn. And the more I thought about things, the worse they seemed to get. I know it's not rational, but that is just the way the mind works.

I know that many people have felt this way. And I'm sure that I haven't always been the best friend to those in need. It's easy to be oblivious to other people's problems. I think that we often are just so busy worrying about ourselves and our own problems that we don't take the time even to look around and notice who else is in need. But fortunately, God notices.

And whether I realize it or not, God sends help to lift my spirits. Sometimes help has come to me from the least-expected people—people I may have turned my back on previously, or people who I didn't think even noticed me. Sometimes it is disguised as someone who was an acquaintance but whom I didn't really know well. Sometimes it's been a teacher or family member. But there we are, two people at the right time and in the right place—placed together to help encourage each other. Coincidence? No, it's a setup from God! He has promised to give us the strength and comfort we need at any time.

And if a human friend is not available, God will still help us through the hard times. The poem "Footprints in the Sand" says, "The times when you have seen only one set of footprints is when I carried you." I love that imagery. I'm sure God has carried me more often than not—thankfully, He doesn't get tired.

When I have difficult times in my life, I know that He will carry me until it's all over. He offers the same help to all of His children. Thank God today for His care and protection.

Why Is That So Wrong?
By Tiffany Rigdon

Likewise the tongue is a small part of the body, but it makes great boasts. Consider what a great forest is set on fire by a small spark. James 3:5.

Have you ever known someone who talks so badly about other people that no one wants to hang out with him or her anymore? Imagine that you and one of your close friends are outside sitting together. You notice that a girl who happens to think you are one of her friends is walking up the sidewalk. She, however, is not one of your favorite people. As she walks by, you give her a friendly smile, but as soon as she is out of sight, the smile fades to a disgusting look of dislike and bitterness. Even though the girl you have just seen has done absolutely nothing to you, you blurt out something about how you can't stand her, or something else you will later regret.

Sooner than you think, you keep going on and on about how you can't stand her, and before you know it, you've told nothing but lies about her. Later, when you are alone, the girl, whom you have said terrible things about, walks up and, with tear-filled eyes, confronts you and asks you why you are spreading rumors and lies about her. You are stunned that she has found out, and in shock you quickly deny everything she has just told you. She walks away knowing that you have lied to her face.

And then you begin to wonder, *Why is that so wrong? Who cares what I say about her?* Even though it seems to us as if no one cares if we gossip, there is Someone who cares. He created us all in His image, and no one is better than another. The apostle James said, "The tongue is a small thing, but what damage it can do." The trouble with our words is that once they are let loose, we no longer have control over where they go. So let's make a promise that the words we say today won't hurt someone else tomorrow.

One of Those Life-changing Experiences

By Stefan von Henner

Filled with compassion, Jesus reached out his hand and touched the man.
"I am willing," he said. "Be clean!" Mark 1:41.

This is a story about a friend of mine whom I will call Peter. He had a good life filled with happiness and joy, but one day he got in a terrible accident. As a result, his left leg was paralyzed. He became an invalid, and every day became one of hardship and pain for him.

After the accident he tried to keep living the same, but he became so depressed that he thought of suicide. The one thing that kept him going every day were the 23 stairs he had to go down and back up again once a day to do his laundry. Those 23 stairs were a great source of pain and agony for him, but he knew that if he could make it down and up again he could live one more day. Knowing that he was destined to live a life of great hardship, his bitterness and depression continued, despite the help his friends and relatives offered.

One stormy night as he was driving, he got a flat tire. Peter drove into the nearest driveway and called for help. The response he got was a little girl who said her father was getting dressed to help him. Quickly he saw the figure of a man coming toward him. He told the man, "I am a cripple and can't change the tire."

The man responded and said, "Happy to help."

As time passed Peter became more and more impatient. He yelled out, "What's taking so long?" Soon after that, he heard the clink of the tire as it came off. Then he heard some scrambling, and before long the job was done.

Peter stuck some cash out the window of the car to the man who had helped him. The man just stood there for a second or two until the girl said to Peter, "Daddy can't see the money."

All of a sudden Peter realized what had just transpired. The man then said, "No problem. Happy to help; I know you would do the same for me."

Are we willing to look past our own problems to help someone else? Jesus did not think about His own discomfort when He left heaven and came to this earth. Let Him use you to touch someone else's life today.

Helpless
By Aimee Garver

For he has not despised or disdained the suffering of the afflicted one; he has not hidden his face from him but has listened to his cry for help.
Psalm 22:24.

Not so long ago I thought I was going to die. It wasn't the kind of near-death experience that happens quickly and then is over. No, it dragged out over a period of weeks, and I could do nothing about it. You see, during the vacation months of June and July, I got very sick.

I didn't experience the kind of sickness that you get rushed to the hospital for, or the kind that you know what's wrong with you. All I knew was that I was in pain and that I wanted it to stop. If I ate anything, my stomach automatically rebelled. I could barely even sleep at night. My days were spent crying, begging and pleading with God to take the agony away.

The first doctor I went to didn't have anything helpful to say. He drew blood, did some tests, diagnosed me with a viral infection, and sent me home with pills for acid reflux. A week later I was no better. In fact, I was worse. My parents were really starting to worry, so they arranged an appointment with a gastroenterologist.

This new doctor did more in-depth tests. In the weeks that followed, I worried that I wouldn't make it to my next appointment, and I was terrified that I wouldn't be able to return to school in August. My helplessness consumed me. I felt that God had left me to fend for myself, something I'm sure the Israelites must have thought after every tribulation. Though God had certainly proved Himself in the past, they didn't think He was still with them. Like them, my faith was tested.

Finally, at my next visit the doctor explained that my misery was the result of stress. He prescribed some medicine to relax my stomach, and he said, "Don't worry so much." Looking back, I cannot believe it took me two months to get the picture. I can't depend on my weak, human self; the only One who can help me—and the One who will gladly help you—is God. Give your worries to Him and save yourself a lot of trouble!

Pride Goes Before a Plunge

By Alisha A. Michael

Therefore, as God's chosen people . . . clothe yourselves with . . . humility.
Colossians 3:12.

I climbed out of my car and drank in a delicious breath of ocean air. The waves beckoned from just beyond a rustling clump of sea oats. A smile crept onto my face at the thought of soaking up rays with no worries of studying or homework or tests. Ah, summer vacation.

Clad in my new bikini, I searched out the prime spot for sunbathing—a few strategic yards from the lifeguard's chair. I could sense him checking me out as I arranged my towel before heading to the water's edge.

While I splashed about like some bona fide bathing suit model, my conscience nagged at me. Was I really tempting him when there were a million half-dressed girls out here to look at? This was the beach! Wouldn't God understand? When Mr. Lifeguard flashed me a smile as I returned to my towel, I was far too satisfied. I brushed off my guilt. The Alisha Show was on!

Unfortunately, his attention was soon thoroughly diverted by several board-toting surfers who had gathered around his post to talk waves. After too many minutes of scratching at the dried salt on my skin in self-pity, I headed for the shower on the nearby boardwalk. I needed to rinse off and perhaps drown out that gentle, yet maddening, voice of conviction in the process.

Once I was soaked, I wove through the field of catamarans nestled in the ankle-deep sand near the dunes. I lifted my gaze from my feet just long enough to notice that the surfers had joined my admirer in observing my return. I decided I would toss my dripping hair and strut a few paces. As I held their gaze, I failed to see the rudder of one of the catamarans in the deep sand. The boys were looking at me, but suddenly I was looking at . . . the sand.

Yes, I had taken a Youtube-worthy nosedive right over that pesky rudder and directly into a full-on belly flop. A single Bible verse kept echoing through my mind as I lay there. "Pride goes before a fall . . . pride goes before a fall." Any pride I might have claimed fizzled when I extracted my face from the grit to see my "hero" rushing from his seat to dig me out.

As I drove home, scraped up and dirty, I knew this lesson in humbleness would stick like those gazillion grains of sand to my wet skin. I realized that putting on humility—as well as some modesty—seemed like a real drag, but it sure was a lot easier to wear than humiliation!

Even When You Don't Know It

By Emmanuel Cabrera

The angel of the Lord encamps around those who fear him,
and he delivers them. Psalm 34:7.

There are many stories about how God has somehow miraculously saved people from certain doom, many examples to let us know that God intervenes in situations that we are not able to control. But just because you may not have a story like this doesn't mean that God hasn't intervened in your life somehow. He watches over us whether we notice it or not, protecting us from things that we have no idea about, or things that are so small that they go unnoticed.

For example, what if someone is riding a bike and needs to cross the street but forgets to look both ways? What they will never realize is that at the last minute the driver of the car behind made a quick turn just before, thus saving the riders from being hit. Little things like this happen to us pretty much every day of our lives. We know about car crashes, but we never know about the ones that could have happened but didn't.

And so we go through our life, not knowing the things that could have happened to us. God saves us, and we keep going on, none the wiser. I'm sure there have been many potential accidents that we won't know about until we get to heaven and our guardian angels will tell us, "See here? If you would have been just a couple more feet in front of the stop sign, you would have been in a terrible accident with that speeding car. But I made that water bottle fall, and you picked it up and didn't even notice that you were spared."

Maybe it won't be things exactly like this, but I hope you understand what I'm trying to say. My suggestion is to pray and thank God every morning for getting you through the past day safely. Then you can ask Him to do it again today. I know that I will. I hope you will realize that God is always taking care of you, even when you don't know it.

Sisters

By Carolina Diaz

A friend loves at all times, and a brother [and sister] is born for adversity.
Proverbs 17:17.

When I was 2 years old, my mom had her second child. It was a girl, Fabiola. My first memory is of the first time I saw her. I was at my grandmother's house, and I saw my mom coming in the living room with something in her arms. It was my newborn baby sister. I didn't know that then, though; I thought she was the neighbor's kid! I was really excited to see such a cute little baby, and I quickly gave her the doll in my hands. It didn't take long to realize, though, that the baby wasn't going anywhere. And we've been together ever since.

We've always shared a room, and we are usually with each other. That is both good and bad. When someone spends too much time with another person, they usually get on each other's nerves. That's exactly what happened to us. The older we were, the more we fought with each other over the dumbest things. Slowly we stopped talking to each other.

Then I left home and started attending boarding academy. During vacation breaks things got better, and we talked a lot and became much closer. Then, in the summer between my sophomore and junior year, I asked her to come to the academy with me. We were both excited about it and have enjoyed our time at school together.

My family moves a lot—I've been in nine different schools. I'm used to always being the new girl and making friends who in a year or two would disappear because we would move again. My sister is the only girl close to my age who has always been there for me consistently. In all my best memories I was with her, and when I needed a friend, even if I was in a new town and knew no one, I knew she would be with me and sit with me the first day of school.

Jesus has given me so many great things, but my family and my sister are my favorite presents from Him. He loves me so much. He knew I was going to need a sister in my crazy life.

What's Best for You?

By Katie Thrash

My salvation and my honor depend on God; he is my mighty rock, my refuge. Trust in him at all times, O people; pour out your hearts to him, for God is our refuge. Psalm 62:7, 8.

God knows what is best for everyone. I once read somewhere, "God is making a beautiful tapestry. Right now we can only see the knots and tangles, but when we get to heaven we'll see the beautiful picture." This is something we can't even begin to imagine. Nothing we have ever seen will be comparable.

I have had a lot of things happen in my life that have hurt me, as I'm sure you have also. But I know that God is in control. He has sent me some amazing reminders that He still loves me and will never leave me. Primarily those reminders come in the form of caring family and friends whom He has placed in my path—people who have loved and prayed for me.

Recently I read a book that conveyed a more modern view of the life of Jesus and what He went through for us. It reminded me that when something bad happens to someone, they often blame God, but this is when God wants us to lean on Him the most. He knows that we are hurting and that we want something to fix it all—and that is God's "job," right?

But we must remember that sin, not God, is the reason for all pain and suffering. God too has been hurt by sin. He gave His only Son to die for us because of sin. Can you imagine the heartache He went through, letting Jesus come to this horrible world?

Though we may not understand our situation when we're in the middle of it, we need to trust God and remember that He will never give us more than we can handle. He will help us grow stronger through our adversity. And then one very special day in the near future, He will show us our beautiful tapestry—our life's tangles and knots that He has turned into a lovely masterpiece.

No Matter How Bad

By Ashton Evans

But now, this is what the Lord says—he who created you, O Jacob, he who formed you, O Israel: "Fear not, for I have redeemed you; I have summoned you by name; you are mine. When you pass through the waters, I will be with you; and when you pass through the rivers, they will not sweep over you. When you walk through the fire, you will not be burned; the flames will not set you ablaze. For I am the Lord, your God, the Holy One of Israel, your Savior; I give Egypt for your ransom. . . . Since you are precious and honored in my sight, and because I love you, I will give men in exchange for you, and people in exchange for your life. Isaiah 43:1-4.

When tragedies occur, feelings of anger, frustration, and sadness seem overwhelming. Over Christmas break my parents confronted me about something that dealt with a certain member of my family. My immediate reaction was anger—anger and hatred toward this person. How could someone so close to me betray me? This was someone I thought would always be there or should always be there in the important events in my life. She never was as active in my life as I would have liked, but I always hoped that one day she would change. But some people will never change no matter how much you want them to. Wishful thinking doesn't change reality.

When life overwhelms you, the best thing to do is lay everything in God's hands. I did that, and in time He took away my anger and sadness. I know that the Holy Spirit is knocking on her heart. All I can do is pray for her every day—pray that God will change her heart and mind.

I once heard a pastor say that bad things happen because the devil is not happy with where we are in our relationship with God. If bad things aren't happening, it's because the devil has nothing to worry about—He has already won us over. After I heard this statement, I looked back at this verse in Isaiah. Read it again.

God cares about us and will never leave us in our time of need. He is always there, waiting for us simply to come and cast all our problems upon Him.

Weeping With Me

By Haruka Mori

Jesus wept. John 11:35.

When there is nothing we can do and we feel hopeless, what do you think Jesus is doing? I was never sure of the answer before, but during one particularly difficult night I definitely understood the character of Jesus better.

The Saturday night before the SAT test, I was studying the SAT prep book in my room. A week before that, the ACT score had arrived by mail, and I realized how poor my English vocabulary was. (Japanese is my first language.) However, when I realized that the next big test, the SAT, was in a week, I felt that no matter how much I studied, I would not be ready and would probably do horrible on the SAT. After doing the English section of the practice test, my most challenging part, I graded it, and I was wrong, wrong, and wrong. Even though I tried my best to solve the problems, I did not have the ability to solve them. I needed to build up my vocabulary, but the test was the next day, and I had put so much pressure on myself. I wanted to do well on the test so that I could excel during my senior year English class. I had no idea what to do, and I started to cry.

After I finished studying, I prayed to God through my tears. "God, I know I'm not ready for tomorrow, and it is my fault that I'm not ready, but the test is tomorrow. Please help me." Then I heard the rain outside. I usually hate rain, but that night it reminded me of something that one of my friends, Shana, had talked about in worship. She thinks of rain as Jesus crying. That story came to my mind, and I felt as though Jesus was weeping with me. I never thought rain was so beautiful before that night. I never thought Jesus would cry with me when I cry, but now I believe He does. It is so comforting to know that God not only loves me but understands me.

Always know that Jesus is beside us, and when we are crying, He is crying for us too. He feels each sorrow we have had or will ever have. Our Savior, Jesus, has a warm heart, and He cares about us through all things.

Drowning

By Michael Brackett

When evening came, the boat was in the middle of the lake, and he was alone on land. He saw the disciples straining at the oars, because the wind was against them. About the fourth watch of the night he went out to them, walking on the lake. He was about to pass by them, but when they saw him walking on the lake, they thought he was a ghost. They cried out, because they all saw him and were terrified. Immediately He spoke to them and said, "Take courage! It is I. Don't be afraid." Then he climbed into the boat with them, and the wind died down. They were completely amazed. Mark 6:47-51.

I know what it's like to struggle neck-deep in water. I almost drowned when I was about 4 years old. The incident happened at my grandparents' house. My cousins and I were all swimming in the pool. I stayed in the shallow end because I was the youngest of the bunch and was still learning to swim. But I decided I wanted to be like the older kids, so I jumped into the deep end without any life vest on or anything. I immediately began to sink. Praise the Lord, my cousin Wayne saw me, came to the rescue, and saved me!

This world has plenty of scary situations just like that. You may not be struggling for your life in a swimming pool, but the devil has you neck-deep in troubles just as bad and worse. Maybe you jumped in over your head in a situation. Just when you think it's all over for you, don't feel alone.

When Jesus walked on the water, the disciples thought He was a ghost when they saw Him! In other words, they didn't think He was real! You're not dealing with anything that even the disciples themselves didn't go through. When you've hit rock bottom and you think that Jesus isn't real because it's not getting any better, when you can't hear anything and your body is weak from fighting the wind and the waves, Jesus speaks! He says loud and clear, "Be of good cheer; it is I. Do not be afraid!"

When you are drowning in the deep end, Jesus sees you, and He refuses to leave you helpless. He said He will never leave us or forsake us! And to top it all off, He will lift us up once and for all when we are caught up in the air to meet Him in the clouds at His second coming! He longs to rescue you—just reach out your hand!

Waiting While I Ran
By Sarah Grissom

My flesh and my heart may fail, but God is the strength of my heart and my portion forever. Psalm 73:26.

The sound of feet hitting the asphalt at a steady rhythm and cool air being breathed in, along with the unexpected silence around me, accompanied me as I ran down the street. I run to stay in shape, and it's how I deal with my emotions. Whenever I'm angry, devastated, or stressed, I deal with it by running. I run as hard and as fast as I can until I can't go any farther. How in the world does that fix anything? I know it doesn't change what has happened, but it gives me time either to not think about it or to get out my anger and frustration.

Early in the school year things were going great. I was doing well in my classes, I had great friends and a loving boyfriend, and I had the best job. Things seemed perfect. Then one night I got a call from my best friend saying he wanted to leave school. My head started spinning! I didn't know what to say or what to do; I was completely confused. I couldn't understand why he wanted to leave. So I did what I knew to do. I ran. I ran farther and faster than I have ever run in my life. Once I was at the point of complete exhaustion I went and sat in the campus gazebo. And that's when it really hit me. With tears running down my face and breathing becoming harder, I slowly began to realize what might be happening. My life might completely change. I started thinking about him not being around, and my heart started to break. The thought of getting to see him only for a few days during spring break and then some during the summer made me sick to my stomach.

He wasn't going to make a decision until after Christmas break. But all through break I struggled. I wanted to be a good friend and support him no matter what, but I didn't want to lose him. This decision was a real strain on both of us. Then, on January 17, when I was to the point emotionally that I couldn't handle it, I fell to my knees and prayed. Asking and pleading for strength, I opened my Bible, and it fell open to Psalm 73:26. And that's when I knew this whole time God was just waiting for me to stop running and ask Him to take my burdens.

We are not meant to struggle alone with heartache and confusion. Give your burdens to Him today!

Let There Be Light

By Rosella Age

You are my lamp, O Lord; the Lord turns my darkness into light.
2 Samuel 22:29.

In August of 2008 I moved into my academy dorm room and rearranged my furniture for the last time. I had two floor lamps, one a five-headed floor lamp with plastic round shades, and the other a single (and rather unappealing) lamp. I decided to light my room with the fun lamp, although the bulbs in it hadn't been changed since I bought it. I tucked the plain lamp in the closet along with my extra stuff.

One evening, several months into the school year, I was knitting comfortably on my bed when one of the lightbulbs abruptly sparked and went out. I screamed before realizing it was just a lightbulb. I didn't have any spare lightbulbs in my room, and since the lighting in the room seemed to be almost the same as before the light went out, I embraced the change and resumed knitting. About a week later I was busy in my room when suddenly another bulb sparked the last of its light and, after that one, another. I gasped, startled. Left with two light-bulbs to illuminate my room, I made the choice to conserve the remaining light by leaving my lights on only when I absolutely needed them. I always turned my lights off when I talked on the phone or even when I left the room for a short period of time. The lighting in my room was as insufficient as that of a cave. I couldn't locate things as easily or see how messy my floor really was. However, I adapted and learned to live in it instead of going to a store and simply buying some new bulbs!

This continued until mid-February, when the dorm students were informed that we would have girls from Great Lakes Adventist Academy staying in our rooms during Week of Prayer. Conscious of my dimly lit room and concerned for my new roommate, I asked around the dorm for a spare lightbulb. Upon receiving one, I rummaged through my closet and pulled out the ugly gray lamp and inserted the light bulb. I noticed that my room assumed a new ambience. What was once tenebrous and ambiguous was now clear.

Like neglecting my spiritual life, I allowed the lights to dim. It's difficult to realize just how great it is to be with God until you get Him back and realize how dark your life was. The only way to improve is to let God back in and allow His light to shine.

Friends Are Special

By Jaz Isom

A perverse man stirs up dissension, and a gossip separates close friends.
Proverbs 16:28.

The way we treat our friends is a very important subject to consider. It is easy for us to criticize how other people treat us, but we are often negligent in the way we treat other people.

Gossip is a massive problem in the world. Anything that can happen to someone can be, and often is, twisted into a terrible, blown-out-of-proportion rumor—all because of gossip. If we hear something about someone, friend or no friend, we should act as a caring and loving person toward them and not gossip and spread rumors.

Of course, nothing we do is isolated. Everyone watches our reactions and actions. If we show love and kindness to our friends, then the people we don't really know that well will more than likely want to be our friends just by watching our behavior. That attitude makes friendship more special. Even if that person doesn't become a close friend, he or she is still blessed, as opposed to having another enemy.

Some people are nice to new people they meet, but to their "friends" they're very sour and coldhearted. I think that happens because they are so concerned with their own appearances that they put on a show for those they don't know. Some people think that the only way to elevate their status is to put others down. This attitude is selfish and unkind.

Jesus, however, offered His friendship to everyone. He was considerate and caring at all times. He was even kind to those who were cruel to Him. Everyone saw how He treated others, and that selfless attitude drew more people to Him. People wanted to be His friend. He was a true friend who did not gossip or disrespect anyone.

Do you want to be like Jesus? Let's emulate His example and show love to everyone.

God Takes Care of Us

By Kyli Jung

Then I said to you, "Do not be terrified; do not be afraid of them."
Deuteronomy 1:29.

When I first came to America from Korea, I was afraid because I didn't speak any English. I was nervous about being in another country, away from all of my friends and family, away from my usual foods and language. I worried about how I would understand people.

I moved into the dorm, and I established a routine so that I felt more comfortable. Things were going pretty well, but then my tooth started hurting, and I had to go to the dentist. That visit was very confusing. I didn't understand what the dentist said to me. I didn't know what was happening, and I was a little afraid. Finally the dentist called a friend of hers who was Korean. The dentist's friend, Mrs. Kim, explained in Korean what was wrong with my tooth and what the treatment would be. Having someone who spoke to me in my own language helped a lot—I felt much more calm.

A few days later Mrs. Kim called to check on me, even though she didn't know me and we had met only that once! But she was so kind and generous. She invited me and some of my Korean friends over to her house to play traditional Korean games and give us a home environment. She thought we probably missed Korean food, so she took all of the Korean students to an Asian restaurant and paid for it. She still helps me—and now she has become like a second mother to me.

I believe God sent Mrs. Kim to me, because she has helped me so much. God knows everything we need, and He takes care of us even when we are in a foreign country.

Take time today to thank someone who has selflessly helped you. And also try to be a helper to someone in need.

That Day

By Alicia Evans

Consider it pure joy, my brothers, whenever you face trials of many kinds, because you know that the testing of your faith develops perseverance.
James 1:2, 3.

How many times a day do we face trials and think *Why is God doing this to me?* I'm sure all of us have had too many to remember. There are trials in our everyday lives we don't recognize as "God-given." And even though God may not cause them, He uses them to give us messages. When someone almost hits your car, God may be trying to say, "Look how fragile your life is." When your Taco Bell lunch goes wrong, God may be testing your patience. He wants our attention, and He'll do anything to get it.

I've had many trials throughout my life, some of them minute and some that gave me a big wake-up call. But one stands out above the rest. I was at Southern Adventist University with no direction as to what career path I would take. But I was happy—I had friends, and I was independent. Life was good! But one day I got a phone call from my dad. He wanted to know how I was doing scholastically. I hated to admit it, but my grades were poor, and my GPA was the lowest I'd ever known it. Dad was stressed because of our financial situation. He had decided that since I wasn't doing well, he would pull me out of school. He needed me to go to the office at SAU and withdraw. I had about a week before the last day I could withdraw.

Leaving my friends and independence was the last thing I wanted to do. I thought God hated me for sure to make me go back home. I became angry toward my parents. I knew that God wanted me to honor and respect them, but I had never known it to be so hard. I withdrew, packed up, and said goodbye to my "perfect life." Throughout the next few months I stayed angry at God and my parents. And then one day I just let it all go. I was tired of being unhappy. I decided to make the best of it, go back to school near home, and try to start a new life. I figured that God needed me to be home for a reason. So I decided to let Him do His thing instead of trying to achieve *my* perfect life.

Never forget that God loves you and has a plan—even if we don't understand it at the time. Learn from me: think before you speak, and respect and love others with all your heart. It'll all pay off on that day Jesus returns.

The Little Things

By Anna Grissom

Similarly, encourage the young men to be self-controlled. In everything set them an example by doing what is good. In your teaching show integrity, seriousness. Titus 2:6, 7.

For the past two years I have worked as a resident assistant (RA) in the girls' dorm. When I first got the job, I saw it as more of a witnessing opportunity than as a job, but that attitude did not last long. After a month or two of very little sleep, I started to see it more as work. Having to deal with people who did not listen to me, or even like me, was really hard—especially during my junior year.

At the start of my senior year, I thought that the year was going to be a lot smoother—I was a veteran RA. This was wishful thinking. If I thought that it was going to be an easier job just because I was a senior, I was very wrong. My senior year was as hard as, if not harder than, my junior year at the job. At the start of second semester, I really didn't feel as though I was doing a good job. I had been slacking off in hall worships, and I didn't really pray personally with any of my girls, so I didn't think that I was helping any of them. But then came Week of Prayer.

During the Week of Prayer I continued doing my job. I helped the deans when they needed me, and I checked to make sure that all of my girls were there at every meeting. After one of the night meetings, I saw one of my girls leaving. She did not look like her normally happy self, so I went over and gave her a hug. She started crying, and I just held her and let her cry. When she finally stopped, I asked if she was OK, and she said that she was and that she had just needed a hug. I really did not think much of it until Sabbath.

At Sabbath school they gave everyone a chance to share their testimony. The microphone was passed around the room as student after student shared what God had done in their lives. I was listening and really enjoying what my fellow students were saying. Then the girl I had hugged earlier in the week raised her hand. I sat up a little straighter to make sure I could hear every word. She talked about how my hug had made the difference. It showed her that there were people who cared about her. I just started crying. I couldn't believe that one simple hug could make such a difference—for her and me.

Don't ever doubt that God can use you to change a life for Him.

Party, Anyone?

By Lauren Cundiff

Therefore keep watch, because you do not know on what day your Lord will come. Matthew 24:42.

I was attending a leadership conference at Nosoca Pines Ranch, learning to become a better class officer, when my RA and friend, Anna, had her eighteenth birthday. Her family had invited everyone to join them on a pontoon boat for a surprise party and a ride on the lake later that afternoon.

I was feeling rather tired from the events of the past few days, so I decided to take a nap before I went; that way I would have energy for partying.

I was planning on taking a 15-minute nap, but I overslept and woke up to the flurry of one of the girls rushing into the cabin to grab a towel. Upon questioning, she hurriedly told me that the boat was leaving in two minutes, and then she swept out the door. I quickly jumped up, put on the first thing my hands touched, and stumbled out. Scampering onto the beach, I watched as everyone floated onto the lake without me. I yelled loudly and waved frantically, but I wasn't seen or heard.

It was then—as I was rooted to the ground, crushed with disappointment—that the parable about the 10 virgins snapped into my mind. They too had planned to go to a big party and had taken a power nap, but five of them didn't have extra oil. When they awoke, they found their oil lamps were out, while the other five girls went to the party. I realized that those five girls had missed their party, just as I had missed my party.

Likewise, we will miss the Lord's return if we are unprepared and "sleeping." We as Christians need to live our lives in such a way that we are always ready for the Lord's return. I believe that He is coming very soon, so let us not fall asleep and miss the signs all around us. Through our actions, thoughts, and words, we should anticipate Jesus' return! We have an invitation to an amazing party; let's not miss it.

Love Grows

By Noelle Stafford

Then the Jews said, "See how he loved him!" John 11:36.

Not so long ago God blessed my household with five beautiful, healthy puppies. With puppies come squeals. Those squeals brought the interest of my other dogs (the older siblings of the puppies). One of them, Squirt, looks at the other puppies and fears that the love her mother gives to her will now shift to the new "things." So she gets extra-clingy, whining whenever her mom goes in with the puppies and following her everywhere she goes to make sure she won't leave. On the other hand, Ricky, another dog, looks at the puppies with curiosity but accepts that he will still be loved the same. So he just sits and waits quietly for his mother to come back from visiting the puppies. He knows that the love for him will never dwindle because something new has come into the picture. He knows that her love only gets bigger—that she will always have enough, no matter how big her family gets.

Sometimes we are like both of these dogs. We don't always think that God can handle our problems. We think that He has too many other things on His plate and can't give us the time of day. So we try to handle our problems on our own. But this usually does not work. There are also those days (which are the best days) we trust Him completely and give Him all of our problems, knowing that He is the Lord of lords, the King of kings—He can deal with all of our problems.

So today and every day, remember that God is big enough to handle all of our problems, and that He loves us no matter what.

God Is Always There
By Shana Byrd

He determines the number of the stars and calls them each by name.
Psalm 147:4.

It was just one of those days. Everything seemed to be going wrong. My horrible day just kept getting worse. From finding out I was failing algebra to my boss yelling at me at work to finally making a fool out of myself that night. At the Acrosports' halftime show for the Bobcats game, I fell doing a cartwheel. For those of you who aren't gymnastics-savvy, a cartwheel is the easiest possible move to do. Therefore, me falling was extremely embarrassing. Where was God that day? I felt foolish and abandoned.

That night on the bus ride back to school, I decided to take a walk with God . . . to let Him reveal something about Himself to me that I had never witnessed before. I prayed and then took in my surroundings. I was on a bus with at least 40 other people who were all asleep. I looked out the window, up into the night sky. It was cloudy and dull, but then I saw a single sparkling star. Suddenly it hit me.

Although the world is full of pollution that distorts the beautiful vision of the stars, they are always there—nothing changes that. Some nights not a single star is visible, but on other nights the sky is a showcase of dazzling specks. This is the way it works with God. Some days you will see Him working through every little aspect of your life, but then on other days you wonder where He is.

We need to remember that like the stars, God is always watching. Even when all you can see is the dark smog that surrounds your life He is there, larger than life, and He will never leave your side.

Riding in that bus after a long, tough day, I realized that life is a gift, that my worst day is still a good day with Jesus, and that I might not have seen the star and received God's message had I been satisfied and asleep.

In the Beginning

By Thana Alley

In the beginning God created the heavens and the earth. Now the earth was formless and empty, darkness was over the surface of the deep, and the Spirit of God was hovering over the waters. Genesis 1:1, 2.

In the beginning God created the earth. We don't know why He decided to do it when He did, or what was going through His mind right then, but we know it was a creative and generous gift.

God reached down and started shaping the earth, breathing life into the void to create a bright and amazing world. But before that shaping began, earth was dark, formless, and empty. Darkness was everywhere.

Today darkness not only means a time you sleep, but it can also be representative of the devil. Think about it: most crimes happen during the dark hours of night; people do not feel as safe at night; predators like to hide under the cover of darkness; most scary stories are set in darkness. Satan specializes in things that are empty of all light. He is the total opposite of God. In fact, we know that God and darkness do not mix. In heaven we will not even need a sun—God Himself will be our light.

In our world of sin, darkness abounds. But it was never God's original plan for us to live like this. Despite humankind's sinful choices, God never leaves us. When we are struggling alone in darkness with family, financial, health, or friend troubles, we may forget that God cares for us. We may even feel as if He has left us. But we can be assured that He is everywhere at all times, for all people. He was there during the Holocaust, He was there during Hurricane Katrina, and He will be there at the end of time. He is there for us in all of our personal challenges. He will not leave us, even in our darkest hours. He wants to take us from the darkness into the light. If we turn to Him and His Word, our lamp, He will light our way and give us warmth, comfort, and hope—even through the night. He is waiting for us simply to accept His offer.

Show Me Some Action

By Jennifer Stollenmaier

"You are my witnesses," declares the Lord, "and my servant whom I have chosen, so that you may know and believe me and understand that I am he. Before me no god was formed, nor will there be one after me." Isaiah 43:10.

Growing up with most of my extended family not being Christians gave me a great opportunity to practice witnessing. With people so close to me who did not have a relationship with Christ, it really struck me that I needed to do something about it. I knew that quoting Scripture and making a biblical analogy out of everything probably would not have a very good impact on them. Instead, it would probably turn them further away from God and label me a fanatic. So I decided that my actions would speak a lot louder than words.

I prayed a lot about it and asked God to help me show His love through me in what I said and did. When I was around the family, I always tried to be aware of my actions. But it seemed as if I were not making any progress at all. Yes, the family respected me and my religion, but other than that, they were not interested.

Finally, after a couple of years, my uncle accepted Christ and became a Christian. It felt so wonderful to finally have someone other than my immediate family to talk to about God.

Even though most of my other relatives still do not have a personal relationship with God, I still see Him working through me to help show them what a great experience they can still have.

Though witnessing can be a scary thing, you can do it in so many different ways. In fact, sometimes it's the words we don't say (swearwords, anger-filled or critical words, etc.) that can make a bigger impact than what we do say. By witnessing through our actions, we can do it in a way that words cannot. Pray that God will use you today to be a witness for Him.

God's Glue

By Ashton Evans

For we do not have a high priest who is unable to sympathize with our weaknesses, but we have One who has been tempted in every way, just as we are—yet was without sin. Hebrews 4:15.

Honesty is the key in any relationship. Sometimes I forget how honest I can truly be with God. It didn't occur to me until my friends Stacy and Guerin encouraged me to be completely honest in my prayers.

I always thought that when I talked to God He couldn't tell how I felt or what I was thinking. Now, I know it seems ridiculous for me to have thought that, but it's true. I really believed that I could hide my true feelings from God. I thought God just wanted to hear all the good things and not the real issues in my life. It finally clicked in my head when Stacy and Guerin both reassured me that God can handle my honesty. He wants to hear what I am actually thinking.

Why withhold that information from Him? God already knows everything in this universe and more. But He wants to be our friend. And friendships can be strengthened only through complete honesty and trust. He wants us to feel completely comfortable with Him, so comfortable that we are willing to share every minute detail of our day with Him. It doesn't matter how bad, mad, or sad we are at God. He can handle whatever we throw His way.

I think we sometimes forget that Jesus Himself was joyful, frustrated, and even overwhelmed while living here on earth. He felt every emotion that we do. He knows how we feel—He can relate to us. He was tempted, yet He overcame and never sinned. And because of His experience, He is able to comfort and save us. We must open up our deepest wounds and let God piece us back together. His healing gift is available to us if we only ask.

No matter the situation or the emotion we may be feeling, God is waiting for His relationship with us to really begin. Be entirely honest with God. Let Him be the glue that holds us together. Honesty is the answer.

Do You Have a Holy Ambition?
By Kevin Worth

Being confident of this, that he who began a good work in you will carry it on to completion until the day of Christ Jesus. Philippians 1:6.

In eleventh grade a buddy and I decided to run together as student body president (me) and executive vice president (him). Then he changed his mind and wanted to run for president. I thought he was too ambitious and wanted all the credit, but I acquiesced, and we flipped positions. Maybe I wasn't motivated enough. In any case, what mattered is that we won the election and accomplished a lot our senior year.

I have always been irritated by ambitious people. And yet part of me envies their strong aspirations. Was I lacking desire and focus? Was I too afraid and simply chose an easier way?

Growing up, I spent way too much time playing video games and watching TV. I collected baseball cards, endlessly studied the player stats, and watched Red Sox games every day of each summer. I would spend countless hours playing basketball with the neighborhood kids, including running out to shoot a few buzzer-beaters during TV commercial breaks. These things weren't necessarily bad, but they were just things I spent too much time doing.

Truth is, I didn't have much ambition for God. Even when I felt spiritually nudged, I stayed in my comfort zone. I refused to surrender fully to God. Apparently I didn't understand that "God did not give us a spirit of timidity, but a spirit of power, of love and of self-discipline" (2 Timothy 1:7). But eventually the seeds planted here and there gave me some direction to stand up for God.

The author John Piper describes a holy ambition as something God has placed on your heart that you really, really, really want to do. Partly because of a past struggle with my belief in God, over time I have developed a new ambition. I am praying that it is a holy ambition to minister to Christian doubters, skeptics, and nonbelievers.

How about you? Is there something that you really care about—and that God cares about too—but you haven't pursued? God can give you the passion for it, and He will support you as you pursue His plans for your life.

You Don't Even Know

By Stephen Drummond

But he was pierced for our transgressions, he was crushed for our iniquities; the punishment that brought us peace was upon him, and by his wounds we are healed. Isaiah 53:5.

Have you ever lost a loved one? Well, I have. Of course, if you've gone through that experience before, you know that it's really painful and takes a while to recover from.

For me, I lost my aunt to cancer in March 2008. I received the news about her death after I came back from a mission trip to Panama. My trip had been wonderful. We had met amazing people and worked to bring them closer to Christ. Every night during the trip I had prayed that my aunt would get well. I almost felt guilty that I was having such a great life-changing experience in an exotic place and that she was suffering through so much back at home. Even though I prayed so hard for her healing, she died. It broke my heart to know she died while I was away having a fun experience for two weeks.

The day after I got the disappointing news my grandma comforted me and told me she was really sorry about what had happened. I know that she loved my aunt, her daughter, very much. She also told me that it won't be long until I see her again and that I will be able to spend eternity with her. Her reassurance made me feel better. We know that cancer was never part of God's plan. He never intended for us to get sick at all! Yet so many people suffer with so much. We must remember that Satan is the reason for all suffering. And that soon Jesus will return to save His faithful followers and take us to a place where there will be no more sadness, tears, or suffering—a place even more beautiful than Panama!

My grandmother's words also reminded me of Jesus' death on the cross. He died for us so that we can have eternal life. Jesus took the second death upon Himself for us. God loved us so much that He sent His only Son to die for us. That is unconditional love! And because of His love, we can spend eternity with our loved ones in heaven. Let us not waste His precious gift.

My prayer today is that angels will comfort all who are feeling the effects of cancer and sickness, and that we will all understand God's gift to us and His wonderful hope and promises as we look forward to His soon return!

When God Says So

By Jennifer Beckham

Then he said to me, "Prophesy to the breath; prophesy, son of man, and say to it, 'This is what the Sovereign Lord says: Come from the four winds, O breath, and breathe into these slain, that they may live.'" Ezekiel 37:9.

I love my mom with all my heart, and no matter what bad things I do, she'll always love me, too. My mom means the world to me. She is my best friend and the most amazing mom.

I never imagined living without my mom until things went wrong after she had surgery on her abdomen. The doctors weren't worried about her vomiting, because they said it was a side effect of the surgery. I became scared, though, because she seemed to be vomiting too much. Sure enough, when I came home from school one day, my aunt called and said that she was going to take my mom to the hospital because she was really sick.

The doctors were predicting the worst, and it felt as if my world were splitting in two. At first I thought that the whole situation was a dream, but when my mom's condition didn't improve, the weight of the whole ordeal hit me like a ton of bricks. My mom's left lung had collapsed, and it felt as if I'd already lost her.

I couldn't control anything. I felt hopeless—so hopeless and alone without my mom. So I did the only thing that my mom had taught me to do when things got tough. I prayed. I prayed my hardest during the weeks that she was in the hospital. I pleaded with God to please heal her and bring her back to me. It was hard to trust God, but I put my faith in Him, knowing that somehow, despite what the doctors said, He'd heal her.

To this day, the doctors don't know how my mom was healed, but I do. The breath of my heavenly Father was breathed into her left lung, and she was given another chance to live.

Our lives are always in God's hands. We may not understand why things happen, but I do know that He is in control and that things will happen when He says so.

Bad Day?

By Stephanie Thomas

So we say with confidence, "The Lord is my helper; I will not be afraid. What can man do to me?" Hebrews 13:6.

Do you ever have those kinds of days? The days that seem as if nothing is going your way, and you feel betrayed and all alone. Well, I recently had one of those days. The day started off as normal. The alarm went off, and I rolled out of bed, somehow found my way through my room, got ready, hopped in my car, and arrived at school right before the bell rang at the tedious time of 7:00 a.m. After lunch I went to my job in the library and had to deal with mindless drama. Finally 5:30 rolled around, and I left for home.

By the time I got home, I was completely exhausted. On top of the huge load of homework and school drama, I found out that someone whom I looked up to and was very close with did something that made me feel extremely hurt, betrayed, and lied to. I was falling apart. I was feeling sorry for myself—as if the whole world were turning against me. The questions flooded my brain. *Why does all of this have to happen? How am I supposed to deal with it all? I mean, I'm only a teenager, for crying out loud!* But in the middle of my pity party I remembered God. I had been so upset and busy worrying about all the bad things that I didn't even acknowledge Him. I decided to give my worries to my heavenly Father. I asked Him to be with me and help me get through everything.

I didn't get a miraculous answer right then, but I felt so much better and did receive a sense of peace. Over the next few days everything worked itself out. I got caught up on my homework, the drama at school died down, and I learned to forgive the person who had wronged me. I was still hurt, but I realized that everyone makes mistakes and no matter how bad someone's mistake is, that person deserves to be forgiven if he or she is truly sorry.

So remember that no matter how bad things may get, in the end everything will work out for good, whether you see it or not. God is always there for you—no matter what! You are His precious child, and He loves you very much.

Bread

By Brooke Wade

I am the living bread that came down from heaven. If anyone eats of this bread, he will live forever. This bread is my flesh, which I will give for the life of the world. John 6:51.

Bread. As one of the single most important foods on earth, every country, region, and culture has bread, in one form or another, as their staple food. The poorest people in the world rely on bread to survive. The importance of bread has spanned the changing ages of time, leaving God with no better way to portray Himself.

When Jesus said He was "the living bread that came down out of heaven," the feeding of the 5,000 was still fresh in the people's minds. As Jesus compared Himself to bread, the people remembered how He had multiplied the bread to feed everyone in the crowd. They realized that Jesus was all they needed to survive. He would grow and multiply, spiritually feeding them through eternity. Everything seemed clear until Jesus told the crowd the bread He would give to save the world was His flesh. How could Jesus expect the world to eat His flesh?

Jesus tells us we are to eat His flesh to live. Today we know this means to have a relationship with Him. We are to fill our minds, hearts, and spiritual stomachs with Him, letting our need for Him increase daily so we can more fully understand His greatness. When Jesus died, He gave us the ability to live forever. All we have to do is "eat" of Him. By accepting His gift of life, we eat His flesh and are guaranteed salvation. But accepting alone is like eating crackers at a feast. God provides us with so much spiritual food that we will never be able to eat all of it, but His challenge to us is to try. Every day we are asked to read God's Word, the bread of life, and to listen and talk to Him—the miracle that multiplies the bread. If we stuff ourselves with all the food Christ has to offer, our spiritual lives will be rich and abundant, making us able to fight in spiritual warfare.

Christ is our salvation. He compares Himself to bread to show us the importance of having Him in our daily lives. Without Him in our spiritual stomachs, we can hardly get through a single day, much less live for eternity. Jesus is the Bread of Life.

Shut Up . . . Shout for Joy!

By Stewart Rosburg

Sing joyfully to the Lord, you righteous; it is fitting for the upright to praise him. Praise the Lord with the harp; make music to him on the ten-stringed lyre. Sing to him a new song; play skillfully, and shout for joy. Psalm 33:1-3.

What is it that helps you worship God best? Is it music? Being still? Loud shouts? Nature? Silence? Do you "shut up"? Or do you "shout for joy"? I believe this psalm lets us know that both are appropriate responses to God's love and power!

For me there are times I just want to be alone with God and be still and know Him. Sometimes other noises can be distracting, and I just crave the silence and reflective communication that God is so good at. I often need just to shut up and listen for a while.

But at other times I want to sing joyfully, praise Him, sing a new song, play skillfully (whatever it is you play—yes, even drums and cymbals), and shout for joy! One of the highlights of my worship and praise of God is joining other musicians and lifting our hearts, minds, and souls to our Creator! This is what worship is all about, giving God the praise for what He has done, is doing, and will do.

To everything there is a season, including worship styles. Take time to enjoy all kinds of worship. Take time to "shut up" and have quiet time with God. And then, sing a new song, and "shout for joy." But above all, always lift Him up!

There's Only Grace

By Patricia Isom

In him we have redemption through his blood, the forgiveness of sins, in accordance with the riches of God's grace. Ephesians 1:7.

I have often asked myself, "Can God really forgive me? I'm a sinner, and I'm not worthy of Jesus' forgiveness." Then I stumbled across this amazing song "There's Only Grace," by Matthew West. This song points out a promise that we should all remember: "There's only grace, there's only love. There's only mercy and believe me, it's enough."

When you think you're not worthy of Jesus' forgiveness, remember that Jesus loves you with an everlasting love, and He yearns for you to repent and turn to Him. You are worthy of His grace. All you have to do is ask Jesus to forgive your sins, and He promises to make you new and whole again.

God Is Merciful

By Ricardo Garcia

I will have mercy on whom I have mercy, and I will have compassion on whom I have compassion. Romans 9:15.

Like most kids, I was given a big birthday party when I turned 1 year old. We had a lot of ice cream, and I, being a toddler with hardly any conscience, ate a lot of it. Since it was a celebration, no one worried about the amount of ice cream I ate. However, that night I got really sick, and my parents thought it was because I had eaten too much. They just gave me some tummy-calming medicine and did their best to take care of me.

The next day I got worse, and my parents and my uncles started to get really worried. So they took me to the hospital because I was not getting any better. In fact, I was actually turning a different a color—my mom said I was turning yellow. So they took me to the hospital, and the doctor told my parents that I was really sick and could even die. The doctor said that I had had a severe reaction to a milk product. No one had previously known that I was severely lactose intolerant.

While my parents stayed with me in the hospital, my uncles went to church the next day and asked my church family to pray for me. My parents also prayed that I would be healed and given a chance to live.

A few days later the doctors were amazed at my improving condition. I was actually getting a lot better, and my skin was turning back to its normal color. After about a week in the hospital, I got to go home. Of course, my parents had to change my diet—no more ice cream—and I've had to be careful ever since!

Remember that whenever you're in trouble or are worried about anything, as my parents and uncles were, turn to God in prayer. Remember that He is our Creator who loves us very much and cares for us. He really wants only what is best for us. And although it doesn't always work out the way we think things ought to, we should be grateful for every miracle in our life. I am very thankful for my second chance. I will not take it for granted.

Stress!

By Carolina Diaz

I am not saying this because I am in need, for I have learned to be content whatever the circumstances. I know what it is to be in need, and I know what it is to have plenty. I have learned the secret of being content in any and every situation, whether well fed or hungry, whether living in plenty or in want. Philippians 4:11, 12.

Going to school at 7:00 every morning, working a three-hour shift, going to after-school activities, and then going back to the dorm to work on homework can really fill a day! Family problems, friends fighting, boyfriend dramas, failing classes, tests to study for, and feeling sick but not being able to take the day off because of the need for more time for everything only adds to the stress. It seems like my to-do list keeps getting longer and longer—and the stress just keeps adding up!

At times during the school year I feel as if I am going to explode and that I can't do it all by myself. I need someone to help me. It didn't take me long last year to realize that I needed Jesus to be a part of my life and that I needed to let Him take my stress away so that I could feel better. When I started praying and asking Jesus to help me put order into my life, things changed for me—for the better! My favorite verse in the Bible is "I can do everything through him who gives me strength" (Philippians 4:13). It is such a great release to know that even though things may seem impossible for me to do, with Jesus nothing is impossible.

Jesus is now helping me find the true sources of my stress. By putting Him first in my life, I have a better grip of my priorities. He's helping me plan ahead, and He has even helped me adjust my lifestyle. Everything is a lot easier for me now. But when I think about it, I realize that I can't get completely away from all stress and worry. Some of it is good for me. I know the idea of not having anything to stress over sounds amazing, but with no challenges or tough decisions, where is the need for Jesus? I think that stress is a reminder that I need Jesus in my life—a reminder that He wants to take over for me and help me out.

Costume Party or Christianity?
By Michael Brackett

A truthful witness saves lives, but a false witness is deceitful.
Proverbs 14:25.

On a warm summer evening in 1978 a nice breeze was blowing through the open front door at a time locked doors weren't particularly necessary, especially out in the country.

As my mother began her triumphant walk down the long hallway back to the living room to relax after getting my brother and me tucked in, she heard, to her shock and horror, painful groans coming from around the corner, where the front door was wide open. Her first thought was that we lived in the country near a local prison. Her imagination ran wild, and rightfully so—there had been a few prison breaks in the years we had been there. The groans became louder as my mother froze in her tracks, right there in the middle of the hallway. Suddenly she saw a hand, low to the floor, reach around the corner. A body followed, crawling, groaning, and lurching forward ever so slowly on his hands and knees. The man was wearing tattered clothes, and his face was cut, with open sores plainly visible. One eye seemed to bulge out, as if it had been severely lacerated. This grotesque figure came closer and closer down the hallway toward my panic-stricken mother. She was so frightened that all she could do was back away from this monster and stammer out small screams of terror. She used the only weapon that she had—a simple flyswatter—to slap at this creature for all she was worth.

My mother would not have lived had my father not taken off his mask. (And it's a wonder that he lived after he did!) You see, Dad owned the most dreadful-looking mask I have ever seen. What made it so scary is the fact that it looked so real.

Do you wear a mask today in your church? Like my father's mask, these masks that we sometimes put on are very scary because they can look especially real. Are we going to a costume party, or are we being true in our Christianity? Jesus says in Matthew 13:25-30 that wheat and tares will grow together in the church until the end. I don't know about you, but I don't want to have a form/mask of godliness, denying the power thereof! I most assuredly don't want to be a tare. They look almost identical to the wheat. Pray that God opens your eyes to your condition. Take off your mask, find salvation in Him, and let His power take you to new heights with Him!

God Leads the Way

By Jacquelyn Plested

Teach me to do your will, for you are my God; may your good Spirit lead me on level ground. Psalm 143:10.

During the spring of 2007 I felt as if my life were falling apart. I had been home-schooled most of my life, which meant I was home all the time. My parents were going through some trouble, and I had a lot of other things going on in my life. I felt as though I just needed to get out of the house.

As summer began I had to decide where to go to school that fall. I had a couple of choices, but was leaning toward homeschooling again because I didn't like the other choices. I prayed so much, asking God to show me where to go. God did not seem to show me, and summer was about to end.

One day a friend told me about Mount Pisgah Academy and mentioned that I should consider going to school there. So I decided to visit and see what it was like. We made the arrangements to visit the very next weekend—only three weeks before school started. I liked it from the moment I arrived. The staff was great, and the summer student workers were very friendly. After we arrived back home, I had to make my decision. I kept feeling this urge to choose MPA, so I ended up attending my junior year.

Living on a campus in a dormitory turned out to be one of the hardest things I'd ever done. I was so far away from home, and I was not able to go home for most of the breaks because of my job. I was so homesick. I considered quitting and going back home several times, but I just couldn't, because I had this feeling I was supposed to be at the academy. I got through the year. I opened up little bits at a time to those around me, and I even ended up becoming an RA in the dorm my senior year.

Looking back, being in a Seventh-day Adventist academy was the best thing that could have happened in my life, in spite of the challenges. I have learned so much from my experiences there. God obviously knew where I was supposed to be. I just had to be patient for Him to show me.

I encourage you to trust God to lead in your life. He will always lead you if you let Him, and it is totally worth it!

Uh-oh!

By Joseph Meneses

I know that you are pleased with me,
for my enemy does not triumph over me. Psalm 41:11.

God never leaves us. Whether we're tempted, in danger, or just going through hard times, He comes to our aid.

One day during my eighth-grade year I stayed after school to play basketball as usual. That day I was playing with some kids I didn't know very well. When we were finished playing, one of them took out a bag with "green stuff" in it. I immediately knew what it was. I was nervous and wanted to get out of there fast.

Quickly I prayed a simple prayer: "God, please help me overcome this." They offered me some. I politely declined, and they walked away without any further pressure. I was relieved. I did not want to be in that situation.

The devil is always trying to trap us and make us do stuff we think is harmless, but underneath it is corrupt. And the world wants us to think that such things are normal. That is part of Satan's trick: everybody is doing it, whether it's drugs, sex, cursing, etc. We are bombarded with media that implies not only that such behavior is harmless, but the message is that if we don't do it, something is wrong with us. Don't listen to the media—and don't listen to your friends if they are into that kind of stuff.

The Bible says in Matthew 7:13 and 14, "Enter through the narrow gate. For wide is the gate and broad is the way that leads to destruction, and many enter through it. But small is the gate and narrow the road that leads to life, and only a few find it."

That is why it is important to have a close relationship with God. He will help us and lead us through that narrow gate if we simply ask Him. We need to be those "few" so that we can have the strength to overcome anything that may come our way.

Blazing Words and a Blistered Witness

By Alisha A. Michael

The tongue . . . corrupts the whole person, [and] sets the whole course of his life on fire. James 3:6.

This outfit is just right!" Many times I'd made this very assessment of my favorite summer top and cutoff jeans. Although my shorts were more appropriate for home or the beach, I wore them to school anyhow. No other set went with my teal-colored tank so perfectly. My best friend would shake her head and make predictions about which teacher would write me up.

"It'll never happen," I'd say. "An honors student can get away with anything."

But one spring day during my senior year those haughty words came back to bite me.

I had never met the girl, but I can still see the smirk on her face. She had just stepped from the classroom I was heading into when she screeched to a halt and eyed me up and down, then she shouted to our teacher. "Mrs. P! Mrs. P! Those shorts she's wearing are against the rule!"

Of course, she meant the very rule my pal had so often warned me I was breaking. If shorts didn't reach the tip of the middle finger when one's hands were by her sides, they were considered too short. My teacher inspected my clothing and informed me I was violating dress code. Embarrassed, I argued that if they were too short, it was just barely.

Mrs. P wouldn't hear it. My thumping heart pushed boiling blood through my veins as I glared at the tattletale grinning at me over our teacher's shoulder. Abandoning restraint, I pointed my finger and spewed curses and insults all over her. The words I said make me blush even now.

By the final bell, everyone knew. The honors student who professed to be a Christian had flown into a verbal tirade and would suffer the infamy of a day of not-so-honorable suspension. How my mouthful of burning words had set the school on fire with gossip! As well as my life. The scandal damaged my witness for Jesus in a way even tearful apologies couldn't mend. How could a girl who loved God speak blessings one minute and brutally curse people out the next?

Although I received much grace and forgiveness, at my 10-year high school reunion some still hadn't forgotten. I had burned them with my thoughtless words, leaving a scar that would sting each time they saw me. I've certainly learned the power of an unrestrained tongue!

He Will Heal Us

By Andrew Grissom

He heals the brokenhearted and binds up their wounds. Psalm 147:3.

On a November afternoon I decided to pick up the *Reader's Digest* that always sits on a side table in our living room. I usually don't read this magazine, but for some reason I decided to read it that day. While browsing through it, I came across a story that demanded my attention. It was "Maja's Dream," by Jennifer Rawlings.

Maja was best friends with her cousin Jasmina, but she unfortunately lost her to leukemia. After Jasmina's death, Maja swore that she would swim with dolphins to honor her cousin's dream.

Tragically, in 1993 during the Bosnian civil war in Yugoslavia, a mortar shell was fired by the Croat separatists and exploded in her backyard. Her six friends were killed. Maja was severely injured. She was taken to a makeshift hospital, where they were forced to amputate her left leg. There was no anesthesia to dull the intense pain. Maja recalled this experience, saying, "They tied me down and put a piece of rubber in my mouth to bite on. I could feel everything." Her wound became infected, and she had to be flown to the United States in hopes that antibiotics and more sophisticated care would save her life.

After spending two long years in a Florida hospital, she was given a prosthetic and released, but this didn't make her happy. Being an athlete, she would try to play a round of golf, but the exertion resulted in pain for days. To unwind, she would go to an aquarium and watch the dolphins swim. Finally, one day there was a bright spark of hope in her eyes. It happened the day she met Winter, a dolphin that had had its tail cut off in a crab trap. Researchers had fitted Winter with a prosthetic tail so that it could swim more efficiently. Mesmerized by this, and feeling a strong connection to the dolphin, she knew she had to swim with him. And she was given that chance. For hours the two swam together. Maja said, "I felt as though I owed someone something, and now I've paid my debt."

A lot of tragic things happen, but good things can always come out of them. God promises to heal our hearts and our wounds. So no matter if you are going through something small or if it is something life-changing, such as losing a leg, God will send blessings your way.

Perfection

By Anna Wurster

Not that we are competent in ourselves to claim anything for ourselves, but our competence comes from God. 2 Corinthians 3:5.

Honestly, I don't think I will ever be good enough to meet my own standards. I can never seem to satisfy myself. I'm very insecure, like many other people. I lack self-confidence. My whole life I've put so much pressure on myself to make good grades, to wear the right clothes, to make the right decisions, to be friends with the right people, to be perfect.

I used to attend public school, and I was so concerned about fitting in. I would pick out my clothes the night before just to be sure I had the perfect outfit for the next day. I started playing sports that I wasn't interested in so that people would think I was more talented. I would tease other kids and gossip about everyone. I changed everything about my personality to be friends with the cool girls. I wanted to be accepted. It worked. I fit in with the right clique, and I was "perfect." But I wasn't happy.

The next school year I left home and enrolled at Mount Pisgah Academy. In my new surroundings, my priorities slowly began to change. I found that it was possible for people to like me for the person I am, no strings attached. I started to think, *What is perfect? How do you define perfection?* By definition, to have perfection is to be free of all flaws. This world is full of flaws. That's what sin is. In my opinion there is no such thing as perfection, with one exception, Jesus Christ. And Jesus doesn't care if you make straight A's or if you always have the coolest clothes. Those things aren't going to get you into heaven. All He is concerned about is building a relationship with you. You just have to be willing to let Him into your life.

I don't try to fit in with the right crowd anymore. I don't have to live up to anyone's expectations. I don't have to fit any mold. I don't have to worry about what my peers think of me, because their opinion isn't relevant. I can be whoever I want to be, and that is a child of God.

Nothing Is Impossible With God
By Ashton Evans

Jesus looked at them and said, "With man this is impossible, but not with God; all things are possible with God." Mark 10:27.

The Bible conference at Cohutta Springs Camp was a blast, with the exception that I tore my anterior cruciate ligament (ACL) while tubing. I had thought that everything was fine and that maybe I had had only a bad fall. I was wrong. My parents encouraged me to get an MRI to make sure my knee wasn't seriously injured. When I went into the orthopedic doctor's office, I was expecting him to tell me everything was fine, just a minor strain in my knee. I was wrong again. He came into the room and told me immediately that I had completely torn my ACL, the main ligament in the knee that keeps the leg from buckling. The way he said it so nonchalantly made it feel so unreal. I couldn't believe this was happening to me. I was the acrobatics team captain at Mount Pisgah Academy at the time, and my doctor was telling me that I couldn't do any physical activity for six months! I just felt like curling up in a ball and crying.

I had surgery about a month later. Everything went smoothly except for the fact that I missed about two weeks of school. When I came back, I had eight back assignments in precalculus plus an entire essay to write for College Composition 101. That was only the start of the back work. I broke down halfway through the week and started crying out to God for help. I realized that I could not do everything myself. I needed help from the only One who could truly make things better.

The week continued on, but it progressively became smoother. Some of my classes that met every day were canceled or let out early. That act in itself was a miracle. I was able to turn in all my back work within two weeks. Physical therapy felt like a breeze as well. The first couple of visits were rough, but after I decided to let the Lord take care of me, I felt increasingly positive about everything. My physical therapist told me that I was ahead of the curve and doing very well for having had the surgery only a month ago. Things were definitely changing.

God allowed me to tear my ACL for a reason. I believe that reason was for me to realize that He is here for me no matter what. I can't do everything myself, but God can do anything.

Trust Him

By Brittany Tompkins

*The Lord is my strength and my shield; my heart trusts in him,
and I was helped. Psalm 28:7.*

Starting over can be very difficult. If anyone knows what starting life over means, it's me. A few years ago my parents made the tough decision to move 583 miles away from my home in Orlando, Florida, to what would be my new home in Asheville, North Carolina.

Ever since I was little all I had known was Orlando. That was my home and it always would be, at least so I thought. Everything I ever knew would be left behind, and a new life was about to begin for me and my family. But I was not looking forward to a move—I was 16 and did not want to start over.

As the big move grew closer we started packing, and I tried to spend as much time with my friends as I could. I knew it would be hard to leave them behind, especially my two best friends, who had always been there for me. I was also going to leave my mom behind temporarily. I thought about how I would have to make new friends with people I had never even met, and that scared me. Starting at a new school in the middle of my sophomore year was very terrifying. I am very friendly, and I like making new friends, but I still knew that it was going to be tough. But I always told myself that God had a plan for me.

I have now been living in North Carolina for several years, and I really love it! I feel as though I have adjusted well and made many good friends. I love my school, and I think that God knew that Mount Pisgah was where I needed to be. I do miss my old friends, my old school, and my family, but I visit often, which makes things a little easier. And all in all, I'm glad that my parents made the decision to move.

Everything happens for a reason, for God's reason. I am thankful that He has led in my life and in my family's move. Things have worked out really well. And I am glad that we are in North Carolina. Trust God—He has a special plan for you no matter if you can't see the good in it at first.

Fight Together

By Clint Martin

You will not have to fight this battle. Take up your positions; stand firm and see the deliverance the Lord will give you, O Judah and Jerusalem. Do not be afraid; do not be discouraged. Go out to face them tomorrow, and the Lord will be with you. 2 Chronicles 20:17.

One night I watched the movie *Remember the Titans.* Something that the coach in the movie said has stuck with me to this day.

The coach woke up the players early one morning for a run. He took the team to where the Battle of Gettysburg had taken place. While at Gettysburg, he gave a speech about working together as a team. One of the many things he said was "If we don't pull together as a team, we all will fall."

This statement got me thinking about how some people go out and try to fight their battles alone. You can try fighting alone, and some people may win. However, most battles are fought as a team and won as a team of two or more people.

If Christians would take Jesus with them everywhere they went, the devil would not have a chance against anyone. However, if we go out and try to fight against the devil by ourselves, the chances of winning the battle are zero—we will always lose against the devil. In order to win the battle against sin, we need Jesus on our side.

I admit that I do not always ask God to be with me. But even if I'm neglectful, He does not leave me. He is ready and willing to help. I just need to be willing to ask for His help.

God states, "I'll never let you down, never walk off and leave you" (Hebrews 13:6, Message). So remember, if you ask for God's help, He will be at your side ready to fight with you. And with God on your side, you are guaranteed a win!

He Brings It Back—*Twice*

By Callie Adams

And my God will meet all your needs according to his glorious riches in Christ Jesus. Philippians 4:19.

My husband and I have a certain amount of money designated in our budget for giving. It's not much, but for us it's one of the fun parts about paying bills. We sit in our living room rubbing our hands together and scheming about who we are going to help with our little donation this month. We had been giving to the same organization for a while, and I had an automatic check that was being sent from the bank to that place. It went out right after we deposited our monthly paychecks.

One month after the check had already been sent but had not cleared the bank, we learned of someone who could really benefit from our little donation budget. We decided to go ahead and use it. Silly me did not think about the fact that my automatic check had already gone out to the previous organization. I went and withdrew the entire budget amount in cash and delivered it to the new recipient. This meant that we had given *double* what we normally gave. After discovering my accounting mistake, I worried and fretted. Should I ask for the money back from one place or the other, or should we go without paying some other bill that month? What if we went ahead and paid all the bills and the grocery budget ran out before the next paychecks arrived? I decided not to ask for the money back, and to pay all the bills, and let God worry about our groceries that month.

The very next day I was talking to my grandfather on the phone, and I was saying that we were putting away money for a new crib for our expected baby. He said he wanted to buy the crib as a gift, and he put a check in the mail for the amount of the crib that day. When I received the check, it was for double the amount of the crib and four times the amount of the budgeted giving. God had brought my donation back to me twice and with a new crib to boot. At the end of the month, we didn't even need to break into the money to buy groceries, so I put it into a savings account. I was so thankful. My friend Beth told me that was God's accounting.

Why So Shameless?

By SangHyuk Lee

You shall not steal. Exodus 20:15.

It was 1:00 in the morning, and everyone in the house, except me, was asleep. That is when I made the most stupid decision I've ever made.

I carefully crept from my bed, trying not to wake anyone up, and went to the room where my mom and sister were sleeping. With a wicked smile on my face I carefully rummaged through my mom's purse. "H'mm . . . there it is!" I carefully and shamelessly pulled out my mom's wallet and stole 300,000 won, the equivalent of US$300.

The next morning, trying to hide my evil happiness from my parents, I quickly left for school. I still remember that day as the fastest school day ever, because I was planning how to use the money I had taken from my mother's wallet. Later I heard from my dad that both my parents were in a panic that morning after I had left for school. Mom had found that the money was missing and was frantically looking for it. (It was very important, because the money had to be returned to her workplace.) In their search they found the stolen money in my room.

I usually hung out with my friends after school until 6:00 or 7:00 each evening before riding back home by bus, but that day my dad came to school to pick me up. On our way home he asked me about school and wanted to know how everything was going. I didn't realize that he was hoping that I might confess to him what I had done. Finally, when we were about five minutes away from home, he stopped the car and asked me if I had anything to tell him. I said no. He drove a few more minutes and asked me again, but I still said no. Then he told me that he already knew everything and had hoped that I would tell him myself.

I cried. I cried in my father's chest as loud as I could. All the shamelessness I had had suddenly came back to me as regret. But my parents still forgave me. They forgave me even though I had stolen the money and had confessed only with prompting.

This experience taught me how great their love is for me. What is amazing to think is that God's love for us, including a child like me, is greater than any love any person can give. I thank God for my parents, who taught me a very valuable lesson that day.

Almost Heaven

By Chelsea Campbell

And if I go and prepare a place for you, I will come back and take you to be with me that you also may be where I am. John 14:3.

It was a beautiful spring day at my home in Asheville, North Carolina. At the time I was almost 3 years old and was playing in the backyard while waiting for my dad to come home from work. My mom was getting supper ready. The sun was getting low, and it illuminated a beautiful, fluffy cloud silhouetted against a deep-blue sky.

My dad arrived, and I looked up into the sky and exclaimed, "Look, look!"

Dad turned around and said, "Look at what?"

I pointed at the cloud and said, "Jesus is coming in that cloud and will take us all to Florida!"

In my 3-year-old mind Florida was the best place in the world. You see, my grandparents lived there, and I always enjoyed going to see them. Dad, of course, told my mom, and that night I heard her talking with my grandparents on the phone. She told them what I had said. My grandfather thought the story needed to be shared. (Yes, I think that he was proud of me.) So he sent the story to Letters to the Editor at the Orlando *Sentinel*. To everyone's delight, they printed it, and the newspaper gave the story the name "Almost Heaven."

They printed the story just as it happened, telling about the "large bright cumulus cloud" and my words, "Look, look, Jesus is going to come, and He is going to take us all to Florida." No doubt I had heard about Jesus' return from my parents and at Sabbath school. "He was taken up; and a cloud received him out of their sight...[and he] shall so come in like manner" (Acts 1:9-11 KJV).

Today, I don't want to go to Florida; I want to go to heaven with Jesus and live in that beautiful home that He has made for you and me. As great as Florida is, it cannot compare to the experience that heaven will be. I can't wait to see *that* cloud!

Miracles Do Happen

By Chloe Howard

"'If you can'?" said Jesus. "Everything is possible for him who believes."
Mark 9:23.

Have you ever wondered if miracles really do happen or if they are just myths? I found out the answer to this question when I was about the age of 4. When I was young, I had constant earaches. My parents never really thought much about it until things got worse. We were riding in the car on a trip when I suddenly burst into an extremely loud cry. My mom quickly looked back at me and saw that my ears were crusty and had pus coming out of them. My dad, being an ER doctor, took a look and knew my eardrums had ruptured. He put me on different kinds of antibiotics in hopes that the earaches would go away. However, nothing changed, and even though they were praying, my parents knew they needed to do something more.

They took me to a local ENT (ear, nose, and throat) doctor. He took one look at my ears and recommended surgery to have tubes put in them. The ENT doctor scheduled a surgery date for one week later. It was soon and overwhelming, but I knew I had to do it. If I didn't go through with the surgery, I could become deaf. The very next day, while my dad was at work, he randomly met a natural medicine specialist whose name was Dr. Block. She believed that everything should be done naturally and with no antibiotics. After my dad told her about my whole situation, she told him she could help me. So I immediately started a weeklong treatment plan that consisted of no antibiotics, no dairy products, and hourly massages of my ears with vitamin E and evening primrose oils, which were to remove the impurities through my lymphatic system. The massages were extremely painful in the beginning, but as the days went on, they actually began to relieve pain and clear my ears. Toward the end of the weeklong treatment, I began to feel much better. My parents took me back to the ENT doctor, and he could not believe what he saw. My ears were completely healed, and there was no sign that I needed the surgery. I was cured!

Although I was young, I still understood what God did for me. No matter how big or small the situation, God can and does perform miracles (sometimes through the capable knowledge of godly people). Never, ever give up on Him.

Everyone Wants a Savior

By Jacob Ballew

Why are you downcast, O my soul? Why so disturbed within me? Put your hope in God, for I will yet praise him, my Savior. Psalm 42:5.

Everyone wants a savior—someone to lean on, to cry on, to look up to, and to be there for them. It's obvious in our world of sin and hurt that we need someone to rescue us from our problems. Every day people have situations that they are not happy to be in. Admit it or not, we need someone to pick us up and rescue us. Look at the media. An overwhelming number of movies or shows feature someone good fighting against evil and saving people. These "heroes" go through great hardship to save their loved ones. They sacrifice their well-being to help others. Some even give their lives.

People look up to these saviors, and it makes them feel good, protected, and safe, but these lifesavers are not perfect. They sin, have problems, and do evil things, just as the rest of us do. Since these saviors are only in movies, it leaves us with the sad reality that they aren't real. So who rescues us in real life when we lose a loved one or a job or face a life-threatening situation? Whom do we turn to? Will someone in colorful clothes come and save us?

I don't know about a man in colorful clothes, but I do know of Someone who will save us. Jesus Christ! He wants to help us with our problems. Every time something troubles us, He is anxiously waiting for us to call to Him. Jesus came to this earth not long ago and died for us so that we wouldn't have to face eternal death. He gave His life for us, and yet people don't appreciate it. All He asks us to do is accept Him as our Savior.

One day soon Jesus is going to come again. He is going to save us from this hurtful earth. He'll take all of our sin and pain and cast it into oblivion. Jesus made us and died for us, and all He wants from us is love and acceptance.

Will you accept Jesus today? It isn't too late to give Him a chance. Let Jesus come into your life and change it for the better. I promise you He will take all the sorrow you have and get rid of it. He wants to love you and take care of you. Put Jesus in your life today and let Him be your Savior!

An Unexpected Gift

By Noelle Stafford

He replied, "If you have faith as small as a mustard seed,
you can say to this mulberry tree, 'Be uprooted and planted in the sea,'
and it will obey you." Luke 17:6.

One summer I worked as a counselor for FLAG (Fun Learning About God) camp. To prepare for our jobs, we had a staff week in which teams from Michigan, Virginia, and North Carolina came together at one base camp. The staff week was held at the North Carolina base camp, where I was scheduled to work the rest of the summer.

The first morning of staff week, while all the other teams were traveling to our location, we had to clean everything. By the time everyone got there I was exhausted, and I still had a while until I could go home.

We ate supper and then headed over to a local church to have a "sat and chat," which is an activity in which everyone gets in two big circles facing each other; then one of the circles rotates so everyone can meet everyone else and learn more about the other team members. Before we did the "sat and chat" we had a little worship.

FLAG camp has a lot of songs that are unique to the camp, and my favorite one is "If You Have Faith Like a Little Seed of Mustard." This song is very active and fun—it reminds me what a little bit of faith can do. In one part of the song when everyone jumps up and moves the way the mountains do when we have faith. That night not very many people were in the spirit to jump up when it was time, but there was one girl from the Michigan team who jumped up and started to do the actions. When she did, it really made my night. The fact that she did not care that she was the only one, no matter how silly she looked, really helped me change my attitude, along with a lot of other people.

This reminded me that no matter what the situation we can always be used for God's benefit. All we need is a little faith, and God can help us move any mountain that needs to be moved, whether we are ready to do it or not. Have faith; be bold!

He's Been Hit

By Rebekah Doying

Are not two sparrows sold for a penny? Yet not one of them will fall to the ground apart from the will of your Father. Matthew 10:29.

Rebekah, get off that phone now! I need to call the vet. Murray has been hit by a car!" My mom yelled as she burst through the door. I immediately hung up without giving an explanation to my friend on the other line. Quickly my mom dialed the numbers. In a blur we loaded into the car, with Murray and me in the back seat. I looked down to meet his droopy eyes. Blood was gushing from his nose, and his breathing was short and painful. The top of his head was all smashed and cut. His white fur was crimson. My eyes darted away; there was no way I could handle seeing this. My baby dog had been hit by a car.

We had just gotten back from our annual summer vacation with our family in South Carolina. We wanted puppies, so we had gotten Murray a girlfriend while we were on vacation. Her name was Maggie, and she was a beautiful black-and-white English springer spaniel just like him. They had barely been together for 15 minutes when Murray had been hit. I was crying as we took him from the car and carried him into the vet's office.

My soul was crushed. I had had that dog since I was 5 years old. I was so mad at God. Every day I cried, prayed for healing, and asked God why my innocent dog had been hurt. After a week of waiting, I decided that God didn't care about healing my dog. People in my church told me they were praying, but I felt it wouldn't do any good. Finally, after a week and a half of long, anxious days, Murray came home. The vet said he had fractured his skull and would have breathing difficulties for the rest of his life. But we still have Murray to this day, and he ended up having nine little babies.

I realize now that God does care. He may not fix the situation as soon as we'd like or exactly how we want it, but He does care! The Bible says that God knows every time a sparrow falls. How much more does He care about you and your family pets? When you feel as if life has hit you the way the car hit Murray, realize that God will not forsake you, even in the hardest times.

You Are My First Priority

By Fabiola Diaz

Be devoted to one another in brotherly love. Honor one another above yourselves. Romans 12:10.

We live in a world that promotes finding our own achievement and reaching personal goals. Getting rich and having the best status in society seems to be all that matters these days. But is this really what we are meant to do? The Bible tells us to love and help each other, like the early church, so that none may be in need.

One of my favorite Bible characters who always comes to mind is Jonathan. Jonathan was Saul's firstborn and was heir to the throne. In ancient times it was normal for the sons of the king to battle each other to gain the throne. Many would kill their brothers and their own fathers to gain rights to it. Selfishness is rooted in the heart from the moment we are born, and competition plays a significant role in our world.

However, Jonathan, heir to the throne, was different. He was not self-centered and envious, nor was he indignant at what fate had torn from him, something that now belonged to David. I can imagine him as a boy, daydreaming about being king. From his childhood he had been raised with the belief that he would occupy the throne one day. That was his future. But that disappeared when God rejected Saul's kingship and when David then showed up. He was even told by Samuel, "As long as the son of Jesse lives on this earth, neither you nor your kingdom will be established" (1 Samuel. 20:31). Jonathan knew that David was in line for the throne, but instead of turning against David and attempting to take the throne by force, he was kind to him, befriending his rival and providing protection from his father's ambition to kill David.

Jonathan knew that God had chosen David as successor to the throne, but he did not resent it. He understood that the key to one's own success depends on doing God's will, and so he devoted himself to help David reach his given place as king. Jonathan did not think of his own future. Instead, he focused on God's plan for himself and David, his friend.

There are many people in the world who think of just themselves, but God looks for those who humbly reach out to others. He is looking for those who will put Him and others before themselves. This is the character of God.

You Never Know When Your Dream Might Come True

By Aimee Garver

I will pour out my Spirit on all people. Your sons and daughters will prophesy. Your old men will have dreams. Your young men will have visions. In those days I will pour out my Spirit on those who serve me, men and women alike. Joel 2:28, 29, NIV.

Everybody knows about dreams in the Bible. Jacob, Joseph, Daniel, and Nebuchadnezzar all had impressive dreams. Does God give real people dreams today? Are dreams important?

I've always been a dreamer. My dreams are colorful and full of detail, and they have always had a real impact on me. But I never imagined that someone else's dream could have a serious impact on my life until I heard the following story.

One dark night about the year 1905, a young mother named Francis Mullinex had a strange dream. In this dream she was greeted by two men who presented her with a book that was surrounded by a shining white light. When she awoke and told Peter, her husband, neither one could make sense of it.

Some time after that, two Adventist colporteurs knocked on the door of their western Nebraska home. As they began their canvas, the young mother immediately recognized the book that they were selling. It was the same book she had seen in her dream! After purchasing the book, *Bible Readings for the Home*, she was convinced that God had given her the dream so she would learn the truth about Him. Eager to learn more, she asked for Bible studies. Following the Bible studies, Francis, her husband, and their three children were baptized, joining the Seventh-day Adventist Church. This devoted wife and mother was my great-great-grandmother!

When the prophet Joel wrote, "In those days I will pour out my Spirit on those who serve me, men and women alike," he had no idea that my great-great-grandmother would be given a dream by God that would influence many generations to follow Him. Most people don't think about God actively intervening in their life by giving them a dream, but God cared enough about that pioneer mother and all her descendants to do just that!

If it hadn't been for that dream and its impact on my family, I most likely would not be a Seventh-day Adventist Christian. The Lord works in mysterious ways, and He will use whatever means necessary to get His message through to His children—even in the middle of the night!

I Remember You

By Guerin Williams

The Lord will keep you from all harm—he will watch over your life.
Psalm 121:7.

In November 2008 our academy acrobatics team went to Southern Adventist University for a gymnastics clinic. One afternoon, since nothing was planned for a few hours, some of us from the team were playing around on the trampoline floor. A trampoline floor is a track of trampoline that is raised off the ground and is used for tumbling. I was doing some tumbling on the floor and practicing some different flips. Everything was going well until I misjudged where I was on the track.

I was doing a bunch a flips in a row, which are called whip backs. I was going to tumble to the end of the track and then do a flip onto the mat at the end. I did probably five or six whip backs before I got to the end and then attempted to do a flip onto the mat. I did the flip fine, but I had hit the end of the trampoline floor, and it had shot me back. My butt hit the end of the mat, and the momentum of the flip slammed my head onto the gym floor. I don't know exactly how long I was out, but the people who saw it happen said I was knocked out for 20 to 30 seconds.

Once I finally came to, I got up and plugged in my phone. I know that sounds pretty random, but it must have been what I was thinking about before it happened. After I plugged in my phone, I walked around for a while to make sure I felt OK. I took a few painkillers, and I felt all right. I praise God that He kept me safe, and the only injury I got was a concussion. Our performance was that night, and I felt OK to perform, so I went ahead and did. That probably wasn't the smartest idea, but God kept me safe through the performance as well. I then took it easy for the next week or so.

I know God was watching over me and keeping me safe, because my injuries could have been a lot worse. God is always watching over us and keeping us from harm, and I thank Him for that every day.

What Are You Worried About?
By Bob Vaughan

You will keep in perfect peace him whose mind is steadfast, because he trusts in you. Trust in the Lord forever, for the Lord, the Lord, is the Rock eternal. Isaiah 26:3, 4.

In the spring of 2007 we were living in the little town of Swansea, South Carolina. I had loved my job in Columbia, and we had lots of really great friends. We were comfortable in our home. God had been very good, and life was, in the words of our son Matt, "pure lushness."

Then things got complicated. My wife and I both knew God wanted our sons to continue with their Adventist education during high school. And after much prayer we were both confident that He wanted us to move near Mount Pisgah Academy, our conference boarding school, to help support their school experience. But there were two enormous hurdles: First, would I be able to find a job in a tight market? Second, at a time when a real estate crisis was rapidly unfolding, would we ever be able to sell our house? We laid it all at God's feet and prayed that if He really wanted us to move to the Asheville area, He would open doors for us.

With the very first phone call I made about a job, God made it clear that we were within His plan. Yes, there was an opening. Yes, I would fit nicely into the spot. And yes, they wanted an interview right away. In short, hurdle number one was only a memory.

When our real estate agent asked about showing our property on Saturdays, Satan filled my mind with excuses: it wouldn't really be work for us; it was for a good purpose; Saturday was the most convenient day for buyers to see the house, etc. But we felt sure that His plan would not involve breaking His law, so we decided not to show the house on Sabbath. The best part about the decision was that it took the stress off us and put it on God—instead of guilt, we felt peace.

The first two months were slow. Nobody seemed to be interested. Doubts about God's will, and our part in it, crept in. I prayed for more faith and for the courage to trust Him. Then, in the third month, God stepped in again. We got an offer. Not the kind of lowball offer almost always given these days, but an offer at the full asking price! God completely blew us away.

I'm no spiritual giant. I have doubts, fears, and too many weaknesses to mention. But God looked beyond all of that and showed me a small glimpse of His everlasting strength. Trust in God no matter what, and in His awesome power you will find perfect peace.

Amazing Escapes

By Jessica Koobs

Now I know that the Lord saves his anointed; he answers him from his holy heaven with the saving power of his right hand. Psalm 20:6.

USA Today reported the following story in December 2001: "The walls, the ceiling, and bookshelves crumbled. [George] Sleigh, 63, manager of technical consistency at the American Bureau of Shipping, crawled from the rubble. He looked up at the exposed steel beams and the concrete underside of the 92nd floor. He didn't know it at the time, but that concrete floor was the bottom of a tomb for more than 1,300 people. Nobody survived on the floors above him. But on his floor and below, an amazing story unfolded: Nearly everyone lived.

"The line between life and death that morning was as straight as a steel beam. Everyone on the 92nd floor died. Everyone on the 91st floor lived.

"When a second jet hit the south tower 16.5 minutes later, the pattern was virtually the same. In each tower 99 percent of the occupants below the crash survived. At the impact area and above, survival was limited to just a handful of people in the south tower who made an amazing escape.

"Four hundred seventy-nine rescue workers died making the evacuation a success. The sacrifice of New York firefighters and police is well known. But 113 others, from low-paid security guards to white-collar workers at the Port Authority of New York and New Jersey, the buildings' owner, stood their ground with firefighters and cops."

Even though this was a very big tragedy, organized by a force of evil against our nation, God still saved a lot of people, and maybe through the stories of those who died someone came to God. We won't know all of the stories until heaven.

We need to live our lives as if any moment may be our last. We must serve and help each other. We should never forget the great tragedies of others and be prayerfully sympathetic to their trials. And we need to make sure our priorities are in order at all times.

Where Was God?

By Rebecca Busche

Do not let your hearts be troubled. Trust in God; trust also in Me. John 14:1.

It was September 11, 2001. As soon as I woke up, I went downstairs, turned on the TV, and saw a huge building on fire. I was only 11 years old, and I didn't really know what the twin towers were. I kept flipping through channels, but I saw the same story again and again. What had just happened? Who did this to our country? Why was there no warning? Where was God?

The World Trade Center had been struck by two planes, and clouds of smoke and fire rose from the tops of them before they collapsed. Terrorists had just threatened our country with violent attempts to destroy our whole nation. People were jumping out of windows and running for their lives as the buildings began to crumble. There were cries for help and prayers being said by everyone. Every eye was watching this horrible tragedy happen, but there was nothing anyone could do about it.

So many lives were lost on that day, but our nation came together and became stronger because of it. In a way, it made us all aware of how fast our lives can end without warning and how we need to make God a part of our lives before we run out of time.

We know through prophecy that things will get worse in this world before they get better and Jesus comes back. We need to strengthen our faith and build up our spiritual muscles while we are in relative safety, knowing that we will need to draw on that strength during difficult times to come.

Do not ignore God's call. He wants to save you from the impending and ultimate destruction to come. He has marvelous plans for your life and wants you to have every advantage.

As our country remembers the horrendous event that happened the day before in 2001, pray for our future and your future, and know that God will soon end all suffering and death. Soon we can be with Him forever in heaven.

Death Is Hard

By Stephanie Hill

Blessed are those who mourn, for they will be comforted. Matthew 5:4.

Death is such a hard thing to understand. It can bring your world crashing down in seconds. It causes you to think unexplainable thoughts and do unexplainable things. It causes you to reach such an emotional low you think you may never laugh again. You think you may never recover.

Not so long ago I went through this when one of my closest friends passed away. When they first told me he wasn't going to make it, I was in complete shock. I had seen him two days before, and he was fine. Now I was being told that he was on his deathbed. They told me he had meningitis and his brain was dead. He couldn't hear us or see us. They said the only thing keeping him alive was a ventilator. In that one moment my safe and ignorant little world fell to pieces. I felt so helpless. I prayed and prayed for a miracle. I held on to the little bit of hope I had that he would make it. When they took me into his room in the hospital to say goodbye, I broke down sobbing the moment I saw his face. He looked so helpless, so vulnerable. He was attached to so many machines just to keep him breathing, just to keep him alive. I went over to his bed and held his hand; it felt way too cold. I stood there for a little while, and suddenly his hand tightened around mine. The doctors told me it was a muscle spasm, but I think he was saying "Goodbye; see you soon."

I was comforted by the thought that I would see him soon. I may miss him now, but I know that I will get to spend eternity with him.

One day we will have no reason to be afraid of losing someone. There will be no reason to cry. We will never have to feel vulnerable, scared, or hopeless again. It may feel as if the world is against us, but God is here and He is helping us. He is preparing a better place for us—a place where we don't have to worry about losing the ones we love, a place where we won't have to be comforted, because there will be no pain. No matter how much pain and suffering we go through on this earth, God is always with us. He never leaves our side. He is with us every step of the way. And soon we will get to spend eternity with our Lord. In the end it is all going to be OK. One day we are all going to be OK.

All the Small Things
By Ian Brewer

For everyone who asks receives; he who seeks finds; and to him who knocks, the door will be opened. Matthew 7:8.

I'm pretty good at saving my money. However, I recently experienced my first real money problem. The senior year of high school is very expensive, and not only for parents. With senior class trip, banquets, and graduation expenses to cover—not to mention my girlfriend, whom I love to buy gifts for—I was broke.

With so much to pay for, I didn't know what to do. I spent a few days ignoring it, going about my normal business, before it occurred to me one night that I should ask God to help me solve my financial crisis. I immediately prayed and asked God to provide me with the money I needed. My motives weren't selfish, so I figured it was a good prayer and I had a pretty good chance of something happening. By the next morning I had forgotten about my request.

That day I was walking the halls of my school when I chanced upon $12 lying on the ground. I picked it up, and not thinking of my prayer, proceeded to ask the closest people how much money they had lost. When I asked Mr. Pelto, he searched his pockets, pulled some bills out, and told me he supposed he'd lost about $10. I said, "Well, this must be yours then," and handed him the money.

For no reason at all Mr. Pelto said, "No, no. It's a finders-keepers thing. You keep it. In fact, here's the rest," and he put three more dollars in my hand.

That night my parents called to tell me they had just transferred $30 into my account, because they figured I would need it. All I could do was thank them, hang up, and sit in wonder at all the riches that were suddenly mine. God had answered my prayer, and it was that simple. I could plainly see that God really cared about the small things in my life and that He was there for me. God is there to answer your prayers no matter how cosmically small the matter may seem.

Choose God and Follow Him!

By James Kim

"Come, follow me," Jesus said, "and I will make you fishers of men."
Mark 1:17.

In life we have many choices, and we have to choose what path we are going to take. For instance, I chose to follow God in my life, but it wasn't the easiest decision to make.

In 2006 I played soccer a lot. I played soccer so much that my grades dropped and my parents were disappointed in me. I played soccer every Sunday. My friends and I made a team, and we met every Sunday and played games with other teams. I usually left home at 8:00 in the morning and didn't get back home until 5:00. I was so into soccer that I really wanted to become a professional soccer player, and I got the chance.

It was Christmas Eve 2006, and our team joined a tournament with about 24 other teams. This tournament was a famous tournament that soccer scouts came to in order to find good players to recruit. Our team played the first game, and we won 7 to 2—I scored three goals. After the first game, the coach of a high school team came to me and gave me his number and said, "If you want to be a soccer player, please call me." I was really happy. I had finally been given the chance to be a soccer player. But if I took him up on his offer, I knew I would have to give up keeping the Sabbath. I was struggling.

A few days later I went to my church as usual. The pastor preached about Exodus 20, and I saw the verse "Remember the Sabbath day by keeping it holy." After I read this text, I suddenly felt that I must choose God and not become a soccer player, because God is my Savior, and He sent His Son to forgive me.

After I made my decision to follow Him, I lived a better life. I lived more spiritually than before. I have a personal devotional time every morning and night. I have never regretted my decision to follow God, and I have confidence that this choice is the best choice that I've ever made in my life.

From Trumpets to Tubas and Solos to Symphonies in the Concert of Life

By Jonathan P. Michael

But I say to every one . . . not to have an over-high opinion of himself, but to have wise thoughts, as God has given to every one a measure of faith. For, as we have a number of parts in one body, but all the parts have not the same use, so we, though we are a number of persons, are one body in Christ, and are dependent on one another. Romans 12:3-5, BBE.

What's the most important instrument in a concert band or symphony orchestra? If I had been asked this question during my seventh- or eighth-grade years, I would have proudly answered, "The trumpet, of course." That's mainly because this was the flashy, commanding instrument I had chosen to play. I wanted my answer to be the same my ninth-grade year, but a lot had changed in my life by then. It was supposed to have been the year I reached the top of the totem pole at my junior high school. I was going to be a big, strapping freshman on campus. (OK, so big and strapping is quite a stretch, but don't miss the point.) Instead, I headed off to an Adventist academy and found myself as a low man on the totem pole in high school.

The Bible says, "Pride goes before . . . a fall" (Proverbs 16:18). And I kept falling. Two weeks before going to academy, I got braces. With my lips still puffy and my gums always sore, I found it almost impossible to play the trumpet. By the end of my disastrous audition before the academy band director, I knew I was in big trouble. I was used to being second seat, and assistant section leader, in a long line of trumpets. Now I was being told that there was no seat at all in the long line of trumpets fit for me, but there was a seat behind the trumpets. The director needed a tuba player! From trumpet to tuba? It made sense—larger mouthpiece, easier to play with braces—but now I felt I was behind the totem pole, or maybe even under it.

Come to find out, I learned a lot playing the tuba. And I learned even more by viewing things from my seat in the back. It was a transition from pride to faith. I now believe every place on the totem pole is needed, every seat in the concert band is important. It takes every person playing every part in every seat to make a concert happen. Pride thinks of the solo. Faith thinks of the symphony. Every person's gifts and talents are needed to make the music happen. God is the conductor, welcoming us to the concert of life. He's hoping we'll each faithfully take our seat, no matter what instrument is waiting there, and join Him in making the music!

The Wind

By Nicholas Ewing

Who comforts us in all our troubles, so that we can comfort those in any trouble with the comfort we ourselves have received from God.
2 Corinthians 1:4.

One beautiful Sabbath afternoon a family packed a picnic in their backpacks and went for a hike. It was a perfect day with a little breeze. They drove about 30 miles on a back road and then parked the car. They had hiked for about two hours when they decided to stop and eat. While they ate, an extremely strong wind came in. At first it was not anything to worry about, but within five minutes it grew into quite a strong windstorm. The wind was so strong that it blew their food and backpacks away. They hopped to their feet and started to chase their belongings. They chased the backpacks until they were blown off a nearby cliff. The father was quite upset because his bag had contained his wallet, which held lots of cash and his driver's license. As they started to leave the side of the cliff, the wind suddenly stopped. This further irritated the father because the timing was frustrating.

With his emotions running wild, the dad let a bad word slip out of his mouth. His little boy immediately said, "Hey, that's not how God wants us to act; I am sure everything happens for a reason." The dad laughed it off, and they started hiking back. Eventually they got back to their car, drove to the house, and started to clean up for the night. That night the family prayed that the wallet would be found, and then they fell into a restful sleep because of the exhausting day they had experienced.

The next day the father went into town and saw that there were posters around that said someone had found a wallet. The father got excited and went to the address that the poster said. When he got to the house, he could not help feeling sorry for the family that lived there, because it was not an actual house—it was a shed filled with six children, two dogs, and a mother. He got out of his car and asked the woman if she had found a wallet. She said they had and showed it to him, asking if it was his. He said no, but thank you. As he handed the wallet back to her, he took out his driver's license and went on his way.

That night he told his family what he had done and how God had used the wind to help out the family in need. He apologized to his family for saying what he did and for losing his temper.

God can use even the wind to help us help others. Let Him use you.

Caught-Off-Guard Moments

By Katelyn Gonzalez

For the Lamb at the center of the throne will be their shepherd;
he will lead them to springs of living water. And God will wipe away
every tear from their eyes. Revelation 7:17.

Some people say that when a disaster happens, God isn't there. They say that when terrible things happen to us here on earth, God leaves us and forgets all about us. It is almost as if to say that God doesn't care about us, His created beings.

Well, I'm not one of those people, and I want to share with you why I believe otherwise. God will never leave His children when we need Him most. Just as Revelation 7:17 reminds us of God's presence and comfort, there are other ways to get the same feeling of encouragement. For example, I love the poem "Footprints in the Sand," because I truly believe that God carries me when I am too worn out to walk. But there is something you have to do. You have to let Him carry you. You have to give Him all of your burdens and troubles. I know you have already heard all of this before, but have you actually tried it? Have you been real with God? God gives us these caught-off-guard moments to make us stronger, not just mentally and physically, but also spiritually.

When I was 11 years old, my grandmother had quadruple-bypass heart surgery. Now, I had never had anyone close to me go through something so serious before. I started praying for her health and for the hands of the surgeons. The surgery was a success, and she is still doing well today.

That surgery was a caught-off-guard moment for my whole family. With the help and strength that God gave us, we were able to get through it and grow closer and stronger as a family. But the best bonus was that my grandmother recognized and acknowledged that the gift she had been given, a second chance at life, was from God, not simply from the surgeons.

About two years after surgery, my father, her son, baptized her into the Seventh-day Adventist Church. The whole experience helped us all grow spiritually and gave us a new appreciation for blessings in the midst of adversity.

Life With a Purpose

Leena Zepeda

And our hope for you is firm, because we know that just as you share in our sufferings, so also you share in our comfort. 2 Corinthians 1:7.

When I was growing up, I thought God was unfair for making me different from the other kids who belonged to good families with two loving parents. I blamed God for giving me parents who apparently hated each other. When my parents got divorced, I felt as if my world had fallen apart and that I was never going to be happy. I also wanted a baby sister, but since my parents were no longer together, that seemed impossible. I thought that I might always be envious, or even resentful of my family situation. I prayed about my life, but from my perspective I couldn't see how things could change. It's been more than 10 years since I last saw my dad, and more than 12 since my parents got divorced. Most of that time I still thought my life would never get any better.

However, things have changed for the better! A few years ago my mom remarried, and since then I've had a wonderful and complete family who loves me. I have a stepdad who cares dearly for my mom and for me, and I am so grateful for his place in our lives. And then the bonus came—I now have a baby sister. What a blessing to our family and an answer to prayer. I love being a part of her life.

All these events in my life have shown me that good things can come out of bad situations. You may have to have a lot of patience, and God may not always answer the way you expect or want, but know that He does want what is best for you. If you are going through terrible things or you're struggling with something that doesn't seem to have a solution, know that God has a purpose for you, even if it takes 11 years to realize it.

Recruiting

By Josh Cundiff

Commit to the Lord whatever you do, and your plans will succeed.
Proverbs 16:3.

My school has a program in the summer called the "recruiting team." It's made up of a group of eight students who spend their summer touring around North and South Carolina. They ride in a shuttle and travel to different towns helping people where help is needed. I have been on the team for the past few summers.

Even though we're called the recruiting team, most of what we focus on is helping churches and families. We've done everything from helping people landscape their yards to preaching evangelistic series. Halfway through the summer of 2008 we spent a week at the Seventh-day Adventist church in New Bern, North Carolina. That was probably the hardest week of my life.

Every day we'd wake up bright and early and go outside and work. The church needed us to repaint their parking lot lines. It would have been easy, maybe even fun, if we had had the right tools. But all we had were rollers and some duct tape. We were out there sweating on the hot pavement for hours. Then toward the end of the day we would go inside, change, and help run a Vacation Bible School program. We were completely exhausted by the end of the week. At first, I didn't see how painting a parking lot and playing a few songs for kids could help anyone; it seemed like pointless, time-consuming work. But at the end of the day the people who attended the New Bern Seventh-day Adventist Church told us how much we were appreciated, and they even brought us food. All of our hard work had been worth it.

I think we did more work at that one church than we did the rest of the summer combined. It was frustrating to work in the heat, and a lot of times I wanted to quit, but we worked together and got the job done. The funny thing is, when it was all said and done, we were closer to the people in New Bern than to anyone else. We took care of them, and they took care of us. Because we worked hard and served the Lord, He blessed us and used us to be a blessing to other people. Try giving your time and energy to bless someone today, and I'm sure God will bless you, too.

The Opportunity of a Lifetime
By Josias Flores

From that time on Jesus began to preach, "Repent, for the kingdom of heaven is near." Matthew 4:17.

Heaven is the one thing that nobody should miss out on. Unfortunately, many people will miss out. Heaven is the place where everything good that you ever wished would happen can happen. The best thing about it will be being with the One who loves us most in this world. Are you excited? Can you feel the anticipation of those around you?

I had not been to Venezuela, my home country, in about five years, but during Christmas break of 2009 my family and I had the opportunity to go there for a visit. As we counted down the days, we were filled with excitement and anticipation. We were looking forward to seeing a lot of family members whom we had not seen in a very long time. These were family members we loved and missed. Our separation from each other over the years had not diminished our love for each other, but it made us appreciate, even more, the opportunity to visit and hug them once again. The excitement was almost too much to hold in.

Why can't we feel this kind of excitement about heaven? Is it not the most important thing on your list of life goals? It is on mine, and it would be great if everyone thought the same way. Get to know the Savior today—love Him, obey His voice, and don't ignore His pleas. Do this and obtain the opportunity that only a few people will accept—the gift to live in a perfect place with other people who sought to do God's will and, even though they stumbled once in a while, came out on top with God's help.

My challenge to you today is to ponder heaven for at least five minutes and think of all the good things you are looking forward to. And then decide how you will spend your day so that you will share the excitement of God's love and promises. Most important, though, think of the Savior, Jesus Christ, and His sacrifice on the cross for all of humanity. Heaven is full of opportunities, a chance for eternal happiness, and no more pain, sorrow, or tears. Don't miss out.

The Greyhound Revelation

By Joy Shin

The Lord Almighty has sworn, "Surely, as I have planned, so it will be, and as I have purposed, so it will stand. Isaiah 14:24.

On one school break I rode the Greyhound bus from my aunt's house back to campus. Since I had never ridden in a Greyhound before, I was pretty scared and worried. I was afraid that I might miss my bus or lose my luggage. As I boarded, I decided to sit in the second seat from the front because I didn't want to be in the back, where it was dark and ominous. Once I got comfortable I looked around to see who my "neighbors" were. I was surrounded by a very assorted group. As I settled into my seat, I looked out the window.

Riding around the city of Atlanta, I was fascinated by the diversity of the people. I saw busy executives, homeless people, thugs, rambunctious kids, and lonely-looking elderly individuals. Sitting there, feeling alone in a crowded bus, I realized that God has style. Every one of us has special qualities and characters that make us individually different. I can tell you that there were some unique people on that Greyhound and on the streets of Atlanta. But the thing is, God loves them all as much as He loves me.

During my ride people got off and on the bus. At one stop a woman with bright-red hair got on the bus and sat in front of me. As soon as we started moving, she took out her phone and started to call someone. I didn't want to get into her business, but I couldn't help hearing her conversation. She was crying and repetitively apologizing to the person on the line. I obviously didn't know her or what she was going through, but I felt sorry for her. That's when I realized that God has a special plan for everyone. God cared about this woman and whatever she was going through—she was not alone, because God was with her.

Someone once told me, "God doesn't have a plan B. God only has a plan A." We just need to follow His will, and we'll be OK. Whatever you are going through—depression, addiction, family troubles—He is always there to lead you to the right path. I still don't know what the red-headed woman was going through. In fact, I don't think that I will ever encounter her again. But what I do know is that Jesus will not forsake her. Every person is important to Him. And I know He has plan A laid out for her and for me. I pray that we will follow His lead.

Where to Find Courage

By Kaylee Couser

When the disciples saw him walking on the lake, they were terrified. "It's a ghost," they said, and cried out in fear. But Jesus immediately said to them: "Take courage! It is I. Don't be afraid." Matthew 14:26, 27.

In 2009 I spent the best summer of my life serving others. I was chosen as one of 16 Mount Pisgah Academy students to spend the summer going from church to church helping with VBS programs, community service, and various other projects. During one week in Hillsboro, North Carolina, my team conducted an evangelistic series. I had never spoken in front of anyone before, so as you can imagine, this was very terrifying to me. This was not at all my idea of fun. I wanted to run away. In an attempt to destroy my chances of having to speak, I decided to try to get sick. I ate a lot of sweets and prayed that I wouldn't have to speak. But even though I thought I couldn't speak, God knew that I could. In no way am I perfect at public speaking, but the thing with God is that He does not need perfection. All He needs is your willingness to serve—He can then use you in a mighty and powerful way.

In Hillsboro I was put out of my comfort zone. But even in my imperfection, God used me to reach other people. He turned my weakness into strength. One of my favorite Bible verses is Philippians 4:13: "I can do all things through Christ who strengthens me" (NKJV). This verse is so powerful! Even though I felt scared and worthless, God showed me how amazing His power is.

At the end of the summer Mrs. Grissom, our leader, gave each of us a little card that said, "Labor in faith and confidence; for the time will never come when I will forsake you. I will be with you always, helping you to perform your duty, guiding, comforting, sanctifying, sustaining you, giving you success in speaking words that shall draw the attention of others to heaven" (*The Acts of the Apostles*, p. 29). God taught me that His love is more powerful than any of my fears. He can do the same for you, too. All you have to do is let Him, and He will use you to reach other people and bring them closer to God.

Everything Happens for a Reason?

By Shana Byrd

O people of Zion, who live in Jerusalem, you will weep no more. How gracious he will be when you cry for help! As soon as he hears, he will answer you. Isaiah 30:19.

Some people say that everything happens for a reason, but this is hard for me to believe. What's the reason for someone we love dying early in life? What's the reason for rape or murder? What's the reason that things like this happen? I never used to think about this until something happened in my life that made me ask why.

On September 24, 2004, 15-year-old Raymond Adam Byrd fell out of the back of a pickup truck and lost consciousness. Emergency personnel airlifted him to Duke University Hospital, where he was placed in the pediatric intensive-care unit for seven days. On the seventh day, which just happened to be a Sabbath, they "pulled the plug." Gruesome expression, isn't it? They pulled the plug on my big brother.

For the first time in years, I prayed. At first I asked, "How could this happen to me? What did I do to deserve something like this?" I still ponder that to this day, but I realized something by going through this experience. You never know when you could die, so why wait to give your life to God? If you wait, it could end up being too late.

Adam's death actually got the attention of many, many people, and I think maybe that's the reason he died. I know for a fact it helped me. I started talking to my mom again (after two years of having no contact). If it wasn't for this experience, I probably would not have made attending Mount Pisgah Academy, a Seventh-day Adventist boarding school, a priority. And I stopped taking my friends, family, and God for granted. God knows everything, and in this situation it took someone dying to bring about changes in many people's lives.

Chains and Cliffs

By Kitty Ratzlaff

But one thing I do: Forgetting what is behind and straining toward what is ahead, I press on toward the goal to win the prize for which God has called me heavenward in Christ Jesus. Philippians 3:13, 14.

I am, generally speaking, not a fan of chains. I don't like the kind worn around the neck, and the ones that hang from belts just annoy me. There are also chains that are meant to bind and imprison someone. I can't imagine anyone liking those. As long as I'm talking about things I dislike, I also really dislike cliffs, especially when I think I might fall off one!

Recently my family and I hiked Angel's Landing in Zion National Park in Utah. It is a strenuous five-mile hike that took us to the peak of a mountain and gave us some amazing views of the park. It does have a sign at the beginning stating, "This hike is not for people who are afraid of heights!" I decided I could push my fears aside and climb to the top. Of course, there are stories of people who have fallen to their deaths along this hike. Just a few months before my hike, a 55-year-old woman fell to her death while attempting to hike this same trail.

I ignored my growing fear and pushed myself up the mountain. With about a half mile left, we suddenly came to a place in the trail where things got dangerous. With precipitous 1,000-foot drops on either side of me, I was left with only a chain to hang on to. I clung to the chain as if my life depended on it—which it did! I kept clinging to the chains and moving slowly up the edge of the mountain. I was beginning to love chains, as they were the only things keeping me from plunging to my death.

As I climbed I realized that these chains represented my relationship with Jesus. Sometimes I think I can move through life by myself. I want to say, "I don't need any help. I am doing fine by myself, thank you very much." Then I get to a precipice, and suddenly I need Jesus. I realize how foolish I've been and how much I need to cling to Jesus to help me through not only the precipices in my life but in everything. I made it to the top and enjoyed the view. I still don't like cliffs, but I have developed a liking for chains, because they remind me that I need to hold on to Jesus because my life depends on it.

Don't Take God for Granted
By Samantha Lee

Who has gone up to heaven and come down? Who has gathered up the wind in the hollow of his hands? Who has wrapped up the waters in his cloak? Who has established all the ends of the earth? What is his name, and the name of his son? Tell me if you know! Proverbs 30:4.

Have you ever complained about the weather—the rain or the heat or the cold? Many times we blame God when we don't like the weather, but have you ever stopped to thank Him for beautiful weather? When you look up at a blue sky, do you thank God? Do you thank Him for the rain that makes the plants grow? Do you thank Him for creating the water that is all around us? We should never take God for granted. We need to thank Him all the time for all the beautiful things He has put in our world.

One day at the beginning of the school year my school was supposed to go on a picnic, and I was very excited about it. However, on the day of the picnic it rained, and I was very angry. I was also mad at my mother because she had told me it would be a nice day.

When it started raining, my mother said that maybe God had other plans for me. This just made me angrier at her and at God because He hadn't given me a nice day for the picnic. Because it was raining, we stayed at the school, but played a lot of games that helped us get to know each other better. At the end of the day, I realized that I had actually enjoyed the day and that it was much better than if we had gone on the picnic. I understood then that my mother was right, that God did have a better plan. After that experience, I realized that when things don't go the way I want, maybe it's because God has a better plan.

The next time you plan a picnic and it rains, instead of complaining take the time to thank God for the rain and all the beauty that He has created in nature. Trust Him in all things. And instead of complaining about your circumstances, try to find the good in your current situation.

The Great Storyteller

By Lauren Lowe

I tell you the truth, anyone who will not receive the kingdom of God like a little child will never enter it. Mark 10:15.

I remember so well sitting in an overstuffed recliner with my grandfather, listening to his incredible tales of his life experiences. I loved to sit and listen without interruption for as long as possible. I heard about the tricks he played on all of his teachers and friends: the time he locked the boys in the outhouse, when he rolled a barrel of rocks down the tin roof of the schoolhouse while all the parents were inside for a teachers' meeting, and playing cowboys and Indians in the dense woods around his home. There were stories of sliding down gutters to escape his classes and teachers or of throwing firecrackers into the potbelly stove, which blew the piping off the wall and filled the whole building with billowing smoke.

He also told me of a time people had very little. He was part of a big family who was excited to get oranges as Christmas presents. They all worked on the farm and used their imaginations to amuse themselves, rather than video games or the computer. He was an all-American boy in the wake of the Great Depression. And he's one of the people I look up to.

My grandfather's stories make me think of an even greater storyteller, Christ Himself. He called the little children to Himself to hear stories and be blessed. I'm sure they listened with rapt attention and admired Him as one of their heroes, just as I did with my grandfather. But they were hearing about the kingdom of God, and they received Christ's message better than even His own disciples. We must become as little children sitting on Christ's knee to enter into heaven. We should look to Him with that kind of devotion, that kind of admiration. Jesus' parables are stories to lead us to Him—Christ gave us many examples through His stories of how to become a true Christian. Like my childhood love of reliving the times of my grandfather's youth, we should also devote ourselves to the Greatest Storyteller.

God Is With Us

By Andrew Linton

For the eyes of the Lord are on the righteous and his ears are attentive to their prayer, but the face of the Lord is against those who do evil.
1 Peter 3:12.

I was so angry and confused that I would vomit on a daily basis from all the stress. My mother was dying of cancer, my younger brother was addicted to every drug in the book, my grades were slipping, and I had just broken up with my girlfriend of 15 months. I fell to my knees and cried out to God, "Lord, why? Send me relief, please, Lord." I cried until my eyes were sore.

That Monday morning I really wanted to give up, but I forced myself to keep going. Later that day I got off work a little late and ran into my friend Ericka. We chatted for a while, catching up on things. I found myself really appreciating her encouragement. That day was service day for the senior class. I made sure I was able to work with Ericka as we worked with the "adopt-a-highway" project. We talked, laughed, and picked up trash until we got to the end of the road. She helped to lift my spirits and make me feel happy again.

We became closer friends as the week went on, and when I least expected it, she surprised me. As I left the Week of Prayer meeting, Ericka asked if I would escort her to the girls' dorm. As we walked, she took an unexpected detour. I turned around to see an army of smiling faces following me to the newly set-up prayer room. I went in, and everyone crowded around me. I was shocked because one by one everyone began to pray for me. I began to cry because I felt loved. I will never forget the way that everyone prayed for me. Ericka assisted in setting up a mass prayer circle just for me. Wow!

I prayed for relief, and the Lord sent me a "family" to love and care for me. I will never forget how the Lord sent Ericka to help me. He relieved my pain and made me feel loved.

Relationships
By Logan White

God has said, "Never will I leave you; never will I forsake you."
Hebrews 13:5.

For years my mom and dad have had problems, but they have always worked through them to stay together for my benefit. Unfortunately, this past year has been another story.

For the past two years my dad has been serving in the military. However, his contract was to end in September, and then he planned to return to his normal job as a mechanic. This was a big issue for him because the military job physically wore him down, which was compounded by two surgeries in the past year. This stress was wearing not only my dad down but also my mom. The arguing soon began, and they were fighting all the time. I would always hear them talking about divorce, which hurt, but I never really believed it would happen.

Well, in October of my senior year, my house went up for sale. My parents were very good about telling me what was going on, but the reality of what was happening still hadn't hit. I cried countless nights and thought there was nothing in my life that was going right. I prayed about it and still felt as though no one was there. After living with both my mom and dad for 17 years, I couldn't help being heartbroken over the thought of not having them both around.

The house sold, and I moved right before Christmas, which made the season especially hard. It was really difficult and hard to understand that it was the last Christmas I would probably spend with the two of them together.

Though I'm going through a really rough time in my life, I know that my mom, dad, and I are learning more about each other and our relationship with God. Recently I have felt that I had no one to help me get through this rough patch. But I know that I'm not completely alone—God is with me all the time. I realize now that He is sad with me, and He wants what is best for all of us. I may not like the situation I'm in, but I know that Jesus will see me through it.

God knows everything before we even think of it, and if we turn to Him and refuse to give up, He will help us every step of the way. Overall, I've learned that challenges are what makes life interesting, and overcoming them is what makes life meaningful. No matter how hard life gets, we will always have at least one Friend who will never leave nor forsake us.

Whom Do You Follow?

By Megan Couser

Then he said to them all: "If anyone would come after me, he must deny himself and take up his cross daily and follow me." Luke 9:23.

When you're a teenager, it is easy to follow the actions, behaviors, or looks of others. Sometimes it may be a style of clothing, a type of music, swearing, or maybe even bullying.

When I was 8 years old, I loved riding my bike. My two sisters and I often rode our bikes around our subdivision. One day my sisters, Melissa and Kaylee, and I, with our neighbor Whitney, decided to play follow the leader on our bikes. My oldest sister, Melissa, led us, followed by Whitney, Kaylee, and then me. Sometimes I have a tendency to "zone out," which is to stare at an object and forget about everything. In this case I was looking at a tree when all of a sudden Melissa stopped, then Whitney, followed by Kaylee. However, I was unaware of this and therefore did not stop in time. Before I knew it, I was on the pavement with my hands and knees scraped, bloodied, and bruised. I had flipped over Kaylee's bike, rolled and skidded, and then landed on the pavement. All I could do was cry. Luckily Whitney's dad heard me, picked me up, and took me to my house, where Mom cleaned me up and bandaged my wounds.

This experience reminded me that in life we follow people, whether it is parents, friends, relatives, or siblings. Which leader are you following—or are you zoning out and oblivious to your surroundings? You should use caution either way. Be aware of your surroundings, your role models, and where you are headed in life.

Whom do you follow? Is it someone who will lift you up in life, or someone who will bring you down and make you bloody and bruised? There is only one Person I know of who will never bring you down—Jesus! So take a proactive approach, be aware of your surroundings, and choose to follow Jesus. Trust me, it's worth it.

Inside and Out

By Bethany Iuliano

Woe to you, teachers of the law and Pharisees, you hypocrites! You are like whitewashed tombs, which look beautiful on the outside but on the inside are full of dead men's bones and everything unclean. Matthew 23:27.

When I was 8 years old, I hated to clean my room! My mom wanted me to clean it quite frequently, and we argued over this issue almost every day. Finally, I gave in to my mom's requests and set out to clean my room. My mom trusted me to do it on my own, but I was overwhelmed. Piles of clothes and toys covered my floor, hiding my carpet. I looked into my empty closet and had a brilliant idea! I packed every last toy and article of clothing into the left side of my closet. I had so much junk all over my room that the pile of stuff almost touched the ceiling inside the closet. The last thing I put on my pile of refuse was a plastic toy shopping cart. The shopping cart had a hard time balancing on all my other things, so I slammed my closet door shut really fast, barely keeping it inside. I made my bed and straightened the things on my dressers. When I stepped back to admire my work, my room looked pretty nice!

When my mom came to inspect my room, she was shocked at how fast I had cleaned it. She told me that it was beautiful and that she was so proud of me. Then, with dread, I watched as she walked toward my closet. When she opened the door, the entire pile of rubbish fell out, and the shopping cart landed right on her head! Needless to say, I was in big trouble, and I spent the rest of the day cleaning out my room for real.

This story reminds me of how many Christians act today. We make sure we look nice and clean on the outside, but inside we are rotten and dirty. Our words are sweet and tender, but our actions are evil. We gossip about others, say mean things behind people's backs, and our hearts are full of hatred toward some of God's children. To be truly clean, we must have a pure heart! We must be clean inside and out.

God and Hair

By Nicholas Ewing

We are bringing you good news, telling you to turn from these worthless things to the living God, who made heaven and earth and sea and everything in them. Acts 14:15.

One day Jonny sat in his Bible class and listened to his teacher talk about how we can see God in everything. The teacher ended the class by challenging the students to find something unique that teaches them a lesson from God.

While walking home from school, Jonny was thinking about the challenge his teacher had given him. He thought for a while, and then it hit him. Hair—hair is like God. That night at the supper table he told his mom and dad what the teacher had challenged him to do. He told them that hair is just like God.

The next day in Bible class the teacher asked the students if any of them had thought about what he had said. Jonny boldly raised his hand and said, "Hair." The class giggled while the teacher looked at Jonny with an inquisitive look on his face that begged him to explain. Jonny started his story very quietly, but got louder as he progressed.

He said, "Many times people run from God and try to cut Him out of their life. But, just like hair, no matter how many times you cut it off, it will always be there. That is how God and hair are alike." Satisfied with his explanation, he promptly sat down.

Eventually Jonny grew up and went to college to become a pastor. As a student or as a future pastor, he plans to tell everyone that no matter what you do, God will never leave you nor forsake you.

Hurricane Isabel

By Nick Cord

I will lie down and sleep in peace, for you alone, O Lord,
make me dwell in safety. Psalm 4:8.

Growing up on the Outer Banks of North Carolina, I experienced plenty of tropical storms and small hurricanes, but only one scared me. Most of the time when a low-pressure system makes it to the North Carolina coast, it is a category one hurricane or a tropical storm—not very frightening. My mom takes a trip to the store and purchases the usual—batteries for flashlights, ice for the fridge, lighters for the candles, and plenty of snacks. Storms are usually a ton of fun.

This time it was a little different. In 2003 Hurricane Isabel came plowing toward the Outer Banks as a category two hurricane with winds up to 110 mph. My family didn't know if it was safe enough to stay in our little old house, so we decided to go to Grammy's house. She lives about an hour north and slightly farther away from the coast. We thought we would be much safer there.

The hurricane hit in the evening, but even if it had happened during the day, the sun had no chance of making its presence known. To be honest, Isabel made me a little nervous, but I didn't get too worked up. That was until century-old trees were shaking the earth as they came down, one after another. Looking through the windows, we could see trees literally splitting houses in half. That's when I got nervous. Soon after seeing another tree fall, a man ran up to our door and knocked on it in the middle of the storm. Yelling, he told us that if anyone was upstairs in our house they'd better come down, because another massive tree was swaying in our yard. Aunt Lori was upstairs in the bathroom, and as soon as she was done, she joined us in the living room. Almost immediately afterward, the entire house shook violently with one of the loudest sounds I have ever heard. After the sound stopped, Papa went upstairs to investigate, and what he saw amazed him—the tree was resting on what used to be the toilet bowl. The girth of the tree filled the whole bathroom.

I'm not sure if the man who warned us was truly a man or an angel, but either way he was sent from God. If my aunt had stayed upstairs, she wouldn't be here today. My grandparents weren't very upset having to pay for the damages, considering what it could have cost us. I'm thankful that God protects His children every day.

Slick Nick

By Callie Adams

*To another miraculous powers, to another prophecy, to another distinguish-
ing between spirits, to another speaking in different kinds of tongues, and to
still another the interpretation of tongues. All these are the work of one and
the same Spirit, and he gives them to each one, just as he determines.*
1 Corinthians 12:10, 11.

While working as a task force dean at Blue Mountain Academy, I had the bright idea to form a drama group. I didn't want to leave anyone out, so we didn't have tryouts and we didn't make cuts. Anyone was welcome, and all were invited. Obviously there were only a few who were dedicated, and these core members were cast in the big play. We started rehearsing months before we were to perform, and I realized as I was casting that the main part of Jonah would have to be someone who was at our meetings every week. There was only one guy who was that dedicated: Nick, my champion member. Unfortunately, he had a terrible stutter, which was bad enough to discourage any aspiring actor, but I decided to go ahead and cast him.

Nick was a happy, fabulous kid, and all the students loved him, but his stutter was severe. I was worried that even though he was well liked, being on stage in front of what should have been an easy crowd would make him nervous and might cause us to have difficulty even getting through our play. I began to pray. When the time came for the performance, Nick had every line memorized, but he couldn't make it through a single sentence without stuttering.

As soon as the performance began, I felt an overwhelming need to pray. I didn't listen to what was going on out on the stage. I simply gathered my troupe members in a circle of prayer. Each member went out on stage at their appointed time, but when they returned backstage, they rejoined the prayer circle. It was an unceasing prayer time throughout the performance. I have never felt so close to God. After the performance, I walked out to the back where the actors were being congratulated by staff members and their fellow students. One staff member came over to me and asked, "How did you get Nick to stop stuttering?"

I was stunned. Since then, I have never heard Nick speak without his signature stutter, but apparently he made it all the way through the performance without once stumbling. He was the hero of the day and my personal answer to prayer.

He Calms Our Storms

By Peter Markoff

He stilled the storm to a whisper; the waves of the sea were hushed. They were glad when it grew calm, and he guided them to their desired haven. Psalm 107:29, 30.

It was a bright sunny day to be out on Lake Keowee. The weather was perfect, and we were headed out in our boat with another family for a day of fun on a lakeside beach. We owned a condo near Lake Keowee, and now we were ready to spend a day by the water.

We parked our boat at a strip of sand and jumped out. Everyone started to enjoy themselves building sand castles, swimming, and having a blast. Suddenly out of nowhere a dark cloud could be seen in the distance. My parents thought it was going the other way, so we just stayed put without expecting much. I kept building my sand castle when I felt a little drop on my nose. I announced the obvious, but all the adults present decided to stay, expecting it to be a little drizzle and then pass. It wasn't.

The rain quickly started to pick up, and soon blew into a huge thunderstorm. Everybody panicked. All at once we grabbed chairs, towels, and whatever we could get our hands on and took it to the boat. Even our dog, almost drowning himself, tried to swim to the boat. It took awhile, but when we had finally gathered all of our loose items into the boat, we set out. We wanted to get home as quickly as possible. My dad started driving, and the rest of us huddled under tubes and towels to try to block the pelting rain from stinging our faces. We were all miserable and soaking wet. We didn't talk at all.

After going a little ways, my dad decided the water was too rough to keep going, and we pulled over to another beach to wait out the storm. All the kids jumped out and sought shelter in the woods until the storm passed.

We all experience storms in our life. It could be anything hard that you are going through with school, family, etc. God helps us through any difficulties we are going through. All we need to do is ask for His help and guidance, and He will get us through our storms. Soon the storm will pass, and we can dry ourselves off and enjoy the sun again.

Second Chances

By Alicia Evans

If you, O Lord, kept a record of sins, O Lord, who could stand? But with you there is forgiveness; therefore you are feared. Psalm 130:3, 4.

Everyone deserves a second chance—and sometimes a third, a fourth, or a fifth. I myself have been given far more second chances than I can count. I know I don't deserve to even be alive, but God is great and merciful. I used to think that God was punishing me and that I deserved to be hurt because I brought it on myself. But I was very wrong. Now that I have had the chance to learn a few of my own lessons, I believe with all my heart that He let me make those decisions on my own, even if He knew my choices would hurt me. This is how we learn, isn't it?

The nice thing is that even if I make another bad decision, He is always right there waiting to give me another try. God never gives up on us!

All of us struggle with sin. Many of us deal with grief, anger, and justification on a daily basis. It's not easy being a Christian, and I easily forget how lucky I am to be a part of this wonderful family of God.

If God kept a book of my daily sins, believe me, it would be a multivolume almanac, I'm sure. But once we have repented and God has forgiven us, we start with a clean slate. God will not bring up the past to punish us. This is not a license to do what we want. True repentance means changing our ways and our attitude—sincerely being sorry.

If you will look at today's Bible verse, it uses the word "feared." I don't think that means that we are to be afraid of God. It simply means that He is all-powerful and we should respect that. Humans have a hard time forgiving and forgetting, but God can do just that! He is amazingly powerful and awesome. And knowing that we are not perfect, He has promised to forgive us again and again.

God has a plan for each of us, and He's prepared to give everyone as many second chances as they need. Thank Him for His mercy and love!

Are You Thirsty?

By Richard Lawrence

Then Jesus declared, "I am the bread of life. He who comes to me will never go hungry, and he who believes in me will never be thirsty."
John 6:35.

Life can be so busy and stressful, especially living on a boarding school campus during the absolutely most draining period of my high school career. Hardly a week goes by that I don't need some encouragement or inspiration that focuses my mind on spiritual things and the goodness of God, thus enabling me to face the week ahead.

In John 7:37 Christ states, "If anyone is thirsty, let him come to me and drink." This water doesn't just quench our thirst; it also nourishes our body and revives our spirit. If you hunger or thirst after something, that usually implies that there's a need. I personally believe that this mind-set is pleasing to God. He likes to see us come to Him and patiently wait for Him to fulfill our needs. I have come to realize that we all need to reguarly take time to pause and spiritually reflect on Christ in order to recharge our batteries and cope with whatever situations in life that come our way.

Establishing a personal relationship with Christ and finding time to study the Scriptures are excellent ways to begin that process. As the apostle Paul wrote: "All scripture is given by inspiration of God, and is profitable for doctrine, for reproof, for correction, for instruction in righteousness: that the man of God may be perfect, throughly furnished unto all good works (2 Timothy 3:16, 17, KJV).

Living in this world can leave you feeling spiritually dehydrated, parched and dry. Take time out of your day to look at God's Word. I've found that all of it points us to Christ, who alone is the living well that provides satisfying water for the thirsty.

I Love You This Much

By Rachel Sheridan

*This is love: not that we loved God, but that he loved us and sent his Son
as an atoning sacrifice for our sins. 1 John 4:10.*

A little boy stood crying, wondering if his daddy loved him, but he thought probably not. He saw his father only about once a year. Each time his father would get ready to leave, the little boy would stand outside in the yard with his arms stretched out as far as they'd go. As tears rolled down his cheek, he would always say, "I love you this much. Do you love me, too? However long it takes, I'm never giving up. No matter what, I love you this much."

As the years went by, the little boy grew to hate his father for what he had done. Then his father died. On the day of the funeral, the young man stood by the casket with tears in his eyes. Standing there in silence, he looked up and saw Jesus on the cross with His arms stretched out as far as they'd go. He then realized that he hadn't been unloved or alone all his life.

Jesus loved him so much that He gave His life on the cross for him—for everyone. At that moment the young man knew that Jesus was speaking to him, and this is what he heard: "I love you this much, and I'm waiting on you to make up your mind. Do you love Me, too? However long it takes, I'm never giving up. No matter what, I love you this much."

When I heard this story, it brought tears to my eyes, because it really made me think about how much Jesus loves me. Even though there have been times I have turned my back on Him, He has never stopped loving me. Jesus died for all of us, nailed to the cross with His arms open wide in love. My prayer for all who are reading this is that you will take a moment to stop and reflect on all that has been done for you. Imagine that Jesus is speaking directly to you, saying, "I love you this much, and I'm waiting on you to make up your mind. Do you love Me, too? However long it takes, I'm never giving up. No matter what, I love you this much."

A Rubik's Devotion

By Jazman Isom

Restore us, O Lord God Almighty; make your face shine upon us, that we may be saved. Psalm 80:19.

We experience numerous trials in this world. I believe it's especially serious in the adolescent years. Satan knows that we are vulnerable to many things, and he knows that we think we have it all figured out and under control already. So we're actually pretty easy targets for him.

You don't have to look far to see teenagers who are quite mixed up. They may not realize it themselves, but from the outside looking in we can clearly see that they are in need of some serious fixing. Don't think that I'm just picking on teenagers—everyone faces times in their lives when they are so tangled that they can get help only through divine intervention. The hard part is learning to let go, give up control, and let God take over. He can see the big picture—where we've been, where we are, and where we need to go.

Have you ever played with a Rubik's Cube and tried to line up all of the colors correctly? I have a variety of Rubik's Cubes in different sizes, and trying to solve them reminds me of our spiritual journey. The cube can get completely jumbled up and can be very difficult to solve. It takes a certain combination of steps to get the puzzle figured out. Some people buy a Rubik's Cube thinking it will be great fun, but then they end up getting frustrated with it, realizing that it's much more difficult than they thought. You can't just solve one side at a time—you must look at the big picture and know the sequence of steps it takes to fix all sides.

From a spiritual standpoint, the mixed-up colors on the puzzle represent our mixed-up lives, which are filled with stress and troubles. We think we can handle the problems, but we just get frustrated and want to give up. Fortunately, God (the true problem solver) knows the solution to any puzzle. He does not get confused or frustrated, and He never gets tired of helping us.

I know one solution for the Rubik's Cube, but God knows every solution to everyone's problems—and I'm glad that I can rely on Him.

Fields of Potential

By Ashley Cale

*It is like a mustard seed, which is the smallest seed you plant in the ground.
Yet when planted, it grows and becomes the largest of all garden plants,
with such big branches that the birds of the air can perch in its shade.
Mark 4:31, 32.*

It was a bitter, blustery morning when six of us headed out to rake terraces and plant trees for a local mission in Fort Defiance, Arizona. Our goal was to loosen the earth on a particular patch of land, dig holes, and then reintroduce native plants to the soil. Unfortunately, the ground was extremely rocky, and no matter how hard we jammed our shovels into the ground, the rocks wouldn't budge. Only when Mr. Grow took swings at the earth with a pickax did the rock-ridden ground finally oblige. Once it did, it was much easier to pull the stones out individually until the hole was large enough. The rocks were heavy, and they left streaks of dirt and sandstone on our gloves. I couldn't believe anything could grow in this, and I sometimes thought that the plants would rather live in a pot than in this seemingly cramped area filled with rocks.

The more I thought about it, however, the more it made me think of how we tend to write people off as unreachable. A few might say that we are wasting our time—that certain people are too far gone, too hard to help, or too hardened to life's troubles to care about what we have to say. Their "soil" can be seen as unfavorable in our eyes. But God has called us to cast seeds on all types of soil. He gave us the Holy Spirit, our metaphorical "pickax" to soften people's hearts so that God's love will be able to grow in unhindered hearts. But this isn't easy work— it involves bending down in the dirt, getting a little dusty, and bearing another's burden. Each new life that is planted stands as a testimony to the boundless love found in us through Christ. Let us plant our own fields daily!

A Handkerchief

By Sarah Grissom

The righteous cry out, and the Lord hears them; he delivers them from all their troubles. Psalm 34:17.

As Kim was sitting in the school office waiting to talk to one of her teachers, a girl came in and asked Kim if she had heard the bad news. Unsure of what she was talking about, Kim shook her head. The girl proceeded to tell Kim of a guy who had attended their school a few years before Kim had come. But the story didn't end well. As he was driving home, he stopped paying attention for just a moment and started drifting off the road. Realizing what was about to happen, he overcorrected and flipped his truck. He never made it home that night.

Uneasy and scared, Kim uttered out the words, "What . . . what was his name?"

"His name was Travis." Kim's heart sank. She had known Travis for many years. They had first met at summer camp and then had bumped into each other just a few months before.

The next few days were a blur. The boys' dean and the principal planned to take several students to the funeral. The thought of even attending a funeral for one of her friends without her parents scared her. The morning of the funeral Kim was overwhelmed by emotions. She felt numb from head to toe and drenched in sadness.

With a sick feeling in her stomach Kim walked in, gave her condolences to the family, and found her seat. At the end of the service she walked to the front of the church where sitting on a table was a wooden box with his name carved in the top and sitting next to it was his hat, the one he had always worn. Bursting into tears, Kim had never felt such a heavy feeling before. All of a sudden she felt someone softly place a hand on her shoulder. She looked up and saw the boys' dean. He stretched out his hand and gave her his handkerchief. After she took it, he turned and walked away. In that moment that's all she needed. By this simple act she saw someone who cared and yet understood her need just to cry.

God is like that with us. When things get thrown at us and we feel as if nothing can help, He stretches out His hand, giving us His handkerchief, showing us He's there for us when we're ready. No, the handkerchief didn't take away the pain, but it made things a little more bearable, knowing someone understood and cared.

Stephanie Thomas

Life as a Car Ride

"Because he loves me," says the Lord, "I will rescue him; I will protect him, for he acknowledges my name." Psalm 91:14.

I was driving home from an overnight backpacking trip when the unexpected and unfortunate event happened. I had barely slept, which caused me to be extremely tired. My goal was concentrating on not falling asleep and to get home quickly, but all of a sudden everything went black, and all I could hear was squealing tires and what sounded like a gunshot. The next thing I remember seeing was a big white bag-type thing in my lap and steam coming from under the hood. I had rear-ended a large white Expedition. The big white thing in my lap was the airbag, which had deployed and caused the gunshot noise I had heard. I was totally freaking out, with tons of questions entering my mind—I was definitely in shock. *How did this happen? Did I fall asleep or what? What will my parents think? How much will the repairs and insurance cost? How will my reputation as a driver change? Is the other driver OK?* While all these questions rushed through my mind, I managed to call 911 and then my mom.

The driver of the Expedition was fine, just a little neck pain from the impact. And the only thing my parents cared about was that I was safe. Unfortunately, the front of my '95 Pontiac Grand Prix was completely totaled. Other than wearing a splint and suffering from a few burn marks on my arm when the airbag deployed, I was fine. I am so thankful and grateful that the accident wasn't worse. I could easily have been hurt worse, but God was looking out for me, as He always does!

A few days after the accident occurred, I was listening to Carrie Underwood's song "Jesus, Take the Wheel," and I thought about how life is like a car ride. Like my accident, a lot of times we get off track because we are distracted or not paying attention. We follow the crowd and don't take time to notice what's going on and what God wants us to do. But even if we make mistakes and crash, God is still there and helps us get right back on track. We just need to tell God to take the wheel that's steering our life and help us back on track to living a life according to His plans.

Love Your Enemies
By Becca Busche

You have heard that it was said, "Love your neighbor and hate your enemy." But I tell you: Love your enemies and pray for those who persecute you. Matthew 5:43, 44.

Enemies are made when we, as selfish human beings, decide not to bother to get to know a person before we judge them. We all do it. We may take one look at someone and decide that they are someone we don't like, someone we don't want anything to do with. We set ourselves up and turn them into our "enemy" without even getting to know them in the first place. We may set up a sort of "brick wall" between us and the situation at hand, and no matter what the other person may say or do, they are always an "enemy."

Attending a boarding school, I've learned that there is a lot more drama that goes on than in other schools because we are all living together on a pretty small campus, and we go through a lot more together. Girls are always talking about other girls and gossiping about things that have happened recently. Someone always ends up getting hurt, but that's just the way it goes. We often argue and complain with the people around us. We live in a world where there is sin, and we can't help having conflicts.

Although we have heard that we should love our friends and hate our enemies, God tells us in the Bible that we should love our enemies and pray for the people who hurt us. God tells us that we can make a difference if we just try hard to be kind to our enemies and love them, even if they treat us badly. So just stop for a minute and think about all those people whom you may have problems with, and choose to make it right with them. I guarantee you will feel better afterward!

Why Are You Afraid?

By Shawntese Smith

He replied, "You of little faith, why are you so afraid?" Then he got up and rebuked the winds and the waves, and it was completely calm.
Matthew 8:26.

I am definitely afraid of a lot of things. My biggest fear, though, is public speaking. During the summers after my sophomore and junior years in academy, I was part of the Mount Pisgah Academy summer recruitment team. Our team traveled around North and South Carolina visiting churches, doing community service, and making friends. I loved the whole experience and felt blessed to have the opportunity to have a job that was so much fun. There was no better way I could have spent my summers.

The second summer I participated, everything was going well until we had to speak up front about who God was to us. We were to present our thoughts at an evangelistic series conducted at a church. I had it in my mind that I was not going to do it. There was no way anyone was going to make me speak, or so I thought. What I never realized was that I had no faith. I thought I was helping myself by easing out of the matter. But believe it or not, God has plans for each one of us. He certainly had one for me. It's funny how you think you can get away with something, but eventually it hits you right back in the face. I sat down and planned out how I was going to escape if I was forced to speak. That's how bad I thought I was at speaking. But God works in ways that are beyond our understanding. He turned my lack of faith into something more than I have ever known. He gave me courage and the strength to know that I am not alone and that there is nothing to be afraid of. So I spoke up front for the first time in my life, and I felt completely calm.

Why was I afraid? I guess it was my own insecurities. But once I realized that it wasn't about me, that it was about God, I felt so much better. If you are facing a challenging situation, don't try to handle it yourself. Give your fears and hesitations over to God. He will work through you—and fear cannot stand in His presence!

Peaceful Disaster

By Alex Faber

Looking for that blessed hope, and the glorious appearing of the great God and our Savior Jesus Christ. Titus 2:13, NKJV.

When I was about 5 years old, I lived on a farm in the small town of Fowler, which is in eastern Ohio. My uncle Wally, who was a doctor, often came to visit my family. One particular time when visiting, he noticed that I looked pale. He urged my mom to take me to the doctor, but she wouldn't listen. "It's Ohio," she argued. "We all look pale."

Five days later I found myself sitting in a chair with a needle in my arm. My mom had finally given in and decided to take me to the doctor to get a blood check. The doctor came back with bad news. "Your son has leukemia," he said, "which is a type of cancer in the blood."

Over the next few years I went through some pretty rough times. Eventually the doctor told my mom that there was no more that they could do. They sent me home with little hope, saying that it could be weeks, maybe months, but I wouldn't be around much longer. My mom sat me down and asked, "Alex, are you afraid to die?" My answer was no. "Why?" she asked. I went on to explain that I would get to see Jesus before her.

Now, I need to explain something. I am a Seventh-day Adventist, as is the rest of my family. We believe, as it states in the Bible, that when someone dies they do not go straight to heaven, but are asleep until His second coming. So when my mother heard my response, she explained to me that I wasn't going to heaven when I died, but that I would stay in the grave until Christ's return. And this is what I said. "I know, Mommy, but the Bible says that when Jesus comes, the dead in Christ will rise first and then the living will rise up to meet them." With this mentality, I felt I could handle anything.

And so now, years later, by the grace of God, a strong family, and the prayers of hundreds of people, I am 100 percent cancer-free. Even though it was rough, God gave me peace through it all, and I know that my future does not end here on this earth.

Torn Apart

Katie Thrash

Jesus said, "Let the little children come to me, and do not hinder them, for the kingdom of heaven belongs to such as these." Matthew 19:14.

When I was 13, I saw my best friend's family torn apart. Sarah's mother, Kate, was trying to raise three children by working a minimum-wage job while Sarah's dad was cheating on her mom. While fighting with her estranged husband over the house and the children, the Department of Social Services had to step in, threatening to take the children away from both Kate and her husband. I watched Sarah go from a carefree 13-year-old to the oldest sibling who had to take care of the younger siblings. Kate continued working hard to support her children while the dad seemed to be taking everything from them, including the roof over their heads.

Sarah and I had attended the same church school since we were both in kindergarten. I had been born into the Adventist Church; Sarah hadn't. Being the only girls in our class, we soon became best friends. Even though we came from different worlds, we had a lot in common. We could spend hours swinging on the tire swings or spinning on the merry-go-round, talking about whatever was the interest of the day. However, in the seventh grade things began to change. We were still best friends, but Sarah was always having to help around the house, and she didn't have time to do fun things outside of school as often.

I don't know how this story ends, because the last day I saw Sarah was the day we graduated from the eighth grade. After we graduated, I hoped and prayed that Sarah's parents would see that the best place for her was our local Adventist academy, but it seemed that they weren't going to send her there.

I know that God had a reason for her attending our church school even though her family members were not Adventists. And even though she was not able to continue school in a Christian environment, I'm sure God is still working on her heart. Sarah has had to face many challenges as a young person, but I pray for her and hope that she is well. One thing I do know for sure is that Jesus loves young people, and He will do all that He can to ensure that we will have a happy home with Him in heaven.

A Close Call

By Allissa Wright

I will not die but live, and will proclaim what the Lord has done. Psalm 118:17.

Every Friday for nine weeks in the winter, students from my school go snowboarding or skiing at a mountain near my house in Vermont. On one of those anticipated days, I woke up excited. I hurried to get ready; I couldn't wait to hit the slopes. My little sister, Julia, and I packed our snowboards and snow clothes into our Suburban and hurried out the door. My mom's parting words echoed in my ears, "Drive safely. The roads could be slippery." I assured her that we would be fine.

Snowboard season was close to being over, so I wanted to make the best of every moment. At the end of a satisfying day (which went by way too fast) I said goodbye to my friends, found my sister, and started heading home. As we drove through our little town and started going down a hill, I lost control. Suddenly our car started sliding on the black ice, and we drifted into the wrong lane. I jerked the wheel to the right to avoid an oncoming car and to try to get back into our lane, but instead we continued to slide to the left, where we hit the bank and bounced back to the wrong lane and hit a minivan head-on. When we finally came to a stop, I was shaking violently and sobbing. Julia looked really scared, but she got out of the car to check out the damage. When I saw the look on her face, I knew it was bad. As I climbed out on the passenger's side, since my door was pressed against a guardrail, I saw a man getting out of the minivan and unbuckling his little baby from a car seat. He yelled to me that they were OK.

Soon fire trucks and an ambulance arrived on the scene. Thankfully nobody was seriously hurt. We walked away with only a few bruised ribs and whiplash. The firemen told me that they see a lot of accidents in that spot since the road is shaded and often stays iced over.

That day I woke up excited, not thinking that something bad would happen. But I could have died and killed three other people. I did total my parents' Suburban and the other car. I wasn't driving fast or recklessly; I was paying attention; but I still got in a bad accident. My point is that you never know what is going to happen. The incident that day made me realize that I need to build my relationship with God, because I never know what the day will bring. I thank God for keeping us all safe that day. And I commit to making Christ a priority in my life. Won't you?

Even When You Least Expect It, God Is Always There

By Shawntez Smith

May the Lord our God be with us as he was with our fathers; may he never leave us nor forsake us. 1 Kings 8:57.

They say it was a miracle, but I say it was the hand of God. October 18, 1991, was just a regular day except for the fact that there was a newborn baby girl fighting for her life. The doctors could not figure out how the first twin came out healthy, all three pounds and eight ounces of her, and how the other twin had to fight for her life. Happily, the story did not end there, for God had a plan for this twin's life.

It has been many years since this incident happened, and I have to say I am strong, for I know that God has a plan for me and for my twin. Yes, there will be times in our lives when things don't go as we plan, but we have to remember that God is in control of our lives. He can make a rainbow shine after a storm. It's not our job to understand the reason things happen, but we can learn from each storm.

When I was born, the doctors didn't think I would make it to the next day, so they all thought that it would be reasonable for me to be with my twin before I stopped breathing. As soon as they laid me beside my twin, the doctor said that something remarkable started happening, something that he had never seen in all his years of being a doctor. I started breathing regularly. In fact, my temperature and body movements became normal.

It's a miracle, some would say, but I say it was the hand of God. Some of us wonder where God is when something happens in our lives, but He's there even when we least expect it. I don't know yet what God has in store for my life, but I do know that whatever it is I am ready to do it.

The Prince on the White Horse
By Alyssa Pelto

I saw heaven standing open and there before me was a white horse, whose rider is called Faithful and True. With justice he judges and makes war. Revelation 19:11.

As a child I loved watching movies about a prince saving a princess from some sort of terror. He would come charging in on his noble steed, clad in armor and ready for battle. The "damsel in distress" would scream his name and call for help. The prince would then charge at the ferocious beast or evil being and fight him to the death. After the prince had won, he would sweep the princess off her feet, and they would ride off into the sunset to his castle, where they would live happily ever after.

Sometimes I find myself wondering if that is what life is really like. Will I ever have a happily ever after? Will a prince come and save me from all the "evil villains" of this world? Is there even a prince for me? Every girl wants some sort of "prince" in her life.

It wasn't until recently that I realized that I do have a "Prince." He lives in a very large castle, where everything is "happily ever after" and there is safety from death, destruction, and evil. When I find myself in trouble or extremely sad, I call to my "Prince" for help. He protects me and puts His comforting arms around me and holds me close. He is my true Prince, Jesus Christ. He will come down to this earth on His white horse. He will have an army on white horses that will follow Him. He is the King of *all* kings and the Lord of *all* lords. He will cast Satan out of existence, saving us all from evil. Soon Jesus will take us to His kingdom, where we will live with Him, happily ever after. I can hardly wait for that day!

The Sorry Card
By Amanda Rojas

My son, keep my words and store up my commands within you. Keep my commands and you will live; guard my teachings as the apple of your eye. Proverbs 7:1, 2.

When I was about 7 years old, my usual routine was to go home after school and watch TV or help my mom around the house. One day my mom and dad asked me to do some chores, but I wanted to finish the show I was watching. They told me I could watch it later, but I defiantly refused. My response did not go over well, and I was told that I would do my chores immediately and then go to my room without any TV.

Instead of just obeying them, I decided to talk back to them. After a couple of minutes of yelling, I was sent to my room without doing my chores. They said that I needed to think about what I had done, and then I could come back out and finish my chores. I went to my room crying, and I sat on the floor underneath my bed. I grabbed some of my books that had Christian stories and started to read. While I read I thought about what my parents had said and what I had done. That's when I bowed my head and prayed to God. When I had finished praying, I got some construction paper and folded it in half. I wrote "To Mom and Dad" on the front of it, and on the inside I wrote, "Dear Mom and Dad, I am sorry for not listening to you tonight. I hope you can forgive me. I love you." I put it in their room where they would find it.

After my mom found the card, she came to me and told me that she loved me but not how I had acted earlier that night. After we talked for a while about what had happened, I went back out and did my chores. My mom generously helped me with them, and I learned a good lesson that night.

I wish I could tell you that after that incident I always obeyed my parents, but I'm human, and I've not always made the best decisions. But I pray that God will help me to obey His commandments and that I will make all of them a part of my life as an internal compass to guide my behavior. Honoring and respecting our parents is important, just as honoring and respecting our heavenly Father is important. And just as my parents forgave me when I was sincerely sorry, God will forgive us when we sincerely repent.

A Light That Never Goes Out

By Ashley Cale

The Lord your God is with you, he is mighty to save. He will take great delight in you, he will quiet you with his love, he will rejoice over you with singing. Zephaniah 3:17.

It was a dark and murky evening, and I was working a weekend supper shift at the academy cafeteria. The last pan was washed, and we were working on closing up for the night when I decided to take out the laundry. Normally I work during the daytime, and laundry is a simple task of walking outside, unlocking the washroom door, and trading the clean cloths for the dirty ones. As was my habit, I asked for the keys and strode out the back door with my regular "daytime" confidence.

It wasn't until I was surrounded with the smothering, black night air that panic struck me. I couldn't see a thing. I could barely make out the shapes of cars in the parking lot. Luckily, my boss had a small light on her key chain, and I fumbled to press the button while holding an armload of laundry. I walked along feeling the pavement under my sneakers, inching toward the door. *Only a little farther,* I told myself. Finally I felt the cold metal of the washroom door, and after many attempts to find the right key, I managed to unlock it. Relief flooded through me as I reached to turn on the much-desired lights. Nothing happened. The lightbulb had burned out a couple days before, and I had forgotten. I was still alone in the total darkness, with my hopes dashed for a morsel of light. I felt a tickle of fear down my spine as I strained to find the detergent and bleach. The only thing I could think of while I was struggling was that "God knows where I am; He has a plan for me; and if it includes getting attacked in the middle of the night, I am just going to have to trust Him."

In the end, I made it back to the cafeteria door, and I was fine. Looking back, I feel like I overreacted a little, but God didn't care. He comforted me in my simple time of need. It reminded me that even when we are surrounded by dark times, and our ideas of what will fix our problems fail, God is still with us. Sometimes we have to be afraid, and not sense His light, for us to appreciate when it's really there.

Our Legacy

By Jennifer Beckham

Those who are wise will shine like the brightness of the heavens, and those who lead many to righteousness, like the stars for ever and ever.
Daniel 12:3.

When a person dies in my family, traditionally the whole family gathers at the deceased person's house to support each other. During my senior year of academy, my aunt died. Her death hit our family especially hard.

When my mom was young, she lost her mother at a young age. So my aunt stepped in and took my mom and her other siblings in as her own, even though she already had kids. Not only was my aunt a mother to my mom, but she was like a grandma to me as well. When I was younger, my aunt used to pick me up from school while my mom worked. She sacrificed her time to come pick me up after she worked all day because my mom couldn't. She'd make me food even if she had only enough for herself.

Not only did my aunt sacrifice for me, but she sacrificed for her children and the rest of our family. Whenever one of her grandchildren was sick, she would take them to her house and fix them dinner after they'd been to the doctor. She loved babysitting her grandchildren and even took one of her grandkids in as her own when the mother wouldn't.

My aunt loved to help people and talk with people whenever she had the chance. Even though she didn't go to church every week, she still loved God and strived to be just like Jesus by helping others. She was extremely friendly and willing to help others. There was never a day that she wasn't down at the homeless shelter or helping out in the community in some way. She loved seeing people smile and making them happy.

Her sacrifice of time and resources reminds me of what Christianity is all about. Jesus showed us that giving of ourselves to help others less fortunate is to be one of our life goals. In an age where the world says to take, take, take, let's instead think of ways we can give, give, give. If we are selfless in our priorities, we will be blessed and happy, and we will leave a legacy our family (and our heavenly Father) will be proud of.

Test Your Teacher

By Cheryl Grant

"Test me in this," says the Lord All-Powerful. "I will open the windows of heaven for you and pour out all the blessings you need." Malachi 3:10, NCV.

Teachers are known for giving tests. Imagine creating a test for a teacher. The teacher could then have the opportunity to prove how much they know. Perhaps we already test our teachers. Daily life experiences give opportunities to examine what has been taught from a teacher. Give a $20 bill to a cashier for a $15 CD and get $5 back with a newly purchased CD—this is proof that our math teacher knew something about subtraction.

God teaches us throughout the Bible, yet there is one time God says, "Test me" (Malachi 3:10). Test Him with what? It's simple—with what we earn (also referred to as tithe). Notice that God does not require tithe for our salvation. Tithing is not mentioned in the Ten Commandments; however, it is mentioned when God is speaking to those (the Israelites) who are struggling to follow Him. Giving tithe is an opportunity to experience God taking care of our needs—it is a way for Him to prove Himself to us. So why is it so difficult to give tithe? Greed, selfishness, independence—these are likely words that come to mind. God is our teacher. He is the authority, the expert, on how to live a life full of hope, joy, and love. For many years I have put God to the test. Here's what I've learned from our Teacher:

Give tithe because you love your heavenly Father, and it is what He has asked of you.

Give tithe because you don't want your treasures on earth to be above God. In your budget, 10 percent comes before car payments, before food, before entertainment.

Give tithe, not because your pastor preaches it (although he probably knows what he's talking about), not because the church expects you to, not because the church member sitting in the pew beside you does, but because it's your choice. God wants us to choose Him; He doesn't demand love from us.

When you give to God out of love and not obligation, He gives back and "[pours] out a blessing so great you won't have enough room to take it in!" (Malachi 3:10, NLT). If you want to experience God, talk to Him daily and listen to Him hourly. Seek to learn more about Him every chance you get, and put your love into action. Test Him—He's ready to prove Himself again and again.

Give Our Time and Tithes to God

By Esther Rue

And this stone that I have set up as a pillar will be God's house, and of all that you give me I will give you a tenth. Genesis 28:22.

How many hours do you spend with God every day?

My friend and I felt bad about the amount of time we spent with God. When we actually added up the time, it didn't seem like much at all.

So my best friend decided to give one tenth of his day to God, which is about two hours and 30 minutes. He told me that we should offer our tithes to God—not only the harvest (our money) that God gives us, but also the time that we are given.

I had never really thought about that before. But the more I did think about it, the more guilt I felt. Sometimes I couldn't spend even five minutes with God. How could I feel good? Five minutes is 0.35 percent of a day. This is not the way that we should worship our God, and it is not the way a good Christian should budget time. One percent of a day is only 15 minutes. Who can't commit to at least this much time? It doesn't seem as though it would be very difficult.

My friend started reading the Bible for two and a half hours every morning, and as a result he says that he feels closer to God every day. (If you want to try this system, but think that so much time all at once is not feasible for you, I think God would understand. No certain hour of the day is more holy than the next, so you could read and pray in the morning, at noon, and/or in the evening.)

To be a doctor, to be a teacher, to be a lawyer—these are not our real goals in life. Our real goal is to go to heaven and live eternally with God. Even though we all know this, we spend our time on things of this world (getting, spending, and wasting).

If we spend more time (one tenth, or even one hundredth of our time) getting to know God and less time doing trivial things, we will better prepare ourselves for an eternity with Him.

Trust

By Lillian Williams

But I trust in your unfailing love; my heart rejoices in your salvation.
Psalm 13:5.

During the summer I work at a pool as a lifeguard. My main job is to watch the pool and ensure that no one gets hurt, and if they do, I am the first to respond. Being a lifeguard is not always an easy job. I am constantly worried that something terrible will happen and I will forget what to do. Knowing that people are counting on me for their safety is a huge responsibility.

The summer between my junior and senior year, while I was on the lifeguarding stand, a little boy jumped in and started to swim. At first he was doing fine; however, after about a minute, he started going under and then popping back up. He could not keep himself up in the deep water. I jumped off my stand and into the water, grabbed him, and brought him to the side. He hung on to me so tightly and would not let me go no matter what, even when we got him out of the water!

This experience really made me realize a lot about trust. That little boy had trusted in me so much and expected me to save him and get him out of the water. He was totally dependent on me.

In the same way, we should always have our complete trust in God. We must totally surrender to Him and let Him save us. In fact, in lifeguarding classes potential guards are taught that it is easier to save a struggling swimmer if the victim will completely relax. In "panic mode," when they are flailing around, swimmers are much more hazardous to themselves and others, including the lifeguard. Only when they allow themselves to trust completely in their savior are they truly safe.

God is on guard all the time, ever watching and ready to save us when we need help. All we have to do is completely surrender to Him, and He will pull us out of harm's way.

Love's Pull
By Gary Bradley

For God did not send his Son into the world to condemn the world, but to save the world through him. John 3:17.

On my first visit to the Pacific Ocean I was really excited. The scene was beautiful. The beach itself was fairly small, but large rocky cliffs boxed in the area. These rocky walls went some distance out into the ocean, causing the waves to become extra big as they came in to shore.

There were at least 10 surfers out that day. They would swim with the wave and effortlessly stand on top of it, or so it seemed to my young boy's mind. We all stood there for some time just watching them. But why were we all just standing there when those surfers were obviously having all the fun? So I did what seemed logical to my 4-year-old mind. I waited for a big wave, and I ran straight for it.

I had seen the surfers stand on the waves coming in, so I thought that I could stand on the waves going out. I ran through the surf as it made its hasty retreat, the sand beneath my feet. As I ran headlong into the ocean, I saw a wall of water heading straight for me. The water I had been running through was gone, and a new wave was coming in. The wall of water looked way bigger up close than what I had just seen the surfers standing on. I turned around and ran back for shore, but it was too late.

The wall of water overtook me, knocked me down, and then tried to pull me back to the ocean as it retreated. Facedown in the sand under the water, I dug my fingers into the sand, desperately trying to keep from being dragged deeper by the retreating wave. Just as my fears reached their peak, I felt the sharp sting of my hair being pulled. The tug was so strong that it stood me on my feet. I was surprised and relieved to see my mother, who was just letting go of me. "Your hair was all I could see to grab," she said. I was embarrassed to be riding in our friend's car all wet, but I was relieved that Mom had pulled me from the ocean.

The world has a way of attracting us, and sometimes we think we are invincible. However, we may be in more danger than we want to admit. I am so thankful that God is our lifeguard and that He will pull us toward Him, maybe even by the hair, and save us from ourselves.

Why Aren't We Grateful?

By Shawntese Smith

But in your great mercy you did not put an end to them or abandon them, for you are a gracious and merciful God. Nehemiah 9:31.

Our academy planned a schoolwide mission trip week. At the time it was announced I was not really looking forward to participating. My main focus and goal was just to get through the school year. I didn't have time for any distractions. I had other stresses to worry about—my social life seemed to be going down the drain, and my entire life seemed like a big tangled knot.

As the school year progressed I thought that maybe a mission trip would be a good way just to take a break and get away from being stressed. So I started to look forward to the trip.

I chose to go on the Washington, D.C., mission option. We stayed at Washington Adventist University and did outreach projects during the day. I got to meet new people and help out at some local charities. Overall it was a fun trip.

One of the things I will never forget about this trip was on Sabbath morning at church. A man had recently returned from a trip to Haiti, and he told us about his trip. The thing that touched me most was his telling us that people there were digging for food and sleeping on the ground while using cardboard for a roof over their heads. Then he told us to listen to the rain outside. It was also raining in Haiti. That's when I realized that the things I thought were so important in my life were really nothing compared to what the people in Haiti were (and still are) going through. His story helped me put my life in perspective.

I am grateful for what I have and what God has done for me. Jesus also loves the people in Haiti. He died on the cross for all of our sins so that we can have an eternity with Him.

Most people in America don't realize how truly blessed we are. I am glad I had a mission trip experience to help me realize what I have and what's important. I want to make sure everyone knows that Jesus came down to earth to give us hope, a better future, and a chance to be with Him.

His Plans
By Elizabeth Vargas

"But I will restore you to health and heal your wounds," declares the Lord.
Jeremiah 30:17.

An event the summer after my sophomore year of high school changed my life. It all started one afternoon while I was at the park with my boyfriend, enjoying the first few days of summer. Everything was going great until I got a slight headache. Painkillers didn't help, and it quickly got worse.

The next thing I knew, I was in the hospital, and I couldn't open my eyes. I found out I had been in the hospital for a week because I had had a brain aneurysm. Hours of surgery left me with 46 staples and bald spots on my head. When I looked in the mirror a week later, I saw a stranger staring back at me. Everything had gone from bad to worse, and I didn't understand why. The one thing that helped me get through this ordeal was all the prayers and support of friends and family.

Before the aneurysm I had hoped to go to academy my junior year, but with all that had been happening, none of my plans were sure. I was devastated. After a lot of pain and many prayers, I went to see the doctor for a checkup. While there, I realized just how serious things were—I should have lost my vision, and I could have died. But God had other plans for me.

I don't know how, and I still wonder why, but I'm alive and I can see. And I started academy in the fall, right on time. I know now that God will never leave my side and that He has great plans for me.

Ultimate Boy Friend
By Karyn Davis

My command is this: Love each other as I have loved you. Greater love has no one than this, that he lay down his life for his friends. You are my friends. John 15:12-14.

It was one of those nights, the kind where you stay up late talking to a close friend about anything and everything. My roommate, Elizabeth Vargas, and I were discussing a wide variety of things when we landed upon the subject of how cool God really is. It was a miracle that Elizabeth was alive, because she had suffered from a brain aneurysm during the summer. We talked about how Jesus never leaves our side or turns away from us, no matter what. He personally wants to be in a relationship with us. This got me to thinking that it's not all that different from boy/girl scenarios. God has all the qualities we could ever want in someone else, and so much more. This is how I saw it . . .

So there's this guy. He's so awesome. I got to know Him better over the summer, and things just keep getting better. I talk to Him all the time; no one understands me the way He does. I'll admit, it's really cool having Him in my life. He's totally changed the way I view things. He's the kind of person I can trust with anything; no one else ever has to know. He doesn't care about my past; He cares about my future. He loves me just the way I am, no exceptions. He would even die for me. You should definitely get to know Him. Our relationship gets stronger every day, and I want to be with Him for the rest of my life.

God is real, and He wants a real relationship with you. He wants to communicate with you. He has your best interest at heart. He is a true friend. But even better than an earthly friendship or relationship, His love lasts forever. What an amazing future we have to look forward to.

Happy Halloween

By Paige Dagnan

He who dwells in the shelter of the Most High will rest in the shadow of the Almighty. I will say of the Lord, "He is my refuge and my fortress, my God, in whom I trust." Psalm 91:1, 2.

One of the best memories of my life happened on October 31 of my senior year of academy. October 31 is known as Halloween, but more important, on this day of that year it was Sabbath. I was super excited about getting away from campus for the weekend and going home to attend my home church in Summerville, South Carolina. I was especially excited to see my mom, best friends, and church family.

When the worship service ended, some of my best friends, whom I hadn't seen in months, picked me up, and we went to Charleston, a seaside town and one of the most beautiful places in South Carolina. We stayed in Charleston until sunset, enjoying each other's company, taking smiling pictures, drinking in the beauty around us, and laughing at the simplest things.

After sunset we went to a local fair, where I had an even greater blessing given to me: the rest of my best friends were there. We all rode rides, laughed, took pictures, and made many amazing memories. The night finally ended when we drove to a parking lot and had a Smarties war—we threw the candies at each other and enjoyed the craziness of our "war."

In this one day I saw the majority of the people I love most in my life. It was amazing! As I went to bed that night, I reflected on the sermon topic from that morning: God can bring good out of anything. He brought something incredible out of a day so feared and so evil. Just because the world presents and promotes something bad doesn't mean we have to be a part of it.

God gave me a gift that day—it was nothing sinister or scary. He gave me a wonderful day and an evening filled with friends and fellowship. It was an amazing "holiday" I will never forget.

Too Much Candy

By Gary Bradley

I denied myself nothing my eyes desired; I refused my heart no pleasure.
Yet everything was meaningless, a chasing after the wind.
Ecclesiastes 2:10, 11.

Trick-or-treating means getting lots of candy. When I was younger, my sister and I looked forward to it for weeks. We would choose our costumes carefully—they had to be something that was fun but didn't upset Mom. We would put new batteries in our flashlights, and we would get the biggest bag we could carry. Finally the big night would arrive, and Mom would say, "It's time to go."

We would run from house to house while Mom followed us in the car. As the evening progressed, we would meet up with several of our friends and compare bags. We would share which houses gave out the best candy and go back to those places more than once.

One Halloween, before the evening began, Mom told my sister and me to eat just a few pieces of candy and save the rest for later. But I was getting a lot of candy in my bag that night and it looked good, so I decided to eat a few pieces after nearly every house.

I knew Mom would not be happy with me eating so much candy, so I had to figure out what to do with all those candy wrappers. I couldn't put them in my bag, or Mom would find them. I couldn't put them in my pockets, or she would find them when she washed my clothes. I couldn't put them in the trash at home, or she would see them. So I just dropped the wrappers along the road when I thought she wasn't looking. I am embarrassed to say that I did a lot of littering that night.

When we got home and emptied our bags, Mom put the candy into plastic containers. My sister had four containers full, and I barely had three. Mom asked me why my sister seemed to have more candy. I made up some excuse about the people giving her more candy because they thought she was cuter. Mom asked me how I was feeling. I told her I had a stomachache. "Most likely because of all the running," I said. Mom knew better. She knew where the extra candy had gone. She asked me, "Do you think that too much of a good thing maybe isn't a good thing?"

Read Solomon's words in today's Bible verse. The world has a way of tricking kids and grown-ups alike that if we have more we will be happier. Don't be fooled!

My Hardest Day
By Katie Brewer

For the Lord comforts his people and will have compassion on his afflicted ones. Isaiah 49:13.

It was the hardest day of my life. That Saturday night, a little more than a week after my birthday, I found out that my grandfather had died. The news hit me like a steel fist in the gut. I know that people die every day, but it wasn't supposed to be him. I knew this person, this victim of time.

Needless to say, I took the news very hard. Harder than most people thought. I fell into a deep depression and felt alone for a good portion of that year. I didn't get along with my parents as well, and I treated my friends badly. Every problem that I came across was handled the wrong way. I didn't want to think about anyone else but him. I had dreams about my grandfather that scared me to the point of waking up crying. For a long time I felt like no one was there to help me through this, no one to see what was going on inside me. I considered turning to God, but instead I turned away in disgust from the One who had taken my grandfather from me. God was not my friend, I thought. I blamed Him for ripping away my happiness.

It took me awhile, but I finally began to really pray again. Instead of yelling, I started talking. Instead of hating, I became curious. Then one night I finally broke down and let God in. I sobbed as I apologized for being so naive. I prayed and prayed for Him to come to me. That night, God saved me.

When you experience a tragedy, don't yell at God and blame Him (although He understands your frustration). Instead, take Him into your heart and trust Him to pull you through it. God does everything for a reason. That reason may not become apparent to you right away, but He knows what He's doing. Just pray, and God will show you the way.

My "Permanent" F

By Josias Flores

For their feet rush into sin, they are swift to shed blood. Proverbs 1:16.

It was a hot, sunny day. I was enjoying a vacation at my grandma's house in Venezuela. I was excited to see my family members, and I started showing off my red New York Yankees cap. Unfortunately, after my cousin Hector had had it for a while, he decided he wasn't ready to give it back. Well, I started growing impatient, and soon we had started an all-out chase throughout the whole property. My cousin, an expert tree climber, decided to scamper up one of his favorite trees, with me following close behind. Earlier on, as I remembered then, my mom had warned me, a city boy, about climbing trees and told me not to do it. Well, I felt pretty confident about my tree-climbing abilities, so I brushed the thought away as my cousin proceeded to climb yet another tree. This tree's location was very interesting. The trunk of it was on one side of a barbed-wire fence, and the branches were on the other side of the fence. My cousin started climbing agilely up the tree, and I, not ready to give up and determined to catch him, increased my speed, but I quickly lost my grip and landed right on top of the barbed-wire fence.

The next few moments passed by in a flash. The next thing I knew, I was looking up at my cousins, my head hanging about 5 inches from the ground, as bare threads from my shorts were still caught on the fence. As I was brought down, I saw it. My legs were a bloody mess, and it was all coming out of an opening that looked like an F. I remembered my mom's words and how I decided to ignore them. Now, unfortunately, I wear an ugly F scar on my leg as a reminder of the day I failed to obey.

Sometimes people just like me know God's plans, but our pride and love of self stand in the way of it guiding and changing our lives for the better. He has given us countless ways to accept His truths, but we abide in our stubbornness and block the paths that He has given us. However, if we follow His ways, we're sure to reach a perfect destination. Have enormous faith in Him, and we'll be a spitting image of His perfect character. I will not have my scar in heaven to remind me of my failings. No, the only scars in heaven will be on the hands and side of our Savior, who gave His all for us.

Place to Place

By Kaylee Couser

I wait for the Lord, my soul waits, and in his word I put my hope.
Psalm 130:5.

In the fall of my junior year of academy I was given the opportunity to go to Bogenhofen, an Adventist school in Austria, as a short-term exchange student. While I was there I experienced many exciting things. One of those experiences was getting closer to God. Before I went to Austria, I didn't have a very close relationship with God. Don't get me wrong; I wanted a relationship with Him, but it was really hard for me to stay connected with Him. As we were on the plane heading to Austria, I asked God to show Himself to me on the trip. Little did I know that my perspective of Him would change dramatically.

While we were on the campus of Bogenhofen, we enjoyed a Week of Prayer at the school. The speaker was Jeffrey Rojas, and he is the most inspirational speaker I have ever heard. When he spoke, I got such a clear image of who God is and what an amazing person He is. During that week, I connected with God in a way I had never done before. I felt revived. Every day I would wake up and talk to God, sharing with Him my feelings, my life, and my fears. I was very confused, though, because I didn't understand why my relationship with Him was drastically different than the relationship I had with Him prior to my trip. Why is it that sometimes people can feel so connected to Him when at other times they feel disconnected? I had trouble trying to comprehend this.

When I got back from my trip, I was so excited to come home with a new perspective on God and on life. Unfortunately, my excitement didn't last. Once I got home my relationship with God vanished. It was as if I had never had a connection with Him. I was so aggravated! Why did my relationship with Him end?

Although it has taken some thinking, I have finally figured it out. In Austria I didn't have as many distractions. So many things can disconnect us from God: TV, books, money, and even friends can lead us away from God. I learned that I need to turn off the distractions and make Christ a priority. There are going to be those days when God feels inseparable, and those other days when you don't feel as close with Him. But the important thing is to keep walking with God. Don't give up. Make Him your priority!

Who Said Faith Was Easy?

By Ashton Evans

And without faith it is impossible to please God, because anyone who comes to him must believe that he exists and that he rewards those who earnestly seek him. Hebrews 11:6.

Working at summer camp is the best experience in the world. So many things have happened to me at camp that I know God is with me. Having faith in Him has helped me through several situations.

One week I was in charge of taking care of the boats at the ski beach at Nosoca Pines Ranch. My friend Alex and I had to take the covers off and gas the boats up every morning and evening. One morning I decided that I wanted to gas the boats up. Alex usually did it, so it was my first time. Everything was going smoothly, and James, the ski beach director, had just left us alone. I was finishing gassing up the last boat when the key chain for the gas cap broke! It had a little float on it, but that doesn't help if the whole chain breaks. I had lost the key! I told Alex, and he just looked at me and started to laugh. I think he thought I was kidding. I told him to come down and help me find the key.

The one thought that kept running through my mind was that James was going to be really upset with me. I had just gotten in trouble with him earlier that week for taking the sailboat out without permission, and now I had lost the key. Alex and I searched the murky, sandy bottom of Lake Wateree for at least 30 minutes, but we couldn't find the key. Alex stopped me for a second and said we should pray. I told him I had been praying constantly, but that it was still a good idea. So we prayed. Alex now told me with confidence that we were going to find the key in three tries. First try, we went down and no luck. Second try, we searched some more, but still didn't see the key. Alex came back up and said that this was the time we would find the key. We both went under water, and guess what? No key. Alex gave up and went back to the shore. I prayed once more, telling God that I knew He could help me find it. I went down again, and right in front of my face was the key! I jumped and shouted to Alex that I had found it!

God can and will help us when we ask. We just need to remember to have faith.

Dancing Around Integrity

By Alisha A. Michael

I know, my God, that you test the heart and are pleased with integrity.
1 Chronicles 29:17.

Integrity. My simple definition of this meaningful word is this: having the guts to do what's right. Some folks seem to be born with the do-right gene, or maybe it is because they have allowed Jesus to move in and rule their hearts so that pleasing Him becomes their greatest ambition.

Others . . . well, not so much.

When I was a teenager, I frequently fell into the "not so much" category. My love for the Lord was genuine. However, I was slow to let His love of all things honest and true and good change the way I operated. If circumstances weren't panning out the way I desired, I could pull a real John Deere and plow right through whatever stood in my way. That usually meant someone got run over. In one particular instance, I left tracks down the backs of two of my dearest friends.

It was almost time for prom. I'd snagged a glittery gown and scored dinner reservations at the most coveted restaurant in town, and I knew exactly how I'd do my hair. The night would be spectacular. That is, with one exception: my date. Early in the school year my best guy pal, Josh, had asked me to go with him. Not considering I might be dating someone when prom rolled around, I said yes. Big surprise when prom rolled around: I was dating someone. The situation was further complicated by the fact that my boyfriend had asked another girl, Heather, to go with him before I entered the picture. Heather just happened to be my best friend.

Here's where integrity did not make a grand, glittery-gowned entrance. In the throes of relationship drama, my boyfriend and I just couldn't bear the thought of prom without each other. We decided at the last minute to dump our dates and go together. Stunned, Heather and Josh made the best of it. I still wince when I see their smile-free prom photo.

Doing what is right might mean sticking it out in a situation that's not ideal. In this case, it would surely have been a challenging evening, but I'm positive I'd be more pleased with myself today if I'd stuck with plan A. And where is the guy I was dating? Beats me. Amazingly enough, Heather forgave me and is still my best friend. And recently, through Facebook, Josh responded to my long-withheld apology with a show of undeserved mercy.

Now, that's what I call integrity.

Why Am I Here?

By Callie Adams

Humble yourselves before the Lord, and he will lift you up. James 4:10.

I am a third-generation Adventist on both sides of my family. I can find pictures of my great-grandparents on the walls of the academy I attended, because they went there when it first opened. By the time I was 25, I had still never stepped foot in a public school, except to vote.

If you have gone to Adventist schools your whole life, you know that you take Bible classes every year. This includes elementary, academy, college, and even graduate school. Then there are church and vespers on top of that! Adventists are some of the most well-educated Bible scholars in the world.

Not only are we Bible know-it-alls, but we have a subculture all our own. We have our own version of Boy Scouts and Girl Scouts called Pathfinders. We have our own hospitals and even our own bookstores and grocery stores. If you live in Loma Linda or a similar community, you could live your whole life and never leave the safe Adventist bubble! As wonderful as all these programs are, we tend to keep to ourselves and are in danger of becoming like the biblical Jews and hiding the light of our truth behind the walls of our well-established church community.

Several chapters in the beginning of Romans talk about the tradition of being a Jew and how they became obsessed with their subculture and hid the light of the truth behind arrogance and complacency. They thought, *We know the truth and are saved. Our destiny is to be in heaven with God. What else is there?* In Romans 12:3 Paul tells the new church, after a long theology lesson about Jewish tradition, "Don't think you are better than you really are. Be honest in your evaluation of yourselves, measuring yourselves by the faith God has given us" (NLT). He is saying that just because you are in the church doesn't mean you can sit back and relax.

If I am not careful, I can become very cocky and academic about my knowledge of Scripture. However, all that knowledge and all the family legacy and tradition of being in this church does not make me a Christian. Unless I have Jesus in my heart, and not just my head, I am nothing.

M&Ms and Angels

By Elizabeth Wilson

An angel from heaven appeared to him and strengthened him. Luke 22:43.

Angels are always with us. Some people have been fortunate enough to actually see them. Even more people have seen them and not even known it. And others meet ordinary people who are being used by God. I believe I'm probably in the last two groups. I haven't seen anyone in a flowing white robe with feathery wings, but there have been complete strangers who have helped me in critical situations.

When I was 5, a group of people from my church, including my family and me, went to Israel. We had been touring everywhere for the past few days. It was hot, I was tired, and soon I was pitching a fit. Long story short, while throwing my temper tantrum, I hurt myself and ended up riding in a taxi to the hospital, screaming all the way.

In the emergency room, we had to wait for what seemed like hours. My arm was hurting, and I was still screaming. My mom was holding me, partly to comfort me and partly because there were no empty chairs. My hysteria got the attention of a woman, Rochelle, who was also waiting. To our surprise, she spoke perfect English. She quickly offered us her chair and tried to calm me down. When it didn't work, she spoke to the receptionist for us. She was speaking in Hebrew, so we couldn't tell what she was saying, but by the woman's face we could tell she wasn't using the most refined language. Whatever she said, we got in to see the doctor, and she translated for us again. Every time my parents had a problem understanding the doctors or got worried, Rochelle would just show up out of nowhere and calm them down, helping in any way she could.

The next morning I woke up in a room with my left arm in a cast and an IV in my right arm. A few minutes later Rochelle showed up in my doorway. She smiled and handed me two packs of M&Ms. As she and my mom talked, we found out that she was born in the U.S. but had moved to Israel to connect with her Jewish roots. We never saw her after that.

I'm not sure if Rochelle was an angel or if she was just letting God use her to help us. But I do know that God is always watching out for us. He sends just the right people at just the right time. And sometimes they come with chocolate.

A Puppy Masquerade

By Nick Evans

Your beauty should not come from outward adornment, such as braided hair and the wearing of gold jewelry and fine clothes. Instead, it should be that of your inner self, the unfading beauty of a gentle and quiet spirit, which is of great worth in God's sight. 1 Peter 3:3, 4.

I recently went to Kenya, Africa, to visit the Masai people. The first thing we noticed when we arrived were the local folks, kids especially, who were so happy to see us.

We were given the chance to tour the local village, or *boma*. It was surrounded by propped-up sticks and brush. This barrier was to protect them from nighttime predators. Inside this walled circle was an entirely new world to me. The stench of cow manure permeated the air. Besides the smell, the first thing I noticed was the cattle corral. The floor of the corral was covered in rancid cow dung. I looked down at my feet and realized I was stepping in some. I jumped out of it only to land in some more.

Our tour guide showed us inside one of the huts. He told us, "These huts are made out of sticks, brush, and cow dung." What a surprise—it seemed to be everywhere. "And at night," he continued, "the villagers bring the baby calves in here to sleep." This was becoming too much.

I scrambled out into the beautiful sunshine and fly-infested air. I walked up the dung trail, turned the corner, and saw grass. Oh, how sweet it was! I walked over to it, and to my surprise, I saw a small puppy curled into a ball, warming itself in the sun. Being the robust guy I am, I refrained from cooing, but I squatted next to it and reached out to pet its soft fur. Suddenly it wasn't a cute puppy anymore! It was a snapping ball of fury. As I ran away, I realized that this puppy, although it looked sweet, was not a normal little pooch. It was a vicious wild African dog.

I learned a lot on my mission trip. Some cute things are dangerous. And some home situations, as gross as they may seem to me, still produce very loving and happy people. God wants us to be genuine. We must show that Jesus lives in us. We must show that our happiness, kindness, and love toward others is not just a big masquerade.

Prayer

By Spencer Williams

Therefore confess your sins to each other and pray for each other so that you may be healed. The prayer of a righteous man is powerful and effective. James 5:16.

On a mission trip to Portland, Oregon, we worked with Bridgetown Ministries, a ministry for the homeless.

One particular night we did something called night strike. This took place under the local bridge and consisted of handing out food and clothes, giving haircuts, talking with our guests, and various other things. Those of us who were not given one of those jobs went on something called a walkabout. Our task was to walk around the city and pray for it and everyone in it. My group had four guys in it, and I had never met any of them before that night. One was a youth pastor, one was a newly homeless man looking for a job, and the last one was an older man named Barry who just came and helped out.

Nothing unusual happened on the walkabout. We went to the designated places on our city map and met a few interesting people. (One guy played Beethoven's music on the harmonica.) But what really changed me that week, and I mean the absolutely greatest thing that could have happened to me, happened after we returned from the walkabout.

It wasn't one of the conversations or experiences with the guests we were having; it was something a lot more simple but also very humbling. Before we parted ways, Barry asked if he could pray for me. His prayer is what really got to me. It wasn't even a long or complicated prayer. He just said something like "Dear God, please be with Spencer. I know You're going to do some really great things with him, and I just want to ask You to keep leading in his life like I see You've been doing already. Amen." That prayer made me feel something new. I've had people pray for me before, but never before has prayer been so meaningful and made me truly feel like God was right there with me.

The next time you feel God impressing you to do something for someone, first pray with and for him or her. If you simply pray, I know God will do something for that person and, in turn, for you. Prayer is a powerful and life-changing thing. Don't miss out.

Bad Decision

By Jennifer Beckham

Do not follow the crowd in doing wrong. When you give testimony in a lawsuit, do not pervert justice by siding with the crowd. Exodus 23:2.

While working as a lifeguard, I met a lot of fun people. Among them was Adam, a flamboyant college guy who lived life as if it were one big party. Adam and I quickly became good friends. I loved hanging out with him because he made work easy and fun.

Adam and I started carpooling to work every day because we lived close to each other. One day when we arrived at work we found that all of the positions were filled for the various pools. This meant that we both were "extras" and were needed only if one of the other guards got sick on duty and needed to go home. So for most of the day Adam and I walked around doing busywork until it was time for us to go home.

When my boss finally dismissed us, Adam and I changed out of our uniforms and went to play in the park. The only problem was that Adam had brought along alcohol, disguised in a water bottle, for us to drink. I knew that drinking was wrong, but I wanted to have some fun, and the thrill of the secret itself was intoxicating.

After several hours in the park Adam and I decided it was time to go home. Unfortunately, we didn't think to call someone to pick us up, and so Adam, who was much more under the influence than I was, got behind the wheel to drive us home. We were almost to my house when Adam skipped three lanes and almost ran into a police car going in the opposite direction. I was so afraid when the police stopped us. I could hardly breathe when Adam got arrested. As the officer walked toward me, I prayed for help. He didn't arrest me, but he did give me a stern warning and left me thinking some pretty heavy thoughts.

I know that I shouldn't have been drinking that day, and I know that I should never have trusted and admired Adam the way I did. Our actions could have injured or even killed people. Fortunately we were spared, and I have learned my lesson. Disobeying God and choosing to disobey the law to have some "fun" is never the right thing to do. I allowed a bad influence into my life—a choice I regret. But God saved me. And I am thankful to Him for my life and another chance to live right and choose Him.

America the Beautiful

By Stella Bradley

But the fruit of the Spirit is love, joy, peace, patience, kindness, goodness, faithfulness, gentleness and self-control. Galatians 5:22, 23.

America the Beautiful" was written by Katharine Lee Bates. She wrote the song in 1893 while on a trip to Colorado Springs, Colorado. After reaching the top of Pike's Peak on a hike, she said, "All the wonder of America seemed displayed there, with the sea-like expanse." The view was so magnificent that it inspired her to write the song that is considered by some to be the country's unofficial national anthem.

It was never intended as a song, but the words fit easily into musical meter. For two years after "America the Beautiful" was written, it was sung to many different tunes, including "Auld Lang Syne." But the tune we've grown accustomed to is from an old hymn by Samuel Augustus Ward called "Materna."

The night Bates wrote the poem she commented to her friends that other countries had failed because, while they may have been "great," they had not been "good." She went on to say that "unless we are willing to crown our greatness with goodness, and our bounty with brotherhood, our beloved America may go the same way." Her insightful words are a challenge for us to rise above the norm and be compassionate and responsible beyond expectations.

Galatians 5:22 talks about the "fruit of the spirit"—qualities we should have if God is in our lives. Goodness is listed; greatness is not.

Today in America we honor our veterans. May we never forget the sacrifices made for our country's freedom, and even more important, the sacrifice made by Jesus for our spiritual freedom. And as we contemplate how blessed we are, let's take Katharine Bates' words to heart. Look at others as brothers and sisters in Christ and treat them accordingly. Let's do our best to be good.

Snow Angel

By Crystal Hattar

Then he calls his friends and neighbors together and says, "Rejoice with me; I have found my lost sheep." Luke 15:6.

Have you ever wanted to break the rules but then ended up doing what you thought was right?

When I was in the sixth grade, my family and I went skiing in Colorado. I was excited because that year my cousin's cousin, Becca, came. We girls wanted to do something exciting by having our own miniadventure during this family ski trip.

Becca and I asked our parents if we could go down a run by ourselves and meet them at the bottom. They agreed, so we started down the mountain. On the way down we noticed a trail toward our right. We both paused, and at the exact same time asked, "Do you want to go down and see where we end up?" Adventure was the only thing on our mind, so off we went. Becca and I landed in some trouble by losing our skis in a snowdrift, plus we had no cell phone service. What were we going to do? Our parents were going to flip out if we weren't at the bottom soon. We did the logical thing: we started digging through the snowdrift looking for our skis. That took about 15 minutes. After finding all but one ski, we decided to head down the mountain, so we started walking. Fortunately, we soon found our "snow angel," a ski patrol officer who came up behind us and asked, "Ladies, can I be of some assistance?"

"Yes!" we exclaimed, and then we explained our whole story to him. He then told us that there was a group of worried people down at the ski patrol center and that he would take us to them.

When we arrived, we found our family. We explained the whole story to them. They simply laughed and told us to be more careful, not to wander off, and to listen to directions. "If you follow the signs, you're not going to get lost." They forgave us and moved on (but to this day they still make fun of me).

The lesson I learned is that God is like the ski patrol guy. He is always there for us even when we wander off the trail. But we don't have to meet trouble if we follow the signs and instructions found in the Bible and heed the warnings.

Don't Give Up
By Christopher Busche

But those who hope in the Lord will renew their strength.
They will soar on wings like eagles; they will run and not grow weary,
they will walk and not be faint. Isaiah 40:31.

Have you ever felt as if you could do anything and everything and never get hurt? Well, I've always felt that way.

Ever since I could walk, I have been one of the most active people I know. My biggest passion is playing sports. Sports are so competitive and challenging—I'm always looking for a battle and some fun. Up until about two years ago, I thought I was invincible. Then suddenly my luck changed. Now it is the complete opposite for me. I can't find a way to stay healthy. From dislocating my shoulder six times to rupturing a tendon in my foot to having two shoulder surgeries, it seems as if I just can't stay out of the doctor's office.

Sitting on the sidelines is very difficult for me. It is not in my nature simply to watch the activity—I want to be in the middle of it. But maybe God has a lesson for me through my trials. Maybe I'm supposed to sit back and observe and cheer for a while. Maybe I need to take a turn in a different role. I have definitely learned to be more patient and to recognize the skills that others have.

Something else I have learned from my "down time" is that it won't last forever! And I don't just mean the healing process here on earth. I am talking about a day to come when there will be no more injuries, no more weariness, no more pain. I don't believe that God has a sedentary life planned for me in heaven. I think I will be more active than ever—playing sports, hiking, biking, and flying all over the universe.

Until that time, I know that I should be thankful for everything and look for the good in all my circumstances. So many things in life distract me from the main purpose of life. But God has promised us that if we live for Him, we will be given eternal life, and then we really will be invincible. I can hardly wait.

Stumped

By Gary Bradley

Children, obey your parents in the Lord, for this is right. Ephesians 6:1.

My dad is an engineer who can build nearly anything. But I think the coolest thing he has ever built was my orange-and-black go-cart. It was the best, with two forwards and a reverse. I took good care of my cherished cart. If I wasn't riding it, I was thinking about it.

My dad let me ride anywhere I wanted except on the neighbor's property. And I obeyed him all summer long.

In the fall my favorite thing to do was to rake up giant piles of leaves and then race full speed through them, blasting a shower of leaves everywhere.

One Sunday afternoon I noticed that the neighbors had an especially large pile of leaves in the woods just beside their house. Now, I knew that Dad had told me not to ride in the neighbor's yard. But as I sat there in my go-cart, I began to reason away my dad's words. After all, I would be on their property for only a short time, and I would rake the pile back up for them. No one would ever really know. Besides, Dad and the neighbors were nowhere in sight.

I revved my motor, shifted into first gear, and floored the accelerator. I picked up speed, then shifted into second. This was going to be the greatest leaf pile whoosh ever.

At this point I remember everything in slow motion. I saw the leaf pile engulf my go-cart and go over my head. *Wham!* I felt a strong force throw me off my go-cart and away from the leaf pile. I felt a sharp pain in my abdomen where the steering wheel had hit me. I struggled for breath as I saw my go-cart's terribly bent fame. Everything was quiet, but I saw my dad and the neighbors running toward me as I lay on the ground.

I was all right—just stunned and bruised. It was pretty apparent to everyone what had happened. The neighbors were very apologetic. "We're so sorry. We raked this big pile of leaves around our big oak tree stump."

Needless to say, I didn't ride my go-cart for some time. Dad eventually repaired it, but that time I rode it having learned an important lesson. I planned to listen much more carefully to my dad so that I wouldn't be stumped again.

The Conscientious Objector
By Andy Rodriguez

*No, in all these things we are more than conquerors
through him who loved us. Romans 8:37.*

It was 1945, and the U.S. Army's 77th Infantry Division had landed on the island of Okinawa after fighting in Guam and Leyte. Japanese soldiers were hidden everywhere and were ready to strike their enemy. American soldiers had to take control of the island, but in order to do so they had to face their greatest obstruction, a jagged 400-foot escarpment. The steep cliff stretched across the island and was heavily guarded by the well-armed Japanese army.

When the order finally came to attack, a man by the name of Desmond T. Doss, a conscientious objector (someone who doesn't carry a gun), said, "I believe prayer is the best lifesaver there is. The men should really pray before going up." After prayer the lieutenant of Company B gave the order to move out. The soldiers laboriously climbed the cliff as bullets whizzed past their heads. They slowly managed to make ground, and soon they had only 50 more feet to go.

As Company B struggled to reach the top of the cliff, they were shot at with heavy enemy gunfire. To their left, Company A was vigorously trying to reach the top as well. Five men were killed in Company A, and casualties rose so high that they could no longer proceed. Company B was now forced to take the escarpment by themselves. Men from Doss's company climbed onto the summit and fought with all their might. They went with guns blazing and shot down not one or two, but nine machine gun turrets. The American soldiers were victorious. Not one person in Doss's company was killed, and the only wound was from a man who got his hand damaged by a rock. It was a miracle, and it was all because of one man who decided to trust God and pray.

There is much more to this story. Read Doss's biography and learn about even more wartime miracles. And remember that prayer and faith in God are very powerful. God cares about you no matter where you are. Commit your life to Him, and you can rest safely in His arms.

Something New!

By Crystal Hattar

*Strengthening the disciples and encouraging them to remain true
to the faith. "We must go through many hardships to enter the
kingdom of God," they said. Acts 14:22.*

Does the past ever haunt you? It takes no prisoners and shows no mercy. What is done is done and is always in our memories—always. No matter how hard we try, we can never take back hurtful words or careless actions. What-might-have-been and what-should-have-happened are all we can talk about now. That is, unless we had a way to go back in time, which I wish could happen, but sadly can't. So if things can't be changed, why do we spend so much time on the problems of our past?

I once heard a fictional story about a room in heaven with different types of clocks. Each clock represented someone's life on earth, and when the clock stopped, so did the person it represented. Only God knew when the clock would stop.

Most people, teenagers especially, don't like to think of when our "time" will end. We all want to live happily ever after. But it's a thought we need to spend a little time on. We don't have time to waste dwelling on the past or not thinking about our future. We need to make every moment count while we still have time.

Remember, the past is just the past. Ask for forgiveness and make things right as best as you can. And then move on! Do what you can in the present to make this world a happier place. Use what you've learned to help others. And when you are discouraged, ask God to lift you up and keep you moving forward.

Don't forget to learn from your mistakes and do everything you can not to repeat them. You can never fully enjoy the present or look forward to the future if you are still living in the past. The clock is ticking.

Spoiled

By Stephanie Thomas

One thing I ask from the Lord, this is what I seek: that I may dwell in the house of the Lord all the days of my life, to gaze upon the beauty of the Lord and to seek him in his temple. Psalm 27:4.

During my senior year of academy I had the amazing opportunity of going on a two-and-a-half-week mission trip to Chetumal, Mexico. We were a fairly large group with diverse talents and assignments. Some students preached the Share Him series at different churches, and others divided up into children's ministries groups and played with the kids while their parents attended the evangelistic meetings.

I was part of the children's ministries group, and I absolutely loved it. Every night we would go to a church and put on a program for the kids. They were always so happy to see us and were thrilled to learn more about Jesus. However, one day about halfway through the trip, I was having a rough time. I missed my family and boyfriend, and I started feeling sick to my stomach. I didn't want to go to the program that night. I just wanted to stay at our comfortable hotel and sulk in my self-pity. I ended up going to the church that night, but I was certainly not cheerful.

As soon as we got to the church, the little kids ran up to us and clung to our arms. They were filled with such happiness and gratitude. The kids were from very poor families. Some kids didn't even have a pair of shoes or a hairbrush. This really struck me and made me start thinking. I often complain about not having a cute pair of new shoes (when my closet is full of many other pairs) or the latest phone style. I realize that I am quite spoiled. I have a roof over my head, food to eat, enough clothes to last for more than a week, a Christian education, and friends and family who love me. But I still complain. What's wrong with this picture?

The kids in Mexico that I met were probably the happiest kids I've ever seen. And this was just because they had Jesus in their lives. They put all their trust, love, and self-worth in God, not in material things. Their happiness was contagious, and I'm glad of it.

I believe that this shows how important it is to have Jesus in our lives. True happiness is found only through Christ.

Many Ways

By Jihun Joung

He restores my soul. He guides me in paths of righteousness for his name's sake. Psalm 23:3.

My home is in South Korea, but I now attend school in America. When I was in elementary school, I was in the national school in Korea. At first it was fine. I had many friends and enjoyed it. But my parents heard that the Seventh-day Adventist school was even better—it promised a good educational environment, and the students and teachers were very kind. So my family moved to a house near the Adventist school, and I started attending. It was my first time to go to a Christian school, and I went with the perception that all Christians are kind and friendly. But I quickly learned differently. At this school the students seemed to be rich and greedy. They didn't like people who came in from the national school, and I was confused by their treatment toward me. It was very hard to find a good friend.

I was very discouraged, and my grades suffered. I could not continue in that school. So I went to the national middle school in my village, but in this school people (adults especially) didn't like Seventh-day Adventists. I was very perplexed, and I struggled with my relationship with God. I did have some friends, and they were more kind to me than the students from my previous school, but it was still difficult.

But one day the local Adventist middle school called my parents and convinced them to send me back. I didn't really want to go, but I gave my best effort. Unfortunately, I felt that I was quickly labeled by everyone and that I couldn't measure up to their expectations. I soon lost interest in school and felt like giving up. So my parents found a school in America for me to attend. I went to Great Lakes Adventist Academy in Michigan, and it turned my life around. People were kind, and I easily made friends and strengthened my relationship with God.

On an orchestra tour our school visited Mount Pisgah Academy, and I was impressed with the school. I felt I was up for another adventure, and the next school year I enrolled at MPA. I like it here. I study hard, exercise every day, and am involved in choir, band, and soccer.

I know that God has allowed me to have difficult experiences for a reason. I plan to continue to grow in Christ and do my best in all things no matter the circumstances.

God Is Amazing

By Kyli Jung

[The Lord] wraps himself in light as with a garment; he stretches out the heavens like a tent and lays the beams of his upper chambers on their waters. He makes the clouds his chariot and rides on the wings of the wind.
Psalm 104:2, 3.

One of the things we studied in my earth science class was the solar system and the universe. When I think about our solar system and how God has placed each planet in its orbit around the sun, I am amazed. God put our planet in exactly the right place. If we were any closer, we would be too hot, and if we were any farther away, we would be too cold. God keeps each planet spinning around the sun in its orbit without any help from us. He put each star in its place and causes the sun to rise in the morning and set in the evening. Each new sunrise is amazing. The colors God uses in sunrises and sunsets are more amazing than any artist could paint.

In biology we looked at and read about cells. Each cell is amazing in the way it is designed. Only God could design such intricate things. Each part of the cell has its own job to do, and each part works with the others. When I think about all the parts of the human body, I am amazed. God designed our body so that each system works together to keep us alive. Our brain is more complex than the best computer. Our heart keeps beating without any help from us, and it keeps sending blood throughout our body even when we are asleep. Our bodies are amazing!

When I look at all the different trees that God has created, I am in awe. The tallest and biggest trees that seem to reach up to the sky all started with a tiny seed. God planned that the seed would have everything in it that it needed to grow into a huge tree. God planned that trees would send oxygen into the air and would provide shade for people and animals. The flowers God created are more beautiful and varied than any person could imagine.

The different kinds of animals that God has created show how amazing and creative He is. I know that God has a great sense of humor when I look at some of the animals He has created—such as the duck-billed platypus.

Everything in nature shows us how awesome and amazing God is. Take time today to look around and thank God for what He has done.

The Ugly Shoes

By Isabel Alvarez

He who is kind to the poor lends to the Lord, and he will reward him for what he has done. Proverbs 19:17.

A few years ago I had the opportunity to go to Africa. While there I had many amazing experiences that were life-changing for me. But one event especially stands out.

Part of my job there was to help with a Vacation Bible School program at a school that had more than 500 kids. All of the children were very enthusiastic, and we immediately got attached to them. So on our last day it was very hard for us. Everyone was saying their goodbyes, with tears in their eyes. Before I left, I noticed a group of boys watching me. I walked over to them, and I felt an instant urge to give them my shoes. I thought for a second. I mean, why would I give one of them my old shoes? Would they even want them? I took off my shoes and handed them to a boy. His eyes shone with excitement as he tried them on. Perfect fit. I can't even start to explain the look of joy on this child's face. It was like nothing I had ever seen before—pure happiness. Why? I mean the shoes were pretty worn and messed up. And actually they were just another item in my big collection of "items not needed." But to this boy, these old ragged shoes meant so much to him. He was thrilled to have them.

I now realize that the less people have, the more they appreciate the little things in life, and that's what God wants. That day I walked back barefooted. But I didn't care. I had made someone happy. Best of all, I know I became a better person through this experience. I knew from that day on I would appreciate every little thing I had—even if it was a pair of ugly, ragged shoes.

By My Side

By Stephen Drummond

Our help is in the name of the Lord, the Maker of heaven and earth.
Psalm 124:8.

I had the privilege of going to Chetumal, Mexico, for two and a half weeks on a mission trip. Forty of us went from our school. I was one of 17 students who volunteered to preach an evangelistic series at a village church. A few days before we left for the trip, I was feeling discouraged and not excited at all. I just couldn't get over the fact that I had to go to a different country to preach 18 sermons at a church by myself for two weeks. What had I signed up for?

During the trip I definitely prayed without ceasing. Every evening before I went up to speak, I prayed that God would be by my side and that He would speak through me.

I know God answered my prayer. The whole trip was truly a blessing. What really made my trip great was the church I preached at. It was a small brick church with open windows and a steel roof. A few fans kept the 30 members somewhat comfortable. But what really made the church great was the people. They were so friendly. They made me feel like I was part of their family, and I felt loved. I admired the fact that they were always happy in whatever conditions they were in. During one of the meetings, I actually went up front and sang a duet with a woman who would sing every evening before I would go up to preach. I never dreamed I would ever do a duet with anyone in front of a church! We sang the song "You Are My All in All" in English because she had already learned the song in English. We sang a cappella, and even the little kids in the congregation knew the chorus and sang along with us. It was an amazing experience.

God was clearly by my side on this trip. He got rid of my negative thoughts and helped me have a positive attitude. I learned that the most important thing is serving the Lord selflessly and sharing Him with others. I learned to rely on the Lord, because He truly is my all in all. I pray that I'll see my new "family" from Chetumal in the kingdom of heaven.

What Does It Mean?

By Olivia Williams

All these blessings will come upon you and accompany you if you obey the Lord your God. Deuteronomy 28:2.

What does it mean to be thankful? Every time Thanksgiving comes around, everyone asks what I'm thankful for and I reply, "My family, friends, food, and a roof over my head." That usually ends the conversation. As I've gotten older, I want to know the deeper meanings of words, events, holidays, etc. So recently I looked up the word "thankful" and it said this: "Thankful—feeling or showing gratitude." As soon as I read that, something hit me. I feel grateful and I talk about it, but do I really show that I'm grateful? I mean, I clean up and put away the dishes, but does that really count as showing that I'm grateful for a good meal?

I read a story about a family who made this huge Thanksgiving meal and then gave it all to a homeless mother who had four children. That would be so hard for me to do. I mean that's giving away the turkey, mashed potatoes, and gravy—not simply sharing it, but giving it *all* away. I would have a difficult time doing that. But the story was inspirational. It planted a desire in me to want to make a difference.

Many families, even in your own town, are not able to eat a Thanksgiving meal. Many people, kids included, do not get three square meals a day. So often we take our meals for granted, never even considering what it would be like not to eat whenever we want.

Looking at the big picture is overwhelming. But if each of us did just a little more to help others, we could share a lot of happiness. We could start with helping more around our own homes, then we could branch out to our local community. No matter if we do something big (such as making a meal for someone) or small (such as taking time to really listen), anything is good. Remember that we can all do great things with God's help. In fact, if we sincerely pray about it, He will place projects in our path. God would love to help us out in helping others. So this Thanksgiving I challenge you to do something for someone. I challenge you to act on the word "grateful."

What Are Your Treasures?

By Stella Bradley

But seek first his kingdom and his righteousness, and all these things will be given to you as well. Matthew 6:33.

Today is Black Friday, the biggest shopping day of the year. Stores, promising doorbuster deals in an attempt to boost their retail sales, will be open long before the sun comes up. Although the day after Thanksgiving has served as the unofficial beginning of the Christmas season for decades, Christmas decorations have actually been up since September in some stores.

I'm not against getting a good deal or enjoying Christmas decorations, but I think that we are easily distracted by the frenzy around us and that our society has complicated the holiday season.

As I look at the decorated trees in the stores and see the beautiful (and often very expensive) ornaments, I can't help comparing them to a rare and precious ornament that adorns my own Christmas tree each year. One of my favorite Christmas ornaments is actually a piece of paper, roughly cut, and colored with crayons. To anyone else it might look worthless, but to me it is a priceless gift from my daughter—something she made when she was 4. No monetary value can be assigned to it. It is irreplaceable to me, and I would never discard it.

So who decides what is valuable and what is not? If you had to think of the most valuable items you have—the two or three things you would save from a fire—what items would you choose? Most likely you would choose irreplaceable possessions such as a picture, a handwritten letter from a loved one, or a sentimental token or gift—things that are beyond monetary value to you, things that could not be replaced at Walmart or the mall.

As we approach the retail world's favorite season, keep in mind that the most important things in life have no price tag. Think about getting creative with your gift-giving this year: write a poem, paint a picture, play a musical piece you've practiced, create a coupon book for chores, organize a scavenger hunt, plan a winter picnic, make a photo collage, etc. Put building friendships with your family, friends, and the Lord at the top of your to-do list this season.

Don't let the scramble for things be your priority. Remember that your true treasure is in heaven.

The Butterfly

By Reyna Torrez

I am the Lord, and there is no other; apart from me there is no God. I will strengthen you, though you have not acknowledged me. Isaiah 45:5.

The sun was shimmering over the trees, and I could hear the birds singing as I walked down the dirt path. I found an open field and plopped down. I was feeling discouraged; I was supposed to speak the next day for church in the afternoon, and I was terrified. I had never told my story to anyone, much less in front of a church and my peers. I had awakened early and gone out to think and pray. I prayed in the open field and told God how I felt. But I felt as though nothing had changed. I was still nervous and scared. I got up on my feet and kicked the grass. I felt angry, annoyed, and frustrated. I walked back to the house, rested on the back porch for a while, and then headed inside. Why couldn't God just take away my fear? Why wouldn't He do it? Then I saw the butterfly.

The delicate creature was stunning—it had orange-and-black spots splashed over its wings. Then it flew by me and bumped right into a window. The butterfly kept banging into the window, trying to fly out. I noticed that there was an open window right beside the closed one, so I tried to push it to the open one, but the beautiful butterfly was determined to get through the closed one.

Wow, I thought to myself. *You are a stupid butterfly. I'm trying to help you, but you've got to let me. I might hurt you if I push you too hard. Let me help you. This way is so much better. You won't be able to get out that way.*

I was beginning to get frustrated, so I trapped the butterfly in my hands and released it outside. I watched as the last flicker of orange and black fluttered off into the woods.

Don't we sometimes act like that butterfly? We think our way is just fine, when in fact we're too blind to see the window that is open right beside us. However, God can see the whole picture even when we can't. Sometimes we tend to push God away when we need Him the most. But if we will let Him, God will get us through anything. He will lead us and take our worries and fight our battles for us. We've just got to let Him.

Music

By Addie Dorough

They sing to the music of tambourine and harp; they make merry to the sound of the flute. Job 21:12.

Music. It is more than just words without meaning or a catchy tune—it is a heart-felt explosion of emotions that is set free to enlighten, inform, and entertain an audience. There is passion behind each song and a fervor that cannot be denied. Music is powerful and has the ability to influence beyond much else.

Not many young people today fall in love with the melodious sound of the harp and flute as stated in Job. However, that was precisely the manner in which God was worshipped back in biblical times. It was the only way people knew how to proclaim their love for Him. From my view it seems that there was simply one style, and that style suited all.

Nowadays, however, we have many styles of music to listen to, and everyone seems to have their individual preference. If a group of four people is in a car, at least one of them is bound not to like the CD or the radio station chosen. Even when it comes to worshipping the one and only God, people cannot agree on one style of music. There seems to be a division between those who want to sing contemporary music and those who would rather sing from the hymnal.

However, one thing that people often overlook is that God still has one style, and one style that will forever suit Him. He simply wants us to praise Him. No matter the style, He will always accept a sincere song. I feel closest to God when I listen to music or am singing. I am not even a musically inclined person (I prefer sports), but I feel God all around me when I listen to Hillsong United and Tenth Avenue North. However, when I listen to secular music, secular ideas start seeping into my brain. I subconsciously begin using more vulgar language and inappropriate innuendos, and consequently, I rely less on Jesus.

Music is extremely powerful. Find the style that fits your taste and lifts your thoughts toward heaven. Be tolerant of other people's choice of spiritual music. And learn to fully appreciate God's gift of music. May we always use it to praise Him.

My Prayers for My Family and My Life

By Lara Woo

And pray in the Spirit on all occasions with all kinds of prayers and requests. With this in mind, be alert and always keep on praying for all the saints. Ephesians 6:18.

When I was 14 years old, I went to the Philippines to go to school. This was the first time I had been away from my family, and I missed them a lot. I thought about my family all the time, always wondering how they were. Every night I would pray for my family before I went to bed. I would ask God to take care of them and keep them happy, healthy, and safe from danger. After I prayed, I was always able to sleep better because I felt at peace and had a sense of calmness. If I ever forgot to pray, the next day I never felt right. Sometimes my friends teased me about praying, but I never stopped. My prayers, I believe, benefited both my family and me.

I want to always stay near God, so I pray to Him every day. When I have a test coming up, I ask God to give me a clear mind so that I can focus on studying. I ask Him to help me study with diligence and focus so that I will do well on my test.

I know that God cares about every part of my life. Once I was having a lot of trouble with one of my friends. She and I had a big misunderstanding, and I had a lot of bad feelings toward her. I asked God to take away all the bad feelings I had. He helped me to be more positive toward her. All my bad feelings were gone, and we were able to become friends again. God cares about all my feelings, and He will help me get rid of all my negative ones.

If I stay close to God and ask Him to come into my life, He will come in and fill my heart with His Holy Spirit. When He is in my heart, I will not have room for bad feelings. It is very important to ask Him to come into my life every day. My prayer for everyone is that they will ask God each day to come into their lives and they will go to Him with all their problems and joys.

My Angel Can Drive

By Carolina Diaz

*But the Lord is faithful, and he will strengthen and protect you
from the evil one. 2 Thessalonians 3:3.*

When I was a little girl, my dad was the pastor of a number of churches near Cancun, Mexico. He liked his work, but the roads that he had to travel were dangerous. One particular road from one of the churches to our house was extremely dangerous. No one ever traveled on it at night, because there were many gangs in that area and they often assaulted people. Even the police were scared of the gangs and avoided that particular road.

One night my family was out until 10:00 p.m. visiting with church members when we decided it was time to start the two-hour ride home. In order to get home, we had to travel that very dangerous road. It was dark and scary. My parents started praying and reciting Psalm 34:7.

Suddenly a car's lights shown behind us, letting us know that we were not alone and making us feel a little safer. The car followed us until we reached the bigger and better-lit highway. Then we lost sight of it.

Starting that night and continuing every time we drove on the dangerous road, that car would show up and follow us all the way to the highway. My parents tried to see what the car looked like, but it was so dark they could see only the car's lights. One night we even pulled over to let the car pass to see who it was, but when we did, the car stopped too. We waited, but the car never moved. So my dad started going again, and so did the car. One night we tried to trick the car, so we stopped our car right past a blind curve in the road. We thought that since it wouldn't see us pulled over, it would pass us and we could get a good look. But the car never passed us, even though it had followed us for the previous two hours. We drove back onto the road looking for the mysterious car, but the road was empty. For the next three years that car followed us. We never drove on that dangerous road alone. People were amazed that we safely traveled that road so often. But we knew we were safe!

The same God who sent angels to take care of my family a long time ago in Mexico still looks after me today! Praise Him!

Successful

By Zeko Burgess

The Lord is good, a refuge in times of trouble.
He cares for those who trust in him. Nahum 1:7.

One morning at home in Bermuda I got a surprise phone call. To my amazement, it was the coach of the Bermuda National Squad for Cricket. He was calling to invite me to train for the Bermuda cricket team. At first I didn't know if I should take his offer, because even though I dreamed of making the team, I wasn't sure if I was really good enough. But it didn't take long to accept his offer and start making plans.

Since Bermuda is a British colony, our two most played sports are football (soccer) and cricket. To represent the country, if I made the team, would be such an honor.

As I arrived at training, I had doubts, because all my club teammates were there and they also were good players, so I knew that qualifying would be competitive. I would have to work hard even to come close to making the team. During our first training session the drills were complicated—I didn't really catch on very quickly, and I didn't do very well. I became discouraged and felt like giving up and leaving, but I didn't want to be seen as a quitter. So I kept pushing myself, and I eventually started to improve and succeed, which was a huge relief.

I was busy for the next several months—all of my free time was spent in practice. Then, the final training session arrived—it was intense! All of the players knew that they would have to make a good impression and work their absolute hardest to be chosen. At the end of the session, we were congratulated for our efforts and told to wait for a phone call to let us know if we had made the team. Later that evening I got the call and found out that all my hard work had indeed paid off. I made the Bermuda National Squad Cricket Team. Victory!

Most worthwhile things in life take effort. And when we want something badly enough we will practice, work, and focus completely on our goals. We should always apply that same principle to our spiritual goals as well. Nothing is more important than having Jesus as our friend and getting to His heavenly kingdom. Let's all do whatever it takes to make His team and hear Him call our name. That will be true victory!

Learning the Hard Way
By Josias Flores

*Therefore, if anyone is in Christ, he is a new creation;
the old has gone, the new has come! 2 Corinthians 5:17.*

One summer I worked for the maintenance department at Mount Pisgah Academy. One day I had to work a little overtime and throw away a bunch of trash from the school cafeteria. I was hot and tired, but luckily my coworker and friend Kyle and I had golf carts that we were using to transport the trash from the cafeteria to the dumpster.

At last we loaded our final bags and boxes of trash. We would soon be free for the day. I was thinking about getting off work as I drove along with Kyle trailing closely behind in his golf cart. I had my cart on full throttle, going down a steep hill leading to the dumpster; just another turn, and I would be there. I barely tapped the brakes and made the turn. Unfortunately, I was going a little too fast, and the boxes I had beside me started sliding toward me, knocking my left leg out of the golf cart. I struggled to hold on as the cart tipped up on two wheels. A loud screeching noise filled my ears as I was engulfed in darkness. I opened my eyes to find myself trapped under the golf cart and surrounded by parts of the windshield and trash everywhere.

Thankfully, Kyle was right behind me and instantly came to my rescue. I was numb—numb to the pain, numb to the people around me, numb to the consequences of my actions. I sat down and took it all in.

After a week of limping and painful road rash, I finally started getting back my driving confidence. (I had a good boss who gave me a second chance.) I certainly drove more slowly and carefully. And I learned not to be reckless with other people's property.

Sometimes we are too reckless with our spiritual life. We speed through our devotions and prayers just so we can get on to other things while still feeling like we did our "job." But this may lead to not-so-good choices that hurt. Instead, we should be focused on spending quality time with Jesus. God has promised us that if we turn to Him He will create us again, taking away our old person of sin. If you sincerely ask Him and do your part, I guarantee that He will come through and transform you into an incredible being.

Kenya

By Timothy Arthur Douglas IV

For the eyes of the Lord range throughout the earth to strengthen those whose hearts are fully committed to him. 2 Chronicles 16:9.

I became a new person in Kenya, Africa, while on a mission trip during my junior year of academy. I was intrigued by the ways of the Christian Masai.

They may not know all the fundamental beliefs. They may not have the Ten Commandments memorized or even understand them all, but in their hearts they know God. They believe in Jesus, and they are hungry to know more about Him and to be like Him. They don't place great value on money and success. The way of life for the Masai warrior is to tend herds of sheep, goats, and cows—just like shepherds in Bible times. The parable about the lost lamb and the story of Daniel in the lions' den are real to them. As they travel on foot for miles through the savanna, there are many dangers—lions, elephants, leopards, and hyenas, to name only a few. But the people know that God loves them and protects them from harm—and that is enough for them.

A lot of their time is spent getting to know God. They talk about Him with their family and friends around the campfire at night. They talk about how they want to treat people better and share their love of God with them. The Sabbath is something sacred and dear to them. No matter what the weather is like, they walk many miles to attend church on Sabbath, their feet tired and dirty when they arrive. But they go. Learning more about God is the most important thing to them.

I wish that we felt that way more often. Television and technology often distract us from experiencing God. It is difficult to hear His "still small voice" above the sounds that overpower it. We must get to the place, like the Christian Masai warrior, that learning more about God is the most important thing to us as we prepare our lives and hearts for His soon coming.

Leading by Example
By Addie Dorough

Follow my example, as I follow the example of Christ. 1 Corinthians 11:1.

When I was in the sixth grade, I made the junior varsity basketball team at my school. Honestly, I was more interested in learning how to play the sport than making friendships and becoming a part of something. In my opinion, the sport itself should have been the sole focus, and I thought I had the right frame of mind. Nevertheless, it turned out that being a team member meant more than having an awesome endurance level and being able to steal the ball, or make every shot I took! It was about working together and anticipating my teammates' moves in order to assist the team as a whole.

Every day before practice began we had a short devotional thought. Coach Eggers often shared some thoughts, that would springboard into a discussion, but she preferred for her players to lead out. She wanted us to come up with relevant topics and issues that could genuinely be helpful to our team. One girl, the best defensive player on the team, always offered to present these devotions—to the point where the coach began to tell her no because she wanted others to have the opportunity to lead out. This girl was not only an amazing player but also a beautiful girl inside and out. She was such a firm believer in God, and every student in the school admired her fiery passion.

I respected her more than almost anyone else I knew. I wanted to be like her in every way possible! Looking back now, I probably annoyed her because I regularly copied her. She never let me know that, though! We would literally sit and just talk about God. My faith grew at lightning speed, and it was because she took the time to lead me. She was just an all-around great person, and everyone knew it. She was trustworthy and kind, fearless yet soft-spoken, and her smile could make anyone's day.

It is my goal to be like my teammate, whom I looked up to. And I hope you will strive to be the person others look up to. And always remember that the best role model has been provided already—Jesus. Strive to be a leader; use God as your example; and proclaim Jesus to the world.

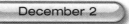

What Do I Do?

By Callie Adams

Never be lazy, but work hard and serve the Lord enthusiastically.
Romans 12:11, NLT.

Be honest! Are you really that great because you know how to pronounce every Bible name? Are you "saved" because you have every Pathfinder honor ever created? Is your faith stronger because you have been a member of the Adventist Church since your dedication at birth? Does following the "rules" (not smoking, not drinking, etc.) make you an effective worker for Christ? No! If you are honest in your assessment of yourself and your faith, you will discover that you are no better than someone who doesn't go to church.

God loves us all the same—we are all sinners. He does not love anyone less; therefore, He does not love anyone more. We do not win some kind of celestial contest when we know every verse and can sing every hymn. We are not to esteem ourselves more than any other human. We are to serve our community in humility and spread His love. His earthly purpose was to show us how to love.

So what do we do once we realize this? Read Romans 12:11 again, and then look inside yourself and decide *why* you are a Christian. Who are you? How do you define yourself? What is your purpose in your church? How can you take all that knowledge, all that tradition, and use it for God's glory? How are you spreading His love to the world?

You have a special function in God's ministry, no matter your age or how long you have been a part of the church. Sitting in a pew after many years of schooling is not Christianity. Living a good life without ever sharing Jesus is not what He intended when He set up the church. God wants you to be a part of the body of Christ. No body part sits around and does nothing.

In your self-evaluation, decide what God is calling you to do. If you truly ask—honestly seeking His guidance—God will put a burden on your heart. There are countless stories of people who honestly sought the guidance of God and when they struck out in faith, their steps were guided in the path He set out for them. He may ask you to go overseas or maybe just across the railroad tracks in your own town. Do not be afraid! You are God's special instrument, and He will use you if you seek Him.

Snow!

By Amanda Skilton

We all stumble in many ways. If anyone is never at fault in what he says, he is a perfect man, able to keep his whole body in check. James 3:2.

All of my friends know that I absolutely love snow. When it snows outside, I go crazy and revert back to acting like a hyperactive 6-year-old child. Snow seems to make the harshness and freezing temperatures of winter worthwhile. For me, it also brings peace and a chance to enjoy a new adventure. And I love the anticipation of getting out of class so I can go play in it. Others don't seem to view snow with as much enthusiasm as I do. Instead, snow is seen as a burden, an obstacle that keeps them stuck at home. Not so for me, but that goes to show how diverse we all are. We may look at someone and judge them because what is getting them "all in a tizzy" just seems like silly nonsense to us. Different things push different buttons for different people.

Teasing is fun. (I should know. I do it quite a bit and receive it just as often.) But be careful of what you say and to whom you say it. A hilarious joke to you could be an offensive remark to others. We have to guard our mouths. Sometimes getting the last word in or having the best "burn" can have a lasting effect on people, whether we realize it or not. I know from experience that words are weapons and can be more painful than a kick in the shins.

God says the ability to watch your mouth can lead to better self-control. Imagine what this world would be like if, instead of seeking the "easy target" to pick on, we looked for people to whom we could lend support and show compassion. I am definitely not saying there is anything wrong with a little innocent teasing among friends, but remember that your jesting words can be a declaration of your character, true or not, to onlookers. Think before you speak, and remember to be like Jesus.

A Mysterious Plan

By Julian Jervis

Dear friend, I pray that you may enjoy good health and that all may go well with you, even as your soul is getting along well. 3 John 2.

One Sunday afternoon my parents decided to treat me and my siblings to a dinner out as a reward for our hard work in school. To make it even better, they decided that we would buy our food and then take it to eat in a park. We enjoyed our picnic, and everything was going perfectly. But after a while I started to find it harder and harder to finish my food, and my stomach began to hurt. I automatically thought it was because I was eating too much. So we packed our food up and went home.

The next day I woke up, and my stomach hurt terribly. I had already skipped school numerous occasions that year from playing sick, and because of that my mother found it hard to believe that I was really sick, so she sent me to school anyway. My brother and I were late and missed the school bus, so we started walking to another bus stop. After about five minutes my mother just happened to drive past the bus stop where we were waiting. Of course, she picked us up and gave us a ride to school.

My stomach started to hurt even worse, so my mother dropped my brother off at school and took me to work with her. Since my mother works at a medical clinic, she got me in to see the doctor right away. After a few minutes the doctor said that I needed to go to the emergency room of the hospital because he was quite sure I had appendicitis. (Appendicitis is an inflamed appendix, and if the appendix is not removed in time, it can burst and the results can be fatal.)

When I reached the hospital, an on-call surgeon confirmed the other doctor's diagnosis and rushed me into surgery to remove my appendix.

When I look back on this experience, I realize that the series of "coincidences" was truly God's leading: missing the bus, my mother driving by, being able to see the doctor at the clinic, and having the surgeon be at the hospital. God had a plan to work a miracle and save my life that day. Thank You, Jesus, for watching over us!

Life Is Precious

By Allissa Wright

He will wipe every tear from their eyes. There will be no more death or mourning or crying or pain, for the old order of things has passed away. Revelation 21:4.

We have our whole lives ahead of us." "Enjoy being young and don't worry about anything." "We are young and nothing can hurt us." I have heard young people say these things before, and I have even thought them myself. But during the summer of 2010 I realized that these statements are not true.

At the beginning of summer break I was riding in the car when I received the phone call that changed my life forever. My closest friend had been in a motorcycle accident and lost his life just eight miles from my house on his way to visit me. When I heard the news, I went into shock. *It couldn't be true*, I kept telling myself. I had seen Nate just four days before; he couldn't be dead. Nate was only 22 years old—I thought people that young didn't die. That week passed in a haze. At the funeral I had to accept that it was indeed true. My best friend was really gone.

The only thing that kept me going and is still helping me today is knowing that Nate had a relationship with God. Nate always put others first and always relied on God. He was not ashamed of being a Christian, and he readily shared God's love with others. Nate's death has made me rethink my own relationship with God. Nate had no idea that that day would be his last, but I feel he was ready. Am I? Are you?

I am never going to say that I have time to change later. None of us know how long we have, and we need to be ready at all times. Throughout this experience God has held me up and kept me moving forward. He gives me the fortitude to face each day. I have rededicated my life to Him. I want to be ready so that if today is my last day, I can one day meet God and see Nate again.

Doomsday Is Coming This Month?

By Stella Bradley

We are hard pressed on every side, but not crushed; perplexed, but not in despair; persecuted, but not abandoned; struck down, but not destroyed.
2 Corinthians 4:8, 9.

No doubt you have heard that something terrible is about to happen this month. Doomsday has been predicted and publicized for years in anticipation of December 21, 2012, a day when the earth will experience dramatic changes according to Doomsday experts. After watching a few History Channel shows, listening to mainstream news broadcasts, and researching some of the origins of the hype, I have come to an interesting conclusion.

Many theories have been attached to this date. Everyone from Mayan scholars, New Age gurus, climatologists, astronomers, NASA scientists, conspiracy theorists, Illuminati whistle-blowers, and even evangelical preachers concur that something big may happen on or around December 21. Could the earth's poles shift? Could a meteor crash into our planet? Is the Age of Aquarius going to enlighten us all and usher in an era of peace? Are terrorists going to wreak havoc? Is the New World Order going to control everything? Is the antichrist going to appear? Will Jesus Himself come to our rescue? Or will it be another ordinary Christmas shopping day and a great disappointment for a lot of the world?

Well, before we spend too much time dwelling on a specific date and what-ifs, let us never forget who seeks to control this world—Satan! So it should be no surprise that bad things will continue to happen and will escalate in intensity before Christ returns. But more important, don't forget who is in control of the universe—God! Hopefully, you put your trust in Jesus Christ who sacrificed to save you from Satan's temporary kingdom.

As events of the world intensify and perhaps even make us a little anxious, keep your eyes on the prize: heaven and eternal happiness with Jesus. Stay focused by reading your Bible—Philippians 4:6-8; John 14:1; John 14:27; Psalm 31:24; and Isaiah 51:11—because within its pages God has given us promises to encourage and strengthen us. Each day we are seeing prophecy fulfilled, and this means that Christ's coming is soon! Stay faithful, share the good news, and rejoice.

Samson's Lesson

By Daniel Lee

Then Samson prayed to the Lord, "O Sovereign Lord, remember me. O God, please strengthen me just once more." Judges 16:28.

In Bible class we studied about the different judges that ruled Israel. I chose Samson for my class report. Samson's mother was told about his birth and given very special directions to follow during her pregnancy. Samson's parents followed God's directions and raised him to know and love the Lord. From the time he was young, he knew that God had a plan for his life. He started out following God's plan, but as he got older he thought less about what God wanted and more about what he wanted. He went against the advice of his parents and made some very bad choices. His bad choices resulted in some very bad consequences. Later Samson realized his mistakes and was truly sorry for not following God's plan. He prayed to God one last time and asked God to forgive him and to help him one more time. Samson was willing to accept the consequences for his bad choices, but he wanted a chance to help other people. God answered his prayer, and Samson died while bringing down the temple of Dagon.

I am like Samson in some ways, because I also have made bad choices and have suffered the consequences of my bad choices. I have gone against the advice of my parents. In my early years in academy, I chose not to study hard or complete all of my assignments. As a result, now that I am a senior, I have to retake all the classes I didn't pass before. I have changed and I am working hard now, but it doesn't take away the consequences of my earlier behavior. I have prayed and asked God to forgive me and to help me get through all of these classes so that I can graduate in May. My advice to fellow students is to listen to your parents and work hard so that God can work out His perfect plan for your life.

I know that God has a perfect plan for each of us, and He wants us to follow Him because His plan will make us happy. When we make bad choices and turn away from Him, it only leads to unhappiness. The good news is that He never leaves us even when we leave Him. He is always waiting for us to come back to Him and ask Him for forgiveness. He will always forgive us and welcome us back with open arms. We just have to do our part.

Closer Than You Think

By Micayla Jones

Then you will call upon me and come and pray to me, and I will listen to you. You will seek me and find me when you seek me with all your heart.
Jeremiah 29:12, 13.

It was the night before a school break, and some of us girls in the dorm were playing around in the hallway. Suddenly, out of the blue, my roommate hit me on my back! Hard! So I chased after her. We ran up and down the hallway a few times before my roommate decided to run to the front lobby. Wanting to tag her back, I ran after her. As I turned the sharp corner toward the lobby, I realized that I could just go to the room and wait for her there. She wasn't looking back to see how far we were apart, so I knew that she would keep running. I turned around to head back to my room and hit the wall with my face!

The side of my head hit the wall first and then my mouth. The wall was a lot closer than I had thought. I heard something fall to the floor, but I didn't immediately pay any attention to it. I looked around the corner and down the hallway to see if anyone had seen what just happened. When I was sure that no one was around to have seen me, I took a really big sigh. When I sighed, I could feel extra air come through my mouth. I thought to myself, *Hold up! That was a lot of air!* I felt my mouth and then looked down and screamed. My tooth had fallen out!

I ran back to my room, slammed the door, locked it, and sat in my closet! I didn't know what to do or who to tell! (Although in hindsight, I should have gone straight to the dean despite my embarrassment.)

Later when I took a look in the mirror I saw that half of my tooth had chipped off diagonally. The next day I went home and got a root canal and a temporary filling. My tooth basically looks normal again. But I've got to tell you, that day at the dentist was not fun.

When I think about that crazy event, it reminds me of how we sometimes feel about our heavenly Father. We mess up, are embarrassed by our own actions, and then go through a lot of pain trying to make things right again. Instead, we should realize that the right thing to do is call on Him in our hour of need, no matter what we've done, and be assured that He will help us.

God Has a Plan
By Kyli Jung

*All that the Father gives me will come to me,
and whoever comes to me I will never drive away. John 6:37.*

I grew up in Korea, and when I was in middle school, my family decided to move to a different city so that my brother could go to a better school. My parents registered my brother in his new school and then started looking for a house. They found a house that would be big enough for us and signed the contract. We were all excited about moving. A few days later we got a phone call telling us that the owner of the house had changed his mind and didn't want to sell it anymore. We were upset about having to start our house hunt all over again. Because the area was known for the good school system, many families wanted to move there. Consequently finding a house was difficult.

We finally found one house, but it was quite small. We prayed and asked God to show us what to do. Many days went by, but we couldn't find any other house, so my father decided that we would have to buy the small house. We kept on praying that God would show us the right thing to do.

Finally my father was ready to sign the contract on the small house when the phone rang. It was my father's friend who was calling to tell my father that he was going to have to move because of a job transfer. He wanted my father to give him some advice about selling his house. My father explained that we were getting ready to buy a new house ourselves. His friend asked where my father was planning on moving, and when my father told him, our friend was very excited because that's where his house was. He suggested that my father rent his house instead of buying a house. This was perfect for us, because we planned on living there only a few years. He gave us a really good price on the rent, and the house was really big and nice.

We were amazed to see God's plan unfold—a plan that included us renting a house that was so much better than any house we had looked at. All the time we had been praying, God had a wonderful plan for us. This experience reminded my family that even when we don't know what God's plan is we need to trust that His plan is better than our plan.

Don't Worry

By James Kim

Therefore do not worry about tomorrow, for tomorrow will worry about it-self. Each day has enough trouble of its own. Matthew 6:34.

On August 9, 2010, I and four friends said goodbye to our parents and boarded an airplane departing from Korea to the United States, where we would be going to school. The first leg of our flight took us to Tokyo, Japan. After a six-hour layover there, we boarded another plane that would take us to Dallas, Texas. Thirteen hours later we were thankful for a safe landing and a change of scenery.

We got off the plane and prepared to pass through immigration. Suddenly I had a stomachache. It was getting worse and worse, and I was about to throw up. I ran into the bathroom. I prayed that God would help me. I didn't want to be sick, and I wanted to pass through immigration quickly. It took a long time for me to feel better, and I was the last person to pass through immigration, but I thanked God for seeing me through.

Next we flew to South Carolina, where we had two more hours of free time, but we ran into another problem. One of my friends had left his wallet on the plane, so we went to the information booth to see where lost and found was. We discovered that we would have to leave the building to speak with the proper agent. We found the office, but it was already closed for the day. We had about 40 minutes left of our free time, so we quickly walked back to the terminal building. Then we discovered our big mistake—we had forgotten to take our passports and flight tickets with us. We could not go through the security check without our passports. The security officers suggested that we go to the American Airlines booth and ask for a copy of our tickets. On my way to the counter I prayed that God would help us with our difficult situation. We got to the booth, and surprisingly, we easily got our tickets. Typically, it is impossible to get tickets without showing a passport, but they printed our tickets anyway. We then went back to the security area, and because we were older than 16, the guard let us pass through the gate.

Some people might think that this was just a coincidence, but I strongly believe that God heard and answered my prayers. I still thank God for His help during that time.

Trapped

By Gary Bradley

*A righteous man may have many troubles,
but the Lord delivers him from them all. Psalm 34:19.*

On a clear autumn Sabbath afternoon, my two children and I took a walk on the mountain behind our home. As we neared the top of the mountain, we noticed a commotion on the trail ahead of us.

As we got nearer to it, we saw large wings flapping about. We were shocked to see a full-grown vulture flapping about in the middle of the trail, but he seemed unable to fly away. I told my kids to wait where they were while I approached for a closer look. I was fully aware that although vultures don't have strong talons, they do have sharp beaks and have been known to defend themselves with projectile vomit.

I slowly made my way toward the big bird. Immediately I saw the problem. Someone had illegally set a steel trap, and the bird's foot had gotten caught in it. The bird had done nothing wrong except be curious about the baited trap, yet its foot was firmly in its grasp. The kids and I were distraught at the sight of one of God's innocent creatures in distress. I wasn't sure if I could free the bird without injuring one of us, but I had to try.

I slowly approached the bird, telling it in a calm voice that I meant it no harm. It seemed to understand, because it turned away from me and lowered its head. I reached for the steel trap and slowly forced it open. The moment the trap was open enough to free its foot, the vulture flew down the mountain at top buzzard speed. My kids jumped up and down in celebration.

Like that vulture, we sometimes are victims in this world. Some people are willing to say and do unkind things to others because they don't know or love Jesus. But regardless of what happens to us, know that God is strong enough to rescue us from any of this world's traps. God will tenderly release us from Satan's entrapments and give us true freedom.

Friendship

By Cassandra Dannenberger

And my spirit rejoices in God my Savior. Luke 1:47.

Life can be messy. When I was younger, in about the seventh grade, I would often imagine how life would test me in the most brutal of ways. I actually worried too much about it. But God helped me to see the light and relieved me of my stress.

But when I started academy, I found myself having trouble with trust. I didn't know who to be completely open with. I needed a friend whom I could completely be myself around and could share everything with. And I needed a friend who needed me. But I was hesitant to let myself be so vulnerable.

As a sophomore in academy, I had become a little more comfortable with myself, but I still felt left out of a powerful friendship. I found myself longing for heaven more than ever before. My rationale was that in heaven I would never be let down again.

Like most of us, my emotions go up and down. I know I need more patience and that I need to trust more. And I pray that God will give me that through some earthly friends.

However, I already have a lasting friend in Jesus. And He is fulfilling my desire for a best friend and confidant. I know that He can keep my secrets and that I can fully trust and love Him. I will never be disappointed or let down by Him.

God has blessed me. My gratefulness for His loyalty and love is too grand for words. I hope you will also find a true friend in Him.

Close to Home

By Beth Grissom

Do not forsake your friend and the friend of your father, and do not go to your brother's house when disaster strikes you—better a neighbor nearby than a brother far away. Proverbs 27:10.

I love to travel! I especially love to fly. I get so excited going to the airport, going through customs, loading the plane, taking off, watching the houses get smaller and smaller, gliding through the air, and then feeling the rush of the engine as the plane stops. Finally, I like waiting for my luggage (hoping it has arrived) and walking out the doors of the airport into a whole new part of this marvelous world. I love it all.

As a staff member at Mount Pisgah Academy, I was extremely excited when I found out that the entire academy would be going on mission trips and I was going along. What could be better—traveling to a new part of this world and having a job to do for God.

My excitement quickly turned to disappointment when I found out that I would not be able to go on the mission trip. I was devastated. I argued with God. I pleaded my case: "Lord, I want to work for You and do something great! Can't I go, please?" I waited, hoping for the answer I wanted. It didn't come. It was clear I was staying home.

A week later I found out I would be traveling with my 90-year-old grandparents to California. My grandfather was going to be honored at his alma mater, and my grandparents needed assistance. I was excited I could travel, and yet disappointed I wasn't going to do mission work.

However, I had no reason to be disappointed. God had answered my prayer. He had a great work for me to do—it was just right in my own family. Sometimes we want to go far and serve people we don't know. The poor in Africa seem more important than our parents or grandparents, brothers or sisters. We must be willing to go wherever God leads us, be missionaries wherever there is work to do, and remember He is doing a mighty work *everywhere!* Just start serving Him now, right where you are.

The Fear of God

By Aimee Garver

The fear of the Lord leads to life: Then one rests content,
untouched by trouble. Proverbs 19:23.

Since I was a little girl, I've always been what people would call a "scaredy-cat." Spiders, roller coasters, the dark—you name it, I was terrified of it. One day when I was 7 years old, I even grew to fear God. I hadn't been good all afternoon, and as my mom finally grew sick and tired of my attitude, she let slip a few words like "bad," "God," and "fire." That caught my attention! That night I prayed the sinner's prayer, but it wasn't until years later that I came to this realization—God doesn't want us to be scared of Him and do whatever He says just to escape punishment!

Of course, that leads us to this question: Why does Proverbs say it's a good thing to fear the Lord? Some people assume that the word "fear" is defined as an unpleasant feeling in the presence of danger, and they use the verse to support their claims of God's cruelty and unfairness. Others take it too far in the opposite direction and use speeches of hellfire and God's wrath to try and scare people into salvation. I disagree with both points of view. The Hebrew word for "fear" that is used in this passage is *yirah*, which can be translated as "reverence" or "piety."

Does this mean that when we respect and obey the Lord we will not be visited by evil? Does that mean Satan won't be able to attack us again? Unfortunately no, but we'll be given aptitude through Christ to overcome whatever hardships Satan throws at us.

This reminds me of Abraham. The patriarch followed God out of awe and adoration, not because he was scared that He'd fry him if he didn't. Abraham also suffered the struggles that come with being human and he made mistakes, but the Lord didn't abandon him. What an example for us!

Who Wants to Prosper?

By John Ratzlaff

But he who trusts in the Lord will prosper. Proverbs 28:25.

When I was a young man, I had a number of girlfriends (not all at once, of course). At least a couple of them were serious enough relationships that I thought about the possibility of marriage. But they all ended for one reason or another, and by the time I was approaching graduation from college and looking forward to starting my career as a teacher, I had no prospects for a wife. I began to feel somewhat concerned—perhaps even alarmed. I was a committed Christian at the time, and so, in my mind, my life was in God's hands. But it's one thing to say that sort of thing, and another thing entirely to confidently move forward believing that God will work everything out. It was kind of scary to permanently leave the security of home and family, move to a new city where I didn't know anyone, and begin my new career.

It was not obvious at the time, but as I look back from the vantage point of many years later, it is clear that God was leading me to that city. I had a very difficult year of teaching—I'm sure that was part of God's plan to make me a better teacher. But more to the point, it was there that I met the girl who would become my wife. Not wanting to sound mushy, I have to say that not a day goes by that I don't thank God for her and for working things out in my life far, far better than I ever could have foreseen. We have been happily married for more than 30 years, and our commitment to each other becomes stronger with the passage of time.

It is clear to me that the best possible course in life is to put one's trust wholly in the Lord and "lean not on your own understanding" (Prov. 3:5). In the case of finding a spouse, for example, it is all too common for young men and women to feel so desperate to marry that they will compromise their principles, rush a relationship, overlook signs of trouble, or accept less than God's ideal for them. I'm grateful that the Lord gave me the faith to trust in Him and that He rewarded my faith in the most wonderful way imaginable! My teaching career has not led me to prosper financially, but I can say with conviction that the Lord has prospered me far beyond what money could buy.

Omnipresent

By Stephen Drummond

Praise be to the Lord, to God our Savior, who daily bears our burdens.
Psalm 68:19.

One day when I was about 7 years old I was riding in the car with my mom and brother on the way home from school. We turned at the light, heading toward the interstate. The sky was mostly overcast, but I noticed that a group of clouds had rays of light shining through them. I marveled at the view and thought to myself, *That's God in His glory shining on the city of Charlotte!*

I seized my brother's and mother's attention, telling them, "That is God shining down on us from His throne!" My brother, with a puzzled look on his face, questioned my comment, stating that what I was seeing was only the sunshine. Because I was 7 years old and thought that I knew everything, I argued with my brother, saying, "That is God shining from the sky!" My mother, attempting to calm us down from our little disagreement, interjected that we were both acknowledging the Creator. She said that I saw the Creator and my brother saw His creation. "There is no need to disagree with each other," she said.

After all these years, I have no doubt that it was indeed God shining His glory on us that day. I have come to realize that it's possible to see God in many ways. We can see God through His creation. In Exodus 20:11 it says that God made the heavens, the earth, the sea, and all that was in the midst. We can also see God through people's benevolent actions and their good characteristics as manifest through the fruit of the Spirit (love, joy, peace, patience, kindness, goodness, faithfulness, gentleness, and self-control).

It's amazing how we can see God in so many different ways, and it's also amazing to know that He is everywhere. Whenever we feel as if we are alone and no one cares about us, remember that God cares for you. He knows your every thought, and He hears you when you call out to Him. Just look for His love all around you.

Fire Changed My Life

By Iyana K. Walker

For it is by grace you have been saved, through faith—and this is not from yourselves, it is the gift of God—not by works, so that no one can boast. Ephesians 2:8, 9.

When I was 13 years old, I had a bad attitude. I wasn't horrible all of the time, but I did give my mom a lot of grief. Part of my attitude problem just came naturally, I guess. But part of it was learned behavior from the rough neighborhood I was in. One weekend I was really getting on my mom's nerves, and to give us both a break from the stress, I asked her if I could go to my cousins' house. Fortunately she said yes, because we both needed a change of scenery.

I had a good time hanging out with some of my cousins, and we spent the day relaxing. That night we wanted to go to the bowling alley, but we didn't have a ride. So we called everyone we knew who had a car, but everyone was busy and couldn't take us. Then I thought to call my aunt who was visiting my mom, nana, and some other cousins at my house. But as soon as she answered her phone, she yelled, "Your kitchen is on fire!"

That got my attention. I was scared that someone was trapped or hurt. I just wanted to get there and be with my family. My aunt assured me that everyone was all right, much to my relief. And in an instant, my priorities lined up properly—trivial things weren't important anymore.

Later on I heard the whole story. Mom was cooking when a faulty wire on the stove sparked the fire. We had asked our landlord to fix the stove, but he had never gotten around to it. My family had managed to put the fire out, but not before our entire home had filled with smoke.

Only now can we see how God used that horrible experience to bring about good. I believe that the fire is just what we needed to get us to move out of that neighborhood so that we could have a better (and safer) life. Instead of growing up in a rough environment surrounded by bad influences, we moved to a nicer neighborhood in a different town. And I am now attending an Adventist boarding school, where my surroundings are centered on God.

Read today's verse again. Only Christ can save us from our earthly environment. He wants to move us to a safe and nurturing place. But it may take something drastic to get our attention. Don't ignore God and His leading in your life.

A Centurion's Superhero

By Terry Sampson

Train a child in the way he should go,
and when he is old he will not turn from it. Proverbs 22:6.

For the last two years at our church I have played the part of the Roman centurion collecting taxes in a live Nativity called "Walk Through Bethlehem." Participants are given a coin upon arrival to "pay their taxes." The role of the centurion is not to make friends but to ensure compliance; therefore, the dialogue is often harsh.

Last year we had completed the last tour and gone indoors to change. I had barely taken a few steps inside when someone stopped me and said, "A mother needs to see the centurion." Our costumes are authentic-looking outfits, so I thought it would be a simple photo request. That idea quickly disappeared when around the corner came a mother holding her two sons by their arms, their eyes full of fear.

"Tell him what you did!" the mom said.

"We . . . kept our taxes," said the boys through their sniffles.

"What did you put in there instead?" asked the mother.

"A . . . a penny," was the sorrowful reply. Tears streamed down their faces.

With the addition of the helmet and its plumage, I stood towering over these two boys by almost twice their height. They looked terrified as I called them over to sit down.

I explained, "Jesus came down here and died for all of my sins as well as yours. If He can forgive me for all of the mean things that I have done as a Roman soldier, then He can forgive you for not paying your taxes." I held out my hand. As they placed the coins in it, I asked, "Are you sorry for what you have done?"

"Yes," the boys said.

"Then Jesus forgives you, and so do I," I replied.

The boys wiped away their tears with relief. I asked if they were going to tell their friends about the tour. They emphatically nodded yes. "Don't tell your friends that you are buddies with the centurion until after they have completed the tour," I added. Their smiles showed they not only had been forgiven but also had made a friend.

Gingerbread Land

Crystal Hattar

Only be careful, and watch yourselves closely so that you do not forget the things your eyes have seen or let them slip from your heart as long as you live. Teach them to your children and to their children after them.
Deuteronomy 4:9.

Remember when you were a little kid and all you wanted to do was stay up all Christmas Eve, waiting with anticipation to open presents. Of course, some kids stay awake because they want to see Santa Claus. They leave him cookies and milk in hopes that he'll leave a nice present or two. I did not believe in Santa Claus as a child, but my younger brother did.

This presented a unique challenge to our family. Although I did not believe in the jolly old man from the North Pole, my family kept the Santa thing alive every year for my brother.

But everything changed one Christmas when my brother was about 5 years old. We went to California to spend the week with my family. We all planned that after my brother went to sleep we would all make it look like Santa had been there. My uncle took a big bite of a cookie and drank some milk. We were just about finished putting fake snow (flour) footprints on the floor when *bang!* We were caught! My brother had awakened and found us in midscheme. He was mad and felt lied to. He ran back up the stairs and sat on my cousin's bed. My mother ran up the stairs to talk to him. He asked my mom, "Why did everyone lie to me, and why couldn't I help with Santa?" She explained to him that we weren't trying to "lie" but were just trying to make his Christmas special. The next day we told him we were very sorry. In fact, it turned out to be one of my favorite Christmases of my life so far. All of my family learned a lesson that day about being more honest with each other.

This story taught me that we should be more honest not only with each other but also with God, because what's the point in trying to hide something from Him if He already knows everything about us? He loves us, accepts us, and sent His Son for us. All we have to do is accept the gift.

A Christmas Story

By Shana Byrd

*Jesus answered her, "If you knew the gift of God
and who it is that asks you for a drink, you would have asked him
and he would have given you living water." John 4:10.*

In the past I procrastinated as much as possible when it came to buying Christmas presents for my friends. I have been known to buy gifts after the holidays and use the excuse "I was able to buy you a better gift because it was on sale!"

My senior year of high school, however, I decided to do all my shopping early. Surprisingly, I actually did it. One gift in particular, for my roommate, I bought two weeks before Thanksgiving. I searched for hours in the local Target for something I thought she would like, but I couldn't find anything at first. Finally, as I was on my way out, I found the perfect gift. I purchased it and traveled back to the dorm. I was ecstatic that I had motivated myself enough to buy her present early.

When I brought it to the room, I forced her to close her eyes and then handed her the bag containing the exotic perfume I had purchased for her. Excitedly I told her to open it, but she refused. She claimed, "It's a Christmas present only if I open it on Christmas."

Obviously, I disagreed. I shoved the present toward her once more and said, "No! I can't keep this in the room! I'm just too excited for you to open it!" After much persuasion, she gave in and dug into the gift bag.

Although my roommate had known something wonderful was right in front of her, she had refused to accept it. My brain still cannot grasp the idea of being offered a gift yet not taking it. However, many people refuse to accept the free gift Jesus has given them—the gift of eternal life. Jesus' death covers any sin we could ever and will ever commit, yet some people refuse to accept it. We know that the present He offers is worth more than anything on this planet, and all we have to say is "Thank You; I appreciate it." Make sure you don't refuse His free gift.

He Is My Snowboard
By McKennan Cook

*Put your trust in the light while you have it,
so that you may become sons of light. John 12:36.*

A few years ago I went snowboarding for the first time. I woke up early in the morning, put on all my gear, and got in the car with my friend Mark. Mark had been pestering me over the preceding few weeks to try snowboarding. It seemed ridiculous to me. I mean the mountain is steep and slippery enough without strapping my feet onto a fiberglass board and forsaking even more control. At first I didn't want to, but eventually I relented. As soon as we got off the lift at the top of the mountain, I knew I had made a mistake. That first day was filled with pain and humiliation. I fell countless times, but somehow I became hooked.

I've been snowboarding for years now, and it is by far my favorite thing to do. Now that I know how to snowboard, I have way more control than I would have simply trying to walk down the mountain on my own two feet.

Since then I've realized that God is like a snowboard. At first it's hard for us to forsake control of our lives and trust Him. It seems as though it would be easier to stand on our own feet. Even when we do decide to give up control, we often lose our trust in God. We try to catch ourselves but end up falling, just as I did when I first began snowboarding. But as long as we don't give up, we will come to realize that strapping ourselves to God gives us more control than we could ever have on our own.

I would encourage anyone who feels that they are falling down the slope of life to try using God to help them maneuver through the obstacles in their way. And to everyone who is already using God as their snowboard, be the "Mark" of my story. Help others to make the decision to strap themselves to God and to put their trust in Him.

When the Going Gets Tough, the Tough Get Stronger

By Rachel Sheridan

So do not fear, for I am with you; do not be dismayed,
for I am your God. I will strengthen you and help you;
I will uphold you with my righteous right hand. Isaiah 41:10.

Everyone goes through a time in their life that things never seem to work out. It seems that every time we turn around something goes wrong. I know this feeling quite well from experience.

My life has never been that easy, but all at once everything fell apart. It all started a few summers back when my family decided to move. My dad is a pastor, and he was called to a two-church district near Waynesville, North Carolina, which would enable me to attend Mount Pisgah Academy. Not long after we made the decision to move, my mom was unexpectedly diagnosed with breast cancer. On top of all that I lost my two cats, our dog, and my best friend. Soon after we made the move, my brother was almost killed in a car accident, and just a few weeks later my mom and sister totaled our van in a car accident. Oh, and did I mention I was really nervous about going to a new school?

Because of everything that had occurred, I became very depressed. I turned my back on God and didn't think I could go on. As I struggled with the weight and stress, I asked again and again, "God, where are You in all this?" I had never felt so alone, but the truth was, I wasn't. God was with me the whole time. I just didn't realize it because I was so focused on everything bad that had happened. I had forgotten about everything good that had taken place and about how much worse things could've been. Even after realizing this, I still asked the question "Why did You let all of this happen to my family?" The truth is, I still don't know why, but I know that no matter how tough things might get, God will give me the strength I need to make it through.

There's one thing that someone very special told me, "When the going gets tough, the tough get stronger." God never said life on earth would be easy, but He did say He'd be there to get us through the storm.

Selfish or Not?

By Ashton Evans

He has showed you, O man, what is good. And what does the Lord require of you? To act justly and to love mercy and to walk humbly with your God. Micah 6:8.

Do we really want a relationship with God or just the benefits? Sometimes we just use people to get the things we truly want from them. Do you have friends like that? Someone once asked the question "Does heaven really matter if God isn't there to spend it with us?" This got me to thinking. Does God seem like the type who wants someone to take advantage of Him for the things He has to offer, such as heaven?

I used to say that I couldn't wait to go to heaven so I could ride on a cheetah's back or pet a lion. I never thought about spending time with God in heaven. Most of us want a relationship with God just so we can go to heaven or get Him to save a loved one. We start with a selfish motive. This is something I, Ashton Evans, want from God. Is it really worth going to heaven if we don't spend time with our Father? But I have good news.

God doesn't mind us being selfish. He wants us to want to know Him better. If we start talking to Him just because we don't want to be lost, it's OK. God just wants a part of us so He can start to change the rest of us. I began my relationship with Him in a selfish way, but eventually I realized that heaven didn't matter that much to me anymore. I wanted to know more about my heavenly Father instead. I found myself reading the Bible in search of that knowledge and praying to really connect with Him.

God takes our selfish motives and works on our hearts. Wanting a relationship with Him just for the perks is all right. He will use this to change our hearts. I want to go to heaven so I can talk with God and spend all the time I have getting to know Him even more. I will get to go swimming with God in the sea of glass. I will get to ride on a cheetah's back with God. I want to be in heaven so I can be in the presence of God. He will change us no matter what our motives are. Just try to get to know God, and He will meet you where you are.

The Other Wise Man

By Callie Adams

*But when you give to the needy, do not let your left hand
know what your right hand is doing. Matthew 6:3.*

Every year since I can remember, my father has read us *The Story of the Other Wise Man* at Christmastime. When he taught in academy, he would rent the movie and show it to the students. No one appreciated his efforts. The book is short and simple. It takes about an hour and a half to read out loud all the way through, but to a 6-year-old who just got presents and wants to play, it is an eternity.

The story is about a fourth Wise Man who follows his friends across the desert to meet Baby Jesus. He sells all his possessions to purchase three jewels to present to the Holy Child. He misses them as they are fleeing to Egypt. He spends the whole book, and the remainder of his life, searching for the Savior. As he searches he helps the needy and uses his jewels to rescue those who are desperate. Finally the Wise Man finds Jesus at the cross. He feels that he is too late, and all his jewels are gone. As Jesus draws His final breath, God speaks to the Wise Man and tells him that he has found the Lord every day as he helped those he encountered on his travels.

This may seem like a touching story to some, but after many years of hearing it again and again, we didn't listen to it anymore. We endured it.

When I was 18, I returned home from school for Christmas break. The time difference caused me to be up earlier than the rest of the family on Sabbath morning. As I sat staring out the window at the newly fallen snow, I noticed my father loading a shovel into the back of his car and driving off. He returned 30 minutes later, before anyone was up, and got ready for church without any indication of where he had been.

At church during the praise time, an elderly woman stood up and said that an angel had shoveled her driveway that morning. She was able to attend church because of this unknown person. I knew who the angel was. That afternoon, as my father read *The Story of the Other Wise Man*, I started to cry. I was overcome by the emotion of knowing that my father was that fourth Wise Man. He had already found the Savior.

Birdmen and Godmen

By Kathy Brannan

"The virgin will be with child and will give birth to a son, and they will call him Immanuel"—which means, "God with us." Matthew 1:23.

Have you heard about the latest extreme sports craze? Jumping from planes or steep cliffs, birdmen and birdwomen fly in specially designed wingsuits that allow them to fly longer than typical skydivers before having to reclaim their humanity and open their chutes.

In 1999 Jari Kuosma and Robert Pecnik were ready to try out their version of the flying suit. However, many other testers had died experimenting with similar wingsuits. This, of course, did not stop Kuosma and Pecnik. They were committed to their product and the advancement of their sport no matter the costs.

This Christmas consider someone else who took a big risk for us—Jesus took an instantaneous skydive from heaven to a young girl's womb to become (not just try to become) a man. He knew the costs. He was coming to do something no human had ever been successful at—to consistently say no to Satan for an entire lifetime.

"Satan in heaven had hated Christ for His position in the courts of God. He hated Him the more when he himself was dethroned. He hated Him who pledged Himself to redeem a race of sinners. Yet into the world where Satan claimed dominion God permitted His Son to come, a helpless babe, subject to the weakness of humanity. He permitted Him to meet life's peril in common with every human soul, to fight the battle as every child of humanity must fight it, at the risk of failure and eternal loss" (*The Desire of Ages*, p. 49).

Willingly He committed everything He ever knew or cared for—His intimate relationship with God the Father and the Holy Spirit, His place as Creator and Ruler of a trillion-plus stars and planets, His perfect home where the streets are made of gold and the angels worship and adore His every word and action. He could have lost it all had He failed.

Wow! What a risk! What love for you and me!

A Holiday Reminder

By Steven Sigamani

Listen, my son, to your father's instruction and do not forsake your mother's teaching. Proverbs 1:8.

It was a scenic but frigid trip, driving up to Connecticut. On the way we saw two or three feet of snow plowed off to the side of the roadway. It had been a long drive, and we were ready to settle down. Everyone was a little irritable, especially me and my mom. We arrived, and after eating were shown our rooms. We started unpacking, and my mom and I began arguing about the next day and that I had not brought enough warm clothes. Our frustration led to me just walking off and going to bed, aggravated that my mom was constantly annoying me.

I went to sleep in a bad mood, and I slept fine until I was jarred awake by a loud thump. I had no idea what it was, but the thump was followed by a loud scream and crying. I lay in bed wondering what in the world it could be. I heard my dad and a few others leave their rooms. Finally I got up and saw everyone at the bottom of the staircase tending to my mom.

I soon found out that my mom had fallen down the whole flight of stairs. We called the paramedics. While they were on the way, my dad asked my mom who I was. I watched my mom struggle, and she answered, "I don't know." Right then I felt absolutely terrible.

I thought about how much I loved her and how much she meant to me. I wished I could take back how disrespectful I had been to her that night. The fact that she didn't know who I was hurt a lot, but it helped me realize how important it is to love and respect our parents and family all the time.

It showed me that life can take turns at any moment. Today I thank God my mom is fine. (She sustained only minor injuries from her fall and has had a full recovery.) But that night taught me a valuable lesson. In the midst of all the holiday hubbub with presents and decorations, remember how blessed you are to have a family.

Seek as for Hidden Treasure

By John Ratzlaff

The kingdom of heaven is like treasure hidden in a field. When a man found it, he hid it again, and then in his joy went and sold all he had and bought that field. Matthew 13:44.

Geocaching is a game of hiding and seeking. Some geocaches are very easy to find, others are deliberately more difficult. Sometimes the difficulty comes from a devious hide. I remember one notorious cache that stumped many geocachers for a long time. It consisted of a piece of silver duct tape stuck to the bottom of a guardrail. Many cachers kept trying and trying until it was finally located. Another memorable cache was hidden in the vicinity of a railroad caboose, and it was so difficult that six months went by before it was found!

In other cases, puzzles must be solved in order to determine the coordinates of the cache. It may be necessary to do some Internet research, decode a message, or figure out clues hidden on the cache listing page. For cachers who enjoy that sort of thing, the reward is usually the feeling of accomplishment for having conquered a challenge.

Jesus talked about seeking for hidden treasure. He suggests that we seek God's kingdom as diligently as we might search for buried treasure, or for a challenging geocache! His parable illustrates the value of heavenly treasure and the effort that should be made to secure it. Just as a geocacher might struggle to solve a puzzle or make repeated attempts to find a cache, the seeker of heavenly treasure must be willing to go to great lengths to gain the treasures of truth. The treasure Jesus refers to is no mere trinket, no fleeting sense of accomplishment. "The value of this treasure is above gold or silver. The riches of earth's mines cannot compare with it.... The Bible is the mine of the unsearchable riches of Christ" (*Christ's Object Lessons*, p. 107).

But it takes earnest study and close investigation to uncover the treasures in God's Word. Just as a halfhearted effort will not solve a challenging puzzle, so "we cannot expect to gain spiritual knowledge without earnest toil. Those who desire to find the treasures of truth must dig for them as the miner digs for the treasure hidden in the earth. . . . It is essential for old and young, not only to read God's Word, but to study it with wholehearted earnestness, praying and searching for truth as for hidden treasure" (*ibid.*, p. 111). The reward will be the riches of eternal life.

God Wants to Hear Us

By Kevin Lee

Peace I leave with you; my peace I give you. I do not give to you as the world gives. Do not let your hearts be troubled and do not be afraid.
John 14:27.

When I was 9 years old, my family and I went as missionaries to Russia from Korea. My father was the pastor of a church with about 150 members. The winters in Russia were very cold, and there was always a lot of snow.

One particular Friday we had a really bad snowstorm, and on Sabbath, when we went to get in our car, we saw that the car was buried under a hill of snow. We knew that the only way we could get to church was by walking.

The wind was still blowing very hard, so my family and I prayed that God would help us get to church safely and that He would also help all the members to safely come to church. We started walking through the snow and the wind. It was very difficult to walk, because we had to walk against the wind. The church was a five-minute drive from our house, but that day it took us 45 minutes to walk there.

We did not know if anyone else would be able to make it to church, but by the time the service started, all the members were there. Everyone had walked to church through the storm. God had answered our prayer and brought us all safely together in the church.

Although the storm was harsh outside, we enjoyed the fellowship and warmth of our little church family. Isn't that the way things are in life, too? The world can be cruel and harsh, yet if we find shelter in Jesus and in the companionship of good Christian friends, we can forget our troubles and lean on each other for strength.

I love Isaiah 43:2 because it reminds me that God is always with us and will never leave us. He was with us through the storm in Russia, and He will be with us wherever we go.

Inside Out

By Matt Vaughan

But the Lord said to Samuel, "Do not consider his appearance or his height, for I have rejected him. The Lord does not look at the things man looks at. Man looks at the outward appearance, but the Lord looks at the heart.
1 Samuel 16:7.

During spring break 2009 my family decided to travel to the fabulous city of Chicago. As we were driving into the city, I was amazed at the wonders of the town. It was huge! Towering skyscrapers outlined the city as far as I could see, and beautiful Lake Michigan was so big it practically looked like an ocean. We were in awe of all that the city had to offer.

One day my family and I decided to go to the top of the Sears Tower, which is one of the tallest buildings in the world. We took the elevator up to the observation tower at 1,353 feet, and when we reached the top, we were all mesmerized at the sights below. We could see for miles and miles.

Standing atop the tower, I looked down on the world below. The people looked like ants! I couldn't tell what their appearance was or what they were doing. All I could see were figures. That got me to thinking about 1 Samuel 16:7—God never looks at the outward appearance; He looks only at our inward selves. Standing at the top of the Sears Tower, I couldn't see their skin color, their wealth, or how popular they were. I just saw people. This gave me a very comforting feeling knowing that no matter how I appear outwardly, God cares about only what's in my heart.

So if you ever meet someone who appears out of the ordinary or different, you should always try to get to know them the same way God would. It can really make a difference in the friends you will make in the future—you never know what person God will bring into your life or for what purpose He'll bring them to you. Never judge too quickly.

Traditions
By Stella Bradley

Then you will have success if you are careful to observe the decrees and laws that the Lord gave Moses for Israel. Be strong and courageous. Do not be afraid or discouraged. 1 Chronicles 22:13.

Now that Christmas is over, folks are planning their New Year's celebration. It's a time to reflect on the past year and plan for the future. Some will make resolutions, or promises, regarding habits they want to stop or start. Some will celebrate with family and others with friends. Many Americans will stay up until midnight and then ring in the new year by singing "Auld Lang Syne." Typically, my family celebrates with sparklers and a meal of black-eyed peas (representing coins) and collard greens (representing dollars). Those foods are supposed to bring wealth and health for the new year. I'm not superstitious, but it's fun to have a tradition.

Around the world people will celebrate New Year's Day in diverse ways. In Brazil people eat lentils to signify wealth for the new year. In Australia families surf and have a picnic. In Korea everyone celebrates their birthday on the new year. South Africans welcome the new year by ringing church bells and firing guns into the air.

Interestingly, not all New Year's celebrations are on January 1. Many cultures celebrate alternative dates for the new year cycle. For Buddhists, the new year is celebrated based on the full moon, which, depending on where the believers live, could be celebrated in January, February, or April.

It is interesting to learn that most New Year's traditions from around the world have to do with superstitions surrounding prosperity and warding off evil spirits. Thankfully, knowledge in Christ has freed us from having to jump over fires or feed statues to try to ensure a good future. In addition to rereading today's verse, look up Deuteronomy 28:1-6, 8, 11-13. Clearly our blessings come from God—He wants us to prosper.

Have fun commemorating the new year in whatever way you and your family and friends celebrate. However, keep in mind that the most important thing you can do to ring in 2013 is to rededicate your life to Christ. Through Him you will find lasting prosperity!

What Are You Going to Do?
By Addie Dorough

But these are written that you may believe that Jesus is the Christ, the Son of God, and that by believing you may have life in his name. John 20:31.

I was 9 years old and attending camp at Nosoca Pines Ranch when I decided that I needed Jesus in my life. As my cabinmates and I sat around a bonfire after the Friday night pageant, I felt a fire in my heart that I had never experienced before. The theme song for the summer—"Above All"—was a powerful song about God's omnipotence and ultimate sacrifice. As my friends and I started to sing, tears began to roll down my face. I am not one of those emotional girls who dramatically display their every sentiment, but I could not restrain myself. Everything began to truly make sense to me, and the effect was overwhelming. This song made me realize what God really did for me by sending His Son to die.

Growing up in a Christian home as I have, although a good thing, has sometimes limited my appreciation of God. I know I have taken for granted all the miraculous stories I was told as a child, and the Crucifixion is no exception. During my early years Jesus' death meant nothing at all to me—it was merely a story. It never "clicked" that Jesus endured the most excruciating pain anyone could imagine. Consider the most pain you've been in, whether it was an illness or the death of a close friend, and multiply it by a million. We take for granted everything until it is taken away from us. Then it becomes real. Jesus did all this for us! He lived as a human and suffered from backstabbing, immature, lying, bothersome, malicious humans only to die because of our stupidity and selfishness. He has the scars. Don't get me wrong; He was overjoyed to take our burdens on His own shoulders, but we need to respect Him for it.

After we finished our worship around the fire, everyone was given a small sheet of paper with a few questions on it. The final question was simple: "What would you like to do about your decision?" I checked the little box next to the phrase "study with a pastor at home to be baptized." My question for you is this: What are you going to do about your decision to follow Christ? The Bible, though sometimes overwhelming, is full of real stories that can change your life. Or maybe it will take only a song for you to discover the truth—I dare you to find out.

All contributors are in some way connected to Mount Pisgah Academy (MPA). Although many of the contributors have now graduated, they wrote these devotional thoughts while they were academy students. Thanks to all the current and former staff and students who told their stories and shared their faith in the pages of this book.

Emily Abernathy graduated from Mount Pisgah Academy in 2008 and now lives in Orlando, Florida. In her free time she likes to play basketball, take pictures, and make videos. **Mar. 9.**

Callie Adams was born in Vancouver, Washington, but spent the majority of her youth in southern Colorado. When she was a staff member at Mount Pisgah Academy, she taught in the computer department, sponsored the yearbook, sometimes taught art, and ran the marketing department. **June 17, Aug. 31, Oct. 4, Nov. 6, Dec. 2, Dec. 24.**

Rosella Age graduated as a four-year senior with the class of 2009. As a student she enjoyed visiting with Mr. Grow, the science teacher, taking precalculus with Mr. Ratzlaff, and singing alto next to her best friend in choir. She is now vice president of her class at Campbell University. Among her hobbies are knitting scarves, playing guitar, singing, and painting. **Feb. 18, Mar. 29, June 6, Aug. 2.**

Thana Alley is from Asheville, North Carolina, and is a member of the class of 2012. Her favorite onomatopoeia is "crackle." Her least-favorite food is Indian food, and her favorite animal is a cow. Her favorite thing about Pisgah is the people. **Aug. 10.**

Isabel Alvarez was a member of the class of 2010. While in academy she was very active in several organizations. She now lives in Spartanburg, South Carolina, with her mom, dad, and two brothers. Her pastimes include listening to music and cooking. She is currently working at a nursing home, where she enjoys being around elderly persons. **Nov. 20.**

Beth Anderson is a school counselor and English teacher at Mount Pisgah Academy. She is married to her best friend, Rick, and they have three grown children. She grew up in Maine and graduated from Pine Tree Academy and Atlantic Union College. She loves the woods and waterfalls, and she enjoys camping, doing yard work, and reading. **Apr. 7, May 13, June 5.**

Rebecca Anderson graduated from Mount Pisgah Academy in 2009. She is currently attending Southern Adventist University and is majoring in public relations. She will forever call Pisgah her home because it gave her the opportunity to thrive spiritually and mentally by being active in Campus Ministries and community outreach programs. While in academy she enjoyed being a part of the recruiting team and traveling with some of her closest friends performing music for churches in the Carolinas. **Feb. 5.**

Rick Anderson is currently the principal of Mount Pisgah Academy and has been involved in education for more than 30 years as a teacher and administrator. Rick enjoys working on home improvement projects, singing in a quartet, jogging, and golfing. The joys of his life are his wife, Beth, their three children, and his faithful dog, Molly. It is a passion of Rick's to work with young people in preparing them for service in this world and life in the hereafter with our Savior. **June 23.**

Jacob Ballew, a 2010 graduate of Mount Pisgah Academy, is from Candler, North Carolina. He enjoys playing his guitar and spending time with his friends. **Apr. 27, July 7, Sept. 4.**

Jennifer Beckham, a 2010 graduate from Mount Pisgah Academy, comes from Charlotte, North Carolina, where she lives with her mom. She says that one of the highlights of the past four years has been meeting her best friends and sharing countless memories at school. She loves to swim, and she became a published author at the age of 17. **May 16, Aug. 15, Oct. 22, Nov. 10.**

Melanie Bethancourt graduated from Mount Pisgah Academy in 2009. She has fond and vivid memories of choir trips (especially to Bermuda), banquets, and other school-sponsored activities. As an academy student she was involved in the Student Association, choir, and volleyball intramurals. She now attends Southern Adventist University and is studying physical therapy. **June 7.**

Michael Brackett proudly graduated from Mount Pisgah Academy several years ago. Now he serves as head pastor of the Mount Pisgah Academy church with his beautiful family. **May 22, June 21, June 27, July 31, Aug. 22.**

Allison Joy Bradley is a homeschooled fifth grader and loves school! She enjoys all subjects. Allison plays violin and piano. She also enjoys swimming, skating, skiing, and making twisty balloon art to give away. She loves to explore nature and learn about all of God's creatures, including insects. She has several pets, including rabbits, dogs, and cats, and she looks forward to having many more pets in heaven. **May 17.**

Gary Bradley taught at Mount Pisgah Academy for 13 years as math and science teacher. He also served as vice principal of student affairs and enjoyed directing Present Truth Drama, the school's drama team. He now teaches science at Canton Middle School. In his spare time he likes hiking with his dog and family, boating, and riding motorcycles. **Jan. 1, Oct. 26, Oct. 31, Nov. 14, Dec. 11.**

Stella Duncan Bradley loves being a mom and an academy English teacher. She has taught for more than 20 years in North Carolina, working at Mount Pisgah Academy since 1996. When not at work, she enjoys spending time with her family. (Her husband, Gary; kids, Allison and Zachary; and mom, Linda Duncan, all have devotionals included in this book.) As a family they like to explore and ride bikes on the mountain trails of North Carolina and beach-comb on the Atlantic coast. She also enjoys reading, having music jam sessions with the family, teaching the kids' Sabbath school classes, and studying end-time and current events. **Feb. 29, Mar. 17, May 18, May 28, June 11, July 13, Nov. 11, Nov. 23, Dec. 6, Dec. 30.**

Zachary Duncan Bradley likes all kinds of animals and has many pets. He also likes to tinker with anything mechanical. He likes skiing; riding his bike and scooter; learning about cars, airplanes, and rockets; and helping cook in the kitchen. He is a homeschooled third grader who loves learning. Zachary plays piano, violin, and harmonica. He is good at making new friends. **Apr. 9.**

Kathy Brannan is the vice principal of academics at Mount Pisgah Academy, her alma mater. She loves the energy and enthusiasm of the students she works with and is always blessed by their testimonies for Jesus. When she is not busy at school, she enjoys exploring nature in the beautiful surrounding mountains with her husband. **Feb. 26, Dec. 25.**

Ian Brewer, a 2010 graduate of Mount Pisgah Academy, comes from Gaston, South Carolina, where he lives with his mom, dad, brother, and sister. He says that his favorite memory of school is his mission trip to Bermuda, where he sang in the choir and repaired churches. While in academy he was the tutoring resident assistant in the boys' dorm and a class officer. **July 2, Sept. 14.**

Katie Brewer is a member of the class of 2012 and is from Columbia, South Carolina. She hates cheese more than any other food, but ironically loves pizza and Easy Mac. Her favorite animals are penguins and ducks. She thinks the words "speckle" and "pickles" are the cutest words in the dictionary. She loves books, but they have to be exciting. The last interesting fact about Katie is that she leaves the lights on in her room 24/7. **Nov. 1.**

Zeko Burgess is in the Mount Pisgah Academy graduating class of 2012. He is from Bermuda, which is a long way from MPA. He loves all sports, but his favorite is baseball. When he grows up, he would like to become a pro athlete or a business owner. **Nov. 28.**

Chris Busche is a 2009 alumnus of Mount Pisgah Academy. While an MPA student he was acrobatics team captain, recreation secretary on the Student Association, and intramural coordinator. He enjoyed playing as many sports as he could make time for. He enjoyed the many friendships he made, but most important, he enjoyed the spiritual atmosphere and chance to grow closer to his Savior, Jesus. Now in college, he is studying physical education and is planning on being a student missionary in the near future. **Nov. 13.**

Rebecca Busche graduated from Mount Pisgah Academy in 2008 and is currently in the nursing program at Southern Adventist University. She is from Asheville, North Carolina, and enjoys playing sports and hanging out with friends. **Sept. 12, Oct. 13.**

Shana Byrd, a 2010 graduate of Mount Pisgah Academy, has fond memories of dorm life and acrobatics trips. She enjoyed working as student chaplain in the campus ministries department and has grown to love leading any type of worship. Shana is now in college and enjoys spending time with her family and friends. **Aug. 9, Sept. 24, Dec. 20.**

Emmanuel Cabrera is a member of the Mount Pisgah Academy class of 2010. He loves the people that make up MPA, and he enjoyed his years there. His favorite pastime is just hanging out with friends. **July 26.**

Ashley Cale, a 2011 graduate of Mount Pisgah Academy, comes from Candler, North Carolina. She lives with her parents and younger brother (who attends MPA). Her biggest highlights during her four years in academy include studying under the direction of great faculty; building relationships with other students and staff; being an exchange student to Bogenhofen, Austria; and all the other remarkable moments shared at Mount Pisgah Academy. **Oct. 10, Oct. 21.**

Chelsea Campbell, a member of the class of 2013 at Mount Pisgah Academy, was born in Asheville, North Carolina. She loves to read, travel, ski, and take pictures. She plays the flute and sings in the choir. She has been on several mission trips to Honduras, and in the spring of 2010 she went on a mission trip to Kenya, Africa. **Sept. 2.**

Abbie Carrillo was a member of the 2011 class at Mount Pisgah Academy. She is a native of Mexico. **Apr. 6.**

Rosa Chavez graduated with the class of 2007 from Mount Pisgah Academy. She was born in northern Mexico but has lived in Chapel Hill, North Carolina, for most of her life. She returned to MPA to work as cafeteria assistant for a year. She has many great memories as both a student and staff member at Pisgah, and the friends she made at Pisgah are like family. **Jan. 19.**

Erin Gosling Ciubotaru, member of the class of 2008, enjoyed dividing her academy years between choir and drama. She now lives in Italy and is pursuing her second degree, which keeps her busy. **Jan. 12.**

Megan Coffey graduated from Mount Pisgah Academy in 2009. She is from Asheville, North Carolina, and is now in college. **Apr. 16, June 20.**

Brittani Coleman's full name is Alexandria Brittani Coleman—yes, her initials are ABC. She graduated from MPA in 2009. She is from Deltona, Florida, but is currently living in Medford, Oregon, where she is taking classes and plans to major in both communications and theater. What she most loved about academy life was all the hugs, high-fives, and encouragement that she both shared and received every day on campus. She loves to spontaneously burst into song, laugh at something that isn't funny, and lift people's spirits. **Jan. 14, Mar. 18, May 4.**

McKennan Cook graduated from Mount Pisgah Academy in 2010. While an MPA student, he was actively involved in the campus ministries department. He enjoys music and videography. He now attends Appalachian State University. **Jan. 30, May 11, Dec. 21.**

Nick Cord, a member of the graduating class of 2011, lives in Durham, North Carolina with his mom, stepdad, and sister. He visits his dad and grandparents in Maryland whenever he has the chance. For 13 years Nick lived on the Outer Banks of North Carolina, where he spent his free time surfing, his favorite thing to do in the whole world. **Oct. 3.**

Kaylee Couser, a Mount Pisgah Academy 2010 graduate, loves singing and playing her guitar. She is now attending a local technical college but plans to soon attend Union College in Nebraska to continue her studies. She loves her friends and family and enjoys spending time with them. Her favorite color is blue, and she hopes to one day live in Australia. **Mar. 2, May 7, Sept. 23, Nov. 3.**

Megan Couser graduated from Mount Pisgah Academy in 2010. She has fond memories of traveling with the academy choir and leading out in music for Mount Pisgah Academy's special events. She is now in college majoring in history, with a minor in Bible. She enjoys hanging out with friends, singing, and playing tennis. **May 8, Sept. 30.**

Melissa Couser graduated in 2007 from Mount Pisgah Academy. She has many fond memories of her academy years. She is now in college. **Jan. 27.**

Victoria Crawford graduated from Mount Pisgah Academy in 2009. While in academy she became a certified nursing assistant (CNA) and has continued to work in that field. She lives in Enka, North Carolina, and enjoys hanging out with her friends. **June 24.**

Josh Cundiff, member of the class of 2011, is from Raleigh, North Carolina. He enjoys playing the guitar, piano, and drums. While attending Mount Pisgah Academy, he was a member of the acrobatics team. His favorite memory from Mount Pisgah Academy is spending the summer on the recruiting team. In his free time he likes to skateboard and snowboard. **Sept. 20.**

Lauren Cundiff, member of the class of 2012, lives in Raleigh, North Carolina. While at Mount Pisgah Academy she really appreciated the supportive staff. One of her favorite academy memories is participating in Trash Night, an annual school event. Lauren's hobbies include photography, listening to and making music, and reading. **Aug. 7.**

Paige Dagnan graduated from Mount Pisgah Academy in May 2010. She loved attending Pisgah because of the family atmosphere. She made a lot of really close friends in academy and says attending Pisgah was one of the best decisions she ever made. She is originally from Ridgeville, South Carolina, a town so small it doesn't even have a traffic light. In her spare time, if she's alone, she writes and also sketches. She reads two or three books a week. Paige also adores her friends and tries to spend as much time with them as she can. **Oct. 30.**

Michael Daily, a 2009 graduate from Mount Pisgah Academy, lives in Cary, North Carolina, but lived for two years in Alaska. He now attends Southern Adventist University and is majoring in business management. He is actively involved in mission work. **Apr. 13.**

Cassandra Dannenberger is a member of the class of 2012 at Mount Pisgah Academy. She enjoys singing and is a member of the choir. In her spare time she likes playing the piano and hanging out with her friends. Even though she has had some struggles, she is proud of the life God has blessed her with. **June 10, Dec. 12.**

Michelle Dannenberger graduated from Mount Pisgah Academy in 2008. She enjoys shopping, helping her grandparents, studying for her online classes, and hanging out with friends in downtown Chattanooga. **Jan. 24, Apr. 19.**

Nicole Dannenberger, a graduate of the Mount Pisgah Academy class of 2007, is now a nightshift nurse at Johnson City Medical Center. Her hobbies include having fun with her sisters and hanging out with friends in Chattanooga. **Feb. 23.**

Karyn Davis graduated from Mount Pisgah Academy in 2011. Her hometown is Kernersville, North Carolina. She enjoyed her time at Pisgah—especially all of the friends she made and the relationship she formed with God. In her free time she likes playing the guitar, singing, and drawing. **Oct. 29.**

Kyle Dennis, a member of the Mount Pisgah Academy class of 2007, enjoyed being on the acrobatics team. He went on to study law enforcement in Tennessee and lives in the Chattanooga area. **Feb. 1.**

Carolina Diaz was born in Cancun, Mexico. She moved to the U.S. when she was 13. She loves to sing and play basketball. Her favorite memories from MPA are the school trips she took and the friends she made. She graduated from MPA in 2010. **Mar. 20, July 27, Aug. 21, Nov. 27.**

Fabiola Diaz is from Tamaulipas, Mexico, but currently lives in North Carolina. She is a member of the graduating class of 2012. She is in the school band and works in the cafeteria. In her free time she likes to read and draw. She plans to be a biologist one day. **July 20, Sept. 7.**

Addie Dorough is from Charlotte, North Carolina. She is in the Mount Pisgah Academy class of 2012 and keeps a busy schedule as its president. She is also a member of the Acrosports team and likes barbeque potato chips. She enjoys writing letters to people and does not like peppermint, unless it's the mocha drink from Starbucks. **Nov. 25, Dec. 1, Dec. 31.**

Timothy Douglas was born and raised in Spartanburg, South Carolina. He is a 2011 graduate of Mount Pisgah Academy. He enjoys long walks on the beach and being with friends. In his free time, when not worrying about school, he likes to skateboard. He also loves tinkering with computers and plans to include that in a career one day. **Nov. 30.**

Rebekah Doying graduated from Mount Pisgah Academy in 2011. Originally from Naples, Florida, her family now lives in Prosperity, South Carolina, in a lake house her great-grandpa and grandpa built. Rebekah loves the beach and warm weather. She hopes to one day be a dental hygienist or a special education teacher. **Sept. 6.**

Stephen Drummond graduated from Mount Pisgah Academy in 2011. He lives in Charlotte, North Carolina, with his mother, father, and older brother. One of the highlights of his academy years was playing basketball. But he especially enjoyed a mission trip to Mexico during his junior year. On the trip he preached an evangelistic series and helped out in the local community. **Aug. 14, Nov. 21, Dec. 16.**

Linda S. Duncan lives in western North Carolina. In their earlier years together, she and her husband spent many vacations exploring North America with their two daughters. And now, as nana of the two most awesome grandchildren ever, the exploring continues . . . especially all facets of nature! She spent many years working in the human resources department at Park Ridge Hospital, but now she has the privilege and pleasure of homeschooling her grandchildren. Her goal is to be ready for Jesus' soon return and enjoy that journey to heaven with all her family and friends! **Mar. 8, Apr. 20.**

Alicia Evans, a 2006 graduate of Mount Pisgah Academy, has many fond memories from her time at MPA: the mission trip to Sonora, Mexico; sitting on the stoop of the old Fleetwood building with friends; and the junior history trip with Mr. Hindman. As an academy student, she was involved in puppet ministry and drama and enjoyed working all four years in the cafeteria. (Five, if you count the one she came back as a supervisor.) **Aug. 5, Oct. 6.**

Ashton Evans graduated from Mount Pisgah Academy in 2010 and is now in college. She lives in Florence, South Carolina, with her mom, dad, and older brother. She says the best part of her high school experience was the mission trip to Portland, Oregon, where she spent time helping the homeless. As a student she served as Acrosports captain, Student Association vice president, and vice president of her class. **July 29, Aug. 12, Aug. 28, Nov. 4, Dec. 23.**

Dustin Evans enjoyed his years at Mount Pisgah Academy and graduated in 2008. His favorite memories include being a part of the music department. During his senior year he was appointed assistant director of the choir. He is now pursuing a college degree and lives in Florence, South Carolina. **Jan. 9, Mar. 24, May 31.**

Lorelle Evans is from Asheville, North Carolina. She graduated from Mount Pisgah Academy in 2009. What she liked most about academy was the incredible staff, working the 5:45 morning shift in the café, and the great opportunities to be involved in organizations. A few of her favorite pastimes are scrapbooking, singing, and playing tennis. **Jan. 6, Feb. 3, Feb. 14, Mar. 3.**

Nick Evans graduated from Mount Pisgah Academy in 2011. Some of his best memories from academy include being on the soccer and basketball teams with his friends. Another highlight was the Africa mission trip he went on during his junior year. While in Africa he enjoyed playing soccer with the little kids and seeing the amazing wild animals on the savannah. **Nov. 8.**

Nicholas Ewing spent 15 years living in Florida before his family moved to Nosoca Pines Ranch in South Carolina. He enjoyed attending Mount Pisgah Academy his junior and senior years (graduating in 2010). He is now in college. Nicholas loves being in the outdoors. **Jan. 3, May 19, Sept. 17, Oct. 2.**

Alex Faber graduated from MPA with the class of 2011. He was part of the gymnastics team and enjoyed playing all kinds of sports. He lives with his parents in Liberty Hill, South Carolina, at Nosoca Pines Ranch. **Oct. 15.**

Cindy Flores is a member of the graduating class of 2007 and is from Ridgeland, South Carolina. She enjoyed making friends at Mount Pisgah Academy. **Mar. 12.**

Josias Flores, member of the class of 2012 at Mount Pisgah Academy, comes from Fayetteville, North Carolina, where he lives with his parents. He originally comes from Venezuela, where he spent nine years of his life. He says that one of his highlights of his past four years was spending a summer with Mount Pisgah Academy's recruiting team. He is a striker/midfielder on the soccer team and is the pastor of his class. **June 19, Sept. 21, Nov. 2, Nov. 29.**

Kristina Forrest is from east Tennessee. She has been riding horses since she was 5, and her favorite sport is basketball. What she liked most about attending Mount Pisgah Academy was the close friendships she built there and the independence she felt being on her own in the dorm. She says that the MPA staff members are awesome and will always be there for her if she needs someone to talk to. **July 1.**

Brittany Foster graduated from Mount Pisgah Academy in 2007. She went on to attend Andrews University. **Mar. 5, Mar. 10.**

Julian Foster graduated from Mount Pisgah Academy in 2008. He is from Greensboro, North Carolina. What he appreciated most about attending MPA were the friendships he made (which are still strong) and the care of the teachers. He has fond academy memories of senior bells, drama practices, basketball intramurals, and late-night talks in the dorm. **Apr. 8, May 12.**

Ricardo Garcia graduated from Mount Pisgah Academy in 2010. He comes from San José, Costa Rica, but now lives in Asheville, North Carolina. Ricardo has one younger brother, Henry, who is a current MPA student. One of the highlights of Ricardo's academy experience was skiing at Sugar Mountain with the school. He loves to play music, hang out with friends, and play all kinds of games. **Aug. 20.**

Aimee Garver is a member of the graduating class of 2011. She comes from Florence, South Carolina, where she lives with her parents and older brother. Some of her favorite activities include writing, drawing, playing in the academy bell choir, and reading a good book. **July 24, Sept. 8, Dec. 14.**

Ryan Gillen graduated in 2009 from Mount Pisgah Academy. He now attends Southern Adventist University and is studying biochemistry. He was a resident assistant for two years in the boys' dorm, class treasurer for three years, and was heavily involved in audiovisual media, Acrosports, and intramurals. He enjoys hanging out with friends and listening to music in his downtime. **Apr. 26, May 29.**

Hector Gonzalez is devoted to being the boys' dean at MPA. He has been a dean for 20 years—serving at Garden State Academy, Columbia Union College, and Mount Pisgah Academy. He has a passion for helping people of all ages. He enjoys watching sports and collecting memorabilia. **Jan. 10, Feb. 10, May 10, July 14, July 15, July 16, July 17.**

Katelyn Gonzalez, a 2008 Mount Pisgah Academy graduate, has numerous memories of acrobatics and choir tours from her four years at MPA. She now attends Southern Adventist University and is always proud to say that she is an alumna of MPA. **Mar. 21, Sept. 18.**

Danielle Grandy graduated from Mount Pisgah Academy in 2007. Her fondest academy memories come from participating on the Acrosports team all four years. Building friendships, learning teamwork, and improving physical fitness were all attributes gained while on the acrobatics team. At the time of this writing she is a health science major at Southern Adventist University, with plans to become an occupational therapist. Her favorite activities include playing intramural sports at SAU, playing racquetball, and rock climbing. **Jan. 28.**

Cheryl Grant is a Mount Pisgah Academy graduate of the class of 1995. She later returned to serve for many years as the assistant food service director at MPA. She was born and raised in North Carolina. Cheryl is blessed with a wonderful husband and two amazing kids. She enjoys anything to do with the arts (music, museums, crafts, culinary, etc.). Cheryl is thankful for the opportunities that God leads her to on a daily basis. **Jan. 20, Feb. 19, June 15, Oct. 23.**

Andrew Grissom graduated from Mount Pisgah Academy in 2011. He lives in Charlotte, North Carolina, and has two sisters. His hobbies are basketball and football. **Aug. 26.**

Anna Grissom graduated from Mount Pisgah Academy with the class of 2009 and has very fond memories of choir trips, resident assistant meetings, and Sabbath afternoons on campus. She is currently using the lessons she learned at MPA as she pursues her nursing degree at Southern Adventist University. **Feb. 12, Mar. 7, Mar. 25, July 12, Aug. 6.**

Beth Grissom, member of the class of 1987 at MPA, is grateful for her high school experience. Beth loved being in the dorm and making friends that have been dear friends for more than 20 years. She also loved being in choir, band, and clown ministry. She is now a staff member at MPA and the proud mother of three MPA graduates. **Dec. 13.**

Sarah Grissom, member of the class of 2011 at MPA, has unforgettable memories of being a resident assistant. She was also on the acrobatics team and very involved in her class. She made the decision to head off to college a year early and is loving all the joys and challenges of being a physical education/wellness major at Southern Adventist University. **Jan. 22, Aug. 1, Oct. 11.**

Linda and **George Grow** lived and worked at MPA from fall 1968 to spring 2011. Now retired near the school, they happily remember their many students, staff, and community friends. They love to experience and photograph natural scenes in North America and share them with everyone. **June 22.**

Aaron Haah attended Mount Pisgah Academy for a while as a member of the class of 2008. Originally from Korea, he now lives in Ohio. For now he is working full-time as a dental technician. From time to time he daydreams about the fun school life he had back at MPA: working at the cafeteria and the dorm, playing ground hockey and volleyball intramurals, doing fun activities with friends, and hanging out in Mrs. Bradley's office. **Mar. 11.**

Moses Haah is from South Korea, and at the time of this writing, he is serving in the South Korean Army as a medic with a rank of sergeant. He graduated from Mount Pisgah Academy in 2007. What he liked the most about academy life was Friday vespers and Sabbath worships. Also, he loved Sabbath lunch at the cafeteria! **Mar. 14.**

Kyle Hano, member of the graduating class of 2011 at Mount Pisgah Academy, comes from Ponchatoula, Louisiana, where he was born and grew up. He moved to the Carolinas at the age of 7. He says that some of his most memorable summers were spent colporteuring and recruiting. He loves to play sports. He also loves to listen to music and likes to play the cello. Kyle plans to pursue a career as a minister. **May 9.**

Jonathan Harris was in the graduating class of 2007. As an academy student he enjoyed being in Present Truth Drama. He lives in Granite Falls, North Carolina, and is a lifelong NASCAR fan. **Jan. 25.**

Crystal Hattar graduated from Mount Pisgah Academy in 2011. She lives in Candler, North Carolina, with her mom and brother. **Nov. 12, Nov. 16, Dec. 19.**

Stephen Herren, a member of the graduating class of 2011, has grown to feel that Pisgah is his home. He credits the school for making him who he is today. He loves basketball. But he wants everyone to know that the most important thing in his life is God. **July 18.**

Carina Herrera was in the Mount Pisgah Academy class of 2008. She is from Wilkesboro, North Carolina. **Mar. 28.**

Stephanie Hill is a member of the class of 2012 at Mount Pisgah Academy. She comes from Asheville, North Carolina, where she lives with her parents and younger sister. She says one of the highlights of the past four years was being able to attend Mount Pisgah Academy and going on a mission trip to Kenya with her classmates. She also enjoys being in the choir. **Sept. 13.**

Brian Hindman is a Bible and history teacher at Mount Pisgah Academy as well as an alumnus of the class of 1993. He enjoys hiking, playing sports, visiting historical sites, and socializing with young people. But above all, his favorite activity is studying the Bible with his students and encouraging them to grow in a relationship with Jesus. Brian has been teaching at MPA for 13 years and hopes to retire there. **Feb. 20, Apr. 18.**

Jamey Holder graduated in 2008 from Mount Pisgah Academy. What he liked most about academy was how close-knit a "family" it was. In his free time he likes to play video games, watch anime, read manga, and draw. **Jan. 23.**

Chloe Howard, member of the class of 2010 at Mount Pisgah Academy, comes from Candler, North Carolina, where she lives with her mom and brother. She enjoys photography, hanging out with friends, and spending time with family. She says that she has learned a lot in her academy years and will use all the knowledge she has gained for the rest of her life. **May 30, Sept. 3.**

Luke Hudgins graduated in 2008 from Mount Pisgah Academy. He comes from Kernersville, North Carolina. He enjoyed the community atmosphere at Pisgah. His favorite pastimes are meeting new people, frolicking in fields, pestering Harvard University, and playing video games. **Feb. 16.**

Anthony Hunt attended Mount Pisgah Academy for his first two years of high school (class of 2012). He was very involved in the music department and was class president his sophomore year. **Apr. 5.**

Michael Huskins was in the Mount Pisgah Academy class of 2007. He enjoyed being on the acrobatics team. He lives in Fayetteville, North Carolina. **Feb. 22.**

Jaz Isom graduated as a four-year senior from Mount Pisgah Academy in 2009. He is from Anderson, South Carolina. What he liked most about Pisgah were the many chances and ways that he could praise God. He especially enjoyed being a member of the praise team, choir, bell choir, and gymnastics team. He is now in college and still involved in music and gymnastics. He wants everyone to remember to trust in God and know that He's there for them and loves them with all of His heart. **Aug. 3, Oct. 9.**

Patricia Lauren Isom is from Fairfield Glade, Tennessee. She graduated from Mount Pisgah Academy in 2009 with high honors. She loved attending MPA for many reasons. MPA is made up of a wonderful staff who are on fire for Jesus and who really care about the students. She enjoyed being involved in music outreach, from leading song service to singing in the choirs. She also loved being a reporter/writer for the school newspaper. **Aug. 19.**

Bethany Iuliano graduated in 2007 from Mount Pisgah Academy. She says that her closest friends are the ones she made in academy. She is from Greeneville, Tennessee, and has recently graduated from Southern Adventist University. She really likes outdoor activities, such as camping, hiking, and backpacking. She also loves reading and creative writing! **Oct. 1.**

Timothy Iuliano graduated from Mount Pisgah Academy in 2010. His favorite academy memories include living in the dorm, being on the acrobatics team, and working with the boys' club to plan events. He currently attends Southern Adventist University as an engineering major. **May 20.**

Chris Janetzko graduated with the class of 2009 at Mount Pisgah Academy. He loved having vespers every Friday with his friends. While in academy he was a part of the drama and acrobatics teams. He also served as a Student Association officer and member of the yearbook staff. He is currently attending Southern Adventist University studying mass communications. **Feb. 7, Mar. 30.**

Julian Jervis is a member of the Mount Pisgah Academy class of 2012. He and his family live in Bermuda. Julian loves to play all sports. **Dec. 4.**

Brandy Johnson graduated from Mount Pisgah Academy in 2007. She fondly remembers singing Disney songs while washing dishes in the cafeteria and going on band, choir, and drama tours. She graduated from La Sierra University in Riverside, California, with a bachelor's degree in music with an emphasis on the bassoon. She is now working on her special education certification. Brandy enjoys counseling at summer camp and spoiling her orange kitty, Isis. **Jan. 29.**

Ryan Johnson graduated with the class of 2007 from Mount Pisgah Academy. He likes backpacking and hanging out with friends. He is now in college and wants to travel abroad. **Feb. 25.**

Micayla Jones currently attends Mount Pisgah Academy and plans to graduate in 2013. Her favorite thing about living in the dorm is the new air-conditioning/heat units! Some of her favorite things to do include singing, playing the piano, and reading. **Dec. 8.**

Jihun Joung lives in South Korea. As a kid he was a little chubby, but he lost 30 pounds in the eighth grade and is now much healthier. He has a lot of good friends in Korea, but did not like school there because he felt the system was always pushing him. However, now that he is in the United States, he pushes himself to do his best, and he is doing well at Mount Pisgah Academy (class of 2012). He misses his family, but wants to show them how independent he has become. **Nov. 18.**

Kyli Jung will graduate from Mount Pisgah Academy in 2012. She comes from Seoul, South Korea, where she lives with her mom, dad, and brother. She says that coming to America has changed her life. She plays the violin, is in the choir, and is a member of the yearbook staff. **Aug. 4, Nov. 19, Dec. 9.**

Denis Kasap, a member of the class of 2009, is from St. Petersburg, Russia. For him the greatest thing about attending Mount Pisgah Academy is that "everybody becomes like a family." He really liked dorm life, especially his senior year, and he enjoyed singing in choir. Going on the Bermuda trip was awesome! And he'll never forget running class with Mr. Hindman, which culminated in running the Conquer the Cove 5K. **Apr. 29, July 6.**

Rachelle Shook Kelley graduated from Mount Pisgah Academy in 2008. She now attends East Tennessee State University, majoring in allied health and military science with a concentration in dietetics and cardiopulmonary. One of her favorite parts of attending academy was the family atmosphere. While in academy she was involved in both choir and acrobatics. She now enjoys hiking and traveling. **Apr. 4.**

Lauren Kenemore graduated from Mount Pisgah Academy in 2011. Lauren was on the yearbook staff for three years. In her free time she likes to hang out with friends, listen to music, and explore Facebook. **Mar. 27.**

Leah Killian, a member of the graduating class of 2009 at MPA, is now attending Southern Adventist University and is pursuing a major in elementary education. In her spare time she likes hanging out with friends, snowboarding, hiking, camping, and anything having to do with the outdoors. **Apr. 1, June 29.**

James Kim, a 2011 graduate of Mount Pisgah Academy, comes from Namyangju, South Korea, where he lives with his mom, dad, and younger brother. During his junior and senior years he was soccer team captain. He says that one of the highlights of his academy years was the experience of deciding to stay with God. **Sept. 15, Dec. 10.**

Junho (Daven) Kim was a member of the class of 2007 at Mount Pisgah Academy. He later studied business at the University of Tennessee at Chattanooga, but returned to his home and now lives in Seoul, South Korea. **Feb. 21.**

Kris Kimbley graduated in 2008 from Mount Pisgah Academy. He has great memories of living in the dorm and traveling with the gymnastics team. He was also involved with the audiovisual media club and the school's newspaper, *Skyliner*. He is now in college studying to become an ESL teacher. **Jan. 8, Apr. 15, July 9.**

A. J. King graduated from Mount Pisgah Academy in 2009. He is from Elizabeth City, North Carolina. He enjoyed his time on the acrobatics team and made many friends at MPA. **Apr. 10, June 16.**

Ross Knight, a 2008 graduate from Mount Pisgah Academy, will never forget his academy experiences—being in the dorm, being a member of the gymnastics team, and preaching. He is now at Southern Adventist University studying theology. **Feb. 11, Mar. 31, June 4.**

Jessica Koobs was a member of the class of 2009. She now lives in Collegedale, Tennessee. She made many good friends while attending Mount Pisgah Academy. **Mar. 26, Sept. 11.**

Richard Lawrence graduated in 2011 from Mount Pisgah Academy. He grew up in South Carolina, but recently moved to the Washington, D.C., area, where he lives with his mom, dad, and older sister. He says that the best things about academy were the friends he made, the college prep experience, and the spiritual growth he experienced. At MPA Richard was involved in the sports program, and he was also quite involved in school ministries and associations. He now attends Washington Adventist University and is pursuing a degree in physical therapy. He is also musically talented and wants to use his talents for God's ministry. **Mar. 13, Oct. 7.**

Charlie Lee or SangHyuk (his Korean name) graduated from Mount Pisgah Academy in 2011. He likes electronics, and he loves taking pictures. **Sept. 1.**

Daniel Lee graduated from Mount Pisgah Academy in 2011. Originally from Korea, he enjoyed his time at MPA. **June 13, Dec. 7.**

Kevin Lee graduated from MPA in 2011 and now attends Southern Adventist University. He calls South Korea home but has attended school in the States since 2008. Kevin loves to play violin and soccer. **Dec. 28.**

Samantha Lee is from South Korea. She is a member of the class of 2012. She loves how Pisgah is like a big family. She enjoys playing piano and cooking. She also loves animals. **Sept. 26.**

Teddy Lin attended Mount Pisgah Academy his senior year, 2009. His home is in Guangzhou, China. He enjoyed making friends at MPA. **May 24.**

Andrew Linton has fond memories of his time at MPA, including geocaching with his favorite teacher. He is now a senior at Western Carolina University. Andrew enjoys science fiction writing and proofreading and editing papers for his friends. The class of 2007 will always hold a special place in his heart. **Sept. 28.**

Shavana Lloyd graduated from Mount Pisgah Academy in 2009. She calls Kailua, Hawaii, home. **May 27.**

Lauren Lowe is from Kernersville, North Carolina. She graduated in 2010 from Mount Pisgah Academy. She has good memories of her time at MPA, including making many great friends, being a part of the choir, and going on the mission trip to the Masai Mara in Kenya, Africa. She is now in college and hopes to pursue more work in the mission field. In her free time she likes to hang out with good friends, go horseback riding, paint, read, and watch college basketball (go Duke!). **Feb. 28, Sept. 27.**

Kari Mann graduated from Mount Pisgah Academy in 2007. **Jan. 15.**

Anders Markoff graduated from Mount Pisgah Academy in 2009. He is from Waynesville, North Carolina. He is now in college. **Jan. 4, Apr. 14.**

Peter Markoff is in the Mount Pisgah Academy class of 2013. He lives in Waynesville, North Carolina, with his mom, dad, and sister. He has an older brother in college. He says that one of the highlights of the past few years was taking a two-month trip to an Adventist school in Austria and traveling while he was there. He is on the Acrosports team at school and enjoys playing music. **Oct. 5.**

Clint Martin graduated in 2008 from Mount Pisgah Academy. He went on to study at Armstrong Atlantic State University. He currently lives in Savannah, Georgia. **Jan. 11, Aug. 30.**

Teddi McAllen graduated with the class of 2007 from Mount Pisgah Academy. After academy she went to Andrews University. Her best memories from academy are spending time with her two best friends her senior year and being a part of the choir and audiovisual media team. **Feb. 24.**

Joseph Meneses was born in Colombia, South America, but was raised in New Bern, North Carolina. He will graduate from Mount Pisgah Academy in 2012. He loves sports, especially basketball and soccer, and music. God is first in his life. **Aug. 24.**

Alisha Michael is a South Carolina girl with a fierce love for the ocean. She and her husband, Jonathan, the associate pastor of the Mount Pisgah Academy church, live on MPA's beautiful campus with their son, Joshua. Along with teaching, Alisha has a passion for writing, cooking, and reading. She also has a heart for ministering to teen girls. **July 25, Aug. 25, Nov. 5.**

Jonathan P. Michael, associate pastor at the MPA church, grew up in West Virginia. He attended Adventist schools in Virginia, Tennessee, and Michigan, and has served as an Adventist pastor in South Carolina, Colorado, and North Carolina with his wife, Alisha, and son, Joshua. He enjoys spending quality time with family and friends, reading, listening to music, watching inspiring movies, communing with God in nature, and sharing insights with others. **Jan. 16, May 2, June 8, Sept. 16.**

Emily Milliner graduated from Mount Pisgah Academy in 2008. What she liked most about Pisgah was dorm life. She loved how close she got to all the other girls on her hall. Her favorite memories include walking around the track with her friends during recreation and sitting on the Fleetwood stairs watching people. Although she's from Tampa, Florida, she says that Pisgah will always be her home away from home! **Feb. 17.**

Sarah Milliner graduated in 2007 from Mount Pisgah Academy. Some of her favorite memories include going on choir trips, having downtime in the dorm, and making lifelong friends. Currently she is pursuing a degree in physical therapy. **Mar. 1.**

Lilly Mitchell, a member of the class of 2011 at Mount Pisgah Academy, was born in Alaska but now lives in Tennessee. In her free time she enjoys reading, swimming, horseback riding, and sleeping. **July 21.**

Haruka Mori graduated from Mount Pisgah Academy in 2010. She is from Kobe, Japan, where she lives with her mom, dad, and older brother. She enjoys playing the piano, as well as doing gymnastics. She is currently attending Southern Adventist University. **Mar. 19, July 8, July 30.**

Makoto Mori, member of the graduating class of 2007, enjoyed singing in an a cappella quartet and quintet while at MPA. He also has fond memories of chilling with his hallmates in the dorm. He is now a premed student in college and is involved in a research project in computational chemistry. **Mar. 6.**

Bonny Musgrave has been food service director at Mount Pisgah Academy since 2003. During that time she has also served as work coordinator and has taught economics, sewing, and looking good. She enjoys keeping up with students, both current and those who have graduated, via Facebook. **Apr. 23, June 28.**

Paul Musgrave keeps the campus running smoothly as codirector of plant services, a job he shares with his son, Jason. In his spare time he can usually be found working in his shop, which is filled with woodworking, metalworking, and auto mechanics equipment. **June 26.**

Jake Nielsen graduated from Mount Pisgah Academy in 2008 and then went on to college. He liked being on the acrobatics team while in academy. He spent many years in Kenya but currently lives in Orlando, Florida. **Mar. 22.**

Jesse Nielsen will graduate from Mount Pisgah Academy in 2012. He was raised in Kenya, Africa, which really shaped his character and personality. He is passionate about art and music and is aspiring to work in the mental health field. **July 19.**

Katie Oates, along with others from the graduating class of 2007, will never forget the wonderful friendships she developed at Mount Pisgah Academy. She will always remember the fun memories they made in the dorm late at night. After graduating from college, Katie hopes to explore the world and its fascinating cultures. **Mar. 4.**

Evan Paradis was in the Mount Pisgah Academy class of 2008. He is currently studying flight and airframe and power plant maintenance at Andrews University. **Jan. 13.**

Brandon Peggau graduated in 2008 from Mount Pisgah Academy. He was on the acrobatics team and made lots of good friends at MPA. He is currently a biology/chemistry premed major at Southern Adventist University. **Mar. 23.**

Alyssa Pelto graduated in 2011 from Mount Pisgah Academy. She is originally from Columbus, Wisconsin, but has enjoyed living on MPA's campus for several years. (Her dad is a faculty member.) She loves the Christ-centered atmosphere of Pisgah and the chances that the school gives their students to help in the community and in other countries. She enjoys the arts, spending time with her friends, horseback riding, playing with her three dogs, and watching football. Her favorite team is the Green Bay Packers. **Feb. 15, July 4, Oct. 19.**

Joy K. Pelto is the wife of MPA music and math teacher Edward Pelto, and mother to Alyssa (class of 2011) and Benjamin (class of 2013). She enjoys writing, reading, crocheting, sewing, and helping save the lives of some of God's creatures by fostering dogs for the local humane society. **Jan. 31.**

Tressa Perry, from Greenville, North Carolina, graduated from Mount Pisgah Academy in 2009. She was in choir all four years of academy and has fond memories of their trip to Bermuda. She is now a college student. In her free time she enjoys playing tennis and learning new sports. **Apr. 28.**

Jacqueline Plested graduated from Mount Pisgah Academy in 2009. She made many good friends at MPA and enjoyed being part of the choir. She also plays violin. Jacquelyn is from Scottsville, Kentucky. **May 3, Aug. 23.**

John Ratzlaff is a math teacher and the network administrator at Mount Pisgah Academy. He lives in Candler, North Carolina, with his wife, Kitty, and son, Mark. He has been a staff member at MPA since 1977. One of his favorite activities is geocaching. **May 21, Dec. 15, Dec. 27.**

Kitty Ratzlaff is the wife of John Ratzlaff, MPA teacher, and mother of Mark Ratzlaff, graduate of MPA. She enjoys working as an endoscopy registered nurse. She just ran her third marathon, and loves getting to know Jesus better every day! **Sept. 25.**

Leydy Reyes graduated in 2007 as a four-year senior from Mount Pisgah Academy. As an academy student she enjoyed being in choir and creative ministries. She enjoyed senior survival and senior class trip. She is now in college and enjoys meeting new friends and keeping up with "old" friends via Facebook. **Feb. 8.**

Jennifer Stollenmaier Reynaert graduated from Mount Pisgah Academy in 2007. As a student she enjoyed being on the acrobatics team as well as being part of the audiovisual media club. She had fun playing on the girls' soccer and basketball teams and being involved with the other intramural sports on campus. She graduated from college in May 2011 with a degree in social work and is continuing her education by getting a master's degree in international social work. She enjoys cooking, reading, traveling, and spending time with family and friends. **Aug. 11.**

Blin Richards graduated from Mount Pisgah Academy in 2009. He enjoyed every minute of academy and loves going back to visit. He enjoys playing all sports and will never forget his friends and teachers at MPA. He is now in college studying aeronautical engineering. **Apr. 30.**

Briana Richards is from Greeneville, Tennessee. She graduated from Mount Pisgah Academy in 2007. While attending Pisgah, she was a part of the acrobatics team and was the pastor of her senior class. Her favorite part of attending Pisgah was the friendships she formed. Now she is finishing her senior year of architecture school at Andrews University, and she enjoys being a part of their acrobatics team. **Jan. 26.**

Tiffany Rigdon is from Sylva, North Carolina. A member of the class of 2011, she includes mall trips, the Bermuda trip, and friendships she made as some of her favorite memories. **July 22.**

Andy Rodriguez grew up in Union City, New Jersey. He graduated from Mount Pisgah Academy in 2011. His hobbies include writing, mixing music, and hanging out with his friends. **Nov. 15.**

Alex Roeder graduated from Mount Pisgah Academy in 2011. She has lived in Asheville, North Carolina, all her life. In her free time she likes to wakeboard and snowboard (depending on the season). **Jan. 21.**

Amanda Rojas graduated in 2011 from Mount Pisgah Academy. While at MPA she was in the choir and bell choir. She was born in Illinois but raised in Winston-Salem, North Carolina. She enjoys riding horses, taking her dogs for walks, reading, cooking, and baking. **Oct. 20.**

Eileen Rojas graduated from Mount Pisgah Academy. While in academy she was a member of the acrobatics team and the choir. She was also very involved in campus ministries. She currently lives near Asheville, North Carolina, and is attending Southern Adventist University. **Feb. 2.**

Eli Rojas graduated from Mount Pisgah Academy in 2007. He has fond memories of going on academy mission trips and is glad that his school had an emphasis on missions. He now attends Southern Adventist University, where he is a theology major, following in his dad's pastoral footprints. He plans to graduate from Southern in 2012. He spent a year as a student missionary in the Ukraine. In his free time Eli enjoys writing. **Feb. 9.**

Anna Romanov was a member of the class of 2008. She went on to study at Southern Adventist University. **May 14, June 3.**

Stewart Rosburg graduated from Mount Pisgah Academy in 2010. He is from Charlotte but also enjoyed living in Asheville as a village student with his dad during his academy years. He enjoys playing drums and is a self-taught artist. **Aug. 18.**

Latavia Rose was a member of the class of 2008 at Mount Pisgah Academy. She made many good friends while at MPA. She went on to study early childhood development. **Apr. 3.**

Jihoo (Esther) Rue is originally from Cheonan, South Korea. She attended Mount Pisgah Academy and graduated in 2009. She later studied at Southern Adventist University. **Oct. 24.**

Sheldon Safrit graduated from Mount Pisgah Academy in 2010. He is from Richfield, North Carolina. **May 5.**

Terry Sampson has two children and is married to an alumna of MPA. They are members of the Kernersville SDA Church in Kernersville, North Carolina, where he is an elder and the Pathfinder director. Terry also has the pleasure of working at Tri-City Christian Academy as the distance learning facilitator. He is an avid mountain biker and enjoys outdoor activities. **Dec. 18.**

Rachel Sheridan graduated with the class of 2011. She hopes to pursue a career in the medical field. She loves photography. She says the highlight of academy was meeting friends who will last a lifetime. **Apr. 17, Oct. 8, Dec. 22.**

Joy Shin, a 2010 graduate, comes from Seoul, South Korea, but resides in Atlanta, Georgia, with her aunt and cousin. She says that a highlight from her time in academy was the mission trip to Mexico, where she helped build a school. She also was the editor in chief of the yearbook her senior year. **Mar. 16, June 25, Sept. 22.**

Steven Sigamani graduated from Mount Pisgah Academy in 2011. He and his family live in Columbia, South Carolina. He says his favorite memories of academy were being on the drama team and preaching in Mexico on a mission trip. He loves playing basketball and served as the senior class pastor. **Dec. 26.**

Mandi Skilton graduated from Mount Pisgah Academy in 2009 and has since been attending Walla Walla University. While at MPA Mandi loved being involved in campus life—she especially enjoyed being part of the drama team. She is majoring in biology, but makes time for such hobbies as mountain biking and rock climbing. **Feb. 6, June 18, Dec. 3.**

Shawntese Smith graduated with the class of 2010 at Mount Pisgah Academy. She is from Sumter, South Carolina. She has a twin sister and seven other siblings. In her spare time she likes to run and watch football. In academy she enjoyed being in three organizations: school newspaper, drama, and choir. She also served as the social vice president of the Student Association and as vice president of the girls' club. Her favorite memory at Mount Pisgah was being on the recruiting team, serving others and getting closer to God. She is currently pursuing a nursing degree at Washington Adventist University. **Apr. 25, June 14, Oct. 14, Oct. 27.**

Shawntez Smith is from Sumter, South Carolina. She graduated from Mount Pisgah Academy in 2010. During her academy years she enjoyed being part of the acrobatics team, choir, and drama. She made many amazing friends at Pisgah. She is now pursuing her bachelor's degree in biology/premed at Washington Adventist University. **June 12, Oct. 18.**

Cassi Sommerville is from Asheville, North Carolina. She graduated from Mount Pisgah Academy in 2008. She liked the atmosphere of Pisgah—it was very friendly and lots of fun! She loved working in the office, going on school trips, and being involved at the school. She was a class officer and an officer in the Student Association. She is now in college studying elementary education and loving it! **June 1.**

Noelle Stafford graduated in 2011 from Mount Pisgah Academy. She lives in Leicester, North Carolina, with her guardian and her 14 dogs and nine cats. She says that some of the highlights of her years at Mount Pisgah Academy are the great friends she made and the amazing mission trips she went on. **Aug. 8, Sept. 5.**

Benjamin Steinkraus was a member of the class of 2007 at Mount Pisgah Academy. He divides his time between North Carolina and New England. He is currently in the U.S. Army, deployed to Afghanistan. In his free time he likes to work out and, when he's stateside, work around the house. **July 5.**

Colton Stollenmaier graduated from Mount Pisgah Academy in 2008. He enjoys staying active and exercising. He has a passion for life and learning about Jesus. He is a student at Southern Adventist University, and he recently returned from being a student missionary overseas. His passion is to serve and share the love of Jesus with others. **Jan. 7.**

Michelle Stollenmaier graduated from Mount Pisgah Academy in 2009. She has fond memories of late nights in the dorm with her friends and traveling with the acrobatics team. She is currently attending Southern Adventist University, with plans to become an occupational therapist. Currently she is a member of the SAU gym team, the Gym-Masters. Her top priority is to spread the love of Jesus and the joy of life to others. **June 9.**

Devin Suarez is a 2009 graduate of Mount Pisgah Academy. He made many great friends in academy and enjoyed being involved in the drama organization. He is currently in college. **May 15, June 30.**

Stephanie Thomas graduated from Mount Pisgah Academy in 2010. She lives in Asheville, North Carolina, with her mom, dad, younger brother, two dogs, and one cat. She says one of the many highlights of her high school years was being an exchange student for one month in Bogenhofen, Austria. She enjoys being social and spending lots of time with her friends, and in the summer she can't get enough of water sports. She was a class officer and on the Student Association at MPA. She absolutely loved attending MPA. **Feb. 13, Apr. 11, Aug. 16, Oct. 12, Nov. 17.**

Katie Thrash is from Asheville, North Carolina. She graduated from Mount Pisgah Academy in 2010. She has fond memories of MPA because of all the friends she made. She loves almost any water activity, such as swimming, waterskiing, and tubing. She also enjoys reading, spending time with friends, and traveling. **Apr. 22, July 28, Oct. 16.**

Brittany Tompkins graduated in 2011 from Mount Pisgah Academy. Born and raised in Orlando, Florida, she now lives in Candler, North Carolina. She loves to watch sports, especially basketball. Her favorite team is the Orlando Magic. She hopes to make a difference in this world. **Aug. 29.**

Reyna Torrez, class of 2010, lives in Charlotte, North Carolina. As an academy student she was involved in the intramural sports program, was a member of the acrobatics team, and enjoyed playing piano and guitar for the praise team. **July 11, Nov. 24.**

Brittany Trosino, member of the Mount Pisgah Academy class of 2011, misses the true friendships she formed at MPA. She is currently a certified nursing assistant and is pursuing her nursing degree. **Apr. 21.**

Jessica Valenzuela was part of the class of 2008. She enjoyed her time at MPA. **Jan. 5.**

Elizabeth Vargas plans to graduate from Mount Pisgah Academy in 2012. She enjoys academy life and the close connection with God that comes out of it. She loves spending time with her friends and her family. After graduation she hopes to pursue a degree in nursing. **Oct. 28.**

Bob Vaughan is the father of two MPA students—Matt is a 2011 graduate, and Luke is a member of the class of 2014. His wife, Tammy (Ellis), graduated from MPA in 1983. **Sept. 10.**

Matt Vaughan graduated in 2011 from Mount Pisgah Academy. He lives five minutes from MPA with his mom, dad, and younger brother. During his academy years he enjoyed being in choir and drama. He also served as vice president of his class, religious vice of the Student Association his junior year, and president of the Student Association his senior year. In his spare time he likes sports—especially tennis and playing forward for the school's basketball team. **Dec. 29.**

Stefan von Henner graduated from Mount Pisgah Academy in 2010. He has great memories of his senior class trip to Florida. He was involved in the school's chapter of the National Honor Society, and he played in the band. He is now in college earning a bachelor's degree in computer engineering. When he's not busy with school, he enjoys spending time with his friends. **July 23.**

Brooke Wade was a member of the 2008 graduating class at MPA. During her four years at MPA she made some of her fondest memories on His Hands creative ministries team and as editor of *Skyliner*, the school newspaper. She is now a senior at Southern Adventist University, pursuing a major in English education with a math minor. **Jan. 2, Feb. 27, Mar. 15, Aug. 17.**

Madeline Wade was a member of the class of 2012 at Mount Pisgah Academy. She greatly enjoyed the mission trip to Mexico in 2010 and the friendships she made while at the school. She was involved in the band; *Skyliner*, the school newspaper; and the creative ministries team. She plans to soon begin college and pursue a career in physical therapy. **July 10**.

Iyana Walker is a member of the Mount Pisgah Academy class of 2013. She enjoys making friends and being part of the choir. **Dec. 17.**

Candis Watterson graduated from Mount Pisgah Academy in 2007 and is now in college, majoring in criminal justice. She enjoys reading and volunteering with animals whenever possible. The Blue Ridge Mountains are not far from her home, and God continues to astound her with their beauty and His presence. **June 2.**

Tiffany Weber lives in Tennessee. She graduated from Mount Pisgah in 2008. She continued her studies at Northeast State University. She made great friends and has fond memories of her academy years. **Apr. 24.**

Logan White graduated from Mount Pisgah Academy with the class of 2010. She is from Columbia, South Carolina. She says that one of the highlights of academy was going to Bermuda for a choir mission trip. As a student she was on the acrobatics team. **Sept. 29.**

Ethan Williams is a 2008 graduate of Mount Pisgah Academy. Although his home is in Leicester, North Carolina, he is currently studying environmental sciences at Canadian University College in Lacombe, Alberta. **Apr. 2.**

Guerin Williams graduated from Mount Pisgah Academy in 2011. He lives in Candler, North Carolina, and has one brother and two sisters. His hobbies are skateboarding and dirt biking. **Sept. 9.**

Lillian Williams graduated from Mount Pisgah Academy in 2009. Her home is in the mountains of Candler, North Carolina. She has two brothers and a sister who have all attended MPA. She says that the best part of being at Pisgah was the close spiritual atmosphere and great friendships, as well as being a part of the gymnastics team and the audiovisual media club. Lillian was secretary of her class for three years and part of the National Honor Society her senior year. She now attends Appalachian State University. **Apr. 12, Oct. 25.**

Olivia Williams graduated from Mount Pisgah Academy in 2011. She is the youngest of six brothers and sisters—all of whom attended Mount Pisgah Academy. She enjoys photography and hiking. **Feb. 4, Nov. 22.**

Spencer Williams has lived in North Carolina, a mile away from Mount Pisgah Academy, since he was 3 years old. He will graduate from MPA in the spring of 2012. His hobbies include painting and playing the violin. He has also been doing gymnastics for more than 10 years. **Nov. 9.**

Elizabeth Wilson is a member of Mount Pisgah Academy's class of 2012. She lives in Asheville, North Carolina, with her parents and standard poodle. She enjoys skiing, backpacking, singing in the choir, watching old black-and-white movies, and reading just about anything, including Wikipedia. Her favorite food is anything chocolate. Her best memory of Pisgah was taking part in the 2010 mission trip to Kenya. **July 3, Nov. 7.**

Lara Woo started attending Mount Pisgah Academy in August of 2010. She is a member of the class of 2011. She is from Seoul, South Korea. She likes the teachers best, because they have been kind to her. She also loves reading, talking with her friends, and playing the flute. **Nov. 26.**

Kevin Worth, vice principal of finance at Mount Pisgah Academy, believes that God is interested in more than just our blind faith. He is richly blessed by his family and enjoys music, sports, and devotional poetry. **Aug. 13.**

Allissa Wright graduated in 2011 from Mount Pisgah Academy. Her home is in Danville, Vermont, where she lives with her family. She has four sisters and one brother. She is also a proud aunt of two nephews and two nieces. She enjoys playing sports, snowboarding, snowmobiling, four-wheeling, reading, and hanging out with friends. She enjoys participating in mission trips, and she loved her recent trip to Kenya, Africa, to work with the Masai people and to share the Word of God in a way that she has never done before. **Jan. 17, Oct. 17, Dec. 5.**

Ericka Wright graduated from Mount Pisgah Academy in 2007. She is from Danville, Vermont. After academy she attended Florida Hospital College, majoring in nursing. While at MPA she was on the gymnastics team for three years, a Student Association officer, and a class officer. She was a four-year senior, and she still loves Pisgah. **Jan. 18.**

Josh Wright graduated from Mount Pisgah Academy in 2009. His home is in Danville, Vermont. He is currently attending the National Aviation Academy in Tampa, Florida, where he is studying to become an aviation mechanic. While at Pisgah he was on the acrobatics team. In his spare time he enjoys four-wheeling and snowmobiling. **May 23.**

Anna Wurster is a 2011 graduate from Mount Pisgah Academy. She is from Sparta, North Carolina. She enjoys photography, and while at MPA she took pictures for the school yearbook. One of her favorite memories at Pisgah is her class spending an entire day caring for the homeless. **May 25, Aug. 27.**

Derek Young graduated from Mount Pisgah Academy in 2009. He enjoyed being on the acrobatics team during his academy years. He loves sports (go Vols!) and now lives in Ooltewah, Tennessee. **May 1.**

Stephanie (Leena) Zepeda was a part of the graduating class of 2009. She is from Raleigh, North Carolina. What she liked the most about attending Mount Pisgah Academy were the close relationships between teachers and students, being able to live with all her friends, and most important, the great spiritual environment. Her favorite pastimes are running, listening to music, hanging out with friends, traveling, and photography. **May 6, May 26, Sept. 19.**